REIMAGINING EMPLOYMENT DISPUTE RESOLUTION AND ENFORCEMENT

This open access book examines the evolution of employment tribunals from a speedy, informal process to a system marked by delays and significant financial and human costs.

Resolving disputes in the workplace is difficult, expensive and emotionally charged. The current system is broken but what is the answer? Using material from a large-scale empirical study, including a survey of over 200 practitioners, the book examines the problems facing the system. It then considers how these problems are addressed in other jurisdictions both in the UK and in other countries.

The book then examines what can be done. It suggests that locating labour law disputes within a contract-tort-human rights frame takes insufficient account of the fundamental emotional and behavioural factors that are in play. The book therefore argues that much can be learnt from the resolution of family law disputes, whether it be in relation to how a relationship that has ended can be satisfactorily concluded, or how a relationship with ongoing ties can be managed going forwards. Utilising this theoretical reframing, the book proposes a blueprint for the future of employment dispute resolution.

This book is for policy makers, practitioners and academics looking for a rigorous empirical and theoretical analysis of what has gone wrong with employment dispute resolution and what can be done about it.

Reimagining Employment Dispute Resolution and Enforcement

Sarah Fraser Butlin
Catherine Barnard
and
Maayan Menashe

• HART •
OXFORD • LONDON • NEW YORK • NEW DELHI • SYDNEY

HART PUBLISHING

Bloomsbury Publishing Plc

Kemp House, Chawley Park, Cumnor Hill, Oxford, OX2 9PH, UK

1385 Broadway, New York, NY 10018, USA

Bloomsbury Publishing Ireland Limited, 29 Earlsfort Terrace, Dublin 2, D02 AY28, Ireland

HART PUBLISHING, the Hart/Stag logo, BLOOMSBURY and the Diana logo are trademarks of Bloomsbury Publishing Plc

First published in Great Britain 2026

A catalogue record for this book is available from the British Library.

A catalogue record for this book is available from the Library of Congress.

Library of Congress Control Number: 2026011087

ISBN: HB: 978-1-50999-053-5
ePDF: 978-1-50999-051-1
ePub: 978-1-50999-052-8

Typeset by Compuscript Ltd, Shannon

For product safety related questions contact productsafety@bloomsbury.com

To find out more about our authors and books visit www.hartpublishing.co.uk. Here you will find extracts, author information, details of forthcoming events and the option to sign up for our newsletters.

PREFACE

'The Employment Tribunal system is broken' is the cry of many practitioners. Confronted by an extraordinarily large number of claims (450,000 multiple claims and 45,000 individual claims),[1] the judges are doing a good job in difficult circumstances. However, it takes two to three years in some parts of the country for a claim to work its way through the system. By then the parties are deeply entrenched in their positions. The dispute that started in the workplace has become highly adversarial, whether there are lawyers representing either or both sides or not. The costs to the individuals involved – the claimant, and any named respondents and managers for the organisation – are significant both financially and emotionally. It is difficult for individuals to navigate the system, particularly without any legal support.[2] The costs to the organisation are also substantial: economically, in paying for representation and with managers distracted by the litigation and taken away from the core business operation; and institutionally, as the individual employee, their co-workers, HR team and managers struggle to interact and engage. And yet, bringing a claim to the tribunal is the first, rather than the last, resort for many people.

Justice delayed is justice denied and there is no access to justice when an individual has to wait for two or three years to vindicate their rights, or for an organisation to be exonerated. Resourcing is a fundamental problem; there are simply too many cases for too few judges and administrative staff. In Scotland and Northern Ireland, the delays are less but the process is still not speedy. The nature and scope of the rights that are now enforceable through the tribunal system have also grown exponentially. We discuss this further in Part I.

So why are there so many cases? We have found that early entrenchment of disputes, particularly with the need to follow a formal grievance process and exacerbated by HR managers who are concerned to follow policies and procedures to the letter, stymies attempts to resolve disputes at an early stage, when creative solutions could be found. Further, Acas Early Conciliation, intended to help find solutions by conciliation, is often seen as a tick-box exercise with little meaningful engagement by the parties. This is partly because employers want to wait and see if the individual is serious about bringing a claim and partly because the conciliators are purely facilitative and there is no 'reality testing' of the claims and responses that are being discussed. We discuss this further in Part II.

[1] Tribunal Statistics Quarterly: January to March 2025: GOV.UK.

[2] N Busby and M McDermont, 'Fighting with the Wind: Claimants' Experiences and Perceptions of the Employment Tribunal' (2020) 49 *Industrial Law Journal* 159.

Claimants – especially those representing themselves – struggle to explain their complaints in a legally coherent way. They have a story to tell, rather than necessarily being able to put their concerns into precise legal boxes. The form (the ET1) does not help them to formulate their issues in the way that lawyers, and the tribunal system, require. We discuss this further in Part III. Once their claim has been presented, the parties are already heavily entrenched. Lawyers are usually involved, at least on the employer's side, and the tribunal system is slow to work. There are few opportunities for the parties to try to resolve their disputes away from the tribunal, although this has been changing with newer models of alternative dispute resolution.

Further, all cases are essentially dealt with in the same way – whether it be a simple wages case or a complex discrimination claim. Different models of adjudication, we argue, are appropriate for different types of case. We discuss this further in Part III. There is a need to seriously consider the role of fees and costs, other enforcement processes and a feedback mechanism so that the findings of the tribunal have an impact on how an organisation operates in future. We discuss this in Part IV.

With the financial support of the Employment Lawyers' Association,[3] we have spent the last 18 months talking with practitioners, judges and academics in the UK and overseas to understand the problems with the UK system and to help us to think about what could realistically be done to change a system which cannot deliver on its original objectives of speedy, accessible, cheap access to justice. We talk about 'grey-sky' thinking, not blue, because we recognise the severe financial constraints on the UK justice system. Advocating for a doubling or trebling of the number of judges and staff, while useful in addressing case load, would have cost implications which the state is unlikely to be able to support. It also does not address some of the more fundamental issues we have identified with the system. In particular, we think many cases should not go to a tribunal at all and should be resolved via alternative dispute resolution, particularly mediation, as already happens in the family law system.

Our fundamental argument is that we need to radically rethink how we understand the role of employment dispute resolution. Traditionally, employment has primarily been conceptualised in three ways: as a matter of contract, as requiring statutory protection, and as incorporating important human rights. Each of these conceptualisations helps us to understand something of the nature of an employment relationship and provides valuable insights into what an employment dispute resolution system should prioritise. These three categories overlap with and inform each other. But what is missing is the recognition that employment is first and foremost about a relationship. It is called an employment *relationship* for a reason: it is a dynamic, changeable, emotional connection, with co-workers, managers, and with the job itself.

[3] Their support has kindly funded one full-time postdoctoral research associate for a year, some student research and bought out some of Sarah Fraser Butlin's time as an academic at Selwyn College.

We will argue that a person's relationship with their job is one of the most important relationships in their lives, arguably second only to that with their spouse or partner and children. A person's job is the source not only of their income but also of their identity, purpose and fulfilment. The loss of a job has been compared by a surprising number of our interviewees to a divorce. When that relationship breaks down, the nature of the connection with the job, the complexities of the dynamics between individuals, and the emotional upheaval caused by the breakdown will inevitably play out within the dispute. And yet, the tribunal system does not recognise this. There are injury to feelings awards for discrimination and whistleblowing claims. But the system itself is not built to manage, address, support or contain the emotional fallout. We therefore propose that parallels with family law and dispute resolution mechanisms used there are particularly instructive. We develop this theoretical underpinning in chapter three.

With that in mind, we have sought to explore what could be done differently. We have drawn considerable assistance in the processes used by family lawyers and the family courts, encouraging mediation and early neutral evaluation; and in Australia and New Zealand, whose systems provide swift, accessible conciliation and mediation followed by rapid adjudication of straightforward matters. We explore the different issues and ideas across different stages of the process: pre-litigation (Part II) and litigation process together with the role of adjudication (Part III) and matters of costs and enforcement (Part IV), before setting out our recommendations and conclusions (Part V). A summary of the individual recommendations relating to the different stages is contained at the start of each part.

ACKNOWLEDGEMENTS

We are enormously grateful to the very many people who have participated in this research, particularly the employment law community in the UK, who generously responded to our survey and discussed the issues vociferously in our focus groups. We benefited enormously from the discussions in the two round table meetings towards the end of the project and are grateful to all the participants. We are grateful to those people who agreed to be interviewed by us, or connected us with the right people to talk to, including Alexandra Heron, Amanda Reilly, Anarkali Musgrave, Andrew Cooper, Andrew Pote, Annmarie Carvalho, Anthony Wood, Danae Shell, Emily Watson, Fatim Jumabhoy, Francis Chan, Jacqueline Marks, Judge Leigh Johns, Kate Nowicki, Katie Sloan, Lynne Passmore, Natasha Pawade, Nicholas Wilson, Rachel Penny, Rachel Rogers, Sharon Bennett, Simranjit Kamal, Susan Baldock, Susan Price, Victoria Speed, members of the Fair Work Commission, Employment New Zealand, the New Zealand Employment Relations Authority. The Presidents of the Employment Tribunals, Barry Clarke, Susan Walker and Maxine Orr, and Lord Fairley, President of the EAT, gave significant amounts of time to speak to us and provided us with valuable assistance, including releasing a small group of regional employment judges to meet with us. There are numerous others we have talked to who do not wish to be formally acknowledged. We are grateful to them all.

We also owe a debt of gratitude to our research assistants Ben Mays, Chris Long and Finn Callow who provided us with help on particular issues, and particularly Oliver Friend-Smith, who worked alongside us throughout the project. While all errors are our own, we are indebted to Charles Wynn-Evans and Peter Frost who read the draft manuscript and provided insightful comments. We have benefited too from many discussions with interested colleagues. We are particularly grateful to Alan Bogg, Alysia Blackham, Emma Hitchings, Felix Steffek and Ravi Chandran.

Finally, this work could not have been done without the financial support provided by the Employment Lawyers Association (ELA), together with the practical support of Catrina Smith, James Jeynes and Paul McFarlane in their different roles within the ELA. The enthusiastic engagement of Caspar Glyn KC, Chair of the ELA, has been a source of constant encouragement. Our thanks also go to all those at Hart who have helped us through the publishing process, especially Roberta Bassi for her editorial skills, Anne Bevan for her careful and patient copy editing and Linda Goss for steering the book through the production process. We could not have completed this project without the emotional and culinary support of our long-suffering families, who have learned to bear with us as we disentangled statistics and systems.

CONTENTS

PART II
RESOLVING DISPUTES WITHOUT LITIGATION

PART III
THE TRIBUNAL LITIGATION PROCESS

PART V
RECOMMENDATIONS AND METHODOLOGY

LIST OF ABBREVIATIONS

After the Event (ATE) insurance premiums

Central Arbitration Committee (CAC)

Conditional Fee Agreement (CFA)

Department for Business, Energy and Industrial Strategy's (BEIS)

Early Neutral Evaluation (ENE)

Employment Agency Standards Inspectorate (EASI)

Employment Appeal Tribunal (EAT)

Employment Claims Tribunal (ECT), Singapore

Employment Lawyers Association (ELA)

Employment Law Association Network (ELAN)

Employment Relations Authority (ERA), New Zealand

Employment Resolution Service (ERS)

Employment Rights Act 2025 (ERA 2025)

Employment Tribunal (ET)

Equality and Human Rights Commission (EHRC)

Fair Work Agency (FWA)

Fair Work Commission (FWC), Australia

Financial Dispute Resolution (FDR)

Freedom of Information (FOI)

Gangmasters and Labour Abuse Authority (GLAA)

Group Litigation Order (GLO)

Health and Safety Executive (HSE)

High Court Enforcement Officer (HCEO)

HM Courts & Tribunals Service (HMCTS)

HM Revenue and Customs (HMRC)

Independent National Whistleblowing Officer (INWO)

Independent Review of Administrative Law (IRAL)

Industrial Relations Act 1971 (IRA 1971)

Labour Abuse Prevention Officers (LAPOs)

Labour Market Enforcement Orders (LMEO)

Labour Market Enforcement Undertakings (LMEU)

Labour Relations Agency (LRA)

Mediation Information and Assessment Meeting (MIAM)

National Industrial Relations Court (NIRC)

Non-Court Dispute Resolution (NCDR)

Notice of Underpayment (NoU)

Parliamentary and Health Service Ombudsman (PHSO)

Pre-Action Protocols (PAPs)

Qualified One-Way Costs Shifting (QOCS)

Reports for the Prevention of Future Deaths (RPFD)

Scottish Public Services Ombudsman (SPSO)

Small Claims Mediation Service (SCMS)

Tripartite Alliance for Dispute Management (TADM), Singapore

Witness Statements (WS)

LIST OF FIGURES

LIST OF TABLES

PART I

Context and Theoretical Underpinnings

The employment tribunal system is no longer delivering on its intended objectives. Created against the background of voluntarism, it was meant to deal with only a limited number of matters and thus a limited number of claims. Its aim was to be quick, cheap and accessible.[1] Tribunals were also considered the forum of last resort when issues in the workplace could not be resolved between an employer and union representatives. Tribunals were given jurisdiction over unfair dismissal claims specifically with speed in mind: claims could be resolved rapidly to provide a viable alternative to industrial action.

That was 1968. Today, the jurisdiction of the tribunals has grown very substantially in both volume and complexity. Consequently, both the employment tribunals – and the Employment Appeal Tribunal (EAT) – are struggling with the number and length of cases. The publicly available statistics and the results from our empirical research show that the current system does not meet its original aims: rather than quick, cheap and accessible, it is slow, expensive and inaccessible. It has become the forum of first, not the last, resort for workers. The system does retain some degree of informality and is still an expert tribunal, albeit with a much reduced use of lay members, but more complex cases increasingly look like High Court cases, with all the meticulous preparation that requires. There is nothing quick and cheap about it.

Employment disputes do not just end up before employment tribunals. Some cases are heard by the Central Arbitration Committee (CAC) and the county/High Court. The CAC retains very specific jurisdiction and operates fairly efficiently in light of quite low numbers of applications. There is very little data on the number of employment claims in the county or High Court. Other enforcement mechanisms – via HMRC, the Health and Safety Executive (HSE), the Gangmasters and Labour Abuse Authority (GLAA) and Employment Agency Standards Inspectorate (EASI) – are largely ineffective in relation to employment matters (as opposed to modern slavery issues) with very few enforcement actions being undertaken.

So, at present employment tribunals are the main forum for addressing employment disputes and the problem of case load is only going to get worse: the

[1] O Franks, *Report of the Committee on Administrative Tribunals and Enquiries* (Cmnd 218, 1957) para 38 (The Franks Report).

Employment Rights Act 2025 (ERA 2025) introduces dozens of new rights that are to be enforced in the tribunal and expands the ambit of other existing rights. It also lifts (from 1 January 2027) the cap on compensation for unfair dismissal, bringing high value claims from the High Court into the tribunal. Its provisions are complex. The ERA 2025 also establishes the Fair Work Agency (FWA), consolidating existing enforcement bodies and becoming the enforcement body for statutory sick pay and the payment of holiday pay, including rolled-up holiday pay. Its remit can be expanded by regulations which may assist low-paid workers if it includes claims for unpaid wages or deductions from wages. However, even if the FWA is properly resourced and potentially takes on some of the smaller claims that currently end up in front of a tribunal, it seems likely that the situation in tribunals is only going to get worse with a growing volume and complexity of claims.

We argue that given this volume of law and thus cases, the time has come for a rethink. The traditional lenses of employment disputes being matters of contract, statute or human rights are overlapping and interlinked but they do not capture the whole picture: the relational, emotional and psychological perspectives on the employment relationship have been forgotten. Where previously a trade union representative and local manager might hammer out an agreement to resolve a dispute, knowing and understanding the personalities and relational dynamics involved, the employment relationship is now highly individualised. HR managers are process driven and rarely feel able to enter the arena. The employment tribunal process is fundamentally a legal process, it is not concerned with the stories, emotions and contextual explanations that people may seek to bring to them. Rather, it is focused on claims and rights and legislative provisions. In considering how the system might be redesigned – from encouraging early dispute resolution in the workplace, to more formal resolution processes before and during tribunal litigation – we argue that the relational context of the employment relationship needs to be put front and centre of any new regime. There are clear parallels between employment law and family law and we argue that the dispute resolution mechanisms in family law are particularly instructive.

1

Evolution of the Employment Tribunal System

I. Introduction

In the introduction to this part of the book we identified the headline issues facing the employment tribunal system: set up to be quick, cheap and accessible, they are proving anything but for many litigants. This chapter will look at the evolution of the employment tribunal system – both the Employment Tribunal (ET) and the Employment Appeal Tribunal (EAT) – from their origins in the early 1970s to where they are today (section II). It will then consider the current challenges facing the employment tribunal system – namely the growth in the jurisdiction of the ET, the volume of claims currently being brought and the level of resources provided to the system (section III). It will then return to the original objectives for the ET system, envisaged by the Donovan Commission, and examine why they are not being met (section IV). Section V briefly examines the literature dealing with access to justice in the employment context, recognising the serious barriers that exist. Section VI considers the potential impact of the Employment Rights Act 2025 (ERA 2025) on the employment tribunal system. Chapter two will examine alternative fora for bringing employment disputes and other government bodies with the power to intervene in employment disputes.

II. Establishment of Employment Tribunals and Employment Appeal Tribunal

A. Establishment and Aims of the Employment Tribunals

When employment tribunals – originally called industrial tribunals[1] – were set up they were intended to be an expert panel that employees and employers could

[1] Employment Rights (Dispute Resolution) Act 1998, s 1. They remain industrial tribunals in Northern Ireland. Claims for discrimination on the grounds of religious belief or political opinion may be heard by the Fair Employment Tribunal rather than the industrial tribunal.

attend in person, as a matter of last resort, to resolve matters between them cheaply, accessibly, informally and speedily.

i. Cheap, Accessible, Informal, Speedy and Expert

The industrial tribunals were created by section 12 Industrial Training Act 1964 to hear appeals by employers against training levies imposed by the government.[2] There was very little public debate about why tribunals rather than ordinary courts should consider these matters. Nor was there much debate about how tribunals should be constituted or their procedures. During the Second Reading of the Industrial Training Bill, the Minister of Labour had little to say about the nature of the industrial tribunals and simply indicated that they would be constituted by a legally qualified chair, an employers' representative and a workers' representative.[3] It seems that the only significant debate concerned whether there should be locally appointed ad hoc industrial tribunals, or a standing tribunal for each region.[4]

Although the origin of industrial tribunals is 'shrouded in silence',[5] their creation came shortly after the 1957 Report of the Franks Committee.[6] This Committee was set up to consider the 'constitution and working of tribunals' and 'the working of such administrative procedures as including the holding of an enquiry or hearing by or on behalf of a Minister on an appeal or as the result of objections or representations'. Marshall noted at the time that '[t]he Committee's general conclusion about tribunals is significant for its rejection of the view that tribunals should be regarded as part of the machinery of administration'. 'Tribunals', the Report states, 'are not ordinary courts, but neither are they appendages of Government Departments'.[7] The Franks Report identified the main advantages of tribunals as cheapness, accessibility, informality, speed and expert knowledge of their subject.[8] Although the Franks Report was concerned with public law challenges rather than employment law, the advantages of tribunals that it identified are mirrored in subsequent discussions concerning industrial tribunals.

By the time of the Second Reading of the Redundancy Payments Bill in 1965, there was more public debate about the nature of tribunals. The Minister of Labour

[2] Coming into force on 31 May 1965 via the Industrial Tribunals (England and Wales) Regulations 1965.

[3] HC Deb 20 November 1963, vol 684, cols 1101–123, col 1010.

[4] J Clark and B Wedderburn, 'Modern Labour Law: Problems, Functions and Policies' in B Wedderburn, R Lewis and J Clark (eds), *Labour Law and Industrial Relations: Building on Kahn-Freud* (Clarendon Press 1983). See also R Wraith and PG Hutchesson, *Administrative Tribunals* (Royal Institute for Public Administration 1973) 85–86.

[5] Clark and Wedderburn (n 4) 174.

[6] O Franks, *Report of the Committee on Administrative Tribunals and Enquiries* (Cmnd 218, 1957) (The Franks Report).

[7] G Marshall, 'The Franks Report on Administrative Tribunals and Enquiries' (1957) 35 *Public Administration* 347, 355.

[8] The Franks Report (n 6) para 38.

again reiterated the advantages of tribunals as cheapness, accessibility, informality, speed and expertise.[9] Dealing specifically with industrial tribunals, he said that, as they became more established and gained experience, 'further functions relating to industrial relations might be given' to tribunals.[10] He considered that they would 'constitute a valuable experiment in our industrial relations system'.[11] At that time, it was anticipated by the Parliamentary Secretary to the Minister of Transport that tribunals would determine claims under the Redundancy Payments Bill 'in a few weeks, at the maximum'.[12]

When the 1968 Donovan Report recommended the creation of a statutory right against unfair dismissal,[13] it also recommended that this right should be adjudicated in the tribunals.[14] Both the Ministry of Labour's evidence to the Donovan Commission[15] and the Report itself[16] said that the aim of the tribunals was – again – to be cheap, accessible, informal, speedy and expert. Moreover, it was expected that the tribunals' jurisdiction would expand over time: the Donovan Report recommended that 'all disputes arising between employers and employees from their contracts of employment or from any statutory claims' should fall within the tribunals' jurisdiction.[17]

Speed was particularly important in relation to unfair dismissal protection because one purpose of introducing the right was to reduce the large number of strikes that were caused by disputes over dismissals.[18] Consequently, the Donovan Commission considered it 'necessary' for dispute resolution to be speedy.[19] In a debate about the Consultation Paper on the Industrial Relations Bill to introduce the right to claim unfair dismissal, the Solicitor-General assured Parliament that it was the 'intention' for the tribunals to be speedy.[20] In debates on the Bill, John Spence MP argued that speedy decision-making was necessary to uphold workers' faith in the industrial relations process, saying that the promptness of a tribunal decision was 'even more important' than the outcome.[21] With cross-party support,[22] the Industrial Relations Act 1971 conferred a right on employees not to

[9] HC Deb 26 April 1965, vol 711, col 46.

[10] ibid.

[11] ibid.

[12] HL Deb 3 August 1965, vol 269, col 227.

[13] Lord Donovan, *Report of the Royal Commission on Trade Unions and Employers' Associations* (Cmnd 3623, 1968) (The Donovan Report) 141–46.

[14] The Donovan Report (n 13) 147–48.

[15] Ministry of Labour, *Written Evidence of the Ministry of Labour to the Royal Commission on Trade Unions and Employers' Associations* (archive.org/details/op1268709-1001/page/n91/mode/2up) 92–93, para 77.

[16] The Donovan Report (n 13) 156, para 572.

[17] The Donovan Report (n 13) 156, para 573.

[18] The Donovan Report (n 13) 143, para 528. See also Clark and Wedderburn (n 4) 174.

[19] The Donovan Report (n 13) 143, paras 528 and 147, para 546.

[20] HC Deb 26 November 1970, vol 807, col 735.

[21] HC Deb 26 November 1970, vol 807, col 677.

[22] Conservative Political Centre, *Fair Deal at Work: The Conservative Approach to Modern Industrial Relations* (Conservative Political Centre, 1968) 35–36. Secretary of State for Employment and Productivity, *In Place of Strife* (White Paper, Cmnd 3888, 1969) 31–32.

be unfairly dismissed and gave the industrial tribunals jurisdiction to hear these claims.[23]

At the same time as the establishment of the new right of unfair dismissal, 'a separate individual grievance conciliation service was established with the twin aims of addressing the high number of collective disputes and proactively dealing with this potential deluge of individual … claims'.[24] This body became Acas.

Sir Diarmaid Conroy, an early President of the Industrial Tribunals,[25] identified a further factor in favour of using tribunals for employment matters, namely, that it was easier to find competent lawyers to be chairmen of tribunals, because they could quickly become experts in a narrower band of law.[26] This theme of the specialist judge is important when seeking to understand the growth of the jurisdiction of employment tribunals. Moreover, the expert knowledge of tribunal members was widely recognised during the parliamentary debates,[27] the Ministry of Labour's evidence to the Donovan Commission,[28] and an influential White Paper in 1969.[29]

ii. Avoiding Lawyers

The idea that lawyers were not necessary for claims before an industrial tribunal has been prevalent throughout the life of the tribunal. This complements the other aims, particularly that the tribunal should be cheap and accessible, but it was also expressed as a self-standing aim. This was because, as Sir Diarmaid Conroy said in November 1970, many ordinary people have 'animosity' and 'fear' of courts and lawyers. He recognised that informal proceedings and conversational proceedings are 'alien' to many lawyers, who are conditioned to be cautious and thorough,[30] but nevertheless thought the informal approach could be justified. In the debates on the Industrial Relations Bill, Philip Holland MP argued that industrial tribunals should remain 'clear of the lawyers' and should not provide 'a field-day for them'.[31] The Under-Secretary of State for Employment (Dudley Smith MP) assured

[23] Industrial Relations Act 1971, s 22(1) and s 106 (IRA 1971).

[24] D Hann, P Latreille, D Nash and R Saundry, 'Custodians of contemporary pluralism? Acas' evolving role in addressing conflict during a time of economic and regulatory flux' [2023] *Industrial Relations* 1.

[25] Barry Clarke, President of the Employment Tribunals (England and Wales), presented a detailed paper on the history of and the work of each of the former Presidents of the employment tribunals at the Industrial Law Society conference, 13 September 2025. It is anticipated this will be available as a paper shortly.

[26] 'Tribunals and the Courts: An Interview with Sir Diarmaid Conroy, President of the Industrial Tribunals for England and Wales' [1970] *New Law Journal* 1069, 1071.

[27] HC Deb 20 November 1963, vol 684, col 1010; HC Deb 26 November 1970, vol 807, col 717.

[28] *Written Evidence of the Ministry of Labour to the Royal Commission on Trade Unions and Employers' Associations* (n 15) 92, para 77.

[29] *In Place of Strife* (n 22) 32, para 106.

[30] Interview with Sir Diarmaid Conroy (n 26) 1070–71.

[31] HC Deb 26 November 1970, vol 807, col 717.

members that informality would be the 'essence' of industrial tribunals, with parties able to proceed without legal representation, and without 'anything of the Old Bailey atmosphere'.[32] The Donovan Report predicted that most tribunal representatives would be union officials or members of employers' associations, rather than lawyers.[33]

iii. Last Resort Measure

During the 1960s and 1970s, the broad consensus amongst workers, trade unions and employers was that the best method of resolving employment disputes was through voluntary means. Recourse to tribunals was seen as an alternative measure when voluntary methods failed. This is reflected in Chapter X of the Donovan Report which said that the 'best way' of resolving employment disputes is through collective bargaining.[34] Tribunals were viewed as an alternative for workers not covered by voluntary machinery, or for disputes that do not lend themselves to voluntary settlement.[35]

Not only were tribunals to be the last resort but there was to be a further stage before a case reached the tribunal. Ministers – in their evidence to the Donovan Commission – and the National Joint Advisory Council (NJAC) considered that there should be conciliation of disputes before any form of tribunal proceedings.[36] Reid, discussing the report from the NJAC, said that:

> The Committee sees the tribunal's function as one of conciliation rather than adjudication, and as a result recommends that this jurisdiction should not be given to the industrial tribunals … Instead, a dismissal dispute should go first to a statutory official (attached to the Ministry of Labour) whose job it would be to establish the facts and if necessary act as conciliator. Failing a settlement at this stage, the parties could have recourse to an impartial tribunal of representatives from both sides of industry, whose chairman need not be legally qualified. Where appropriate the tribunal could attempt conciliation, whether or not the statutory official had already done so.[37]

While the Donovan Report recommended that unfair dismissal protection should fall within the industrial tribunals' jurisdiction, it also emphasised the need for tribunals to seek to settle disputes amicably through conciliation wherever possible. This is where Acas fitted in.[38]

[32] HC Deb 14 December 1970, vol 808, cols 1071–72.
[33] The Donovan Report (n 13) 159, para 585.
[34] The Donovan Report (n 13) 155, para 568.
[35] ibid.
[36] *Written Evidence of the Ministry of Labour to the Royal Commission on Trade Unions and Employers' Associations* (n 15) 92–93, para 77; *Dismissal Procedures: Report of a Committee of the National Joint Advisory Council on Dismissal Procedures* (HMSO 1967) 42, para 151.
[37] J Reid, 'Report of the National Joint Advisory Council Committee on Dismissal Procedures' (1968) 31 *MLR* 64, 68.
[38] The Donovan Report (n 13)148, para 549.

Given this context, it was thought that the employment tribunals would not have a significant workload. For example, in the debates on what became the Redundancy Payments Act 1965, Lord Lindgren predicted that the volume of work of industrial tribunals 'will not be on a scale approaching anywhere near' the case-load of the local appeal tribunals under the National Insurance Scheme, which dealt with around 36,000 cases a year.[39] In 1970, the Under-Secretary of State for Employment said that the aim of the Industrial Relations Bill was not to encourage large numbers of tribunal claims.[40] He suggested that, once the new law on unfair dismissal had operated for some years, the 'court aspect' would '[fade] more and more into the background as better practices develop and there is greater harmony throughout industry'.[41] While this may now seem like wishful thinking, it highlights the emphasis on tribunal litigation being the exception rather than the norm and the expectation that disputes would generally be resolved by other means, and without lawyers.

iv. Appropriate Breadth of Functions

The early debates also indicate that the functions of the tribunals should be restricted to allow tribunal members to develop expertise in industrial relations. This, it was thought, would make it easier to find judges who could quickly become experts in a narrow band of law.[42] This was the basis for the Donovan Report's recommendation that tribunals should not be concerned with disputes between employers and trade unions and that those disputes should be left for the ordinary courts,[43] a divided jurisdiction which continues today.

On the other hand, widening the functions of industrial tribunals would avoid the split of jurisdiction to hear employment disputes between tribunals, county courts, the High Court and magistrates' courts. A division of jurisdictions between these different fora was considered to cause 'waste', 'frustration' and 'delay'.[44] Moreover, although a narrower range of functions would make it easier to find tribunal judges, a wider range of functions was thought to make it easier to find 'good calibre' judges.[45] Additionally, it was considered that giving tribunals more jurisdiction would build their legitimacy in the eyes of employers and workers.[46] It is the latter framing that has taken precedence; with the growth in individual rights, the jurisdiction of the employment tribunal has substantially expanded over the years. We turn to consider this in section III after briefly exploring the origins of the Employment Appeal Tribunal (EAT).

[39] HL Deb 3 August 1965, vol 269, col 243.
[40] HC Deb 14 December 1970, vol 808, col 1071.
[41] ibid.
[42] Interview with Sir Diarmaid Conroy (n 26) 1071.
[43] The Donovan Report (n 13) 156–57, para 576.
[44] The Donovan Report (n 13) 155, paras 569–70.
[45] HC Deb 26 April 1965, vol 711, col 46; HC Deb 17 November 1966, vol 736, col 798.
[46] HC Deb 26 April 1965, vol 711, col 46.

B. Establishment and Jurisdiction of the Employment Appeal Tribunal

i. The Origin of the Employment Appeal Tribunal

When industrial tribunals were created in 1965, appeals lay on a point of law to the High Court. This does not seem to have been particularly controversial. When the Donovan Report recommended the creation of a statutory right against unfair dismissal and the expansion of the jurisdiction of industrial tribunals,[47] there was no lengthy discussion of appeals from industrial tribunals. Instead, the Report simply recommended that '[a]n appeal should lie on a point of law to the Queen's Bench Division of the High Court'.[48]

The Industrial Relations Act 1971 (IRA 1971) created the National Industrial Relations Court (NIRC). Some appeals from industrial tribunals went to the NIRC, while others remained in the High Court. However, the NIRC was a controversial body because it had original jurisdiction to hear complaints of 'unfair industrial practice',[49] including the calling of strikes by unregistered unions,[50] as well as various complaints relating to collective bargaining and other trade unions matters.[51] Moreover, there was considerable criticism of its President, Sir John Donaldson, in relation to secret exchanges with ministers and civil servants on questions of general industrial relations policy.[52] Sir John was considered politically partisan, as a member of the Conservative Party,[53] and because he held meetings with representatives of an employers' association to discuss the operation of the IRA 1971.[54] He was therefore thought to have conducted himself in a manner that 'verged on the injudicious as well as the unjudicial',[55] resulting in a motion before Parliament in late 1973 to consider his dismissal as President of the NIRC.[56] He was not dismissed but the NIRC was instead abolished by the Trade Union and Labour Relations Act 1974, and appeals from industrial tribunals returned to the High Court.

The EAT was created by the Employment Protection Act 1975. Debates on the Employment Protection Bill do not give many indications as to why the EAT was created. When summarising the Bill in the House of Lords, Lord Hughes simply outlined that

[47] The Donovan Report (n 13) Chapters IX and X.
[48] The Donovan Report (n 13) Chapters IX and X, and 159, para 586.
[49] s 101 IRA 1971.
[50] ibid, s 96.
[51] eg, ss 7, 11, 14, 17, 37, 45, 51 and 112 IRA 1971.
[52] M Spencer and J Spencer, 'The Judge as "Political Advisor": Behind the Scenes at the National Industrial Relations Court' (2006) 33 *Journal of Law and Society* 199, 201.
[53] ibid, 210.
[54] HC Deb 11 June 1973, vol 857, col 989.
[55] C Monaghan, 'Controversial Judicial Decisions and Security of Tenure: Reflections on *Trump v United States*, the *Miller* Litigation, and the Attempt to Remove Sir John Donaldson in the 1970s Labour government' (2024) 29 *Judicial Review* 215, 227. See also HC Deb 7 May 1974, vol 873, cols 239–40.
[56] Early Day Motion No 49. HC Deb 22 November 1973, vol 864, cols 1554–55.

> the Employment Appeal Tribunal is to be a new specialist body with High Court status to hear appeals from industrial tribunals on questions of law, and appeals from the decisions of the Certification Officer on questions of fact or law. Its constitution is to mirror that of industrial tribunals, but with a judge as legally qualified chairman, and side members drawn equally from employers' and workers' representatives. Decisions of the new Tribunal will be subject to further appeal on points of law to the Court of Appeal, in Scotland to the Court of Session, and to your Lordships' House.[57]

ii. Jurisdiction of the Employment Appeal Tribunal

Appeals from the Industrial Tribunal and Fair Employment Tribunal in Northern Ireland go directly to the Northern Ireland Court of Appeal. Some participants in our research noted that sometimes the Court of Appeal did not appear to appreciate the informality of employment tribunal proceedings and that the tribunal was not set up to adjudicate in the same way as a High Court. This presented particular challenges in the Northern Ireland system.

In England, Wales and Scotland most appeals from employment tribunals are heard in the EAT.[58] However, the EAT has jurisdiction to hear appeals from employment tribunals only if statute confers that jurisdiction.[59] Where statute has not granted jurisdiction to the EAT, appeals from employment tribunals, on a question of law, lie to the High Court.[60] Appeals from the Certification Officer also go to the EAT[61] as do some appeals from the Central Arbitration Committee (CAC).[62] However, the EAT does not have jurisdiction to hear appeals against the CAC's decisions on trade union recognition and de-recognition. Instead, these are subject to judicial review in the High Court.[63] The EAT is also the forum in which applications for penalty notices are determined – by way of original jurisdiction – in relation to certain employee information and consultation and employee involvement obligations.[64]

[57] HL Deb 7 August 1975, vol 363, col 1851.

[58] See the Employment Tribunals Act 1996, s 21(1) (ETA 1996).

[59] *Pendragon Plc v Jackson* [1998] ICR 215; *Refreshment Systems Ltd v Wolstenholme* UKEAT/0608/03 [8].

[60] Tribunals and Inquiries Act 1992, s 11. As to appeals that go to the High Court, see s 24 Health and Safety at Work etc Act 1974 (eg *Wilcox v Survey Roofing Group Ltd* [2016] EWHC 868 (Admin)). For a critique of this see B Hepple et al, *Industrial Tribunals* (JUSTICE 1987) 50–51, para 4.17.

[61] Concerning the internal operation of trade unions, including s 9(1) and (2), s 45D, s 56A, s 95 and s 108C Trade Union and Labour Relations (Consolidation) Act 1992 (TULRCA 1992).

[62] eg, Transnational Information and Consultation of Employees Regulations 1999, reg 38(8).

[63] For a discussion about whether these appeals should also go to the EAT see Law Commission, *Employment Law Hearing Structures: Report* (Law Com No 390, 2020) paras 9.8–9.10.

[64] Regulations 20(7), 21(6) and 21A(5) Transnational Information and Consultation of Employees Regulations 1999; reg 22(6) Information and Consultation of Employees Regulations 2004; and reg 20(6) European Public Limited-Liability Company (Employee Involvement) (Great Britain) Regulations 2009.

As the jurisdiction of the employment tribunals has grown, so has the jurisdiction of the EAT, along with a consequent growth in the number of appeals.[65] In 1976, just 427 appeals were registered.[66] By 1996, this figure had risen to 1,465.[67] The way the data was collected changed in 2004/05 but the figures appear to be relatively stable since then. In 2004/05, 1,876 appeals were received;[68] 1,963 were received in 2009/10; 1,207 were received in 2014/15; 1,407 in 2019/20;[69] and 1,805 in 2024/25.[70] There was a brief dip in receipts in from 2015 to 2017 which was likely to be due to the introduction of employment tribunal fees and the consequent reduction in claims before the tribunals. The backlog of cases before the EAT was relatively static from 2011 to 2023, at around 300–400 cases outstanding each year, save for the period of fees and for a short period thereafter.[71] However, the backlog appears to be growing with 496 open cases in 2024 and 598 cases in 2025. No statistics are publicly available in relation to the time it takes for an appeal to be heard.

As an appellate body, the EAT can interfere with the decision of an employment tribunal only if there was an error of law.[72] This requires the appellant to establish that (a) the employment tribunal misdirected itself as to the applicable law, (b) there was no evidence to support a particular finding of fact, or (c) the decision was perverse.[73] Once an appellant has lodged an appeal and it is confirmed that it has been instituted in time and in compliance with the Rules,[74] then it is considered by a Judge of the EAT on the papers.[75] Appeals are 'sifted' and where the grounds of appeal are reasonably arguable then directions will be given for it to proceed to a full hearing. If the judge considers that there may be grounds that are reasonably arguable – or where clarification is required in relation to certain grounds – then the appeal will be listed for a preliminary hearing, either with both parties present or just the appellant for oral consideration of the issue of whether the appeal should proceed.[76] However, where there are no reasonably arguable grounds of appeal, the appeal is dismissed.[77] An appellant may renew their appeal

[65] There are a number of limitations in relation to the public data for the EAT. This is addressed in Appendix 1.

[66] Lord Chancellor's Office, *Judicial Statistics for the Year 1976* (Cmnd 6875, 1977) 90. From 1976 to 2003, the *Judicial Statistics* publication records the number of appeals 'registered' by the EAT. This excluded some appeals which were not registered after an initial sift.

[67] Lord Chancellor's Department, *Judicial Statistics for the Year 1996* (Cm 3716) 72.

[68] Employment Tribunals Service Annual Report & Accounts 2004–05, 9.

[69] Employment Tribunal and Employment Appeals Tribunal Annual Tables 2023/24, Table E_11. These tables were published together with Ministry of Justice, Tribunal Statistics Quarterly: April to June 2024.

[70] See: www.gov.uk/government/statistics/tribunals-statistics-quarterly-january-to-march-2025/tribunal-statistics-quarterly-january-to-march-2025#employment-tribunals.

[71] Ministry of Justice, Tribunal Statistics Quarterly: January to March 2025, Table S_1.

[72] s 21(1) ETA 1996.

[73] *British Telecommunications Plc v Sheridan* [1990] IRLR 27, 30.

[74] EAT Rules 1993, r 3.

[75] EAT Practice Direction 2024, pt 4.

[76] Para 4.3.6 EAT PD 2024.

[77] EAT Rules 1993, r 3(7).

at an oral hearing under rule 3(10) of the EAT Rules. If they are successful, then the claim will proceed to a full hearing on another day. If they are unsuccessful then the appeal stands dismissed. Where grounds of appeal are considered totally without merit, then the appellant has no right to a hearing under rule 3(10).[78] Appeals against decisions of the EAT are made to the Court of Appeal in England and Wales or the Court of Session in Scotland.

The 'sift' process reduces the number of appeals that are heard by the EAT considerably (see Table 1.1).

Table 1.1 Employment Appeal Tribunal Disposals 2009–24[79]

		Type of disposal						
Financial Year	**Total appeals disposed**	**Appeals rejected as out of time**	**Appeals rejected as no reasonable prospect of success**	**Appeals withdrawn prior to registration**	**Appeals withdrawn after registration**	**Appeals struck out**	**Appeals dismissed at preliminary hearing**	**Appeals disposed at full hearing**
2009/10	1,848	244	839	169	115	22	56	403
2010/11	2,001	279	959	167	150	23	60	363
2011/12	2,217	283	1,040	179	128	26	55	506
2012/13	2,155	302	1,042	187	114	30	46	434
2013/14	1,684	232	592	162	123	83	41	451
2014/15	1,392	164	374	113	89	196	30	426
2015/16	1,055	117	311	102	68	87	36	334
2016/17	905	62	380	61	58	58	45	241
2017/18	905	81	412	67	49	23	27	246
2018/19	1,086	133	543	55	68	35	25	227
2019/20	1,092	47	604	100	69	4	16	252
2020/21	1,001	78	512	165	64	20	19	143
2021/22	961	132	470	157	44	12	15	131
2022/23	885	66	579	92	19	4	24	101
2023/24	1,006	55	729	48	36	23	26	89

[78] EAT Rules 1993, r 3(7ZA).

[79] Data collated from Employment Tribunal and Employment Appeals Tribunal Annual Tables 2023/24, Table E_11. These tables were published together with Ministry of Justice, Tribunal Statistics Quarterly: April to June 2024.

Although the sift process is fundamentally different, there are other features of the EAT process that mirror the employment tribunal. The EAT is composed of a legally qualified judge, ranging from recorders through to High Court judges depending on the complexity of the appeal, who may sit with non-legal members or may sit alone.

The procedure in the EAT is relatively informal. Sir John Wood, a former President of the EAT,[80] said that an 'essential part of the function of the EAT' is that it is 'A people's Court ... a place where individuals are not afraid to approach that judicial body in person'.[81] However, other commentators have argued that a degree of juridification has been inevitable. For example, Sir John Waite, also a former President of the EAT,[82] pointed out that '[a] single-minded pursuit of the Franks/Donovan objectives of informality, speed, cheapness and accessibility is bound sooner or later to come into conflict with the aim of certainty'.[83] Employment law is required to achieve a balance between these conflicting principles. However, others are critical of the loss of the distinctive nature of the employment relations context because of the reduction in the use of non-legal members and the fact that appeals from the EAT feed into the civil appellate hierarchy.[84]

III. The Challenges Facing Employment Tribunals

Having looked at the origins and aims of the employment tribunals, we now want to examine the challenges currently facing the tribunals. We identify two: first, the rapid expansion in jurisdiction and second, the increase in number of cases.

A. Growth in the Jurisdiction of the Employment Tribunal

As we have seen, tribunals were initially given jurisdiction over unfair dismissal complaints. However, the number of rights over which tribunals have jurisdiction has grown substantially. Initial extensions of the jurisdiction of industrial tribunals covered relatively straightforward issues: challenges to state duties and

[80] He was President from 1988 to 1993. He also described the post as a 'stinking job' due to the complexity of employment law and the highly political nature of employment law: www.thetimes.com/uk/article/sir-john-wood-6h62ctvgk?msockid=12a1a9a397c965352b54bd4896f16455.

[81] J Wood, 'The Employment Appeal Tribunal as it Enters the 1990s' (1990) 19 *Industrial Law Journal* 133, 134.

[82] From 1983 to 1985.

[83] J Waite, 'Lawyers and Laymen as Judges in Industry' (1986) 15 *Industrial Law Journal* 32, 39. See also R Munday, 'Tribunal Lore: Legalism and the Industrial Tribunals' (1981) 10 *Industrial Law Journal* 146, 153.

[84] S Corby and P Latreille, 'Employment Tribunals and the Civil Courts: Isomorphism Exemplified' (2012) 41 *Industrial Law Journal* 387, 394–96.

determinations (training levy assessments,[85] selective employment tax,[86] and the meaning of dock work[87]) and simple employer–employee issues (statutory redundancy payments,[88] and the failure to give written particulars of employment).[89]

However, since then the jurisdiction of the employment tribunals has expanded substantially across a spectrum of individual and collective rights. In the period from 1965 to 2024, we have identified 64 different pieces of legislation introducing new rights over which the employment tribunals have or have had jurisdiction.[90] One piece of legislation might introduce a right in relation to a very specific area (such as the Employment (Allocation of Tips) Act 2023 which creates only three potential claims)[91] or may introduce a whole raft of different rights, substantially expanding the jurisdiction of the tribunal (eg, the Public Interest Disclosure Act 1998).[92] Moreover, legislation that is primarily concerned with consolidating or amending pre-existing rights often includes additional rights.[93] The President of the Employment Tribunals said that the employment tribunals 'decide well over one hundred types of claim'.[94]

This is also apparent from the public statistics addressing the case-load of the employment tribunals.[95] In 2000/01, 130,408 claims were accepted addressing 218,101 different jurisdictional complaints.[96] That means that each claim included an average of 1.67 different types of complaint. In 2012/13, 191,541 claims were accepted addressing 332,859 different jurisdictional complaints, that is, an average of 1.74 different complaints were made per claim.[97] The employment tribunal system changed its case management system in 2021. This new system, called Reform, has been progressively rolled out to different groups of users. Data is available only in relation to cases on the Reform system (which does not capture all claims) but this does show that of those cases, there was an average of 2.2 different complaints made

[85] Industrial Training Act 1964, s 12 and Industrial Tribunals (England and Wales) Regulations 1965 SI 1965/1101.

[86] Selective Employment Payments Act 1966.

[87] Docks and Harbours Act 1966, s 51(1).

[88] Redundancy Payments Act 1965, s 46(1)(a).

[89] ibid, s 38.

[90] There is no central database containing all employment legislation that is within the tribunals' purview, therefore it is somewhat difficult to be confident that every item has been found.

[91] A complaint by an employee about how or when tips are dealt with (s 27K(1) Employment Rights Act 1996), a complaint by an agency worker in relation to the same matters (s 27K(2)) and a complaint about a failure to comply with the requirements as to a written policy or records (s 27N(1)).

[92] Introducing rights relating to whistleblowing, including protection from detriment, unfair dismissal and unfair selection for redundancy.

[93] See, eg, the Equality Act 2010 which was primarily concerned with harmonisation and consolidation but also introduced protection from indirect discrimination in relation to disability and discrimination arising from disability.

[94] See: www.judiciary.uk/speech-by-judge-barry-clarke-discrimination-in-employment-industrial-courts/.

[95] There are a number of limitations in relation to the public data for employment tribunals: Appendix 1.

[96] Employment Tribunals Service Annual Reports and Accounts 2000–01.

[97] Ministry of Justice, Tribunal Statistics Quarterly: July to September 2023 Main Tables, Table ET_1.

per claim in 2024/25.[98] However, the Impact Assessment for the ERA 2025, in relation to cases brought, says that the 2023 figures indicate the average number of jurisdictional complaints is 4.1 per claim.[99] Even these figures do not represent the full picture; a jurisdictional complaint is simply the broad area of complaint but may contain a number of different claims. For example, disability discrimination is a jurisdictional complaint but might encompass direct discrimination, indirect discrimination, discrimination arising from disability, and a failure to make reasonable adjustments, as well as harassment and victimisation. Similarly, sex discrimination is identified as a jurisdictional complaint and might likewise cover direct and indirect discrimination, victimisation and harassment, discrimination because of marriage and civil partnership and gender reassignment.[100]

Whatever the precise number of claims over which they have jurisdiction, the jurisdiction of employment tribunals has grown considerably in volume and complexity. The growth can be considered in relation to six key areas.

First, in relation to unfair dismissal. This right was established under section 106 IRA 1971 and placing it within the jurisdiction of the tribunals was the first significant development in their work. This was a home-grown right arising out of the Donovan Report 1968. At that time, it was concerned with 'ordinary' unfair dismissal, that is where the reason was conduct, capability, redundancy or non-compliance with a statutory requirement.[101] It also extended to dismissals relating to the enforcement of a closed shop, strikes and lockouts.[102] Tribunals must now also consider claims for automatically unfair dismissal in the context of issues including leave for family reasons, working time, protected disclosures, flexible working requests, blacklists and Sunday working.[103] An ordinary unfair dismissal may also be for the potentially fair reason of 'some other substantial reason' capturing quasi-redundancies and other business reasons.[104] There are added complexities where the decision to dismiss an employee engages issues relating to their right to a private life under Article 8 of the European Convention on Human Rights (ECHR).[105]

The ERA 2025 significantly extends the right to claim unfair dismissal by reducing the current requirement for employees to have worked from two years to six months before being able to claim. In addition, and more significantly, the

[98] Ministry of Justice, Tribunal Statistics Quarterly: January to March 2025 Main Tables, Table ET_1_R.

[99] See: assets.publishing.service.gov.uk/media/6842fa6e4d039a010411f076/employment-rights-bill-economic-analysis.pdf.

[100] Ministry of Justice, Tribunal Statistics Quarterly: January to March 2025 Main Tables, ET_1_R, note 7.

[101] ss 22–23 IRA 1971.

[102] ibid, ss 25 and 26.

[103] Pt X, Employment Rights Act 1996.

[104] For critique of the approach taken to identifying the reason for dismissals see P Collins, 'Finding Fault in the Law of Unfair Dismissal: The Insubstantiality of Reasons for Dismissal' (2022) 51 *Industrial Law Journal* 598.

[105] *Pay v UK* [2009] IRLR 139 [2008] ECHR 1007 in which an employee was dismissed because of his performances in fetish clubs which were considered incompatible with his role as a probation officer working with sex offenders.

cap on compensation is to be removed, meaning that many high value claims that would previously have been heard in the High Court are likely to be heard before the tribunal.

Second, there has been major growth in protection from discrimination. While initially a home-grown right, starting with the Equal Pay Act 1970, the Sex Discrimination Act 1975, the Race Relations Act 1976 and the Disability Discrimination Act 1995, the scope of discrimination law has subsequently been significantly reshaped and expanded by European Union (EU) law. Protection was extended to cover discrimination because of sexual orientation, religion or belief, and age in order to implement the EU Framework Directive 2000/78.[106] The scope of the rights within domestic legislation now includes associative direct discrimination,[107] discrimination by perception[108] and associative indirect discrimination.[109] The employment tribunal's jurisdiction has continued to expand. For example, section 1 of the Worker Protection (Amendment of Equality Act 2010) Act 2023 gives jurisdiction to the employment tribunal in relation to the newly created duty on employers to take (all)[110] reasonable steps to prevent sexual harassment of employees.

The complexities in discrimination law cannot be overstated. This is apparent from the volume of appellate case law covering, among other things, the construction of the comparator,[111] the operation of the burden of proof,[112] the interplay with the ECHR,[113] and the meaning of work of equal value.[114]

The third area of growth arises solely from the implementation of EU Directives. This has resulted in legislation in a number of mainstream employment areas including the transfer of undertakings[115] and – two areas that have given rise to very substantial litigation[116] – protection from discrimination for part-time

[106] The EU Framework Direction establishing a general framework for equal treatment in employment and occupation: [2000] OJ L303/16.

[107] Case C-303/06 *Coleman v Attridge Law* ECLI:EU:C:2008:415.

[108] *English v Thomas Sanderson Blinds Ltd* [2008] EWCA Civ 1421.

[109] Introduced as s 19A Equality Act 2010 in light of the CJEU decision in Case C-83/14 *CHEZ Razpredelenie Bulgaria AD v Komisia za zashtita ot diskriminatsia* ECLI:EU:C:2015:480.

[110] This word is to be added by the Employment Rights Bill.

[111] See, eg, *Hewage v Grampian Health Board* [2012] UKSC 37.

[112] *Igen v Wong Ltd* [2005] EWCA Civ 142.

[113] With regard to worker status, see *Gilham v Ministry of Justice* [2019] UKSC 44. As to religion and belief discrimination, see *Higgs v Farmor's School* [2025] EWCA Civ 109.

[114] *Asda Stores Ltd v Brierley* [2021] UKSC 10.

[115] See The Transfer of Undertakings (Protection of Employment) Regulations 2006 SI 2006/246 replacing SI 1981/1794, implementing the Acquired Rights Directive 77/187/EC and Transfers of Undertakings Directive 2001/23/EC respectively.

[116] Particularly large-scale multiple claims. For example, in relation to pension provision for part-time workers see Case C-393/10 *O'Brien v Ministry of Justice* ECLI:EU:C:2012:110 and *Miller v Ministry of Justice* [2019] UKSC 60. In relation to holiday pay claims see *HMRC v Stringer* [2009] UKHL 31 and *Chief Constable of the Police Service of Northern Ireland v Agnew* [2023] UKSC 33.

workers[117] and working time.[118] The question of how to calculate holiday pay has been particularly vexed resulting in lengthy litigation on a number of issues, including what happens to a person's entitlement to holiday pay when they are off sick and whether rolled up holiday pay is permissible.

Issues of working time have also led to employment tribunals being given jurisdiction in relation to niche and specific contexts such as the Merchant Shipping (Working Time: Inland Waterways) Regulations 2003 and Cross-border Railway Services (Working Time) Regulations 2008. These claims required employment tribunals to interpret domestic legislation in light of the wording and purpose of the original EU Directives which they implement and have given rise to difficult questions of EU law. Although the UK has now left the EU, most of the implementing legislation remains in place and there is now the added complexity of how the various pieces of Brexit legislation including the European Union (Withdrawal) Act 2018 and the Retained EU Law (Revocation and Reform) Act 2023, fit with EU law already on the statute book.

The fourth area relates to claims concerning trade union membership and activities. While voluntarism was understood to be the foundational feature of the employment dispute system when tribunals were introduced, legal issues relating to trade unions nevertheless arose. These were primarily addressed in other fora: by the CAC,[119] the Certification Officer[120] or in the High Court.[121] The employment tribunal's jurisdiction, however, is concerned with the rights of a trade union member vis-a-vis their employer. Even in this sphere, complex questions of law have had to be addressed by tribunals: for example the interpretation of legislation providing protection from an employer offering inducements to employees to give up collective bargaining rights[122] and the interplay between the domestic legislation and freedom of association rights under Article 11 ECHR, where a worker is subjected to a detriment short of dismissal for participating in strike action.[123]

Fifth, there has been a significant growth in 'family-friendly' legislation. Initially the Employment Protection Act 1975 extended the jurisdiction of the industrial tribunals to include claims concerning the newly created rights to maternity pay. There is now a panoply of rights relating to family life which have arisen from a variety of sources, including EU law. These include rights relating to parental

[117] The Part-time Workers (Prevention of Less Favourable Treatment) Regulations 2000 SI 2000/1551 implementing the Part-time Work Directive 97/81/EC.

[118] The Working Time Regulations 1998 SI 1998/1833 implementing Council Directives 94/104/EC and 94/33/EC.

[119] eg, recognition: sch A1 TULRCA 1992.

[120] Primarily internal union affairs: ss 45C and 55 TULRCA 1992.

[121] Including for an injunction where the requirements for industrial action in TULRCA 1992 have not been met.

[122] *Kostal UK Ltd v Dunkley* [2021] UKSC 47.

[123] *Secretary of State for Business and Trade v Mercer* [2024] UKSC 12.

leave and pay,[124] shared parental leave and pay,[125] flexible working,[126] and, more recently, parental bereavement[127] and neonatal care leave and pay.[128] These do not simply confer the right to leave and to pay but also provide protection from detriment and unfair dismissal.[129]

Sixth, and most recently, jurisdiction has been given to employment tribunals in relation to claims concerning precarious work. The introduction of the national minimum wage[130] can now be seen as the start of a growing body of legislation aimed at protecting low paid, vulnerable workers. The right to written particulars was extended to workers, not just employees from 6 April 2020.[131] Concern about zero hours contracts has been particularly acute and resulted in the Exclusivity Terms in Zero Hours Contracts (Redress) Regulations 2015[132] which provide for claims to be brought to a tribunal concerning unfair dismissal or detrimental treatment for breaching a provision that was an exclusivity term. Further rights have been provided for in the ERA 2025, introducing highly complex provisions relating to guaranteed hours[133] and reasonable notice of shifts[134] for zero hours / low paid workers, which also extend to agency workers.[135]

Alongside this growth, in legislation the employment tribunal also has jurisdiction over certain breach of contract claims. Here a claimant has a choice over whether to bring the claim before the tribunal or to take it to the county court. The advantage of the former is that the tribunal is generally a costs-free jurisdiction. However, tribunals may only consider breach of contract claims that are not concerned with personal injury, are up to a value of £25,000, and concern breaches arising on or are outstanding at the termination of employment.[136]

Despite repeated attempts to consolidate these many and various rights, they remain scattered across many different sections of Acts and provisions in secondary legislation.[137] They have required interpretation of EU Directives and case

[124] The Maternity and Parental Leave etc Regulations 1999 SI 1999/3312, as amended; the Paternity and Adoption Leave Regulations 2002 SI 2002/2788 as amended.

[125] Shared Parental Leave Regulations 2014 SI 2014/3050.

[126] Employment Rights Act 1996, s 80F.

[127] Parental Bereavement (Leave and Pay) Act 2018 and Parental Leave Regulations 2020 SI 2020/249.

[128] Neonatal Care (Leave and Pay) Act 2023 and Neonatal Care Leave and Miscellaneous Amendments Regulations 2025 SI 2025/375.

[129] See, eg, regs 19 and 20 Maternity and Parental Leave etc Regulations 1999, as amended.

[130] National Minimum Wage Act 1998.

[131] Reg 13 Employment Rights (Miscellaneous Amendments) Regulations 2019/731 amended s 11 Employment Rights Act 1996.

[132] Exclusivity Terms in Zero Hours Contracts (Redress) Regulations 2015 SI 2015/2021.

[133] The ERA 2025 inserts new sections into the Employment Rights Act 1996 as ss 27BA–27BF.

[134] Inserted as new ss 27BJ–27BW Employment Rights Act 1996.

[135] Inserted as new Schedule A1 Employment Rights Act 1996.

[136] Employment Tribunals Extension of Jurisdiction (England and Wales) Order 1994 SI 1994/1623.

[137] See, eg, the Employment Protection (Consolidation) Act 1978, Trade Union and Labour Relations (Consolidation) Act 1992, Employment Rights Act 1996 and the Equality Act 2010.

law. Unsurprisingly this growth in rights has also resulted in a dramatic increase in both the number of claims brought before tribunals and the length of time required to determine them because the law is often highly complex and with it has come greater involvement of lawyers, significant increases in costs and, inevitably, a greater formalisation of the process.

B. Volume of Claims before the Employment Tribunals

The statistics dealing with the volume of claims accepted by the employment tribunals reveal a steep upward trajectory (see Figure 1.1).[138] In 1972, only 14,857 claims were accepted. In 1975, a step change occurred with numbers increasing to 35,897.[139] The numbers remained relatively stable until 1991/92 when there was another change, up to 67,448.[140] A further increase occurred in 1994/95 with numbers rising to 88,061.[141] An unusual peak in the number of claims can be seen in the 1995/96 figures (108,827 claims) which is largely attributable to the part-time employee pension cases.[142] Numbers steadily increased with another significant peak in 2000/01 at 130,408[143] arising from large-scale equal pay claims and ongoing part-time employee pension cases, before settling back to around 90–115,000 claims per year until another rise to 132,577 in 2006/07[144] and again in 2007/08 to 189,303.[145] In both of these years there were a large number of equal pay claims brought by multiple claimants, and in 2007/08 the number of working time claims doubled compared with previously. Very high claim numbers can also be seen in 2009/10 and 2010/11 at 236,103 and 218,096 respectively, primarily driven by multiple claims of working time rights – claimed in relation to both the Working Time Directive and unauthorised deductions from wages[146] – before declining again to 186,331 in 2011/12 and 191,541 in 2012/13.[147] Thereafter, numbers have remained stable in the 100,000–120,000 range, except for the period in which fees were introduced where the number of claims dropped significantly.

[138] For the limitations in the data see Appendix 1.

[139] Department of Employment, *Employment Gazette* November 1984, 488.

[140] B Hawes, 'Setting the Pace or Running Alongside? ACAS and the Changing Employment Relationship' in B Towers and W Brown (eds), *Employment Relations in Britain: 25 Years of the Advisory, Conciliation and Arbitration Service* (Oxford University Press, 2001) 19.

[141] ibid.

[142] ibid.

[143] Employment Tribunals Service Annual Reports and Accounts 2000–01.

[144] Employment Tribunal and EAT Statistics (GB) 1 April 2006 to 31 March 2007.

[145] Ministry of Justice, Tribunal Statistics Quarterly: July to September 2023 Main Tables, Table ET_1.

[146] They were predominantly multiple airline industry cases that were resubmitted every three months: Employment Tribunal and EAT Statistics 2009–2010 (GB) 3.

[147] Ministry of Justice, Tribunal Statistics Quarterly: July to September 2023 Main Tables, Table ET_1.

Figure 1.1 Tribunal claim numbers from 1972 to 2025[148]

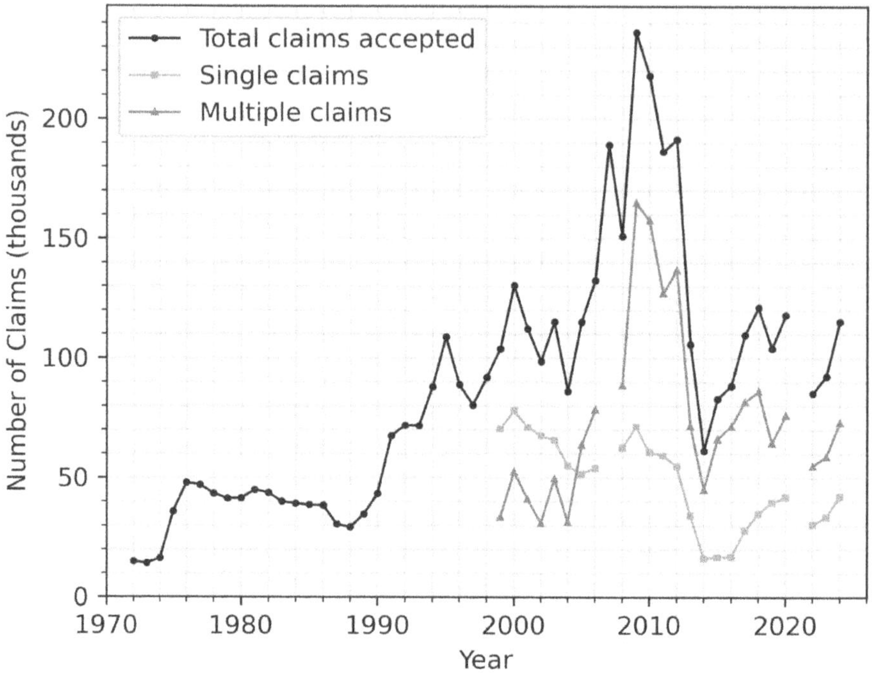

The data on the number of claims disposed of is somewhat less clear. The numbers gradually increased from 37,910 in 1985/86 to 92,938 in 2000/01.[149] Thereafter the number of claims disposed of remained relatively stable in the range of 90,000 to around 120,000 from 2000/01 to 2012/13.[150] There was an increase in 2013/14 to 148,387 and then a dramatic rise in 2014/15 to 312,773 which is almost entirely explained by the disposal of some 293,934 multiple claims, predominantly on working time. Since then the number of claims disposed of has dropped

[148] The data for Figure 1.1 was collated from the sources identified in nn 143–47 above.

[149] See *Employment Gazette* October 1987, 499–504; *Employment Gazette* May 1989, 258–60; *Employment Gazette* April 1990, 214–18; *Employment Gazette* May 1991, 304–06; *Employment Gazette* May 1991, 304–06; *Employment Gazette* November 1993, 528–31; *Employment Gazette* November 1993, 528–31; *Employment Gazette* October 1994, 368–71; Office for National Statistics Labour Market Trends July 1996, 306–10; Office for National Statistics Labour Market Trends April 1997, 152–54; Office for National Statistics Labour Market Trends April 1997, 152–54; Office for National Statistics Labour Market Trends September 1999, 494–96; Office for National Statistics Labour Market Trends September 1999, 494–96; Employment Tribunals Service Annual Reports and Accounts 1999–2000; Employment Tribunals Service Annual Reports and Accounts 2000–01.

[150] Employment Tribunals Service Annual Reports and Accounts 2001–02; Employment Tribunals Service Annual Reports and Accounts 2002–03; Employment Tribunals Service Annual Reports and Accounts 2003–04; Employment Tribunals Service Annual Reports and Accounts 2004–05; Employment Tribunals Service Annual Reports and Accounts 2005–06; Employment Tribunal and EAT Statistics (GB) 1 April 2006 to 31 March 2007; Ministry of Justice, Tribunal Statistics Quarterly: July to September 2023 Main Tables, Table ET_2.

significantly: to 49,529 in 2015/16 and remained at around 35,000–50,000 until 2022/23 when the numbers rose to 72,894.[151] Although it is difficult to know exactly what caused this drop, recent statistics show that the proportion of complex cases that are being brought has increased.[152] We were told that over the last five years the percentage of receipts of the more complex cases, assigned to the open track, has been growing and now sits at about 60–65 per cent of the case-load. These will inevitably take longer to deal with. Moreover, 13 per cent of receipts over the last year were disability discrimination claims. We were told that the disabilities relied on were predominantly mental health disabilities which also necessitated more time to be given to support claimants bringing those claims.

In recent years, the number of cases disposed of has been volatile (Figure 1.2): the numbers rose to 72,894 in 2022/23 and again to 104,587 in 2023/24. However, they then fell to 71,430 in 2024/25. Much of this volatility can be explained by the disposal of large-scale multiple claims, such as the settlement of equal pay claims against Glasgow City Council in November 2023.[153]

Figure 1.2 Number of disposals of claims by the ET[154]

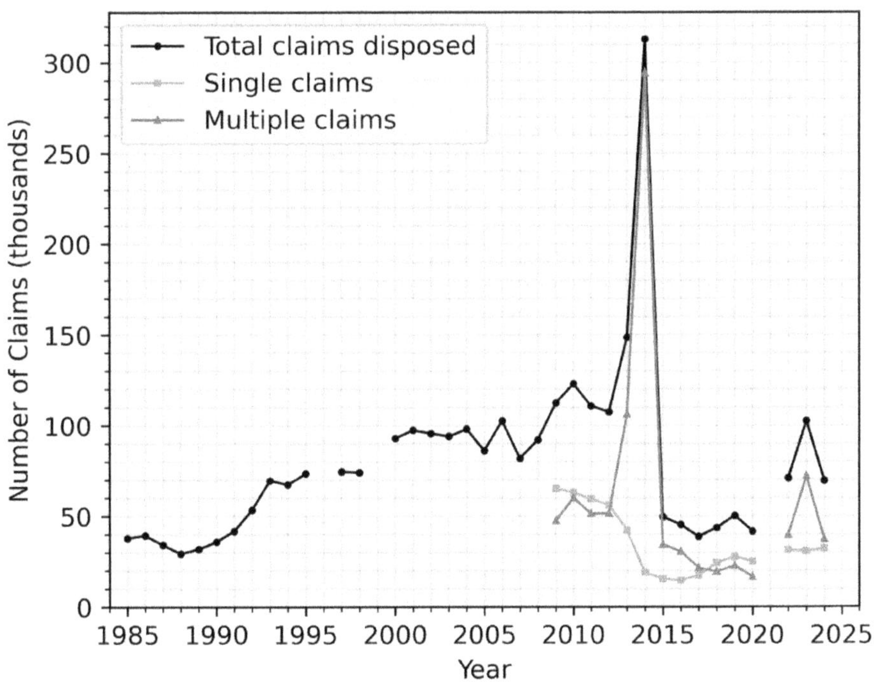

[151] Ministry of Justice, Tribunal Statistics Quarterly: January to March 2025 Main Tables, Table S_1.

[152] See: www.gov.uk/government/statistics/tribunals-statistics-quarterly-january-to-march-2025/tribunal-statistics-quarterly-january-to-march-2025#fn:2.

[153] ibid.

[154] The data for Figure 1.2 was collated from the sources identified in nn 149–52 above.

The backlog remained relatively steady between 2010 and 2020 in the region of 400,000, peaking at 609,251 in March 2013 and dipping to 219,045 on 31 March 2015. However, since 2020 it has been in the region of 450,000–510,000 cases.[155] Much of the backlog arises from multiple claims.[156] The extent of the backlog has significant implications for the timeliness of tribunal hearings, which we address below.

C. Resources

The public data dealing with the funding allocated to employment tribunals is not available in one place nor is it clear whether it is directly comparable. However, following a Freedom of Information (FOI) request, the operational costs, excluding any share of digital or property overheads, were as follows (Table 1.2):

Table 1.2 Funding of employment tribunal system

Financial Year	Operational Costs (£m)
2015/16	41.8
2016/17	38.1
2017/18	40.0
2018/19	43.3
2019/20	53.8
2020/21	56.4
2021/22	65.2
2022/23	68.2
2023/24	73.6
2024/25	80.8

The table shows that funding of tribunals has doubled over the last 10 years, but other publicly available figures[157] suggest that the funding has remained relatively

[155] See: www.gov.uk/government/statistics/tribunals-statistics-quarterly-january-to-march-2025/tribunal-statistics-quarterly-january-to-march-2025#fn:2.

[156] Ministry of Justice, Tribunal Statistics Quarterly: July to September 2023 Main Tables, Table S_4.

[157] Different figures are shown in other sources including Michael Gibbons, 'Better Dispute Resolution: A Review of Employment Dispute Resolution in Great Britain' (Department of Trade and Industry, March 2007) 22: webarchive.nationalarchives.gov.uk/ukgwa/20090608233228/; www.berr.gov.uk/files/file38516.pdf; Ministry of Justice, 'Press Release: Employment Tribunal Fees to Benefit Business and Taxpayers': www.gov.uk/government/news/employment-tribunal-fees-to-benefit-business-and-taxpayers; D Pyper, F McGuinness and J Brown, 'Employment Tribunal Fees', *House of Commons Library Briefing Paper* Number 7081 (18 December 2017) 22: researchbriefings.files.parliament.uk/documents/SN07081/SN07081.pdf; and Question to the Ministry of Justice (tabled on 3 April 2025, answered on 10 April 2025): questions-statements.parliament.uk/written-questions/detail/2025-04-03/44114/.

flat over the last 20 years at around £70 million to £80 million per year. If that is correct, then according to the Bank of England's inflation calculator,[158] the funding should now be £125 million just to stand still. The difficulty is that it is unclear what is included in the different funding calculations.

Perhaps a more helpful way of considering the resources of the employment tribunal system is to consider the staff and judicial head-count over the last five years. The number of HM Courts & Tribunal Service staff in the employment tribunal system, and agency staff, has ranged from 565 in 2020, increasing to 618 in 2021 and then gradually declining to 545 in 2024.[159] As at September 2025, 23 per cent of staff were agency workers. However, this varied across regions with 17 per cent and 18 per cent of staff being agency workers in the South West Region and London Region respectively, but 63 per cent of staff in Wales and 43 per cent of staff in the Midlands Region.[160] There were 317 employment tribunal and EAT judges across England, Wales and Scotland in 2020. This increased to 425 in 2022 but has then steadily declined to 346 in 2025.[161] The judicial head-count however, is for salaried and fee paid judges. Fee paid judges only sit for a limited number of days each year. We were told that in England and Wales, about 70 per cent of sitting days were undertaken by salaried judges; in Scotland the figure was about 90 per cent. There are particular difficulties recruiting salaried judges in London and the South-East. In April 2024, a recruitment round for salaried employment judges in London and the South-East yielded 32.4 per cent of the number of judges sought;[162] it was said that '[t]he likeliest explanation for the shortfall is the cost of living in London and the South East'.[163]

Despite the reducing head-count of judges, the number of sitting days has increased. In 2020/21, there were 30,000 sitting days in the employment tribunals and 35,000 in 2021/22. There were 34,000 sitting days in 2024/25.[164] In the EAT, there has been a similar gradual increase in sitting days, from 397 days in 2020/21 to 591 in 2024/25.[165]

Given the substantial growth in case load and complexity of the jurisdiction of the tribunals, it is notable that there has been little increased resource. Judges have nevertheless increased sitting days even with a reduced head-count.

[158] See: www.bankofengland.co.uk/monetary-policy/inflation/inflationcalculator?number.Sections%5B0%5D.Fields%5B0%5D.Value=700000&current_year=78.1118333333333&comparison_year=139.343.

[159] Question to Ministry of Justice (tabled on 1 April 2025, answered on 7 April 2025): questions-statements.parliament.uk/written-questions/detail/2025-04-01/43047/?utm_source=chatgpt.com and Judicial Appointments Commission, 'Statistics about Judicial Appointments': judicialappointments.gov.uk/statistics-about-judicial-appointments/.

[160] Data obtained via Freedom of Information (FOI) request.

[161] There were 138.9 FTE salaried judges (including the President and Regional Employment Judges) as at 1 April 2025 in England and Wales.

[162] It was 52% in the 2023 recruitment round.

[163] See: www.judiciary.uk/wp-content/uploads/2024/05/15-April-2024-NUG-Minutes-ET-.pdf.

[164] Data obtained via Freedom of Information (FOI) request.

[165] Ministry of Justice, Tribunal Statistics Quarterly: January to March 2025 Main Tables, Table JSFP_1.

IV. Are the Original Aims of the Employment Tribunal Being Met Today?

It will be recalled that the original aim of the employment tribunals was that they should be cheap, accessible, informal, speedy and expert. These aims are deeply rooted in the psyche of most employment lawyers and in the system as a whole. It was particularly evident in many of our discussions in the focus groups. Yet, as we have already indicated, the employment tribunals currently do not live up to this billing. We turn now to examine this in more detail, drawing on insights from our survey data and focus groups.

A. Speedy

The need for a speedy resolution to stop cases from being protracted and allow individuals to move on with their lives has long been seen as an important objective of the employment tribunals. However, the statistics – and our empirical study – show very clearly that the employment tribunal process is not speedy. The higher courts have also been concerned about delay. For example, the Court of Appeal in *The Kingdom of Spain v Lorenzo* noted the very lengthy period over which a case had been heard:

> 33. I must record my dismay at the fact that we are now nine years from Ms Lorenzo's alleged constructive dismissal, without the merits of her case yet having been tried. It was entirely sensible for the ET claim to be stayed in September 2016 for what turned out to be just over a year until the Supreme Court had delivered judgment in *Benkharbouche*. But after that judgment had been given the case was before the employment tribunal for a further three years and eight months and the Employment Appeal Tribunal for almost two and a half years, including ten months during which judgment was reserved. If the case cannot now be settled it should be heard on its merits in the ET without further delay. Whatever its outcome, Ms Lorenzo may understandably feel that the English ET system has not treated her well.[166]

The available data on timeliness of hearings is limited. However, in 2012 the median 'age' of case at disposal was 29 weeks.[167] In 2013/14 it was 104 weeks.[168] More recent data deals with single claims separately from multiple claims. In 2020/21, the median stood at 33 weeks for single claims and 70 weeks for multiple claims.[169]

[166] *The Kingdom of Spain v Lorenzo* [2024] EWCA Civ 1602, [33].

[167] Ministry of Justice, Tribunal Statistics Quarterly: October to December 2013 Main Tables, Table 4.1.

[168] Ministry of Justice, Tribunal Statistics Quarterly: October to December 2015 Main Tables, Table 4.1.

[169] Ministry of Justice, Tribunal Statistics Quarterly: October to December 2021 Main Tables, Table T_1.

Timeliness data is now only available for single claims that are on the Tribunal's new 'Reform' database. In 2024/25, the median age of case at disposal for this (limited) category of single claims was 18 weeks.[170] There is no publicly available data in relation to the timeliness of EAT hearings.

These figures somewhat under-represent the reality of the position; there is significant regional variation. This can be seen in the minutes of the October 2025 National User Group for employment tribunals in England and Wales:

a. For shorter hearings of 1–2 days' duration, the majority of the regions were still listing them in either the second half of 2025 or the first half of 2026. However, in the South West and North West regions they were listing them in the second half of 2026, and in London South they were being listed in the first half of 2027.
b. For hearings of 3–5 days' duration, these were mostly being listed in the first half of 2026. The Midlands East, Midlands West, London Central, South West, South East (Watford and Reading) and Wales (North and South) were listing them in the second half of 2026 and London South was listing them in the second half of 2027.
c. For hearings of 6–10 days' duration, the picture is mixed. London East and the North East were listing these cases in the first half of 2026; Midlands West, the South West and Wales (North and South) in the second half of 2026. Everywhere else was listing these cases in 2027, except Watford who were listing in the first half of 2028.
d. For hearings longer than 10 days, hearing dates ranged from the first half of 2026 in London East and the North East, the second half of 2026 in the South West and Wales, the first half of 2027 Midlands West and Bury St Edmonds, and the second half of 2027 in Midlands East, the North West, London Central and South East. However, Watford was listing these cases in the first half of 2028, and London South was listing them into February 2029.[171]

In Scotland the picture is better: in October 2025, the first case management preliminary hearing in open-track cases were being listed about 10 weeks after the claim was received and final hearings were being listed in December–February 2026.[172]

Participants in our research were very concerned about the long waiting times, especially in Watford and London South. We understand that the employment tribunals in these locations particularly struggle to recruit employment

[170] Ministry of Justice, Tribunal Statistics Quarterly: January to March 2025, Main Tables, Table T_1.
[171] See: www.judiciary.uk/courts-and-tribunals/tribunals/employment-tribunal/employment-tribunal-england-wales/national-user-group/.
[172] See: www.judiciary.uk/courts-and-tribunals/tribunals/employment-tribunal/employment-tribunal-scotland/employment-tribunal-user-group-minutes-for-scotland/.

judges and there are a number of judicial vacancies. In the survey, participants were asked to indicate how problematic they perceived certain issues to be for the tribunal system (see Figure 1.3). One of those issues was the time taken for a case to go from start to finish. Fifty-eight per cent of participants considered it to be 'very significant' and 37 per cent considered to be 'quite significant'. It was the most significant issue for most participants out of the seven factors they were asked about.

Figure 1.3 Survey data showing how problematic particular issues were perceived to be

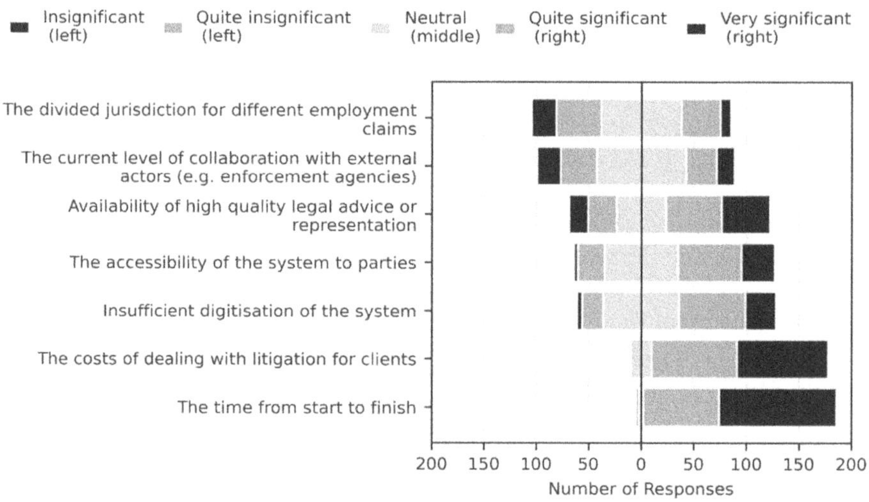

There was no significant difference in that view between participants from different types of practice (solicitors, barristers, trade union representatives), years of professional experience or the percentage of their practice that was concerned with claimants or respondents. Geographical location yielded some differences in that the time from start to finish was somewhat less significant in Scotland and a little less significant in Northern Ireland compared with other regions.[173] The delays appear to be less lengthy in these regions.

Participants in both the narrative sections of the survey as well as in focus groups and interviews overwhelmingly pointed to the lengthy waiting times for the listing of hearings. They noted that while preliminary hearings tended to be listed quite quickly, it was taking around two to three months to process a claim; around six months for the preliminary hearing; and around two to two and a half years for the final hearing. This delay between the preliminary and

[173] Where a scale of -2 (insignificant) to +2 (significant) was used, the mean across the UK was 1.534 (standard deviation 0.622). However, the mean for Scotland was 0.571 (albeit with a standard deviation of 1.134) and for Northern Ireland it was 1 (standard deviation of 0).

final hearing meant that claimants were rushed to initiate their claim within the limitation period and swiftly attend a preliminary hearing, and then had to wait several years to address the substantive issues. In addition to the costs and stress involved, the parties 'move on' during this time. Participants also said that hearings were often postponed at the last minute, sometimes just the day before due to a lack of resource and were not then rescheduled for another six months to a year.

This highlights the very significant issues in relation to meeting the original aim of employment dispute resolution through the tribunals being achieved speedily. The current situation is a very long way from the expectation that matters would be dealt with within weeks.

B. Accessibility and Informality

As noted above in Figure 1.3, participants in our survey were concerned about the availability of high-quality legal advice or representation and the accessibility of the tribunal system; matters which go hand in hand. By assigning a number to the significance rating,[174] a mean value can be calculated. In relation to high quality legal advice the mean was 0.429 (standard deviation of 1.259) and for accessibility of the system it was 0.476 (standard deviation of 0.988). These both sit between the neutral and quite significant bracket.

There was some differentiation in how important these issues were to different groups. In relation to the availability of high-quality legal advice or representation, this was generally perceived as a significant issue among all types of practitioners, although views varied more strongly among those working in trade unions, as sole practitioners, in city law firms, and in a regional firm with a substantial employment team. Geographically, participants' views were quite divergent and there was no particular trend in relation to the different regions.

In relation to the accessibility of the system to the parties, this was generally perceived to be a significant issue among most practitioners, except for those working in a generalist chambers with an employment team. There was a greater variety in the responses for those with 0–5 years of experience. It was perceived as a neutral issue for those in Scotland and North West England.

When participants were asked about the relative importance of the complexity of the procedural rules in relation to the time cases take to be resolved, this was considered mildly insignificant. The mean value was -0.109 (with a standard deviation of 1.089). There was no obvious pattern or diversity across different participant groups.

[174] Insignificant -2, Quite insignificant -1, Neutral 0, Quite significant +1 and Significant +2.

Figure 1.4 Survey data showing how significantly particular issues were perceived to be as a cause for delays

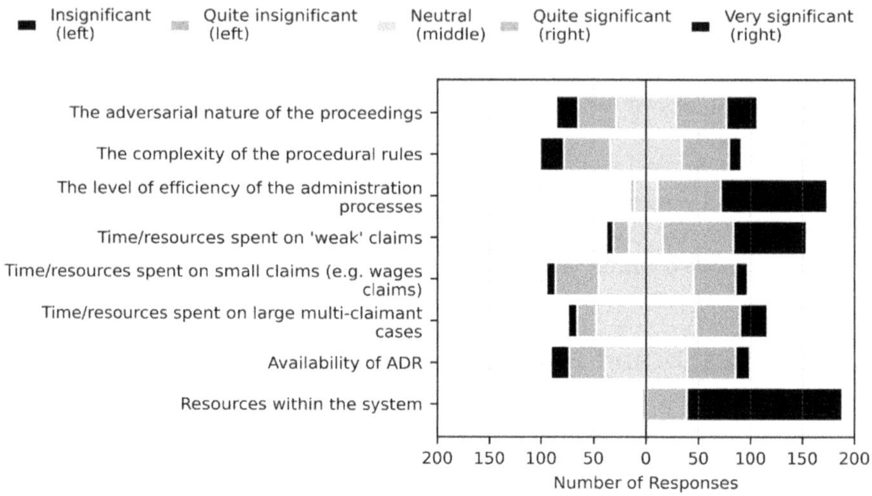

In focus groups, the procedural rules were not seen as a particular problem, although various suggestions were made to improve the efficiency of the process overall (these are considered in chapter seven). Despite this, participants overwhelmingly said that the tribunal process was inaccessible to litigants in person, whether as a claimant or a respondent. This was primarily because the litigants were deeply involved in the dispute and the 'emotional baggage' made it difficult for them to engage objectively. It was noted, for example, that litigants in person often struggled to detach their emotions from the facts and overemphasised motives of the individuals involved, rather than focusing on the legal issues. This was noted to be particularly so when dealing with disclosure and witness statements, with many litigants in person providing large numbers of irrelevant documents. Participants noted that neurodiverse litigants in person face particular challenges in accessing the tribunal process.

Additionally, participants noted that many litigants in person have difficulties in trusting either the legal representative for the other side or the system as a whole. This is particularly challenging for claimants who may have been representing themselves through a lengthy process prior to the tribunal, perhaps facing significant obstacles (and sometimes divergent advice) during that period.

The main obstacle that participants said they thought litigants in person faced was a lack of knowledge of the litigation process: the law and procedure are highly complex and require a lot of specialised knowledge that is not available in the public domain. Even the vocabulary used, it was said, is specialised; many litigants would not know what a 'bundle' is. One focus group participant said: 'I would never, ever advise anybody to turn up at a tribunal hearing without representation just because it is so, so complicated'. Consequently, participants noted, the efficiency of the process suffers: litigants in person overcomplicate their claim or response, fail to focus on key issues, or fail properly to articulate their points in legal terms. Significant tribunal time is required to assist litigants to clarify their claims and remain focused on the real issues. This also increases the costs for the other party. The situation today, we were told, is that without legal representation, litigants are submitting weak claims that should not have entered the system in the first place (or defending the indefensible) or are submitting legitimate claims/responses which are badly pleaded and/or in which they lack the capacity properly to handle the litigation process.

The view of the judges we spoke to was subtly different: they emphasised that litigants in person were not a 'problem' per se. They told us that it was much more challenging to manage a case where parties were badly represented than when they were unrepresented. They said that unrepresented parties were often very open to their case being managed so that the issues were narrowed. The issue, as they perceived it, was that parties did not understand the legal labels that should be put on claims and were worried about missing things out that might be important. However, with input from a judge at a preliminary hearing, a case could usually be brought within sensible limits. Nevertheless, they also recognised that there is a small proportion of litigants in person who were extremely challenging and who therefore took up very substantial resources.

C. Cheapness and Avoidance of Lawyers

The percentage of claimants who are legally represented at the time they make their application to the employment tribunal is surprisingly high. In 2005/06, it was 59 per cent[175] and it gradually increased to 86 per cent over the years to 2016/17.[176] It has since declined to 56 per cent in 2019/20[177] before rising again to between 59–61 per cent between 2021 and 2024.[178] However, the figures are very different at the point of a final hearing. In 1985/86, 31.2 per cent of claimants were legally represented and 42.7 per cent of employers.[179] However, this declined for claimants to just 25.8 per cent in 2016/17, but rose to 51.6 per cent for employers in the same year.[180] There are no up-to-date figures available at the time of writing. Statistics are also not available in relation to the percentage of legal representation before the EAT.

[175] Employment Tribunal and Employment Appeal Tribunal Annual Tables 2021–22, Table E_1.

[176] Tribunals and Gender Recognition Statistics Quarterly: April to June 2018.

[177] Ministry of Justice Tribunal Statistics Quarterly: April to June 2020.

[178] Ministry of Justice Tribunal Statistics Quarterly: October to December 2022; Ministry of Justice Tribunal Statistics Quarterly: April to June 2023; Employment Tribunal and Employment Appeal Tribunal Annual Tables 2023–24, Table E_1.

[179] *Employment Gazette* October 1987.

[180] Survey of Employment Tribunal Applications 2018, Tables 3.5 and 3.7.

The previous section indicated that despite the numbers of litigants in person, the fact that there is a burgeoning industry of employment lawyers emphasises the loss of another original aim of the industrial tribunal, that is, the avoidance of lawyers. This is unsurprising given the complexity and volume of the legislative provisions that provide for the rights that are being claimed. And with lawyers come costs.

The financial cost of litigation was a significant issue for participants, not least because of the use of legal representation. As noted above in Figure 1.3, participants in our survey were concerned about the costs of dealing with litigation for clients. The mean was 1.314 (standard deviation of 0.744),[181] which is above the 'significant' category. There was a high consensus about the significance of the costs of litigation as an issue, across all years of professional experience and types of practice that participants were working in. It was identified as significant in all regions, save that it was a little less strongly significant in Northern Ireland.

Participants said that the efficiency of the tribunal process, along with the long delays, were closely related to the costs of the process – significantly increasing the parties' financial, emotional, and mental-health related costs. Participants noted that, unsurprisingly, the longer the process takes, the greater the legal costs.

Furthermore, participants highlighted that the high costs have implications in terms of the availability of high-quality legal representation. In conversations with practitioners, we consistently heard that the lengthy tribunal procedure and its inefficiencies often make it economically unviable for legal representatives to take on certain cases. This is especially true in claims relating to basic rights infringements, where the potential compensation is far too low to justify the legal costs involved. This means that workers who seek legal representation may in practice face financial pressure to accept undervalued early settlement offers, in order to avoid paying all or a considerable proportion of their compensation towards legal costs. Lawyers too are incentivised to accept high value claims, rather than lower value basic rights claims.

Moreover, where lawyers do take on lower value cases, they would often have to do it, as described by a focus group participant, in the most 'cost-efficient' way. Inevitably, the quality of the representation might suffer as a result. Indeed, participants raised concerns about the low quality of many of the pleadings prepared by some legal representatives. Bad representation and a lack of 'collegiality' were identified as contributing to the inefficiencies of the tribunal procedure, particularly where lawyers failed to comply with court orders. Participants were concerned that, for some representatives, there were negative incentives operating in relation to early settlement, as they sought to increase their billable hours. However,

[181] By assigning a number to the significance rating of Insignificant -2, Quite insignificant -1, Neutral 0, Quite significant +1 and Significant +2 the mean can be calculated.

for scrupulous representatives, it was not worth taking on low value claims which crucially, then, leaves the most vulnerable workers facing a significant barrier in terms of access to legal representation.

D. Expertise

Initially, tribunals were tripartite bodies, comprised of a chairman (now called an employment judge) and two lay members, one from a trade union background and one from an employer/HR background.[182] This structure was adopted to ensure that the industrial reality of situations was properly addressed. In 1993, limited options were created for the chairman to sit without wing members, including applications for interim relief and unauthorised deduction from wages claims.[183] More substantive changes were made by the Industrial Tribunals Act 1996. Section 4 specified the types of cases that could be heard by an employment judge sitting alone. These included cases where the parties 'have given their written consent to the proceedings being heard' by a single judge and proceedings in which 'the person … against whom the proceedings are brought does not, or has ceased to, contest the case'. However, a full tribunal could hear a case where relevant factors tipped the balance in favour of doing so, particularly where there was likely to be a dispute on the facts. Further claims were added to the list of matters that could be heard by a judge alone in 1998, including claims of deduction from wages in relation to union dues,[184] collective redundancies,[185] written particulars of employment,[186] and redundancy payments.[187] In addition to other small changes that were made over the years, in 2012 the Employment Tribunals Act 1996 (Tribunal Composition) Order 2012 added unfair dismissal to the list of claims that a judge could hear alone. This was a significant departure from the pattern of the previous cases that could be heard by a judge sitting alone which were predominantly technical and legal in nature; unfair dismissal claims often involve disputes about facts.

In January 2024, the Employment Tribunals and Employment Appeal Tribunal (Composition of Tribunal) Regulations 2024[188] delegated to the Senior President of Tribunals the power to make provisions for determining the composition of employment tribunals.[189] The Senior President of Tribunals was

[182] Regulation 5 Industrial Tribunals (England and Wales) Regulations 1965 SI 1965/1101 and Employment Protection (Consolidation) Act 1978.
[183] Trade Union Reform and Employment Rights Act 1993, s 36.
[184] s 68A TULRCA 1992.
[185] ibid, s 192.
[186] Employment Rights Act 1996, s 11.
[187] ibid, s 163.
[188] Employment Tribunals and Employment Appeal Tribunal (Composition of Tribunal) Regulations 2024 SI 2024/94.
[189] Art 3.

required to have regard to the nature of the matter, the means by which it is to be decided and the need for members of tribunals to have particular expertise, skills or knowledge. The Composition in the Employment Tribunals and Employment Appeal Tribunals Practice Direction[190] came into force in October 2024 which said that most proceedings would be heard by a judge sitting alone unless a judge decides that a full panel is required, having regard to the interests of justice and the overriding objective to deal with cases fairly and justly.[191] The Presidential Guidance emphasises that the factors that are relevant to the decision as to panel composition will vary 'from case to case. They need not lead inevitably to a conclusion one way or the other, but are for the judge to weigh in the balance'.[192] A full tribunal will usually be used in final hearings relating to discrimination and whistleblowing.

At EAT level, in January 2023 the Senior President of Tribunals reported that: 'Since 25 June 2013 the EAT has been composed of a judge sitting alone by default, with a discretion to sit with a panel. That discretion is currently exercised in about 15% of cases'.[193] The Senior President of Tribunals issued a new Practice Direction on panel composition in October 2024 but this did not significantly change how EAT panel compositions are determined.[194]

Consequently, the role of lay members has considerably diminished. Arguably this changes the nature of the tribunal's expertise. Corby and Latreille argue that the reduction in the use of non-legal members has increased the juridification of the employment tribunal system, making it more like the ordinary civil courts through 'the subordination of employment relations practice to legal norms and values'.[195] This legalisation of claims has exacerbated the issues of a lack of accessibility, lack of informality and increased costs due to the greater use of lawyers.

One of the major issues identified by our research participants with the employment dispute resolution process was its inefficiency. Some participants raised concerns about the use of employment judges who were not specialist employment practitioners: participants observed that today some judges are appointed without having an employment background and that their lack of

[190] See: www.judiciary.uk/wp-content/uploads/2024/10/Practice-Direction-on-panel-composition-in-the-Employment-Tribunals-and-Employment-Appeal-Tribunal-Oct-2024.pdf.

[191] At paras 3–6. Rule 3(1) The Employment Tribunal Procedure Rules 2024 SI 2024/1155.

[192] Produced by the President of the Employment Tribunals (England and Wales) and the President of the Employment Tribunals (Scotland): www.judiciary.uk/wp-content/uploads/2024/10/Practice-Guidance-on-panel-composition-in-the-Employment-Tribunals-and-Employment-Appeal-Tribunal-Oct-2024.pdf.

[193] Senior President of Tribunals, 'Consultation–panel composition in the Employment Tribunals and the Employment Appeal Tribunal' (January 2023): www.judiciary.uk/wp-content/uploads/2023/02/ET-EAT-Panel-composition-consultation.pdf, para 12.

[194] Senior President of Tribunals, 'Practice Direction: Panel composition in the Employment Tribunals and Employment Appeal Tribunal' (29 October 2024) para 7.

[195] Corby and Latreille (n 84) 394–96.

expertise and familiarity in the field often resulted in inefficient hearings and process, adding to the costs of the parties. It was accordingly suggested that judges should be employment specialists. Participants also referred to the role of lay members and many participants observed that their contribution was very important, especially in more complex issues such as discrimination claims. Many participants considered that they should be used in unfair dismissal claims as well. One survey participant said 'they are good at giving the Tribunal an industrially-rounded and realistic view'. For this reason, many participants suggested that their involvement should be increased.

E. A Matter of Last Resort

Finally, it will be recalled that tribunals were intended to be used as the last resort in disputes. This is no longer the case. First, with the decline of trade union representation in terms of both coverage and density[196] and the growth in individual rights, the focus has inevitably shifted away from collectively bargained resolution of disputes. Indeed, even in 1968, Reid was questioning whether the underlying premise that 'voluntary machinery is better than statutory intervention' held true. She said:

> [I]it may be that the fear of statutory intervention often expressed by both trade unions and management has been too indiscriminate. Few people would after all criticise the redundancy payments scheme or the Contracts of Employment Act solely on the grounds that they originated in statute-law rather than in voluntary negotiations; and even if one accepts that collective bargaining is 'better', the fact that the superior advantages it can offer are enjoyed by the employees of only 20 per cent of all private firms might lead one to conclude that, at least in quantitative terms, legislation could do the job more effectively.[197]

Trade union density has declined significantly since then: in 2024, just 11.7 per cent of employees in the private sector were trade union members.[198] With this loss of the emphasis on voluntarism, it must be questioned whether the importance of informally resolving disputes, away from litigation, has inevitably also been lost. The number of claims that are brought in the employment tribunal (see section III.B) indicates that recourse to the tribunal is no longer the last resort.

[196] See: www.gov.uk/government/statistics/trade-union-statistics-2024/trade-union-membership-uk-1995-to-2024-statistical-bulletin. See also G Gall, 'Union recognition in Britain: the End of Legally Induced Voluntarism?' (2012) 41 *Industrial Law Journal* 407.

[197] Reid (n 37) 68.

[198] See: www.gov.uk/government/statistics/trade-union-statistics-2024/trade-union-membership-uk-1995-to-2024-statistical-bulletin.

V. Access to Justice and Article 6 of the European Convention on Human Rights

There is a very rich seam of literature dealing with access to justice across the court system and particularly how well access to justice is realised in the present system. We will limit our consideration to the issues relating to employment disputes. As the previous sections have shown, it is quite apparent that at present there are very serious problems with access to justice in the employment context. There are a number of dimensions to this. The timeliness of hearings is one, the lack of legal representation another, but these are not the only matters. The law itself is problematic as is the enforcement of any awards.

Davies has argued that the law applied in employment tribunals is often complex, and so '[t]he idea that litigants will be able to represent themselves without disadvantage is not plausible'.[199] Busby says that the tribunal system is a 'legalistic, adversarial and often very formal arena', where 'Even those who do [pursue a claim] are often left without any sense of having achieved justice, not least because of the difficulties in enforcing awards'.[200] Because of this, she says that the complexity of employment law and its application should be acknowledged rather than brushed under the carpet. She argues for greater investment in the system and for the purposes of providing good quality independent legal advice and representation for all those who can not afford it or access it by other means.

Similarly, Busby and McDermont argue that

> the failure to deliver individual justice may appear to have no wider significance than the direct impact on those unfortunate individuals. An alternative narrative recognises the substantial public benefits lost. The social and economic costs of not providing justice to those most in need are inestimable and are exacerbated and reinforced by wider inequalities within society including poverty across all life stages. Individual health and well-being suffers, and the suppression of conflict can have severe and deep-seated effects on organisations with lower productivity and an inferior delivery of public services. However, overriding all of these concerns and in line with an understanding of the civil justice system as a critical component in the realisation of the rule of law is the belief that every individual matters and that each and every one of us is entitled to the law's full protection.[201]

Any dispute resolution system must meet the requirements of Article 6 of the European Convention on Human Rights. This requires that there is a fair and

[199] A Davies, *Valuing Employment Rights: A Study of Remedies in Employment Law* (Hart Publishing 2024) 24.

[200] N Busby, 'The costs of justice: barriers and challenges to accessing the employment tribunal system' in S Kirwan (ed), *Advising in Austerity: Reflections on Challenging Times for Advice Agencies* (Bristol University Press 2016) 80 and 88.

[201] N Busby and M McDermont, 'Fighting with the Wind: Claimants' Experiences and Perceptions of the Employment Tribunal' (2020) 49 *Industrial Law Journal* 159, 198.

public hearing within a reasonable time by an independent and impartial tribunal established by law. When additional procedural hurdles to bringing a claim were introduced by the Employment Act 2002, concerns were raised that they would result in a breach of Article 6.[202] The issue now is primarily the significant delay in hearing claims raising concerns about whether the requirement in Article 6 for a hearing to take place 'within a reasonable time' is being met. Our research shows that there are significant barriers to access to justice, and potential issues of compliance with Article 6, in relation to employment claims, impacting individuals, organisations and wider society.

VI. The Employment Rights Act 2025

The Employment Rights Act 2025 (ERA 2025) has been hailed by the Labour government as 'delivering the biggest upgrade to rights at work for a generation, boosting pay and productivity with employment laws fit for a modern economy'.[203] It introduces significant changes to existing rights and introduces many new rights. We think that – at the time of writing – the ERA 2025 introduces approximately 25 new claims that could be made by individuals before the employment tribunal. They range from rights to guaranteed hours for zero, or low, hour contract workers, to reasonable notice of shifts and to payment for cancelled, moved or curtailed shifts.[204] These rights are also extended to agency workers.[205] Third-party harassment provisions are to be added to the Equality Act 2010.[206] Provision is made to protect workers from detriment short of dismissal for taking protected industrial action.[207] Other pre-existing rights are to be expanded and will therefore enable a wider pool of people to bring claims: the qualifying period for parental leave is to be removed and for unfair dismissal reduced to six months, parental bereavement leave is to be expanded and protection from dismissal in relation to statutory family leave is to be amended to include dismissal after a period of bereavement leave.[208] In addition, the cap on compensation for unfair dismissal is to be removed meaning that calculating the compensation in some claims will become far more complicated and high value claims that would otherwise have been brought in

[202] B Hepple and G Morris, 'The Employment Act 2002 and the Crisis of Individual Employment Rights' (2002) 31(3) *Industrial Law Journal* 245.

[203] Angela Rayner, 10 October 2024: www.gov.uk/government/news/government-unveils-most-significant-reforms-to-employment-rights.

[204] To be inserted as s 27BA–s 27BU Employment Rights Act 1996.

[205] To be inserted as s 27BV and Schedule A1 Employment Rights Act 1996.

[206] As new s 40(1A)–(1C) Equality Act 2010.

[207] To be inserted as s 236A–D TULRCA 1992. This follows the Supreme Court declaration of incompatibility in *Mercer v Secretary of State for Business and Trade* [2024] UKSC 12.

[208] In addition, new rights are created relating to access agreements for trade unions to be able to engage with workers in a workplace, with enforcement operating via the CAC: Pt 4 of the ERA 2025.

the High Court as contractual claims are likely to be brought in the tribunal in order to avoid the costs rules in civil litigation.

As many commentators have noted, the new provisions are complicated and difficult to interpret, particularly those relating to guaranteed hours and reasonable notice of shifts.[209] The number and complexity of the new rights in the ERA 2025 will inevitably increase the burden on the employment tribunal system. The impact assessment for the ERA 2025 notes that it 'is difficult to accurately predict' the impact of the ERA 2025 on the tribunal system 'because the number of cases that enter the system each year fluctuates and the impact depends on behavioural factors'.[210] Even excluding changes that will not be implemented for a few years (including the changes to tribunal time limits), the 'overall quantifiable impact is expected to be an increase of around 15% in cases to the 'individual enforcement' system'.[211] Moreover, this assessment was undertaken before the plan to remove the unfair dismissal compensation cap was announced. As this chapter has already indicated, these changes will put a significant further burden on an already over-stretched system.

VII. Conclusions

It is clear from the publicly available data and the empirical material that the employment tribunals no longer meet their original aims: they are no longer a forum of last resort, they are slow, expensive and inaccessible. While the tribunals retain a degree of informality in terms of process, the extensive growth in volume and complexity of legislation has resulted in greater legal representation and with it, more formality and cost. The composition of the tribunal panel has changed significantly over time: the norm has moved from a tripartite body to a single judge. We would argue that this has changed the expertise in the tribunals: there is far less expertise in the industrial relations landscape and the practical realities of working life. However, employment judges retain significant legal expertise and the tribunal remains, in that sense, an expert, specialised body: our participants expressed no concerns about the quality of justice when they were in front of the tribunal. Nevertheless, it is hard to get speedy access to justice from the employment tribunal system. So what about the other fora which hear employment disputes or other states bodies which have jurisdiction to intervene in employment matters? We turn to examine these in chapter two.

[209] eg: www.lewissilkin.com/insights/2025/03/13/employment-rights-bill-unpacked-will-guaranteed-hours-guarantee-flexibility-for-both-parties; www.linklaters.com/en/insights/blogs/employmentlinks/2025/may/employment-rights-bill_guaranteed-hours-for-zero-and-low-hours-workers; and rangeofreasonableresponses.com/2024/10/16/the-employment-rights-bill-the-right-to-guaranteed-hours/.

[210] See: assets.publishing.service.gov.uk/media/6842fa6e4d039a010411f076/employment-rights-bill-economic-analysis.pdf, section 14.

[211] ibid.

2

Other Fora for Employment Claims

I. Introduction

In the UK, employment rights are mainly enforced by individuals bringing a claim before an employment tribunal. We considered the challenges faced by the individual enforcement model in the previous chapter. Some claims can also go to the county courts and High Courts which we consider in section II of this chapter where we also consider the work of the other quasi-judicial body in the employment field – the Central Arbitration Committee (CAC).[1] However, the UK system does also have a role for state enforcement either in addition to, or instead of, individual claims, which has until now been somewhat residual. Participants in our survey were neutral as to there being any issues in relation to the current level of collaboration between employment tribunals and external actors, such as enforcement agencies.[2]

With the establishment of the Fair Work Agency (FWA) by the Employment Rights Act 2025 state enforcement may come to play a more central role. The FWA will bring under one roof the different agencies that currently operate; we discuss this in chapter twelve. Until the FWA is set up, the existing enforcement agencies will continue. Therefore, in this chapter we briefly consider the work of the Gangmasters and Labour Abuse Authority (GLAA) dealing with gangmasters and modern slavery, HM Revenue and Customs (HMRC) in relation to the national minimum wage, the Health and Safety Executive (HSE) concerning working time, the Employment Agency Standards Inspectorate (EASI) regarding Employment Agencies, and conclude with the work of the Director of Labour Market Enforcement which has had a coordinating function across these agencies since 2016 (section III). Section IV concludes.

II. Other Judicial/Quasi-Judicial Bodies

We begin by considering the role of the other judicial or quasi-judicial bodies with jurisdiction to deal with employment disputes apart from employment tribunals.

[1] We have not included consideration of the work of the Certification Officer because they only hear matters relating to internal trade union or employer association matters which fall outside the scope of this book.

[2] The mean was -0.0904 with standard deviation 1.088.

A. Central Arbitration Committee

The Central Arbitration Committee (CAC) is a non-departmental public body that determines applications about trade union recognition,[3] disclosure of information in collective bargaining,[4] European works councils,[5] the European Public Limited Liability Regulations 2009[6] and the mechanism for information and consultation under the Information and Consultation of Employees Regulations 2004.[7] It may also arbitrate industrial disputes.[8]

The number of applications to the CAC are limited, totalling just 1508 from 2001/02 to 2024/25.[9] Between 2001/02 and 2004/05 there were around 90–110 applications each year, around 45-–60 each year until 2019/20 when there was a small peak of 86 applications. Similar peaks occurred again in 2022/23 and 2023/24 with 86 and 87 applications respectively.[10] The applications over the whole period were almost entirely concerned with trade union recognition (71.22 per cent of total applications) and information for collective bargaining (12.33 per cent). The average time that elapsed between receipt of a recognition application and a declaration of recognition or non-recognition (including cases where a ballot was required) ranged from 16 weeks to 30 weeks.

Cases are heard by a tripartite panel with a legally qualified chair together with lay members drawn from employer and union backgrounds. Hearings before the CAC are flexible and often informal. The Guide to recognition proceedings notes that 'The procedures will be as user-friendly for both employers and trade unions as possible'.[11] The Guide also says that the CAC's approach will be as 'flexible as possible' and will focus on 'problem-solving' to 'help the parties, where possible, reach voluntary agreements outside the statutory process'.[12] A case manager is appointed when an application is made and remains the point of contact for parties throughout the process. They will make

[3] Sch A1 Trade Union and Labour Relations (Consolidation) Act 1992 (TULRCA 1992).

[4] s 183 TULRCA 1992.

[5] Under the Transnational Information and Consultation of Employees Regulations 1999 SI 1999/3323.

[6] European Public Limited Liability Regulations 2009 SI 2009/2401.

[7] Information and Consultation of Employees Regulations 2004 SI 2004/3426.

[8] s 212 TULRCA 1992.

[9] See Central Arbitration Committee Annual Report 2002/03, 2003/04, 2004/05, 2005/06, 2006/07, 2007/08, 2008/09, 2009/10, 2010/11, 2011/12, 2012/13, 2013/14, 2014/15, 2015/16, 2016/17, 2017/18, 2018/19, 2019/2020, 2020/2021, 2021/22, 2022/23, 2023/24 and 2024/25 available at: www.gov.uk/government/publications/cac-annual-reports and webarchive.nationalarchives.gov.uk/ukgwa/20140701192835/; www.cac.gov.uk/index.aspx?articleid=2213.

[10] With the new rights of trade union access to a workplace under the Employment Rights Act 2025, the workload of the CAC is likely to increase.

[11] See: www.gov.uk/guidance/statutory-recognition-guidance-on-part-i-of-schedule-a1#cac-proceedings.

[12] CAC guide (n 11) 3.5.

> enquiries of the parties on the instructions of the Panel. The case manager will ensure that correspondence and documents are cross copied between the parties and the panel as appropriate. Case managers will do all they can to explain the statutory procedures and help both parties understand the implications of the legislation, as well as resolve difficulties.[13]

There will be times where more formal processes are required for the CAC to reach decisions, and the Guide reminds parties that the onus is on them to raise any issues they wish to be considered by the CAC.[14] Some applications may be heard on the papers while others require a hearing. In the latter scenario:

> [P]arties will be asked to submit and exchange evidence in the form of written submissions prior to the hearing. New evidence will only be admitted at hearings for good reasons and at the discretion of the panel and, where it is admitted, parties can request that the panel allows some additional time, such as a short adjournment, to consider the new evidence. The parties will be asked to inform the CAC panel in advance of the names of the speakers and any witnesses proposed for the hearing. Speakers should be persons who are capable of representing the positions of the parties and who can contribute appropriately to the evidence required to assist the panel's considerations at the particular stage in the statutory procedure. The parties may appoint representatives but there is no requirement to use lawyers.[15]

Thereafter the hearing is held

> in as informal a way as is consistent with clarity and fairness. Each party will be asked to comment on and amplify its written statement and to comment on the other's evidence and to answer questions put by the CAC panel. Speakers and any witnesses may be cross-questioned where factual issues are in dispute, at the discretion of the chairman of the panel.[16]

So, in common with the objectives of the employment tribunals, there is an emphasis on informality, accessibility and speed. However, the relatively small number of applications means that these objectives are easier to deliver.

B. County Court and High Court Claims

High Court claims arise generally within six contexts: (1) breach of contract claims concerned with bonuses; (2) injunctive relief in relation to disciplinary procedures and dismissals; (3) injunctive relief enforcing restrictive covenants; (4) construing collective agreements; (5) matters relating to directors' duties; and (6) injunctive relief relating to industrial action. Data is unavailable

[13] CAC guide (n 11) 3.4.
[14] CAC guide (n 11) 3.5 and 3.6.
[15] CAC guide (n 11) 3.15.
[16] CAC guide (n 11) 3.12.

relating to the volume of these claims: the Royal Courts of Justice Annual Tables are published alongside the Civil Justice Statistics Quarterly but there is no separate classification for employment disputes;[17] they are likely to fall within the broader categories of breach of contract or miscellaneous. A search for the period of 25 June 2023 to 25 June 2025 of Bailii's database of cases from the King's Bench Division (KBD) on the terms 'employment', 'bonus', 'restrictive covenant', 'directors' duties', 'collective agreement' and 'trade dispute', matters most likely to be heard by the KBD, yielded 18 relevant cases.[18] This does not include cases from Scotland or Northern Ireland, nor does it capture cases that have settled at the door of the court (particularly likely in restrictive covenant cases where undertakings may be given). Nevertheless, this snapshot indicates that there are not very many cases that are being dealt with in the ordinary court system.

County court claims are likely to concern simple claims for notice pay, holiday pay and unpaid wages. Employment claims are not separately identified in the Ministry of Justice's Civil Justice Statistics Quarterly, and would simply fall within the category of 'Money claims'. Anecdotally, we understand there are very few employment claims in the county court.

Where cases are heard in the county court or High Court then the stricter rules relating to evidence under the Civil Procedure Rules will apply and the full costs regime will bite.[19] This creates a significant incentive for parties to go to the Employment Tribunals.

C. Using Other Judicial Fora

The participants in our survey primarily practised in the employment tribunal (see Figure 2.1). Ranking different jurisdictions from 0 (not at all) to 4 (most often), the mean for the frequency of practice in the employment tribunals was 3.8. The High Court was ranked second with a mean of 0.81. Our

[17] See: www.gov.uk/government/statistics/civil-justice-statistics-quarterly-january-to-march-2024.

[18] In relation to 'employment': *Woodhead v WTTV Ltd and Anr* [2025] EWHC 1128; *Chanel Ltd v Skeens* [2025] EWHC 619; *Assensus Ltd v Wirsol Energy Ltd* [2025] EWHC 410; *Chassy v Left Shift IT Ltd & Ors* [2025] EWHC 225; *Morretti v Leone & Anr* [2025] EWHC 145; *Smith & Ors v Surridge & Ors* [2025] EWHC 74; *Simon-Hart v Standard Chartered Bank* [2024] EWHC 2957; *Crabb & Ors v TUI Airways Ltd* [2024] EWHC 3581 and [2024] EWHC 2589; *Duke v Moores & Ors* [2024] EWHC 2746; and *Titan Wealth Holdings Ltd & Ors v Okunola* [2024] EWHC 2718. In relation to 'bonus': *Gupta v DB Group Services Ltd* [2024] EWHC 2297. As to 'restrictive covenant': *Kau Media Group Ltd v Hart* [2025] EWHC 553; *Dare International Ltd v Soliman & Anr* [2025] EWHC 227; *Amberside Energy (Development) Ltd & Ors v Ahmed & Anr* [2024] EWHC 3077; *Proactive Group Holdings Inc & Anr v HJ 2024 Ltd & Ors* [2024] EWHC 2821; and *Literacy Capital PLC v Webb* [2024] EWHC 2026. As to 'collective agreement': *Nistor v USDAW* [2024] EWHC 1165. As to 'trade dispute': *Warrington Borough Council v Unite the Union* [2023] EWHC 3093.

[19] See further ch 11.

participants had much less to do with the county court (mean of 0.5) and CAC (mean of 0.24).

Figure 2.1 Survey data showing participants' frequency of practice in various jurisdictions

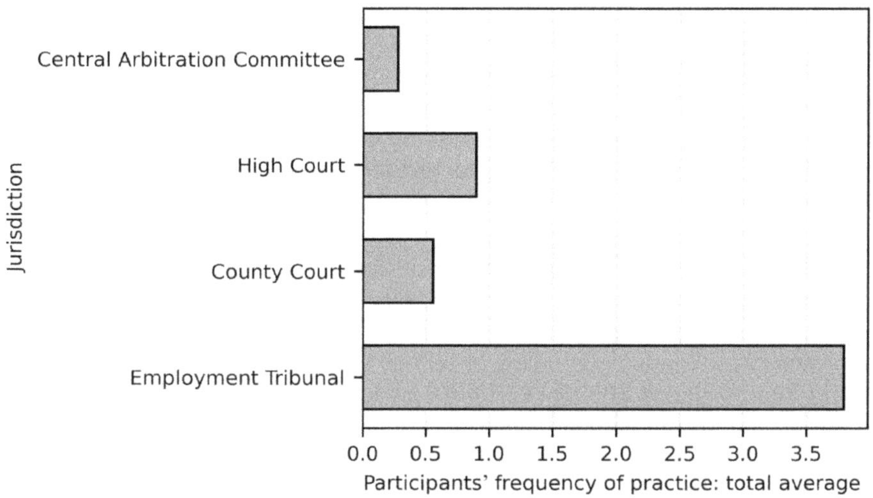

When participants were asked about the significance of the divided jurisdiction for different employment claims, their response was that it was neutral to quite insignificant (mean of -0.1789, standard deviation 1.0539). It is apparent, therefore, that the use of other fora for particular claims is not understood to be particularly problematic. This is probably because of the specialist nature of those claims. Moreover, the number of such claims appears to be very limited.

III. Other Enforcement Mechanisms

We now turn to look at the state agencies currently used to enforce employment rights: the GLAA, HMRC, HSE and EASI.

A. Gangmasters and Labour Abuse Authority

The original Gangmasters Licensing Authority (GLA) was given the task of licensing gangmasters and enforcing the requirements of the Gangmasters (Licensing) Act 2004 (GLA 2004). The Gangmasters and Labour Abuse Authority (GLAA) continues to deal with the licensing of gangmasters in the designated sectors of agricultural work, gathering shellfish, and processing or packaging agricultural produce, shellfish, or fish.[20] The detail of the gangmasters licensing regime and the work of the GLAA in enforcing the relevant requirements goes beyond the scope of this book.[21] Our focus is on employment rights.

In April 2017 the GLAA was given new powers and the role of Labour Abuse Prevention Officers (LAPOs) was created giving them powers under the Police and Criminal Evidence Act 1984 to arrest and search in relation to 'labour market offences' across the entire labour market.[22] These offences ('trigger offences') include offences under the Employment Agencies Act 1973, the National Minimum Wage Act 1998, and the GLA 2004. Specific offences under the Modern Slavery Act 2015 were also included. The GLAA is focused on tackling 'high harm, low volume cases of exploitation falling short of those tackled by the National Crime Agency'.[23]

The GLAA enforcement policy makes it clear that the GLAA uses 'a range of civil and criminal options from simple advisory letters, licence decisions and advisory letters (notifying labour providers to apply for a licence), a warning letter regarding future conduct, or the use of Labour Market Enforcement Undertakings (LMEU) and Orders (LMEO) to a criminal prosecution'.[24] The GLAA has the power to request an LMEU where they believe that a person has committed or is committing a trigger offence.[25] It must give notice to that person and invite them to give an undertaking to comply with any prohibitions, restrictions or requirements.[26] In addition (or more usually as a subsequent alternative),[27] the GLAA may apply to a court for an LMEO.[28] An order will be granted where it is shown that, on the balance of probabilities, the person has committed or is committing a trigger offence and the court considers it just and reasonable to make the order. The order prohibits or restricts a person from doing anything set out in the order or requires them to do something. A breach of an order is punishable by a maximum sentence of two years' imprisonment.

The GLAA was unable to provide any data on the number of enforcement actions taken against companies between 2010 and 2023. However, using the information on the website and news stories, we have identified that the number

[20] Gangmasters (Licensing) Act 2004, s 3(1) (GLA 2004).

[21] For a more detailed study of the issues see C Barnard and S Fraser Butlin, 'Where Criminal Law Meets Labour Law' in A Bogg, J Collins, M Freedland and J Herring (eds), *Criminality at Work* (Oxford University Press 2020).

[22] Immigration Act 2016.

[23] See: assets.publishing.service.gov.uk/media/5f298236d3bf7f1b17facdc9/BIS-15-549-tackling-exploitation-in-the-labour-market.pdf.

[24] See: www.gla.gov.uk/our-impact/how-we-inspect-and-prosecute/enforcement-policy-statement para 5.

[25] s 16 Immigration Act 2016.

[26] ibid, s 15(1)(b).

[27] Home Office, 'Code of Practice on Labour Market Enforcement Undertakings and Orders' (Crown November 2016): assets.publishing.service.gov.uk/government/uploads/system/uploads/attachment_data/file/572991/Code_of_Practice_Print.pdf.

[28] s 18 Immigration Act 2016.

of LMEUs each year ranged between 3 and 8 from 2019/20 to 2023/24. In 2018/19 there were 14 LMEUs and the only LMEO was made in the same year.

We recognise that this is an incomplete picture of the enforcement work of the GLAA, but it does appear that the formal enforcement work it undertakes is limited. Moreover, the GLAA's work is primarily focused on very serious breaches of the relevant regulations and is targeted at issues that would usually be considered at the cusp of modern slavery.

B. HMRC

While an individual worker can bring a claim for failure to pay the National Minimum Wage/National Living Wage either as a breach of contract claim in the county court or the employment tribunal, or as a claim for deduction from wages under section 23(1)(a) Employment Rights Act 1996 in the tribunal, HMRC is also given the task of enforcing the national minimum wage. The National Minimum Wage Act 1998 (NMW Act 1998) provides for both civil enforcement and criminal investigation, the latter being reserved, according to the Policy on Enforcement, for 'a small minority of employers that are persistently non-compliant, refuse to cooperate with compliance officers or where there is a broader public interest in prosecution'.[29]

Civil enforcement starts with an investigation and the Policy says that 'A Notice of Underpayment (NoU) should be issued where a compliance officer finds that arrears of minimum wage were outstanding at the start of an investigation' although HMRC officers have some discretion in this regard. The Policy also says that NoUs should be issued from the outset even where the 'employer claims that the underpayment of minimum wage was accidental'.[30] The NoU sets out the arrears of national minimum wage to be repaid and the penalty for non-compliance.[31] The penalty is set at 200 per cent of the total underpayment for each worker, with a minimum penalty of £100 and up to a maximum of £20,000.[32] When an employer fails to comply with the NoU then payment may be pursued via the civil courts[33] or in the employment tribunal,[34] and the penalty can be pursued in the civil courts.[35]

In addition, employers who fail to pay the national minimum wage may be publicly named. The aim of this policy is to 'raise awareness of minimum wage enforcement and deter employers who would otherwise be tempted to break

[29] See: www.gov.uk/government/publications/enforcing-national-minimum-wage-law/national-minimum-wage-policy-on-enforcement-prosecutions-and-naming-employers-who-break-national-minimum-wage-law (NMW Policy on enforcement) section 3.

[30] ibid.

[31] National Minimum Wage Act 1998, s 19A(1) (NMW Act 1998).

[32] s 19A NMW Act 1998.

[33] ibid, s 19D(1)(c).

[34] ibid, s 19D(1)(a).

[35] ibid, s 19E.

minimum wage law'.[36] An employer is named where an NoU remains unpaid for 28 days without an appeal having been lodged. This power has been used extensively, with media posts from the Gov.uk website saying that 191 employers were named between 2011 and 2018[37] and 524 were named between 2015 and 2023 (with an obvious overlap in relation to the years 2015 to 2018).[38] The majority of the failures to pay the national minimum wage were noted as relating to deductions being made, for example, for uniforms and expenses, taking the pay to a level below the national minimum wage or for failing to pay workers for all the time they had worked, such as mandatory training and travel time.

The number of matters addressed by HMRC is limited. At its peak 7,256 cases were closed by HMRC, but the range was more usually between 2,000 and 4,000 (see Figure 2.2). In 2023/24, 4,642 cases were closed.[39]

Figure 2.2 Number of cases closed by HMRC[40]

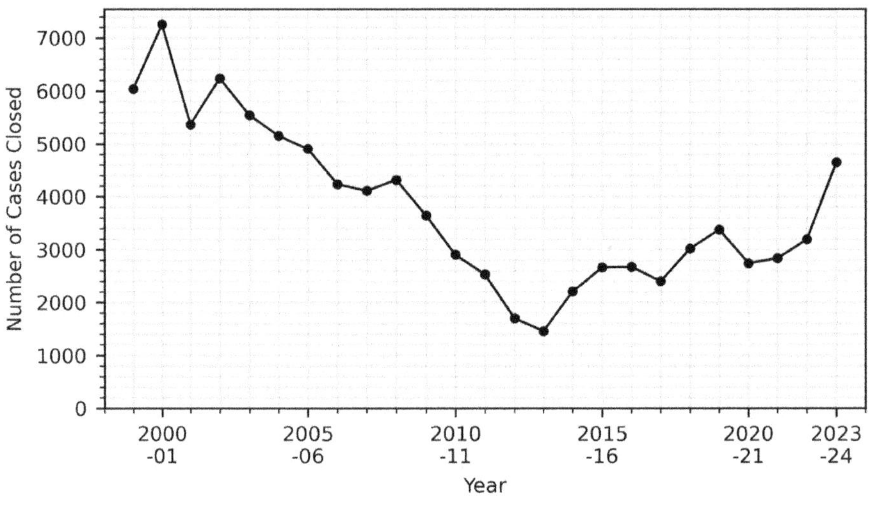

There was a similarly low number of penalties imposed on employers, ranging from 372 over a three-year period (2005/06 to 2008/09) to 1,008 from 2018 to 2019 (see Figure 2.3). An average of 723 penalties were charged in each year between 2021 and 2024.

[36] NMW Policy on Enforcement (n 29), section 5.

[37] See: www.gov.uk/government/news/employers-named-and-shamed-for-paying-less-than-minimum-wage.

[38] See: www.gov.uk/government/news/over-500-companies-named-for-not-paying-minimum-wage.

[39] National Living Wage and National Minimum Wage: Government evidence on enforcement and compliance in 2023 to 2024: assets.publishing.service.gov.uk/media/68dfdf26ef1c2f72bc1e4dc1/national-minimum-wage-enforcement-and-compliance-report-2023-2024_1.pdf. See also C Barnard, F Costello and S Fraser Butlin, *Low-Paid EU Migrant Workers: The House, the Town, the Street* (Bristol University Press 2024) ch 4.

[40] Data obtained via FOI request.

Figure 2.3 Number of penalties imposed by HMRC[41]

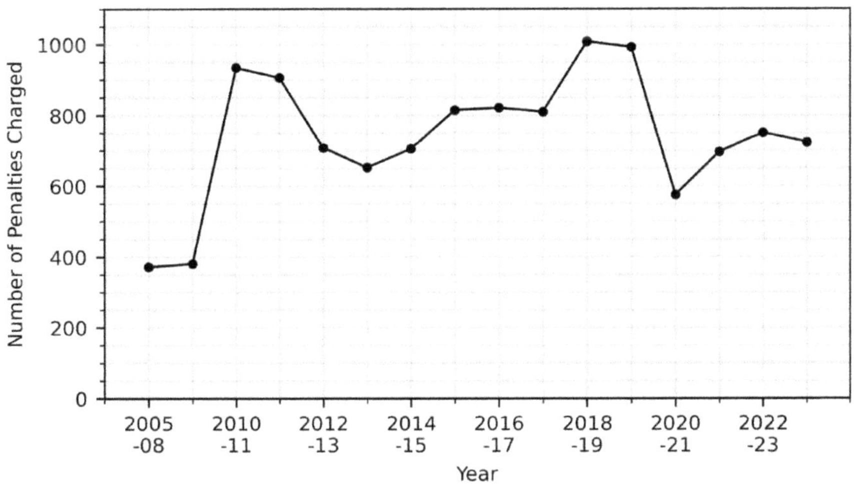

A report in September 2023 by the Low Pay Commission said that

> very few workers continue to report underpayment, despite the abundant evidence and anecdote suggesting it does in fact take place at a considerable scale. The circa 3,000 contacts HMRC receive each year do not compare favourably to the overall estimates of hundreds of thousands of underpaid workers, or to the volumes received by comparable points of contact. The pipeline to HMRC is only delivering a trickle of cases.[42]

HMRC also undertakes proactive work, alongside reactive work responding to complaints. In 2021/22, targeted enforcement accounted for 71 per cent of closed cases that year.[43] Nevertheless, the number of matters addressed is low.

Moreover, investigations take considerable time:

> Closing an enforcement case is not a quick process. In 2021/22, around 40 per cent of HMRC's caseload was closed within 120 days … the length of the process contributes to the resource bottleneck and is perhaps the most salient feature of the enforcement process for employers and (especially) workers. Even if a case is resolved within (for example) three months, it still represents a meaningful wait for low-paid workers short of money they are entitled to.[44]

[41] Data obtained via FOI request.

[42] See: www.gov.uk/government/publications/compliance-and-enforcement-of-the-national-minimum-wage.

[43] See: www.gov.uk/government/publications/national-living-wage-and-national-minimum-wage-government-evidence-on-enforcement-and-compliance-2022.

[44] See: www.gov.uk/government/publications/compliance-and-enforcement-of-the-national-minimum-wage at paras 2.27–2.28.

C. Health and Safety Executive

The Working Time Regulations 1998[45] provide workers with rights in relation to maximum weekly work,[46] night work,[47] work patterns that put a person's health and safety at risk,[48] and compensatory rest.[49] Employers are required to keep relevant records.[50] The Health and Safety Executive (HSE) is under a duty to 'make adequate arrangements for the enforcement of' these rights, except where workers are employed in premises for which a local authority is responsible. Importantly the HSE does not enforce time off, rest break entitlements, or paid annual leave entitlements, and individuals cannot bring a claim under the Working Time Regulations in relation to the rights that the HSE is responsible for enforcing. Broadly an HSE Working Time Officer will investigate complaints and try to obtain informal compliance. Thereafter they will follow up with prohibition notices and ultimately prosecution.[51]

There is very little official data on the extent of enforcement by the HSE in relation to working time. However, a Freedom of Information (FOI) request made on 27 August 2024, identified that the number of complaints that were made to the HSE via their online concerns portal totalled 241 complaints from 2017 to 2024 (see Figure 2.4).

Figure 2.4 Number of complaints to the HSE concerning working time[52]

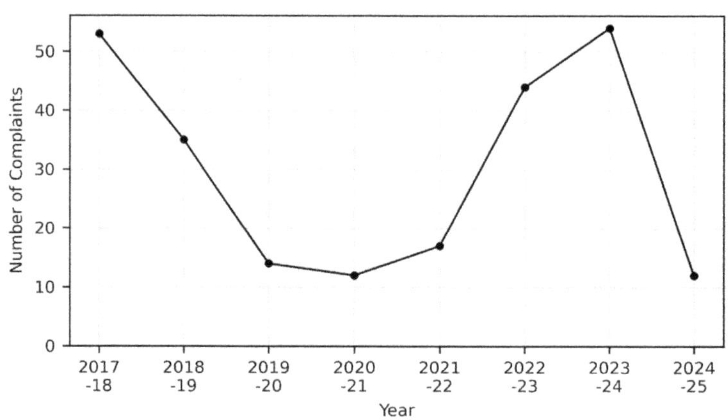

[45] Working Time Regulations 1998 SI 1998/1883.
[46] ibid, reg 4(2).
[47] ibid, regs 6 and 7.
[48] ibid, reg 8.
[49] ibid, reg 24.
[50] ibid, reg 9.
[51] ibid, reg 29(1). The regulation provides that employers are guilty of an offence where they fail to comply with a relevant requirement and are liable to a fine. This is an either way offence (as a summary offence or on an indictment in the Crown Court). In addition, employers will be guilty of an offence under s 33 Health and Safety at Work Act 1974 where they, for example, contravene a requirement imposed by an inspector, contravene a requirement or prohibition imposed by an improvement notice or prohibition notice, prevent or obstruct the work of an inspector, or provide false information to them.
[52] Data obtained from FOI request.

Of these 241 complaints, 218 were followed up or investigated and 23 were closed as 'not investigated'. The HSE said that there had been no improvement notices served or prosecutions taken for breaches relating to working time in the seven years from 2017 to 2025. However, they said that in line with their Enforcement Policy,

> inspectors can and do take other measures to ensure compliance with the law, including issuing a notification of contravention, providing verbal advice or directing duty holders to guidance on our website. These other means of intervention are regularly used and often negate the need for further enforcement action.[53]

Once again, we see that the extent of enforcement work is very limited indeed.

D. Employment Agencies Standards Inspectorate

The Employment Agencies Standards Inspectorate (EASI) is the enforcement body that ensures compliance with the Employment Agencies Act 1973 and the Conduct of Employment Agencies and Employment Businesses Regulations 2003[54] (2003 Conduct Regulations). The key provisions of the 2003 Conduct Regulations prohibit an agency from making the provision of work to a work seeker conditional on using other chargeable services or hiring or purchasing goods;[55] provide protection from detriment to workers who terminate a contract with the agency or employment business;[56] restrict the use of transfer fees;[57] restrict the withholding of wages from workers;[58] and require the agency or employment business to provide, in writing, specific information to hirers and work seekers and obtain agreement to terms and conditions with work seekers.[59] Individuals can bring claims for breaches of the 2003 Conduct Regulations where damage has been caused,[60] and failure to comply with their requirements constitutes a criminal offence.[61] Section 3A EASI 1973 provides that the Secretary of State may apply to an employment tribunal for a prohibition order where a person 'on account of his misconduct or for any other sufficient reason' is unsuitable to run an employment agency. Any failure to comply with such an order is a criminal offence.[62]

The work of the EASI was relatively significant in the period from 2003 to 2008 with the number of complaints received in the region of between 1,000 and 1,400. The number of complaints received peaked in 2009/10 at 1,714. There was then a significant decline in the number of complaints with the figures in the region

[53] See: www.hse.gov.uk/pubns/hse41.pdf. See also: www.hse.gov.uk/enforce/enforcement-management-model.htm.

[54] Conduct of Employment Agencies and Employment Businesses Regulations 2003 SI 2003/3319.

[55] ibid, reg 5.

[56] ibid, reg 6.

[57] ibid, reg 10.

[58] ibid, reg 12.

[59] ibid, regs 13–19, 21.

[60] ibid, reg 30.

[61] Employment Agencies Act 1973, s 5(2). Moreover, s 6 makes it an offence for an employment agency or business to demand or receive a fee from any person for finding or seeking to find them employment.

[62] ibid, s 3B.

of 600–830 from 2011/12 to 2016/17. They have climbed gradually over time since then with over 2,000 complaints in 2021/22 and 2022/23 (see Figure 2.5).[63]

Figure 2.5 Number of complaints received and cleared by EASI[64]

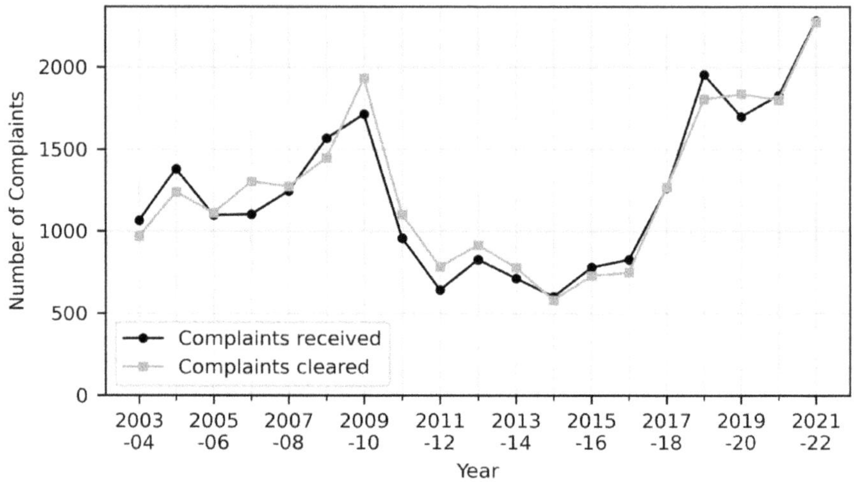

The number of complaints cleared each year broadly tracked the number of complaints received. In addition, the EASI undertakes targeted investigations with a particular focus on specific sectors, for example on adult social care in 2022/23[65] and construction in 2019/20.[66]

The EASI Enforcement Policy makes it clear that they will only intervene when 'necessary' and they seek to achieve compliance through 'support and education' first.[67] The Policy states that after an investigation or inspection then 'any breaches of the legislation will be brought to the attention of the employment agency or employment business and followed up by the issue of a warning letter'. Where an agency or business does not promptly respond to the warning letter, then the EASI will move to other enforcement action such as an LMEU/LMEO, prosecution and prohibition. In 2022/23, out of the 2,300 complaints that were received and

[63] See Annual Accounts and Reports at: www.gov.uk/government/collections/employment-agency-standards-eas-inspectorate-annual-reports and webarchive.nationalarchives.gov.uk/ukgwa/20091002200806/; www.berr.gov.uk/whatwedo/employment/employment-agencies/index.html.

[64] Data collated from Annual Accounts and Reports (n 63).

[65] 2022/23 Annual Accounts and Report (n 63).

[66] 2019/20 Annual Accounts and Report (n 63).

[67] See: www.gov.uk/government/publications/employment-agency-standards-eas-inspectorate-enforcement-policy-statement/employment-agency-standards-eas-inspectorate-enforcement-policy-statement.

267 targeted inspections completed, only 385 warning letters were issued, there was one prosecution and one LMEO.[68]

E. Office of the Director of Labour Market Enforcement

The Office of the Director of Labour Market Enforcement was established via the Immigration Act 2016 as a coordinating body, bringing together the work of HMRC, the EASI and the GLAA. The role of Director of Labour Market Enforcement and Exploitation was created to 'achieve a single set of priorities across enforcement bodies and more flexible allocation of resources'.[69] The Director's role is to enable better coordination and focus by the individual enforcement agencies, who remain separate and distinct bodies, and to 'form a coherent view of the nature and extent of exploitation and non-compliance'.[70] The 2024/25 strategy recorded the four themes that the Director had 'promoted previously', namely improve the radar picture, improve focus and effectiveness, engage and support and better joined-up thinking.[71]

The Office of the Director of Labour Market Enforcement has long been in favour of establishing a Single Enforcement Body and in their 2023/24 strategy noted that it would provide benefits, including 'making it easier for workers to know where to go for help, more effective use of resources and pooling of intelligence, better support for compliant employers, and new powers and sanctions'.[72] The 2023/24 strategy also noted certain 'crucial enforcement gaps' including enforcing holiday pay for vulnerable workers and regulation of umbrella companies. Some of these issues are dealt with in the Employment Rights Act 2025 through the establishment of the Fair Work Agency which we consider in chapter twelve.

IV. Conclusions

Forums other than employment tribunals are little used to enforce employment rights. There is no useful data about employment claims in the High Court and county court. State enforcement bodies have limited impact on enforcing rights

[68] 2022/23 Annual Accounts and Report (n 63).

[69] BIS, 'Tackling Exploitation in the Labour Market: Consultation' (October 2015) [66]: assets.publishing.service.gov.uk/government/uploads/system/uploads/attachment_data/file/471048/BIS-15-549-tackling-exploitation-in-the-labour-market.pdf.

[70] ibid, 71.

[71] See: assets.publishing.service.gov.uk/media/673236dc0d90eee304badb89/uk-labour-market-enforcement-strategy_2024-25-accessible.pdf.

[72] See: assets.publishing.service.gov.uk/media/65324da6e839fd001486724f/uk_labour_market_enforcement_strategy_2023_2024_accessible_version.pdf, 1.1.2.

because they deal with a relatively small number of complaints and issues. As we discuss in chapter twelve, the Fair Work Agency has real potential to make a difference, if it is well enough resourced to address a large volume of issues and to do so swiftly. This will require considerable leadership. However, in the meantime, employment tribunals remain the principal avenue of redress to enforce employment rights and, as chapter one has shown, are struggling to address the many and varied claims before them in a reasonable time. It is clear that the current system cannot continue as it is, and a radical rethink is required. We turn to consider the theoretical underpinnings for that rethink in the next chapter.

3

Theoretical Underpinnings of Employment Law and Dispute Resolution

I. Introduction

Where employment law sits within the taxonomy of law is a deeply debated subject. Even choosing to call the subject 'employment law', rather than 'labour law', is divisive because it could denote a focus on individual employment matters to the exclusion of collective trade union matters. However, referring to labour law may be understood as something of a historical anomaly dating back to a time when trade unions were central to the employment relationship.[1] Because our focus is on the resolution of disputes between worker and employer, we will refer to employment law.[2]

But where does this employment law sit? It is 'not primarily a legal relationship or one that in practice fits neatly into established legal forms'.[3] Collins has said that 'Labour law in Britain has always been conceived as a contextual field of legal study rather than a doctrinal category. Textbooks on the subject range broadly over private law and public law, touching on contract, tort, trusts, company and judicial review'.[4] In this chapter we do not attempt to cover the whole field but rather focus on the three main understandings of employment law in order to appreciate their implications for dispute resolution. We discuss this in section II.

Traditionally, employment law is viewed as a species of contract law but, given the significant overlay of statute now, it could be considered through the prism of an autonomous form of public law.[5] Relatedly, there is another analytical overlay

[1] See further A Bogg, '"Labour Law is a Subset of Employment Law" revisited' (2020) 43(2) *Dalhousie Law Journal* 479.

[2] By using this term we are seeking a neutral descriptive term to capture the primary ambit of our study rather than making a normative or philosophical choice. For an interesting discussion of the normative conceptions of the different terms, see H Collins, G Lester and V Mantouvalou, 'Does Labour Law Need Philosophical Foundations?' in H Collins, G Lester and V Mantouvalou (eds), *Philosophical Foundations of Labour Law* (Oxford University Press 2018) 7.

[3] S Honeyball, 'Employment Law and the Primacy of Contract' (1989) 18 *Industrial Law Journal* 97.

[4] H Collins, 'The Productive Disintegration of Labour Law' (1997) 26 *Industrial Law Journal* 295.

[5] Freedland argues that it is neither contract nor status but is 'a mixed domain of voluntarily agreed arrangements and imposed norms': M Freedland (Gen Ed), *The Contract of Employment* (Oxford University Press 2016) 12. See also M Freedland and N Kontouris, *The Legal Construction of Personal Work Relations* (Oxford University Press 2012), 222–245.

based on human rights, which has come to the fore mainly since the incorporation of the European Convention on Human Rights (ECHR) into UK law via the Human Rights Act 1998. However, we shall argue that none of these frameworks fully captures the human/emotional element of an employment *relationship* and this has implications for the way that employment disputes are resolved. This chapter therefore considers three questions.

First, is employment law fundamentally a matter of contract law? After all, the employment relationship is founded on the employment contract. Or do those usual rules of contract have to be modified to such an extent, in recognition of the unequal bargaining power of the parties, that it can no longer be described as purely a matter of contract law? This leads some to suggest that it is a relational contract with particular rules that operate in circumstances where the contract is incomplete and long term. Others suggest it should be analysed as a psychological contract. We ask whether this brings any additional insights.

Second, as we have discussed in chapter one, there has been an exponential growth in legislative intervention in the employment contract, and with the courts in *Autoclenz*[6] and *Uber*[7] placing emphasis on the purpose of that legislation, rather than the minutiae of the contractual agreement, have we moved to a position where employment law should be categorised as a matter of status and statutory protection rather than of contract?

Third, some of the protections arise from fundamental human rights which raises further questions of how human rights law operates within and alongside employment law. Would a purely rights-based approach encapsulate the nature and scope of employment law?

We argue that none of these three understandings can be considered in isolation; they are interlinked and interrelated. Moreover, even taking the three understandings together, there is still a missing element, namely, that at its heart, employment is a relationship: it is a relationship between the worker and the (anthropomorphised) employer, their manager and their colleagues. The emotional, relational and psychological perspectives of the work relationship have been largely overlooked by a system understandably focused on what the law is and how it applies to the facts of a case (section III). This appreciation has an impact on how to determine the optimal design for a dispute resolution system.

We argue that strong parallels can be drawn between workplace disputes or the loss of a job, and the breakdown of family relationships and divorce. By looking to the underlying rationale of family law, and the impact this has had on the dispute resolution process in the family courts, we can learn a great deal about how the emotional, relational and psychological perspectives that have been overlooked in employment law can be brought to the front and centre of any new system (section IV).

We start by analysing the three traditional approaches to analysing employment law.

[6] *Autoclenz Ltd v Belcher* [2011] UKSC 41.
[7] *Uber BV v Aslam* [2021] UKSC 5.

II. The Three Understandings of Employment Relationships

A. Employment Relations as a Contractual Relation

i. Employment Law and Contract Law

At its heart, the employment relationship is contractual: there is an agreement for the individual to do work in exchange for pay.[8] Thus, standard contractual principles are often applied by the employment tribunals. For example, the contractual mantra that an unaccepted repudiation is 'a thing writ in water' was relied on in *Societe Generale v Geys*[9] when the Supreme Court rejected an argument that an employment contract could come to an end by the unilateral actions of one party which were not accepted by the other (the automatic theory). Rather poetically, Lord Hope said:

> In proposing that the court should [e]ndorse the automatic theory, the Bank invites it to cause the law of England and Wales in relation to contracts of employment to set sail, unaccompanied, upon a journey for which I can discern no just purpose and can identify no final destination. I consider, on the contrary, that we should keep the contract of employment firmly within the harbour which the common law has solidly constructed for the entire fleet of contracts in order to protect the innocent party, as far as practicable, from the consequences of the other's breach.

In so doing, the Supreme Court emphatically delineated the nature of the employment relationship as contractual.[10]

The application of normal contractual rules can also be seen in relation to collective agreements. Terms of employment derived from collective agreements bind the individual worker through the contractual lens of the incorporation of terms, whether or not the individual employee is a member of the trade union.[11] When collective agreements were widespread, the 'principal

[8] Freedland has identified three principles that are descriptive, and he argues also normative, that underpin the contract: the exchange principle (that the contract essentially consists of an exchange of work and remuneration); the integration principle (that thereafter the worker should be regarded as integrated into the enterprise); and the reciprocity principle (the worker and employer should be regarded as being committed to reciprocal cooperation): M Freedland et al (eds), *The Contract of Employment* (Oxford University Press 2016) ch 2. The argument that these are normative principles is criticised by P Elias, 'Changes and Challenges to the Contract of Employment' (2018) 38 *OJLS* 869.

[9] *Societe Generale v Geys* [2012] UKSC 63, [97].

[10] It is a decision that has been criticised as being 'at the expense of logic' 'since it seems that the employee who keeps the contact alive cannot sue for wages but can only claim damages and, critically, remains under an obligation to mitigate his loss. So he can keep the contract alive, but must try and secure other employment which will perforce bring it to an end': Elias, 'Changes and Challenges' (n 8) 878.

[11] *National Union of Rail, Maritime and Transport Workers v Tyne and Wear Passenger Transport Executive t/a Nexus* [2024] UKSC 37, [1]. Described by Collins as 'merely a rather obtuse way of describing the reality of the collective determination of terms': Collins, 'The Productive Disintegration of Labour Law' (n 4) 298.

function of the contract of employment was to provide the vehicle by which the collective terms were given legal effect by being incorporated into the contract of employment'.[12] Even now when collective agreements are less prevalent, the Supreme Court has held that ordinary contractual principles apply to the interpretation of a collective agreement incorporated into individual contracts of employment and guaranteeing retained pay as a 'permanent feature' of their contractual entitlement.[13]

Another example is where strike action is taken: it is considered to be a repudiatory breach of contract. Where part of the contract is performed, an employer is nevertheless entitled to refuse to pay for any performance that has been rendered.[14] English says that such an approach means that 'the law in relation to substantial performance in employment contracts is out of kilter and counterintuitively harsher on the employee than the approach taken to the construction of commercial contracts'.[15] Nevertheless, it is the law of contract that is used to determine whether a worker is entitled to pay when taking industrial action.[16]

However, there is a fundamental difference between commercial and employment contracts, namely that 'the employment contract is one by which one party – the employee – voluntarily agrees to be subservient to the other … The employer's power to direct his employee is an incident of the contract: it is still at heart *master and servant*'.[17] Another way of looking at the same point is that there is a fundamental inequality of bargaining power in most worker–employer relationships. The worker is almost invariably in a weaker position than the employer and the traditional contractual assumption that each party is in an equal position of power to determine the terms on which they contract, does not apply. It is this difference which has required the modification of contractual principles to address the reality of the employment relationship and to protect workers from exploitation. Consequently, mitigating the weaker bargaining power of the worker is 'justifiably' seen by the 'majority of labour law scholars' to be the purpose of employment law.[18]

This has led to the modification of standard contractual principles and, most notably, to the development of implied terms which are specific to the employment relationship. Accordingly, implied terms – implied by law as a necessary incident

[12] Elias, 'Changes and Challenges' (n 8) 870.

[13] *Tesco Stores Ltd v USDAW and others* [2024] UKSC 28.

[14] *Wiluszynski v Tower Hamlets London Borough Council* [1989] ICR 493.

[15] J English, 'Substantial Performance in Employment Contracts' in A Bogg and P Davies (eds), *Private Law and the Employment Contract* (Hart Publishing 2025) 64.

[16] For a detailed analysis of strikes and breach of contract see P Elias, 'The Strike and Breach of Contract: A Reassessment' in K Ewing, CA Gearty and BA Hepple (eds), *Human Rights and Labour Law: Essays for Paul O'Higgins* (Mansell 1994) 257.

[17] B Langstaff, 'Changing times, Changing relationships at work … changing law?' (2016) 45 *Industrial Law Journal* 131. See also G Davidov, 'A Theory of the Contract of Employment' [2025] *Industrial Law Journal* forthcoming.

[18] Elias, 'Changes and Challenges' (n 8) 872.

of the employment relationship – now require an employer 'to care for the physical, financial and even psychological welfare of the employee'.[19] As Mummery LJ said in *Commerzbank AG v Keen*:

> The employment relationship contains implied duties which do not normally feature in commercial contracts sued on by businessmen in the Commercial Court or in the exercise of public law discretions challenged by citizens in the Administrative Court. Employment is a personal relationship. Its dynamics differ significantly from those of business deals and of State treatment of its citizens.[20]

The development and modification of normal contractual principles is seen most starkly in the establishment of the implied term of mutual trust and confidence. This implied term, developed from the usual contractual duty of cooperation, goes much further than the 'distinctly limited role' which 'confines itself to rendering illegitimate certain behaviour by one party which seeks to make it more difficult, or has the predictable effect of making it more difficult, or impossible for the other person to perform'.[21] The implied term of mutual trust and confidence requires that an employer shall not 'without reasonable and proper cause, conduct itself in a manner likely to destroy or seriously damage the relationship of confidence and trust between employer and employee'.[22] This captures more than matters that make it more difficult to perform the contract. In light of the extensive number of implied terms, a number of academics argue that there is now a duty of good faith in an employment relationship,[23] and others argue that the employment contract sits within the category of contracts that are relational contracts.

ii. Relational Contracts

Lord Steyn, in his dissent in *Johnson v Unisys Ltd*, said that 'it is no longer right to equate a contract of employment with commercial contracts. One possible way of describing a contract of employment in modern terms is as a relational contract'.[24] A relational contract[25] is one where there is

[19] *Spring v Guardian Assurance* [1995] 2 AC 296, 335 (Lord Slynn).

[20] *Commerzbank AG v Keen* [2006] EWCA Civ 1536, [43].

[21] D Brodie, 'Beyond Exchange: The New Contract of Employment' (1998) 27 *Industrial Law Journal* 79, 80.

[22] *Malik v BCCI SA* [1997] UKHL 23.

[23] See, eg, Brodie, 'Beyond Exchange' (n 20) and K Banks, 'Good faith obligations in employment law' in G Davidov et al (eds) *The Oxford Handbook of the Law of Work* (Oxford University Press 2024).

[24] *Johnson v Unisys Ltd* [2001] UKHL 13, [20]. See also Lord Hodge and Lord Kerr in *Braganza v BP Shipping Ltd* [2015] UKSC 17.

[25] Fraser J, *Bates v Post Office (No 3)* [2019] EWHC 606, 725 identified the following as features of a relational contract: 1. There must be no specific express terms in the contract that prevents a duty of good faith being implied into the contract; 2. The contract will be a long-term one, with the mutual intention of the parties being that there will be a long-term relationship; 3. The parties must intend that their respective roles be performed with integrity, and with fidelity to their bargain; 4. The parties will be committed to collaborating with one another in the performance of the contract; 5. The spirits and

> the expectation of a longer-term business relationship; investment of substantial resources by both parties; implicit expectations of co-operation and loyalty that shape performance obligations in order to give business efficacy to the project; and implicit expectations of mutual trust and confidence going beyond the avoidance of dishonesty.[26]

The fundamental feature of a relational contract is that it is 'incomplete by design',[27] arising from the long-term nature of the relationship such that 'the performance obligations and the desired outcome of the transaction are deliberately incompletely specified'.[28]

Certain attributes of employment law have been identified as indicating that the employment contract should now be considered to be a relational contract: the fact that the interpretation of contracts is undertaken in a deeply contextual way; the dynamic variation and adjustment of contractual obligations in light of the changing needs and requirements of the employer; the recognition of binding intermittent contracts in the context of a long-term, ongoing business relationship; and the application of a mandatory obligation to perform the contract in good faith.[29] Thus, the 'more diffuse obligations' such as 'implied terms about loyalty, obedience, and health and safety' could be said to have moved the employment contract away from being an exchange transaction to be 'merged or subsumed into the personal employment contract as a relational contract'.[30]

While this may be helpful as a descriptive tool, to explain and rationalise the fact that a different approach is taken to employment contracts as compared with more general (commercial) contracts, it is equally difficult to see what assistance can be derived from this categorisation as opposed to simply acknowledging that 'there is considerable scope for the common law of contract to respond to the particular needs of the parties to an ongoing relationship'.[31] Moreover, we would argue that the employment relationship is more than a relational contract because work is a distinctive form of commodity that is integral to the personhood of a human being.

However, the benefit of describing employment relationships as relational is that it recognises a broader human dimension of work which is not captured by

objectives of their venture may not be capable of being expressed exhaustively in a written contract; 6. They will each repose trust and confidence in one another, but of a different kind to that involved in fiduciary relationships; 7. The contract in question will involve a high degree of communication, co-operation and predictable performance based on mutual trust and confidence, and expectations of loyalty; 8. There may be a degree of significant investment by one party (or both) in the venture. This significant investment may be, in some cases, more accurately described as substantial financial commitment; 9. Exclusivity of the relationship may also be present.

[26] H Collins, 'Employment as a relational contract' (2021) 137 *LQR* 426.

[27] H Collins, *Regulating Contracts* (Oxford University Press 1999) 161.

[28] Collins, 'Employment as a relational contract' (n 26) 450.

[29] ibid, 428.

[30] M Freedland, *The Personal Employment Contract* (Oxford University Press 2003) 92.

[31] D Brodie, 'How relational is the employment contract?' (2011) 40 *Industrial Law Journal* 232, 238. See also D Brodie, 'Relational Contracts' in M Freedland (Gen Ed), *The Contract of Employment* (Oxford University Press 2016), 145–166.

the terms of the contract, however detailed. Relational contract theory argues that 'parties to contracts develop a relationship between one another that incorporates planning, trust and solidarity that far exceeds the terms of the original document'.[32] Relational contracts are founded not just on law but also on norms which, for Bird, are 'perceived as law more than laws are', that is, 'virtually every aspect of the employment relation that falls outside the treatment by contract lawyers – corporate culture, office politics, future planning, and the complex social matrix of organizational life – is the exclusive domain of norms'.[33] Yet we know, that these are often the very things that give rise to a dispute or militate in favour or against that dispute being successfully resolved. We return to this issue in section III.

Similarly, Collins says that a distinctive feature of employment contracts is the 'multilateral relations of association', that is:

> [T]he goods and services produced by a productive organization must be largely the outcome of teamwork. Employees have to constantly interact with managers and colleagues and subordinates within the organization in order to get the job done efficiently and successfully.[34]

These interactions may be governed by rules in a handbook, perhaps backed up by a contractual sanction but they are often 'guidance rather than commands, aspirations rather than specific obligations' so are not contractual obligations. Moreover, the interactions 'depend on personal relations and expectations of reciprocal assistance between the members of the organization' between 'whom there is no direct contractual relation'.[35]

We would argue that it is this relationality that is fundamental to understanding the employment relationship and ultimately how disputes can be resolved because 'contract law, although not wholly incompatible with employment, does not fully account for the broad range of relational interests and contexts present in employment relationships'.[36] Even with the extensive use of implied terms and a contextual interpretation of the underlying contract, the complex relationships that operate in the workplace – not just between parties to the particular contract – require a different perspective beyond an analysis of even a relational contract when the resolution of disputes is being considered. We return to this point in section III.

iii. Psychological Contracts

What about 'psychological contract', a descriptor that commentators use in organisational theory? The 'classic' definition of a psychological contract 'refers to the perceptions of mutual obligations to each other, held by the two parties in the

[32] R Bird, 'Employment as a Relational Contract' [2005] 8 *University of Pennsylvania Journal of Labor and Employment Law* 149, 151.

[33] ibid, 150.

[34] H Collins, 'Relational and Associational Justice in Work' (2023) 24 *Theoretical Inquiries in Law* 26, 34.

[35] ibid, 34–35.

[36] Bird (n 32) 158.

employment relationship, the organisation and the employee'.[37] It is concerned with 'the subjectivity inherent to all employment contracts'.[38] By contrast, Rousseau defined the psychological contract as 'An individual's belief in mutual obligations between that person and another party such as an employer',[39] that is, an entirely one-sided 'contract'. A further definition of the psychological contract is that there are in fact 'an infinite number of potential contracts' with any number of individuals within the organisation.[40]

We do not consider that the concept of a psychological contract is of particular assistance in understanding how employment disputes can be addressed. The language of contract, used here where there may be no shared agreement or any intention to create legal relations, is problematic to us as lawyers. However, the recognition of multifarious relationships[41] within an organisation with varying degrees of significance for the individual is helpful as a means of recognising that these may have 'a powerful effect on [the person's] behaviour'.[42] Indeed, academics have posited that where a person considers their contract to be transactional rather than relational, they are more likely to adopt a more pragmatic stance to any perceived breach,[43] whereas a breach of a psychological contract 'yields deeper and more intense responses, akin to anger and moral outrage'.[44] The parallel in dispute resolution is obvious: the dynamics of a particular employment relationship need to be considered in the dispute resolution process because it is out of these relationships that the dispute is likely to have arisen.

iv. Challenges of a Contractual Analysis of the Employment Relationship

The problems with viewing the employment relationship through a purely contractual lens is that, as Collins puts it, it 'constructs an image of the human association that reduces its complexity to the elements and trajectories that have significance within the contractual framework'. He continues:

> The contract thinks about events, for instance, by examining human actions and words within a narrow time frame. The prior pattern of the social relation between

[37] A Marks, 'Developing a multiple foci conceptualisation of the psychological contract' (2001) 23 *Employee Relations* 454, 455.

[38] L Millward and P Brewerton, 'Psychological Contracts: Employee relations in the twenty-first century?' in I Robertson, *Personnel Psychology and Human Resources Management: A Reader for Students and Practitioners* (Wiley-Blackwell 2015) 387.

[39] D Rousseau and S Tijoriwala, 'Assessing psychological contracts: Issues, alternatives and measures' (1998) 19 *Journal of Organizational Behavior* 679. See also D Guest, 'The Psychology of the Employment Relationship: An analysis based on the psychological contract' (2004) 53 *Applied Psychology* 541, 544–45.

[40] Marks (n 37).

[41] ibid, 464.

[42] Millward and Brewerton (n 38) 388.

[43] ibid, 404.

[44] D Rousseau, 'Psychological and Implied Contracts in Organizations' (1989) 2 *Employee Responsibilities and Rights Journal* 121, 128.

> the parties and their sentiments of trust and loyalty are irrelevant to this construction of knowledge. The contract thinks, for instance, about a promise, whether it was made, what the promisor intended by the commitment, and whether the promise has been kept. This construction of the event ignores most of the context in which the promise was made, how it fitted into a prior relation between the parties, how it affects other people, and how performance of the promise serves the interests and aspirations of the parties.[45]

For us, that is the essence of the problem. An employment relationship generally does not ignore the context of the promises that were made, nor the prior pattern of social relations between the actors. The emphasis on contract reduces the reality of employment to a degree that renders it too simplistic and too short term. As Gardner says:

> The problem is not that the extant law of contract regards us as 'unrelated humans' but that it regards us as *merely contractually related* humans … So the problem is not that the law of contract fails to do justice to contractual relations. The problem, rather, is that it does justice *only* to contractual relations. It fails to do justice to other relations, such as that between employer and employee, because it insists, reductively, that they are but types of contractual relations.[46]

Moreover, the modification of ordinary contractual principles specifically for the context of employment law, itself highlights that a purely contractual analysis is incomplete when measured against the real world. As Coester says:

> An important difference exists between an employment contract and other contracts creating obligations, such as a sales contract: the employment contract is not fulfilled in a single and not even in a repeated exchange of goods and/or services, but rather the employee with his or her individual rights submits him- or herself to the organisational and jurisdictional control of the employer, spending significant portions of his or her active life 'on the job'. As a result, the employee is not only subject to the employer's influence with respect to his or her work, but also with respect to his or her physical and mental well-being, giving rise to a need to be protected.[47]

Much of that protection now arises through legislative intervention.

v. *Contractual Perspectives and Dispute Resolution*

An emphasis on the contractual perspective of employment relationships would require a dispute resolution forum to perform a careful analysis of the contractual rights and entitlements that have been, or generally are, agreed in employment

[45] Collins, *Regulating Contracts* (n 27) 15–16.

[46] J Gardner, 'The Contractualisation of Labour Law' in H Collins, G Lester and V Mantouvalou (eds), *Philosophical Foundations of Labour Law* (Oxford University Press 2018) 41. He goes on to argue that the contractualisation of labour law has resulted in work being a cost or sacrifice to the employee such that work is seen only to contribute instrumentally to a person's life, giving them a way of supporting the rest of 'life', rather than contributing constitutively, having a place within one's wider life and therefore contractualisation acts as a threat to freedom: 45–47.

[47] M Coester, 'Protection of Employees' Individual rights in the Employer-Employee Relationship' in K Zielger (ed), *Human Rights and Private Law* (Hart Pubishing 2007) 133.

contracts. It results in a focus on the financial costs and benefits of continuing or ending an employment contract. There will be some employment relationships which are transactional, where the employer and the employee see their relationship as a matter of economics and the outcome of the dispute is simply a matter of assessing the relative costs and gains to each party and the risks of those outcomes accruing. In those sorts of disputes, a purely contractual approach is clearly appropriate: it calls for a straightforward, speedy and efficient economic analysis of the position and any dispute resolution system needs to build in capacity to address such straightforward matters in that way.

However, these are also unlikely to be the cases that end up in tribunals because if they are considered dispassionately as transactional arrangements that need to be unravelled, the parties are likely to be able to resolve the issues themselves. In reality, the problem with a highly contractual approach is that:

> The assertions of entitlement and correlative obligation, which fuel the legal process of litigation and adjudication, tend to exacerbate the conflict between the parties. They shift the discourse away from the normative framework of preserving the business relation and ensuring the mutual benefit to be derived from the deal towards the legalistic assertion of contractual rights.[48]

This, in turn, unravels the 'ties of trust and confidence in commercial relations' and prevents 'accommodation which preserves the benefits expected from the transaction for both parties. Social order is only preserved at the cost of economic disintegration.'[49]

Moreover, the emphasis on identifying the 'events' of the contract, ignoring the context and the 'prior pattern of the social relation', is divorced from the reality of employment relationships. This disjunction prevents parties from addressing the real issues in a dispute.

If the dispute resolution system is modelled solely to enable assertions of entitlement and obligation, it is likely to cause entrenchment of disputes and the raising of the temperature of the conflict. This is particularly damaging where the individual remains employed by the organisation. Thus, while the fundamentally contractual basis of employment law and the importance of business efficacy for the employer needs to be considered, any dispute resolution system will need to go beyond a process that is solely concerned with allocating the costs and benefits of the relative rights and obligations of the parties and take a more holistic approach.

B. Statutory Protection

i. Introduction

So far we have discussed the legal but also the psychological limits of conceiving of the employment relationship solely through a contractual lens. We turn now to

[48] Collins, *Regulating Contracts* (n 27) 321.
[49] ibid.

see how the employment relationship is increasingly being conceived through a regulatory prism, replacing the more traditionally contractually focused analysis which in turn had replaced the focus on a collective reading of the employment relationship. Indeed, historically, 'the common law was a mere footnote to the social institutions of collective bargaining and strike action' and 'private law was generally regarded as an instrument of repression wielded against workers and trade unions by unelected judges'.[50] Thus, contract law was sidelined in favour of a worker-protective perspective founded in collective bargaining.

The role of trade unions in the workplace is now much reduced but in its place, there is a mass of legislative intervention seeking to address the inequality of bargaining power inherent in every contract of employment. Has this statutory perspective – and the requirement to hold a particular status to access those statutory rights – replaced contract law?

The focus of the debate in relation to employment status versus contract has been on the approach that should be used to determine whether someone falls within the ambit of the protection of certain legislative provisions. To claim most rights, a person must be a worker within section 230(3)(b) Employment Rights Act 1996, and cognate legislation, that is, they must have a contract personally to do work. For unfair dismissal and redundancy protection, they must be an 'employee', having a contract of employment defined as a contract of service. The distinction between the employed and the self-employed, the worker and the employee, is a dichotomy that 'was, in reality, imposed or maintained by legislation' and was one where 'the search for a clear conceptual distinction showed that, ultimately, to be as elusive as the search for the Philosopher's Stone'.[51]

The issue for the courts has been what approach should be taken when the written arrangements have no bearing on the reality of the relationship on the ground. The Supreme Court in *Autoclenz Ltd v Belcher*[52] determined that a 'purposive approach' should be taken, that is, the relative bargaining power of the parties must be taken into account in deciding whether the terms of any written agreement in truth represent what was agreed and the true agreement will often have to be gleaned from all the circumstances of the case, of which the written agreement is only a part'.[53] This was clarified in *Uber BV v Aslam*[54] when the Supreme Court held that whether a contract is a worker's contract within the legislation is 'not to be determined by applying ordinary principles of contract law'[55] but, in light of the inequality of bargaining power of the parties and that

[50] A Bogg and P Davies, 'Private Law Perspectives on the Employment Contract' in A Bogg and P Davies (eds), *Private Law and the Employment Contract* (Hart Publishing 2025) 1.

[51] M Freedland quoted in S Deakin 'Does the "Personal Employment Contract" provide a basis for the reunification of employment law?' (2007) 36 *Industrial Law Journal* 68, 70.

[52] [2011] UKSC 41.

[53] ibid, Lord Clarke at [35].

[54] [2021] UKSC 5.

[55] ibid at [68].

the rights 'were not contractual rights but were created by legislation',[56] by applying a purposive approach.

Bogg argues that in light of *Uber*

> purposive should be understood as the general statutory purpose of worker protection in employment protection legislation … the task of tribunals will now be focused on applying the statutory protections purposively and realistically, sensitive to the realities of control and dependence in working arrangements.[57]

Instead of a 'narrow contract-based analysis of the parties' relationship', Atkinson and Dhorajiwala say that the courts must now undertake 'a broad enquiry into the reality of the relationship … constructed in a manner that protects individuals performing work in positions of subordination and dependency'.[58]

In many ways, this returns the focus of employment law to a sociological perspective and the underlying assumption of Kahn-Freund's collective laissez faire model that labour law 'should address and seek to relieve a fundamental social and economic problem in modern society: the subordination of labour to capital, or of employee to employer'[59] (albeit that he viewed collective bargaining as central to the labour market with legislation only operating as an auxiliary function) as opposed to viewing the relationship in transactional terms. However, this perspective is insufficient on its own because so much of the statutory protection is built on contractual concepts.

ii. Interplay between Contract and Statute

While a purposive approach to determining whether someone falls within the ambit of legislative protection is an important development, we would argue that saying that employment law is now all about status and statutory protection, and has nothing to do with contract, goes too far.

Kahn-Freund described the contract of employment as the 'cornerstone' of modern labour law. Deakin says that this description captures precisely the dual nature of the contract of employment:

> [O]n the one hand, it underpinned the common law of 'managerial prerogative' through the open-ended duty of obedience, while simultaneously supporting the edifice of social legislation aimed at providing the individual with protection against the economic risks.[60]

[56] ibid at [69].

[57] A Bogg, 'For Whom the Bell Tolls: "Contract" in the Gig Economy': ohrh.law.ox.ac.uk/for-whom-the-bell-tolls-contract-in-the-gig-economy/.

[58] J Atkinson and H Dhorajiwala, 'The Future of Employment: Purposive Interpretation and the Role of Contract after *Uber*' (2022) 85 *MLR* 787, 789.

[59] H Collins, 'Labour as a vocation' (1989) 105 *LQR* 468, 469.

[60] S Deakin, 'The Contract of Employment: A study in legal evolution' (2001) ESRC Centre for Business Research, Working Paper No 203, 32.

Thus, he says that from a historical perspective 'not only is the contract of employment a more recent innovation than many have thought, but that its essential features owe as much to legislation as they do to the common law of contract'.[61] Freedland also acknowledges the interplay between the two saying that 'employment legislation has continued to interact with the common law of the contract of employment, in the sense both that legislation has invoked that body of common law and has had a major substantive impact upon it'.[62]

The primary location of this interplay is where the contract of employment operates as the gateway to many statutory rights.[63] But it also arises in other parts of the statutory framework for example, section 95(1)(c) Employment Rights Act 1996 defines dismissal – for the purposes of claiming unfair dismissal – as including constructive dismissal, ie where 'the employee terminates the contract under which he is employed (with or without notice) in circumstances in which he is entitled to terminate it without notice by reason of the employer's conduct'. This statutory provision relies on utilising contractual concepts about what constitutes a repudiatory breach of contract. Thus, contractual principles once again operate as a gateway to accessing statutory rights.[64]

Ultimately there must still be an agreement between the parties – at the very least to do work in exchange for remuneration.[65] It is not possible entirely to jettison contract law.[66] Statutory rights are 'grafted onto specific types of contractual relation … [which] represents a kind of 'hybridity' in legal form'.[67] Another

[61] ibid, 4. For a more detailed treatment of this point, see S Deakin and F Wilkinson, *The Law of the Labour Market: Industrialization, Employment and Legal Evolution* (Oxford University Press 2005).

[62] Freedland, *The Personal Employment Contract* (n 30) 3.

[63] In addition, it might be noted that statute has been used by the courts to prevent the development of a common law contractual remedy in relation to wrongful dismissal in circumstances where Parliament had already occupied the field in unfair dismissal: *Johnson v Unisys Ltd* [2001] UKHL 13. For further discussion, see C Barnard and L Merrett, 'Winners and Losers: *Edwards* and the unfair law of dismissal' (2013) 72 *CLJ* 313 and ACL Davies, 'The Relationship between the Contract of Employment and Statute' in M Freedland et al (eds), *The Contract of Employment* (Oxford University Press 2016). Any lifting of the cap on compensation for unfair dismissal may change this.

[64] For other examples of the interaction between statute and common law see Freedland, *The Personal Employment Contract* (n 30) 3–4.

[65] B Hepple in his seminal work 'Restructuring Employment Rights' (1986) 15 *Industrial Law Journal* 69 argued that statutory employment rights should not be 'built on the traditional "cornerstone" of the common law contract of service' and proposed a wider concept of an employment relationship. However, he also acknowledged that his formulation could still be regarded as contractual. For a more recent reflection on this issue, see P Davies and M Freedland, 'Changing perspectives upon the employment relationship in British labour law' in C Barnard, S Deakin and G Morris (eds), *The Future of Labour Law* (Hart Publishing 2004).

[66] Nor would jettisoning contract law be beneficial to workers or employers who depend on the predictability of the contractual obligations. In addition, there are of course some statutory rights that expressly operate by modifying the underlying contract, see for example, the equality clause in equal pay (s 66 Equality Act 2010).

[67] A Bogg, 'Common law and statute in the law of employment' (2016) 69 *Common Legal Problems* 67, 70.

conceptualisation may be that the two are 'mutually supporting elements of an overarching purposive approach'.[68]

Status (and statutory protection) is necessarily overlapping and interrelated to contract.[69] However, even viewing the employment relationship as both a matter of status and contract does not get to the heart of how an individual interacts with their employer and other individuals in the organisation. Taking a purposive approach helps to capture the essential vulnerability of many workers, but we would argue that it does not fully encapsulate the importance of work in a person's life or the nature and complexities of the relationships in a workplace.

iii. Statutory Protection and Dispute Resolution

What does a statutory perspective mean for the design of a dispute resolution system? By focusing on employment as requiring statutory protection there is a need to look to measures to rebalance the relationship of unequal bargaining power between an employer and an employee. It requires a system that is protective of the weaker party, but only within the ambit of the statutory provision that has been made. That is generally carefully calibrated to restrain the worst excesses of subordination without unduly preventing an employer from running their business.

The purposive approach to statutory rights means that any dispute resolution system must focus on the worker's protection and their ability to enforce their rights against the strong employer. At one extreme it might necessitate another person stepping in to enforce the individual's rights for them because they lack the power to do so, thus also reflecting the public quality of employment rights.[70] That is an important element to consider going forward: where a worker is particularly vulnerable or lacks the ability to enforce their employment rights, it may be necessary to provide a mechanism whereby those rights are enforced by an external enforcement body.

However, this does not represent the reality for the majority of employees, even with the establishment of the Fair Work Agency. Very often there is an inequality of bargaining power but not of the magnitude that requires them to have a third party acting on their behalf. Moreover, it is important to recognise that this is still a contract-oriented relationship with a transactional element. Thus, while steps must be taken in the design of the dispute resolution system to ensure that employees are not disadvantaged, and that their weaker bargaining position is accounted for, the economic perspective (ie, the need for employers to be able to run their business and the need to ensure fairness to other workers) must also be considered.

[68] Atkinson and Dhorajiwala (n 58) 791.

[69] See further: ACL Davies, 'The Relationship between the Contract of Employment and Statute' in M Freedland (Gen Ed), *The Contract of Employment* (Oxford University Press 2016), 73–95.

[70] See further Bogg, '"Labour Law is a Subset of Employment Law" revisited' (n 1).

C. The Employment Relationship and Human Rights

i. Human Rights as the Basis for the Employment Relationship

So far we have looked at the employment relationship as a sub-species of contract law and through the perspective of statutory protection. We turn now to consider the increasing framing of the employment relationship through the prism of human rights.

With the introduction of the Human Rights Act 1998, there was considerable speculation about whether 'bringing these rights home' would have any significant impact on employment law.[71] Hepple argued that the incorporation of human rights into domestic law – 'those moral rights which one has simply because one is a human being' – would 'have a profound effect on private employment' as well as public employment.[72] In reality, the impact of human rights arguments derived from the ECHR has been more limited than perhaps was expected. Human rights arguments have primarily been used to modify the usual domestic principles in some way. For example, when considering the question of whether a person was unfairly dismissed, in circumstances where their fundamental rights are engaged, a tribunal must consider whether the interference with their Convention right by dismissal is justified in addition to the usual considerations of fairness under section 98 Employment Rights Act 1996.[73]

Human rights have been used in whistleblowing claims and discrimination matters to extend protection to groups that would otherwise have remained unprotected. Consequently, in *Gilham v Ministry of Justice*,[74] the statutory provisions in relation to who may bring a whistleblowing claim were read down so as to include judges because their exclusion constituted a breach of Article 14 (non-discrimination) read together with Article 10 (freedom of expression). In *National Union of Professional Foster Carers v The Certification Officer*[75] the definition of worker in the context of listing a trade union was read down to ensure there was no breach of Article 11 (freedom of assembly and association). In *Higgs v Farmor's School*[76] a requirement to justify direct discrimination in relation to the manifestation of religious belief was read into the Equality Act 2010 to ensure compliance with Article 9 (freedom of religion).

[71] See, eg, B Hepple, 'Human Rights and Employment Law' (1998) 8 *Amicus Curiae* 19.

[72] ibid, 22.

[73] eg, *X v Y* [2004] EWCA Civ 662 and *Pay v UK* [2004] EWCA Civ 776 and [2009] IRLR 139 (ECtHR). For a detailed analysis of these two cases see: V Mantouvalou and H Collins, 'Private life and dismissal' (2009) 38 *Industrial Law Journal* 133; J Atkinson, 'Taking Human Rights Seriously at Work: The Past, Present and Future of Employment Law' (2025) 54 *Industrial Law Journal* 744.

[74] *Gilham v Ministry of Justice* [2019] UKSC 44.

[75] *National Union of Professional Foster Carers v The Certification Officer* [2021] EWCA Civ 548.

[76] *Higgs v Farmor's School* [2025] EWCA Civ 109, in addition to a reading of the legislation in accordance with domestic principles.

Taking an instrumentalist approach,[77] human rights have been utilised 'principally through techniques of statutory interpretation of existing "private" rights, such as unfair dismissal'.[78] It had been argued – pre-*Uber* – that where fundamental rights were at stake, 'the common law tests for employment status should be strongly purposive in character' to ensure that the underlying rights were upheld.[79] The impetus for this appears less now that a strongly purposive approach has been taken in any event under common law. Nevertheless, it seems that human rights are primarily useful when interwoven in general common law reasoning, modifying contractual principles or requiring purposive statutory interpretation rather than as a stand-alone classification.[80] We would accept that 'the province of employment rights … is co-extensive with human rights … It would require significant intellectual effort to disentangle employment law from human rights law and to still provide a coherent account of the law without using the grammar of human rights',[81] albeit that it is not a complete categorisation of the discipline.

There are strong normative arguments in favour of aligning employment law and human rights. It has been said that 'If workers' rights can be viewed as fundamental or human rights, these are stringent entitlements with an increased moral and legal force'.[82] Moreover, both employment law and human rights 'are motivated by a desire to improve the human condition, and both are often seen as protecting human dignity'.[83] In practice however, we would argue that employment law should not be conceptualised as a matter of human rights alone. Human rights have not comprehensively occupied the field: Atkinson acknowledges, even from a normative perspective, that 'human rights will likely only provide partial foundations for labour law … [although] the fact that some labour law norms do not have their foundations in human rights does not prevent human rights from playing an important role in justifying the discipline'.[84]

[77] For the different approaches that are taken in the literature, see V Mantouvalou, 'Are labour rights human rights?' (2012) 3 *European Labour Law Journal* 151 and A Bogg, H Collins, ACL Davies and V Mantouvalou, *Human Rights at Work* (Hart Publishing 2024) 4–5.

[78] Bogg and Davies, 'Private Law Perspectives on the Employment Contract' (n 50) 5.

[79] Bogg, 'Common law and statute in the law of employment' (n 67) 108.

[80] Bogg has argued that human rights should be treated as a 'seamless element integrated into general common law reasoning' rather than a 'separate legal compartment of legal reasoning governed by the Human Rights Act 1998': ibid, 110. Perhaps to an extent, this is already being achieved.

[81] Bogg et al, *Human Rights at Work* (n 77) 11.

[82] Collins, Lester and Mantouvalou (n 2) 9.

[83] J Atkinson, 'Human Rights as Foundations for Labour Law' in H Collins, G Lester and V Mantouvalou (eds), *Philosophical Foundations of Labour Law* (Oxford University Press 2018) 124.

[84] Atkinson takes a normative approach to the issue examining human rights as a matter of theory rather than an instrumentalist approach, concluding that human rights can provide the foundations of labour law but not completely: Atkinson, 'Human Rights as Foundations for Labour Law' (n 83) 137. See also H Collins and V Mantouvalou, 'Human Rights and the Contract of Employment' in M Freedland (Gen Ed), The Contract of Employment (Oxford University Press 2016), 188–208.

While a human rights analysis has not had the dramatic impact on the employment relationship first anticipated, it is worth stepping back and recalling the importance of a rights discourse more broadly:

> [R]ights are not simply about making the wage-work bargain more efficient. They are an expression of our common humanity. Rights at work – such as the rights to equality, to freedom of association, to job security, to decent working conditions, and to combine family and working life – express the moral judgment that 'labour is not a commodity or article of commerce', and that all human beings are entitled to be treated with equal dignity and respect … our rights at work are 'precious jewels' that give us a sense of identity, self-worth and emotional well-being and so enable us to contribute to society.[85]

However, as with the other two perspectives, a human rights discourse tends to focus on the atomised individual, removed from the social ties of interconnectivity in the workplace.

ii. Human Rights and Dispute Resolution

In many ways there is little to add to the analysis in relation to contract and statutory protection because human rights have tended to be used as an additional perspective or as a basis for modifying contractual principles or statutory interpretation. The rights perspective reminds us of the need to accord dignity and humanity to all participants in any system. A dispute resolution system must also meet the requirements of a fair trial in Article 6 ECHR: that there is a fair and public hearing within a reasonable time by an independent and impartial tribunal established by law.[86] We note particularly the need for the hearing to be within a reasonable time and that any hearing is fair.

III. Employment Relationships and Dispute Resolution

A. The Breakdown of Employment Relationships

> Work is one of the most fundamental aspects of a person's life, providing the individual with a means of financial support and, as importantly, a contributory role in society.

[85] B Hepple, *Rights at Work: Global, European and British Perspectives* (Sweet & Maxwell, 2005) 1–2. See also Bogg et al, *Human Rights at Work* (n 77) 310–11.

[86] This generally does not give an individual the right to legal representation at internal disciplinary proceedings, unless there is a substantive correlation between the outcome of the internal proceedings and a related subsequent decision that is within the ambit of Article 6, eg, a decision of a professional regulatory body preventing the person from practising their profession: *R(G) v Governors of X School* [2011] UKSC 30. For discussion on the issues that arise, see A Sanders, 'Does Article 6 of the European Convention on Human Rights apply to disciplinary procedures in the workplace?' (2013) 33 *OJLS* 791. We discuss Article 6 in the context of our recommendations in ch 13.

> A person's employment is an essential component of his or her sense of identity, self-worth and emotional well-being.[87]

In many ways this is a statement of the obvious. A person's identity is heavily influenced by their work and 'there is a dynamic interaction between identity and work environments such that they influence each other reciprocally'.[88] Practically, individuals spend substantial amounts of time at work, maybe spending more time with colleagues than even a spouse or partner.

Self-evidently then, a dispute at work will strike at a person's identity and constitute an 'identity threat'.[89] That may arise from actions of the employer, such as a challenge to a person's conduct or capability or through a reorganisation of the business, or of colleagues, particularly where there is interpersonal conflict or discrimination.

We want to argue that with the growing juridification of employment law, the relationship perspective of employment has been sidelined. Historically when there were difficulties in the workplace, the local trade union representative would hammer out an agreement with the local manager. If they could not resolve the issue then matters would be escalated through the chain of management and the trade union structures. Ultimately there might have been strike action but cases brought to the courts were limited and before a dispute reached the seriousness of industrial conflict, local and regional managers and representatives would have met and discussed and argued about how to resolve the problems. Wood says:

> Traditionally, industrial relations in the United Kingdom has been firmly rooted in its own culture and has operated largely separate from the legal system … Relationships [between trade unions and managers] were felt to be so personal that interference, either by legislation or recourse to the courts, was resented as unwarranted and felt likely to be destructive of understandings painfully built up over the years.[90]

More fundamentally, the issues were addressed first at a local level, with the trade union representative operating as a third-party 'voice' for the worker, as well as a sounding board and adviser for them. The managers and the trade union representatives generally knew and understood the relationships and organisational dynamics that were involved in any disputes. Today, without significant trade union presence, localised resolution by people who are attuned to the relational aspects of the dispute has been lost. Moreover, the role of trade union representatives has changed from 'co-regulators of terms and conditions of employment, to monitors and enforcers of employees' legal rights'.[91] This inevitably results in an emphasis on seeking legal recourse where rights are violated.

[87] Dickson CJ, 'Re Public Service Employee Relations Act' [1987] 1 SCR 313, 368.
[88] D Miscenko and D Day, 'Identity and identification at work' (2016) 6 *Organisational Psychology Review* 215, 216.
[89] ibid, 223.
[90] J Wood, 'Dispute Resolution – Conciliation, Mediation and Arbitration' in W McCarthy (ed), *Legal Intervention in Industrial Relations: Gains and Losses* (Blackwell 1992) 241.
[91] Deakin and Wilkinson, *The Law of the Labour Market* (n 61).

There has been a growing focus on process and procedure. Importantly where previously these processes would have been rules that were agreed between managers and trade unions, the position 'has been transformed into the observance of what are believed to be the norms set by legal institutions'.[92] This has had an impact on how human resources teams address disputes, with much greater emphasis on process and procedure, and how individuals view issues with their focus turning to vindicating their rights and entitlements.

We would argue that we need to return to a recognition that employment is fundamentally relational and the more high-trust the relationship the greater the need to understand the psychological dimension of the relationship breakdown. Deakin and Wilkinson distinguish between (1) 'low trust' employment relationships – where workers are managed closely with tight supervision, detailed rules and the use of punishment where standards are not met and (2) 'goodwill trust' relationships which involve 'both parties being willing to perform over and above the literal terms of their contract' and which are often long term and open ended.[93] They recognise that the latter type of relationship 'exposes each party to a high risk of opportunism – because the degree of lock in is greater, each side has more to lose, and the opportunities for effective retaliation may well be more limited'.[94] We would add to that the challenges that arise when there is a dispute, namely that where there has been a goodwill trust relationship, any dispute is likely to involve much greater emotional factors and prove to be much more complex to resolve.

We would argue that there is a real need when seeking to locate employment matters to acknowledge that they are fundamentally about relationships. We should not shy away from the reality that there are significant emotional and psychological factors that are involved in how employment relationships operate – taking it beyond questions of the transactional (contract) and the worker-protective (statutory). It is crucial to recognise the centrality of the employment relationship to people's lives and their sense of identity, together with the complex, multifaceted relational context in which the relationship operates.

Watt, having described different academic 'proposals for the regulatory principle governing the employment relationship', concludes that a 'bespoke design intended to reflect the specific features of the employment relationship' is required. He concludes that 'Most importantly, however, if the regime fails to acknowledge the centrality of the work relationship to peoples' lives, the regulatory regime will fail to achieve that which is demanded from it'.[95] We would wholeheartedly concur.

[92] B Hepple, 'The Fall and Rise of Unfair Dismissal' in W McCarthy (ed), *Legal Intervention in Industrial Relations: Gains and Losses* (Blackwell 1992) 91–92.

[93] S Deakin and F Wilkinson, 'Labour law and economic theory: a reappraisal' in H Collins, M Davies and R Rideout (eds,) *Legal Regulation of the Employment Relation* (Kluwer 2002) 56–57. Fox distinguished between 'high trust' and 'low trust' roles: A Fox, *Beyond Contract* (Faber 1974).

[94] Deakin and Wilkinson, 'Labour law and economic theory' (n 93).

[95] B Watt, 'Regulating the employment relationship: From rights to relations' in H Collins, M Davies and R Rideout (eds,) *Legal Regulation of the Employment Relation* (Kluwer 2002) 346.

B. Employment Relationships and Dispute Resolution

How do these emotional and psychological aspects of the work relationship have an impact on the dispute resolution process? At present, the costs of employment litigation are very high: a number of participants in our research identified the significant financial, time, emotional and health costs that litigants, on both sides, faced. Participants noted that litigants often became unwell during the process which exacerbated the delays in the process, which in turn caused increased ill-health. A particular concern was the cost of litigants having to relive events through the litigation process, especially during cross-examination. One focus group participant said: 'I felt my clients never won. They won money and they won compensation, but basically they had a whole year of stress and all of these complex legalities.' The emotional and health costs of litigation were noted to be particularly severe for claimants who were claiming maternity discrimination because of the stress of pregnancy, childbirth and dealing with the early months of motherhood, alongside the litigation.

We would argue that we need to take these emotional and health costs seriously. The corollary of recognising the relational perspective of employment relationships is that an effective dispute resolution system must operate in a way that limits those emotional and health costs. Understanding the emotional factors in litigation and dispute resolution may help to achieve that aim. Bies and Tyler identified that interpersonal connections were crucial to employees deciding whether to litigate disputes and that

> the creation of formal, procedural safeguards, intended to restore trust, may actually contribute to a growing adversarial climate in which trust is undermined anyway … the quality of interpersonal treatment … has an independent influence on procedural justice, as do inferences about trustworthiness of the manager … Specifically, the dilemmas caused by formalization can be managed by enacting procedures properly and in interpersonally sensitive ways.[96]

However, as Liddle says,

> conflict is not logical; it is irrational. Conflict is not black and white; it is grey. Conflict can be overt or it can be subtle, it can be simple or it can be incredibly complex. Conflict is deeply human and it can't be resolved by reducing it to right/wrong, good/bad, defend/attack or win/lose.[97]

What is clear from the literature is that economic models (based on the maximisation of economic utility) do not explain human behaviour in litigation particularly where conditions are uncertain 'such as those involving the risky choices available to litigants who are considering whether to settle for a certain outcome or pursue

[96] R Bies and T Tyler, 'The "Litigation Mentality" in Organizations: A test of alternative psychological explanations' (1993) 4 *Organization Science* 352, 362.

[97] D Liddle, *Managing Conflict: A Practical Guide to Resolution in the Workplace* (Kogan Page 2023) 123.

a more attractive but uncertain outcome at trial'.[98] Consequently, 'non-value-maximising considerations can affect decisions about whether to settle or try disputes'. Three elements tend to influence whether parties settle: (1) how the offer is framed; (2) the status of the relationship between the parties; and (3) who makes the offer of settlement.[99] Thus, there is once again an interpersonal element that affects the likelihood or otherwise of settling a dispute outside of court.[100]

Moreover, the role of anger has been identified as playing a significant role in disputes. Robbenolt and Sternlight, in their book *Psychology for Lawyers*, note that anger tends to arise from many types of conflict in the legal arena including 'violations of autonomy, perceived injustice, and violations of procedural justice'. They say that 'anger tends to result in decreased trust and a decreased concern for the other's interests'.[101] This loss of trust in others will, we would argue, inevitably affect a person's ability to engage in processes seeking resolution in the workplace or externally during litigation. Moreover, Robbenolt and Sternlight identified that:

> The feeling of certainty associated with anger can also lead an angry person to be less receptive to advice … [and] the certainty associated with anger tends to result in an increased reliance on more intuitive processing and schemas such as stereotypes.[102]

It is important to recognise the role of anger and its impact on an individual's understanding of the dispute and their ability to take advice and understand the risks involved in litigation.

How do these psychological insights have an impact on the design of a dispute resolution system? A key feature is that the process must provide 'the opportunity to have one's say and procedural fairness'.[103] This is echoed by Robbennolt and Sternlight who identify four elements in a psychologically-sustainable dispute resolution system:

> First, people are concerned about voice – having an opportunity to participate in the process, to state their case, to provide their views on what they see as a just result.

[98] T Wayte, J Samra, J Robbennolt, L Heuer and W Koch, 'Psychological issues in civil law' in J Ogloff (ed), *Taking Psychology and Law into the Twenty-First Century* (Kluwer Academic 2002) 327.

[99] R Korobkin and C Guthrie, 'Psychological barriers to litigation settlement: an experimental approach' (1994) 93 *Michigan Law Review* 107, 109–11. Other theories include the Framing theory, which predicts that litigants behave differently depending on how a litigation decision is framed, ie, whether it is seen as a loss or a gain from a perceived position: J Rachlinski, 'Gains, losses and the psychology of litigation' (1996) Cornell Law Faculty Publications, Paper 795. The Regret Aversion theory posits that the value of a decision option is 'a function not only of its outcome but also of the feelings associated with the outcomes of foregone options' ie, what someone anticipates they will regret if they choose to settle: C Guthrie, 'Better Settle than Sorry: the regret aversion theory of litigation behavior' (1999) 1 *University of Illinois Law Review* 43, 72.

[100] See also: Wayte et al (n 98) 360. See also: A Damasio, *Descartes' Error* (Avon Books 1995); J Robbennolt and J Sternlight, *Psychology for Lawyers: Understanding the Human Factors in Negotiation, Litigation and Decision Making* (American Bar Association 2021) 87; and S Bandes, 'Empathy, narrative and victim impact statements' in S Bandes et al (eds), *Research Handbook on Law and Emotion* (Elgar 2021) 517.

[101] Robbennolt and Sternlight (n 100) 95–96.

[102] ibid.

[103] Wayte et al (n 98) 331.

> Second, consistent with popular notions that justice is blind and that playing fields should be level, people care about the neutrality of the process or forum. A procedurally just process is one in which decision makers are unbiased, decisions are based on rules and objective criteria that are consistently applied, and explanations are given for the decisions reached. Third, the trustworthiness of the authority or process is important. People prefer processes in which the relevant authority is concerned about their interests and well-being, listens to their arguments, and genuinely tries to reach the right result. Finally, a procedurally just process is one in which participants are treated with dignity and respect.[104]

These are all factors that we, as lawyers, consider must be a core part of any dispute resolution system. They also coincide with the requirements of Article 6 ECHR.

Considering the highly relational and emotional factors in employment litigation – and the parallels drawn by our research participants between divorce and the loss of a job – we turn now to consider how family dispute resolution occurs and the premises on which that is based to see if there are lessons that can be learned for employment dispute resolution.

IV. The Theoretical Underpinnings of Family Law and Family Dispute Resolution

Family law is no longer a discipline 'concerned with rights and responsibilities within the intact family' but is 'one that largely focuses on the aftermath of relationship breakdown'.[105] Thus the starting point of family law is often the same as employment law: the law is attempting to deal with a complete breakdown in the context of the termination of employment or a partial breakdown of relationships at work.

One conceptualisation of family law is a functional approach in which it is argued that family law seeks to pursue three goals: protective (guarding family members from harm), adjustive (helping families that have broken down to adjust to new lives apart), and supportive (to support family life).[106] Again, there are interesting parallels here with employment law in its role protecting vulnerable employees as well as helping them to adjust to changes.

Another key principle in family law is autonomy. Herring says that autonomy means that

> in the case of disputes between the parties, we should respect their decisions about how to resolve them. The State should not be telling people how to run their families or imposing solutions to their disputes. Autonomy appears to be playing a more

[104] Robbennolt and Sternlight (n 100) 295–96.

[105] J Masson, R Bailey-Harris and R Probert, *Cretney's Principles of Family Law* (Sweet & Maxwell 2008) 2.

[106] J Eekelaar, *Family Law and Social Policy* (Weidenfeld & Nicholson 1984), discussed in J Herring, *Family Law* (Pearson 2025) 17.

> prominent role in family law with increasing weight being placed on enabling couples to resolve disputes themselves and with the law taking a less interventionist stance.[107]

The emphasis on autonomy has led to a drive to promote a settlement culture and to discourage the use of legal proceedings. In addition to saving legal and court costs, this is because, as Lowe et al say:

> The 'win-lose' essence of adversarial legal proceedings may antagonise and add to the general unhappiness and bitterness associated with the breakdown of a relationship and this may be emotionally and psychologically damaging to any children affected. Court orders and legal rules are blunt instruments for dealing with complex human problems, and the legal process is ill-equipped to provide the full range of support needed by family members going through crises and change. They may be particularly inappropriate where there is a need to preserve and foster a relationship notwithstanding a change in legal status.[108]

But what role does law have in family disputes? Mnookin and Kornhauser see

> the primary function of contemporary divorce law not as imposing order from above, but rather as providing a framework within which divorcing couples can themselves determine their post-dissolution rights and responsibilities. This process by which parties to a marriage are empowered to create their own legally enforceable commitments is a form of 'private ordering' … This new perspective and the use of the term 'private ordering' are not meant to suggest an absence of important social interests in how the process works or in the fairness of its outcomes. The implicit policy questions are ones of emphasis and degree.[109]

This private ordering is facilitated by extensive use of Alternative Dispute Resolution (ADR), especially mediation, an issue we return to in chapter five.

The advantages of 'private ordering' are that it 'aims to contain and reduce conflict' where adversarial proceedings are 'prone' to inflame it, as well as enhancing autonomy and enabling more creative solutions to be reached.[110] We would argue that there are useful parallels with employment disputes which often, as Lowe et al say, involve 'complex human problems'. The parties are autonomous and should have a strong say in how their dispute is resolved, particularly where there remains an ongoing work relationship.

However, concerns have been raised about an emphasis on autonomy in family law both in terms of whether the inherent individualisation represents the reality of social relationships,[111] and that it overlooks the vulnerability of some parties.[112]

[107] Herring, *Family Law* (n 106) 27. See also A Diduck, 'Autonomy and family justice' (2016) 28 *Child and Family Law Quarterly* 133.

[108] N Lowe, G Douglas, E Hitchings and R Taylor, *Bromley's Family Law* (Oxford University Press 2021) 12.

[109] R Mnookin and L Kornhauser, 'Bargaining in the Shadow of the Law: The case of divorce' (1979) 88 *Yale Law Journal* 950, 950–51.

[110] A Barlow, R Hunter, J Smithson and J Ewing, *Mapping Paths to Family Justice: Resolving Family Disputes in Neoliberal Times* (Palgrave Socio-legal Studies 2017) 4.

[111] J Herring, 'Relational autonomy and family life' in J Wallbank, S Choudhry and J Herring (eds), *Rights, Gender and Family Law* (Routledge 2010) 299.

[112] J Herring, *Vulnerable Adults and the Law* (Oxford University Press 2016).

There have been a number of steps in family law to address concerns about domestic abuse being perpetuated in non-court dispute resolution processes, including not requiring mediation to be used or to use a different form of mediation.[113] It is important to bear in mind the risks, and to build in safeguards, in employment disputes where parties are vulnerable.

Another concern about the emphasis on autonomy is raised by Herring who argues that family life is being privatised, with the law regulating less and less of it.[114] This is particularly apparent in the increased use of mediation. Moreover, Diduck says that parties' choices 'cannot be detached from legal principles developed to take account of the public, social context in which they are made and experienced or from the social and political consequences they engender' and there is a risk that an emphasis on private decision-making will result in the law approving a 'problematic status quo' particularly in relation to the role of women in the family.[115] Herring has argued that post-divorce financial arrangements cannot simply be seen as a 'private' matter since 'the wider community has a legitimate and powerful interest' in the distribution of income and assets between former spouses.[116]

In contrast to these concerns, Mnookin and Kornhauser note that individuals in a number of contexts 'bargain in the shadow of the law' such that 'preferences of the parties, the entitlements created by law, transaction costs, attitudes toward risk, and strategic behavior will substantially affect the negotiated outcome'.[117]

Many of the same issues can be identified in relation to employment law.[118] The conflict is fundamentally relational, addressing the complexities of a relationship breakdown. There are significant benefits to enabling and supporting the autonomy of the parties and the 'private ordering' of their dispute, particularly where the relationship is ongoing. However, there are also wider public interests in ensuring that employers do not break the law and that employment standards are maintained. The dispute resolution system for employment disputes needs to meet both of those fundamental elements.

V. Conclusions

We have argued that the traditional lenses of understanding employment law – as matters of contract, statute and human rights – are interlinked and overlapping. However, they do not fully explain the complexities of the relationships, both in terms of the people who are involved in a dispute and the emotional,

[113] See ch 5.
[114] J Herring, *Relational Autonomy and Family Law* (Springer 2014).
[115] Diduck (n 107) 134.
[116] See also ibid, 140.
[117] Mnookin and Kornhauser (n 109) 997.
[118] Arguably they could both be considered a part of a broader idea of the 'law of persons'.

psychological and behavioural factors that are at play. This has implications for the reform of any employment dispute resolution system. We would argue that there are strong parallels with family law. It is fundamentally relational, dealing with the messiness and complexity of multiple human relationships and the need to help parties make the transition to a new way of functioning, while safeguarding the important public and social function of the law of ensuring that just outcomes are achieved and the vulnerable are protected. This has influenced the model that is used in family law and we would argue should provide a useful framework for helping to re-imagine the employment dispute system. We argue it should focus much more on early dispute resolution, particularly ADR. This is the subject of chapter four.

PART II

Resolving Disputes without Litigation

> The adversarial model is an admirable model but does not deliver justice – or access to justice – for the vast majority of disputes that arise for most of the population and the majority of businesses in the country, either because it is too expensive a model, or too slow, or too adversarial when people need reconciliation.[1]

When, in 1996, Lord Woolf published his final report on Access to Justice[2] he described a 'new landscape' in civil litigation that would result from his proposed reforms. That included a feature that 'litigation will be avoided wherever possible … people will be encouraged to start court proceedings to resolve disputes only as a last resort, and after using other more appropriate means when these are available'. We want to argue that the spirit motivating the Woolf reforms should apply equally to employment law: litigation in the employment tribunals must be a last resort – as it was intended to be when the tribunals were first established. To achieve that, a radical repositioning is required, of both the employment dispute processes and the mindsets of practitioners. We want to advocate for greater intervention from hands-on Human Resource (HR) managers and far greater use of alternative dispute resolution (ADR), drawing inspiration from family law.

In this part of the book we consider the current structures supporting the early resolution of disputes in the workplace (chapter four). Success is limited. Therefore, we look at four alternatives within the UK: an initiative of Welsh Health making disciplinary hearings a matter of last resort; ombuds schemes; the use of pre-action protocols in personal injury and clinical negligence claims, and the use of mediation in family law disputes, to consider what lessons could be learned from them (chapter five). Both the Welsh and family law experiences speak strongly to the importance of recognising the relational and emotional context of employment disputes. As one interviewee said: 'Losing your job is like a bereavement, it is existential'. Many interviewees drew parallels between an employment relationship breakdown and a family breakdown. In family law, mediation is used extensively.

[1] C Hodges, *Delivering Dispute Resolution: A Holistic Review of Models in England and Wales* (Hart Publishing 2019) 22.

[2] See: webarchive.nationalarchives.gov.uk/ukgwa/20060213223540/; www.dca.gov.uk/civil/final/contents.htm.

Mediation was described as particularly valuable because 'we allow them to vent a little bit because … in a court process, judges [are] just not interested in the emotions … But actually you can't really bury those things, because those are the obstacles to reaching resolution'.[3] Because of that, mediation may be particularly successful in achieving a resolution that looks beyond the financial value of a claim and can explore the resolution of the dispute from a different perspective.

However, there is significant value in having a suite of non-court dispute resolution mechanisms to use separately or in combination, according to the particular needs of the individuals involved and the particular context of the dispute. Three international jurisdictions approach employment dispute resolution from a very different starting point from that in the UK: ADR is much more the norm. In chapter six, we explore the processes that are used in Singapore, Australia and New Zealand which all emphasise mediation, with it being described as the 'pinnacle' of dispute resolution in New Zealand. There are cultural differences which make the Singapore model less appropriate to translate into the UK, but the models in Australia and New Zealand provide useful examples of how lower value, less complex claims might be addressed through an emphasis on early mediation.

Recommendations

Arising from our analysis in chapters four, five and six, we make the following recommendations:

1. The Acas Code should be amended to make it clear that there is no requirement to follow a formal grievance procedure before bringing a claim to the tribunal. It should be emphasised that parties must make attempts to resolve the issues informally. The uplift/reduction in damages should be retained but applied only where informal resolution attempts have not been made. Grievances should be renamed as, for example, 'matters of concern'.
2. The Acas Code of Practice on Disciplinary and Grievance Procedures should be amended to specify that the disciplinary procedure should be used as a matter of last resort in most cases.
3. An Employment Resolution Service (ERS) should be established. This body should be the first port of call for all employers and employees seeking information and advice about issues in the workplace. It should provide comprehensive information and advice, with longer appointments where more complex advice is required. It should also actively encourage, support and facilitate internal workplace mediation.
4. Where further assistance is required, the ERS should operate as a triage service directing enquiries to the Fair Work Agency (FWA) for matters of

[3] Interview, 17 July 2025.

enforcement of basic rights, to a phone conciliation service for issues that appear to be possible to resolve straightforwardly or to an online mediation service staffed by experienced and highly capable mediators.

5. Parties should be required to attend either a phone conciliation appointment or online mediation appointment according to the complexity of the matter. These sessions should be resolution-focused, rather than problem-focused, and should include an element of 'reality testing', rather than being purely facilitative. The specific type of mediation should be tailored to the circumstances of the case. Where required, such as in certain discrimination matters, the mediation should follow a 'trauma informed' approach or transformative mediation approach.
6. Where conciliation or mediation is unsuccessful in resolving the dispute, the ERS should certify that the parties have attended to permit them to bring or defend a claim in the tribunal. However, judges should readily send cases back to the ERS for further mediation.

4

Early Resolution of Disputes

I. Introduction

Participants in our study overwhelmingly told us that the earlier that resolution of disputes was attempted, the more likely it was to succeed. They said that formal grievance processes were counterproductive, resulting in the parties digging in and becoming defensive; they were also sceptical about the usefulness of Acas early conciliation, with many seeing it as a tick-box exercise. So the question is how can early resolution of disputes be achieved and what might a system look like that encouraged this most effectively?

In this chapter, we define key terms including mediation and conciliation (section II). We explore how disputes can be currently resolved in the workplace (sections III and IV) and the steps a worker and an employer must or may take before a claim is brought to an employment tribunal (section V). We set out in more detail our empirical findings in relation to early dispute resolution and Acas early conciliation, as well as examining three related pre-action issues: time limits, the Acas arbitration scheme, and pre-action disclosure (section VI).

Our findings point to the need to have a system that emphasises early dispute resolution which is *informal* and is initially focused in the workplace; strict processes and formalities are generally counterproductive to achieving a resolution. When a resolution cannot be achieved, participants considered that external support may be helpful to mediate a resolution before matters proceed to the employment tribunal. However, these things take time and the current time limit for the presentation of claims of (in most cases) three months is too short to enable dispute resolution; more optimism was expressed about the planned extension of limitation to six months in the Employment Rights Act 2025 (ERA 2025).

II. Terminology of Alternative Dispute Resolution

A. Introduction

Alternative dispute resolution (ADR) is a broad term encompassing all forms of dispute resolution other than court adjudication. The glossary of the White

Book defines ADR as the 'collective description of methods of resolving disputes otherwise than through the normal trial process'.[1] Similarly, Bartlet says ADR involves 'processes for resolving disputes that are alternative or complementary to court adjudication. Many of these processes include a neutral third party supporting a negotiation settlement. The term is generally used to include arbitration and sometimes internal dispute resolution'.[2] Waters et al explain that

> a strict and comprehensive definition for the processes encompassed within the term ADR is elusive. The processes may be adjudicative or agreement-based, and though they may be prescribed to an extent by legislation (as under the Arbitration Acts), they are shaped by the requirements and wishes of the parties, and may be influenced by the ideologies and approaches of the third-party facilitator. Hence, rather than restrict the scope of ADR processes, we may be flexible and creative and adopt a wide range of possibilities under its umbrella.[3]

For the purposes of this book, we shall focus on the main types of ADR: mediation, conciliation, arbitration, and early neutral evaluation.

B. Mediation

Bartlet defines mediation as 'third party facilitated negotiation', and he defines civil mediation specifically as 'voluntary, flexible, and confidential third-party facilitated negotiation in which the parties remain in control of the decision to settle and the terms of resolution. It can take place either in prospect of litigation or as an attempt to settle litigation'.[4] The mediator acts as an unbiased and neutral third party without the power to impose results. Instead, the parties retain full control over the outcome, while the mediator 'uses skills to assist parties to negotiate settlement terms and arrive at their own resolution'. As we shall see, depending on the form and style of the mediation adopted, the mediator may express some views on the merits of issues; these views are non-binding.[5]

While adjudication of disputes emphasises impartiality, objectivity, adherence to precedent and a focus on facts rather than individuals, mediation centres on collaborative decision-making, is voluntary, confidential and informal, and prioritises the interests of the parties involved rather than their legal rights. In that sense, while adjudication emphasises what has happened in the past,

[1] Lord Justice Coulson (ed), *Civil Procedure: The White Book Service* (Vol 1, Sweet & Maxwell 2025) Section E – Glossary.

[2] M Bartlet, *Mediation and other Forms of Alternative Dispute Resolution* (Routledge 2025).

[3] B Waters et al, *Brown & Marriott's ADR Principles and Practice*, 4th edn (Sweet & Maxwell 2018) s 1-052. See also the 'mediation grid' created by L Riskin to classify mediator orientations, strategies and techniques: 'Understanding mediators' orientations, strategies and techniques: A grid for the perplexed' (1996) 1 *Harvard Negotiation Law Review* 7.

[4] Bartlet (n 2).

[5] Waters et al (n 3) s 2-033.

mediation 'seeks to maintain relationships and is future focused, looking to agreed outcomes'.[6] It is eminently suitable as a dispute resolution tool in employment disputes which are almost invariably dealing with personal, and sometimes ongoing, relationships.

Mediation is generally categorised into three main types: facilitative, evaluative and transformative. There are, however, other less common types, such as narrative mediation, problem-solving mediation, as well as hybrid forms. We shall focus on the main three, and also briefly touch on problem-solving mediation.

i. *Facilitative Mediation*

In facilitative (or shuttle) mediation, the mediator 'focuses on underlying interests and problem solving and allows parties maximum autonomy to determine creative outcomes'.[7] The mediator 'does not take a role in evaluating the respective claims of the parties'.[8] In purely facilitative mediation, mediators do not express their views on the dispute and do not challenge parties' existing perceptions of the merits of their position; the parties are thus not directly influenced by the mediator.[9] However, 'the mediator's role is not a passive one' – the mediator performs crucial functions that seek to guide the parties towards settlement.[10] For some mediators, facilitation is viewed as 'the "one true way" of mediation because mediation draws its legitimacy from its purported non-evaluative character'.[11]

In practical terms, facilitative mediation involves meetings facilitated by the mediator, some with both parties present and others held separately. In these sessions, the parties determine the content of the negotiation, while the mediator manages the overall process.

Facilitative mediation is used by Acas in the context of early conciliation:[12] '[o]riginally, this was an evaluative mediation scheme, but now, in common with the more widespread trend towards facilitative rather than evaluative

[6] G Morris, 'Mediation styles used in New Zealand Employment Disputes' (2015) 33 *Conflict Resolution Quarterly* 203, 208. See also S Blake, J Browne and S Sime, *A Practical Approach to Alternative Dispute Resolution* (Oxford University Press 2018) s 14.51.

[7] ibid.

[8] Bartlet (n 2) 5–8.

[9] Waters et al (n 3) s 2-034.

[10] According to Blake, Browne and Sime (n 6): 'The mediator will: ask questions that test the strength and weaknesses of each side's case; explore each party's situation and help them to identify what they really need or want to achieve from the dispute; encourage the parties to think about the likely outcome of litigation and the costs of obtaining that outcome; focus each party's attention on their underlying objectives and needs, rather than on a strict analysis and evaluation of the merits of their case; and help them to work out a creative solution that is in their best interests … The facilitative mediator will also help the parties to negotiate more effectively, formulate offers in a way that will be attractive to the other side, and give guidance about the timing and staging of offers and concessions' ss 14.52, 14.53.

[11] J Stempel and K Kovach, 'The Inevitability of the Eclectic: Liberating ADR from Ideology' (2000) 2) *Journal of Dispute Resolution* 247, 249 though he himself considers that mediation should be 'eclectic' in style.

[12] See section V.

mediation, the mediator will not make judgments or determine the outcome for the parties'.[13] However, many participants in our study said facilitative mediation was not suitable for employment disputes, calling for a much more 'hands-on' and proactive approach from the Acas conciliators – in particular one which involves some kind of evaluative element (see also section V.B).

ii. Evaluative Mediation

Evaluative mediation may be defined as a 'style of mediation in which the mediator takes the role in evaluating the respective claims of the parties'.[14] The focus is on rights and duties.[15] The mediator thus helps the parties assess what a court or tribunal might determine in relation to their claims. In some evaluative mediations, the mediator might even recommend to the parties a particular settlement arrangement. Blake et al say:

> The evaluative mediator will evaluate the dispute, exert more control over the process, challenge the parties to re-evaluate their assessment of the case, and give an opinion on the likely outcome. The evaluation will be carried out in a legalistic way, with emphasis on the legal and factual issues and an evaluation of the evidence in relation to the issues ... The evaluative mediator may also be asked to recommend a form of settlement, or a range of options for settlement.[16]

We would argue that evaluative mediation is a better 'fit' for employment disputes. Our empirical research suggests that because many claimants do not have access to high-quality legal advice, they may avoid early settlement because they are uncertain about whether a proposed settlement is fair. These findings point to the value of having some kind of authoritative and reliable assessment of their case at an early stage that could guide them as to the boundaries of a potential settlement and help them accept good offers.

iii. Transformative Mediation

Transformative mediation is a 'style of mediation which prioritises the relationship between the parties over the settlement of the dispute between them'.[17] It 'emphasizes mediation's capacity for fostering empowerment and recognition'.[18] The mediator 'focuses on empowerment and allowing parties to transform their

[13] In collective mediation, however, 'the Acas mediator may be more active in making non-binding recommendations for settlement of the dispute': Blake, Browne and Sime (n 6) s 18.72. See also: Waters et al (n 3) s 13-013.

[14] Bartlet (n 2) xv.

[15] Morris (n 6).

[16] Blake, Browne and Sime (n 6) ss 14.57, 14.59.

[17] Bartlet (n 2) xv.

[18] R Bush and J Folger, *The Promise of Mediation: The Transformative Approach to Conflict* (Jossey-Bass 2004) 12.

understanding of the conflict and their relationship'.[19] It seeks to harness the conflict resolution process to empower the parties and improve their relationship, leading to a 'more humanising, constructive, connecting, positive communication, despite the issues between the parties remaining unresolved'.[20] The focus in transformative mediation is 'to help the parties to improve their communication so that they can resolve their own dispute. The parties themselves will control the nature of the discussions, with the mediator primarily providing a reflective role'.[21] This approach may be of particular benefit in workplace disputes where there is a continuing employment relationship.

There is a parallel with 'therapeutic mediation' in family law where a family consultant or family therapist may also be brought into the mediation to support the parties to process the emotional aspects of the dispute. While there may be some employment disputes where a more therapeutic approach would be beneficial, this is unlikely to be appropriate for most workplace disputes.

iv. Problem-Solving Mediation

A fourth, less common, type of mediation is problem-solving mediation, namely, a 'style of mediation in which the mediator plays a proactive role in helping the parties shape a resolution to their dispute'.[22] The mediator asks the parties to 'explore the original cause of the dispute and discuss ideas for a solution. The dispute is seen as a problem to be solved by mutual agreement and creative thinking'.[23] The mediator can bring 'logic and clarity from an independent perspective and help as an agent of reality in checking the various actions that are necessary for the settlement to be fulfilled'. While the mediator may suggest possible solutions, this must be done 'with a light touch' so that 'both the definition of the problem and its solution are derived from the parties' preferences'.[24]

Problem-solving mediation is beneficial for the settlement of workplace conflicts. Mediators who participated in our empirical study confirmed this approach, noting that in the adversarial court or tribunal process the actual needs of the parties are 'masked' behind formal legal claims and rights, and so do not directly address the real issues that are at play. They therefore emphasised the need to explore with the parties their true problems and concerns (rather than the formal legal rights) and to work with the parties creatively to find a solution.

[19] Morris (n 6) 208.
[20] Bartlet (n 2) 6.
[21] Blake, Browne and Sime (n 6) s 14.65. See also L Bingham, C Hallberlin, D Walker and W Chung, 'Dispute System Design and Justice in Employment Dispute Resolution: Mediation at the Workplace' (2009) 14 *Harvard Negotiation Law Review* 1.
[22] Bartlet (n 2) xvi.
[23] ibid, 6.
[24] ibid.

C. Conciliation

In UK law there is a mandatory requirement for claimants to contact Acas for Early Conciliation prior to any litigation (and there are also further options for 'conciliation' after a claim has been presented).[25] Corby defines conciliation as 'a strategy whereby a third party assists the parties to the dispute to reach a settlement and, importantly, it is a voluntary process in that it can be declined by either party'.[26] Conciliation 'is virtually identical to mediation', and the terms 'conciliation' and 'mediation' can be used to describe the same process,[27] although there is some variation of understanding as to how it differs or indeed whether or not it is different. Some regard it as more proactive and evaluative than mediation, others take the opposite view and see it as informal and exploratory with no evaluation possible. There is no consistency of usage of the term'.[28]

When it comes to the UK's employment dispute resolution context, however, there is a practical differentiation between these terms, as they are referring to two different services offered by Acas:

> Acas conciliation is also a facilitative and non-evaluative mediation process. The only difference lies in the fact that Acas state on their website that conciliation is the term used if an employee is making a specific complaint against their employer and where there is a potential or actual claim to the Employment Tribunal rather than more general employment matters.[29]

In response to questions, Acas said that 'Conciliation is a facilitative process and conciliators provide parties with information to assist them in making informed decisions … For Acas to offer an evaluative service would breach our impartiality'.[30] There is also a difference in terms of the timing of when Acas 'conciliation' and Acas 'mediation' are used: Acas 'conciliation' describes the process offered by Acas to employees before they can make a claim to an employment tribunal (Early Conciliation), and Acas can continue to offer 'conciliation' to the parties after the claim has been made up until the date of the Employment Tribunal hearing (Post-Claim Conciliation). The term 'mediation', in contrast, is used by Acas to refer to the process it offers 'to resolve workplace disputes with the aim of restoring and maintaining the employment relationship between the parties'.[31] In terms of its timing, Acas mediation can occur

> at any stage in the conflict as long as any ongoing formal procedures are put in abeyance, or where mediation is a stage in the procedures themselves. It can be used before

[25] Or the LRA in Northern Ireland.

[26] S Corby, *Resolving employment rights disputes through mediation: the New Zealand experience*, Institute of Employment Rights (IER) Comparative Notes (1999) 2, 2–3.

[27] Blake, Browne and Sime (n 6) s 20.01.

[28] Waters et al (n 3) s 2-035.

[29] Blake, Browne and Sime (n 6) s 18.71.

[30] Response to questions from the authors.

[31] Blake, Browne and Sime (n 6) ss 20.06, 20.07, 20.10.

a formal grievance has been identified. It can be used after a formal dispute has been resolved to rebuild relationships.[32]

D. Arbitration

Arbitration may be defined as a 'process by which parties to a dispute contract to be bound by the decision of an arbitrator or arbitral board who will make a binding determination of the issue brought before them'.[33] Similar to litigation then, the dispute is settled by a neutral third-party who makes a binding enforceable decision. However, unlike in litigation, the parties have the freedom to choose their arbitrator, decide which legal rules or standards will govern the decision, and determine the procedures to be used.[34] Arbitration in the UK is regulated by the Arbitration Act 1996, as amended.

In the employment dispute resolution context, Acas can provide arbitration as an alternative to resolving disputes through employment tribunal proceedings. This option is available in relation to industrial disputes ('collective arbitration') and, under the Acas Arbitration Scheme, individual employment disputes concerning flexible working or unfair dismissal. By entering the Acas Arbitration Scheme, the parties contract out of the jurisdiction of the employment tribunals.[35]

E. Early Neutral Evaluation

Early neutral evaluation is a 'voluntary, without-prejudice process by which parties and their legal teams put their case to a neutral party to obtain an evaluation of what might happen if the case goes to trial'.[36] Early neutral evaluation is not binding, but is intended to help the parties in their decision-making. Early neutral evaluation may also help the parties narrow and define issues. By doing so, it may promote efforts to settle.[37] Judicial assessment is offered in most employment tribunals, as part of the litigation process, for longer cases (see chapter ten).

Our empirical analysis shows that there is a need to better manage parties' expectations, in relation to both likely remedies and their prospects of success, at an early stage. The study has also highlighted the need to limit the areas of disputes, which are currently much broader than merited. These issues could be addressed by better use of early neutral evaluation.

[32] Acas, 'Mediation: An Approach to Resolving Workplace Issues' (2013) 11: www.acas.org.uk/sites/default/files/2021-03/mediation-an-approach-to-resolving-workplace-issues.pdf.

[33] Bartlet (n 2) xv.

[34] Waters et al (n 3) s 2-020.

[35] ibid, s 13-014. See further: Acas, 'Arbitration': www.acas.org.uk/arbitration.

[36] Bartlet (n 2) xv.

[37] Waters et al (n 3) s 2-028.

Having addressed the key terminology in ADR, we turn to consider particular issues relating to the pre-litigation process, starting with grievances.

III. Internal Grievance Procedures

Although an employer or a worker is not required to go through any internal procedure as a condition of making or defending an employment tribunal (ET) claim, the failure to do so may have an impact on both the success of the claim and the level of compensation payable. If an employer fails to follow their internal disciplinary procedure, any subsequent dismissal is likely to be unfair. Moreover, if they unreasonably fail to follow the Acas Code of Practice on Disciplinary and Grievance Procedures then the ET can increase the employee's unfair dismissal compensation by up to 25 per cent.[38] Likewise, where a worker has unreasonably failed to follow an Acas Code of Practice, usually by failing to raise a grievance about the substance of their subsequent claim, then any compensation awarded if the claim succeeds may be reduced by up to 25 per cent.[39]

The requirement to go through a disciplinary/grievance procedure was introduced for the best of motives: to encourage early resolution of employment disputes. However, paradoxically it has had the opposite effect: it raises the stakes and encourages both sides to dig in. As a very large number of participants in our empirical study noted, raising a grievance is, or becomes, a highly formal process. This is because many employers, often led by geographically remote HR employees, adopt a risk-averse approach, sticking rigidly to the Acas procedure which prevents real engagement with the underlying problems and issues.[40] Mr Justice Underhill, as he then was, has expressed similar concerns about 'a blind faith in the process'[41] and that 'formalism and [a] process-driven approach' may have 'got in the way of a more humane and straightforward resolution' of issues.[42] Saundry et al observe this too. They note that because, in many workplaces, there has been a decline in union membership, more emphasis has been placed on the confidence and competence of managers whose general preference for pragmatic conflict resolution has in turn been replaced by a close adherence to process and

[38] Trade Union and Labour Relations (Consolidation) Act 1992, s 207A(2) (TULRCA 1992). In Northern Ireland, they may be subject to an uplift of up to 50% where there is an unreasonable failure to comply with the Code of Practice on Disciplinary and Grievance Procedures published by the Labour Relations Agency: Article 90AA Industrial Relations (Northern Ireland) Order 1992 (NI 5).

[39] s 207A(3) TULRCA 1992.

[40] Focus Groups: 11 November 2024, 14 November 2024, 19 November 2024 (12pm), 20 November 2024 (12pm), 25 November 2024, 29 November 2024, 5 December 2024, 10 December 2014 (1.30pm), 12 December 2024, 13 December 2024; Interview: 29 April 2025.

[41] *Mental Health Care (UK) Ltd v Biluan* (UKEAT/0248/12/SM) [36].

[42] *Royal Bank of Scotland v Morris* (UKEAT/0436/10/MAA) [35].

procedure. These managers may have become more isolated as HR functions have become less localised and more 'strategic'.[43]

The *Keep Britain Working Report* identified one of 'three persistent problems' in dealing with employees who are unwell: 'a culture of fear, that is felt by employees and, differently, by employers, especially line managers. This creates distance between people and discourages safe and early disclosure, constructive conversations and support just when they are needed most'.[44] Employers reported to them that they 'fear … doing the wrong thing and that raising health issues or disabilities might cause offence, trigger grievances, or escalate into a tribunal'[45] which 'often leads to distance, adversarial processes, and reliance on tribunals – outcomes that rarely benefit either side'.[46] They say:

> Over time, workplaces have become increasingly procedural and risk-averse. Too often, employees are treated as risks rather than as people to invest in. We need to rebalance this by reducing perceived risks, fostering constructive dialogue, and taking a person-centred approach that considers what is right for both the individual, and the employer, in their specific circumstances.[47]

Focus group participants also said that the grievance process entrenches both sides in their position and inherently focuses on the problems rather on possible solutions. This was described by one focus group participant as a 'sort of battle' which, once launched, is 'quite difficult to climb down from'.[48] By the time a worker raises a grievance, participants considered that the issues had already intensified towards something that is contentious and focuses by its nature on 'everything that's gone wrong'.[49] The process is geared towards allegations against the other side. Liddle describes 'traditional grievance, discipline and performance management procedures' as 'broken, corrosive, retributive, adversarial, damaging and harmful … these processes offer a mirage of justice and an illusion of fairness. They act as the incubators for the toxic work cultures and the broken workplace relationships which, ironically, they are designed to resolve'.[50] We think that many of our participants would agree.

[43] R Saundry et al, 'Reframing resolution' Acas Discussion Paper 2014. See also: R Saundry and G Dix, 'Conflict resolution in the UK' in W Roche, P Teague and A Colvin (eds), *The Oxford Handbook of Conflict Management in Organisations* (Oxford University Press 2014). Similarly, Kirk describes the professionalisation of HR managers and the juridification of labour law and raises concerns about the mobilisation of law by HR professionals to suit certain ends, underpinned by a business-capitalist ideology: E Kirk, 'Law and legalities at work: HR practitioners as quasi-legal professionals' (2021) 50 *Industrial Law Journal* 583.

[44] *Keep Britain Working: Final Report* (2025) 4: www.gov.uk/government/publications/keep-britain-working-review-final-report/keep-britain-working-final-report.

[45] ibid, 17.

[46] ibid, 40.

[47] ibid, 22.

[48] Focus Group, 19 November 2024.

[49] Focus Group, 13 December 2024.

[50] D Liddle, *Managing Conflict: A Practical Guide to Resolution in the Workplace* (Kogan Page 2023) 1.

Moreover, because a grievance often serves as the first step in the process of bringing a tribunal claim and the complaint and response must be in writing, participants said that employers invariably respond defensively because it is not in their interests to admit anything that might be used against them in subsequent litigation.[51] Therefore, as one participant said, often the employer is not genuinely investigating the grievance with an open mind but is following the process merely to provide 'cover' to achieve a predetermined outcome.[52] Trade unions, by contrast, recognised the value of bringing a grievance not least because it enabled them to represent their members and gain access to information that the employer might hold on the individual.[53]

Our focus group participants said that the adversarial nature of the process meant that grievances were rarely successful in resolving issues and that they often shut off other routes to an early resolution of the issues. Many participants said that because of the contentious nature of the grievance procedure, employees who raise grievances are overwhelmingly likely to lose their jobs.[54]

Moreover, participants reported that the emotional and health costs for employees engaged in a grievance procedure were very high.[55] The work conducted by Welsh Health, which we address in chapter five, goes further. They suggest that the costs are felt by all the participants in a formal process on both 'sides' of the complaint, as well as by HR advisers and the organisation as a whole.[56]

A recurring theme within our focus groups was on the desirability of resolving employment disputes at the earliest stage before they escalated into what is essentially an adversarial process.[57] Specifically, they argued for the need to change workplace culture so that employees feel more comfortable sharing their concerns and seeking to address them as soon as an issue arises and before it escalates. They also identified a need for HR and line managers to be better trained to deal with problems informally and creatively, rather than feeling constrained automatically to pursue formal processes. Participants considered that HR professionals should be more willing to consider the full range of ways to address problems, while line managers should be empowered to be more engaged and to have difficult conversations with employees to address ongoing issues and to build trust. This would be especially beneficial, it was emphasised, since problems would be addressed at the

[51] Focus Groups: 11 November 2024, 14 November 2024, 19 November 2024 (12pm), 19 November 2024 (3pm), 25 November 2024, 29 November 2024, 12 December 2024, 13 December 2024.

[52] Focus Group, 11 November 2024.

[53] Meeting with trade unions, 17 December 2025.

[54] Focus Groups: 11 November 2024, 14 November 2024, 19 November 2024 (12pm), 19 November 2024 (3pm), 20 November 2024 (12pm), 25 November 2024, 5 December 2024, 10 December 2024 (1.30pm), 12 December 2024, 13 December 2024.

[55] Focus Groups: 11 November 2024, 19 November 2024 (12pm), 29 November 2024, 12 December 2024, 13 December 2024. Interview, 22 November 2024.

[56] Interview, 29 April 2025.

[57] Focus Groups: 11 November 2024, 19 November 2024 (12pm), 19 November 2024 (3pm), 20 November 2024 (3pm), 25 November 2024, 5 December 2024, 12 December 2024, 13 December 2024. Interview, 22 November 2024.

lowest level within the workplace, rather than it escalating away from the people involved in the issue.[58]

There is strong academic support for this view. Saundry et al argue that more integrated approaches that locate conflict management as central to HR strategy are needed, using by way of example, 'integrated conflict management systems' in the US, which is a systematic approach to preventing, managing and resolving conflict within the organisation.[59] Lucy and Broughton note the need to avoid escalation by reinforcing procedural and interaction justice within organisations and the significant role that line managers play in this regard.[60]

Employee voice more generally has been identified as key to avoiding disputes escalating.[61] Charlwood and Pollert found that among their sample of low-paid, non-unionised workers, those who could meet regularly with management about workplace issues were less likely to experience a problem that they considered to be a rights infringement, and they were more likely to seek, and succeed in obtaining, an informal resolution to any problems.[62]

So what can be done? Participants in our focus groups highlighted the need to have an early and speedy mechanism to address disputes before matters escalate or 'drag on and just … poison the relationships'.[63] Such a mechanism, it was noted, should be based on constructive dialogue that facilitates a solution-based approach. Participants considered that parties should be guided towards focusing on the future rather than on the past and to focus on seeking a resolution rather than on allegations of past mistreatment. Participants noted that this would require claimant representatives to take a different approach: instead of conveying workplace issues as legal arguments, which are framed as blaming the other side, they needed to assist employees in thinking about what they want to achieve and exploring different ways of getting there.[64] We therefore propose some practical steps. The grievance procedure could be replaced by a 'statement of concern'. Given the lack of trust in HR, larger firms could be required to have an ombuds who might be an employee of the company but with a specific remit of independence or may be external to the company. They could also facilitate workplace mediation.

[58] Focus Groups: 11 November 2024, 19 November 2024 (12pm), 19 November 2024 (3pm), 20 November 2024 (3pm), 25 November 2024, 5 December 2024, 12 December 2024, 13 December 2024. Interview, 22 November 2024.

[59] P Latreille and R Saundry, 'Toward a System of Conflict Management? Cultural Change and Resistance in a Healthcare Organization' in D Lipsky, A Avgar and J Lamare (eds), *Managing and Resolving Workplace Conflict* (Emerald Publishing, 2016).

[60] D Lucy and A Broughton, *Understanding the Behaviour and Decision Making of Employees in Conflicts and Disputes at Work* (2011) BIS Employment Relations Research Series No 119. See also A Bogg and T Novitz (eds), *Voices at Work* (Oxford University Press 2014).

[61] Focus Group, 19 November 2024 (3pm).

[62] A Charlwood and A Pollert, 'Informal employment dispute resolution among low wage, non-union workers: Does managerially initiated workplace voice enhance equity and efficiency?' (2012) 52 *British Journal of Industrial Relations* 359.

[63] Focus Group, 13 November 2024.

[64] Focus Group, 13 December 2024.

IV. Workplace Mediation

Many of our focus group participants felt that there should be much greater use of workplace mediation. They noted that mediation could be a highly effective alternative to the grievance procedure, particularly where it was solutions-focused. Participants suggested that workplace mediation should be promoted more, with better education for workers and employers about the benefits of internal mediation both to solve workplace problems and to avoid future litigation.[65] One focus group participant told us,

> if employers were told the success rate of workplace mediation in terms of avoiding a claim and avoiding the cost of the grievance, the investigation … and it's going to take months, I mean honestly. Whatever it costs … [it is a] drop in the ocean compared to all of that cost.[66]

For workers, it was noted that they should be made more aware of the risks and costs of litigation, as compared with mediation. Some suggested that mediation should be a compulsory step before litigation; others suggested that there should be an informal pathway beginning with mediation before moving on to a grievance procedure.[67]

However, participants were also realistic about the existence of barriers to achieving early resolution of problems in the workplace. Many participants said that employers are generally reluctant to engage properly in early mediation in the absence of a credible or reliable threat to pursue litigation, instead waiting to see how the issue unfolds. Moreover, without having any formal document setting out what the complaint actually is, it is hard for employers to assess the potential merits of it.[68] Employers that do agree to settle at this early stage, it was noted, generally agree to do so because the settlement undervalues the claim.[69] Consequently, from the worker's perspective, they may pursue a formal grievance in order to signal to the employer the seriousness of the issue and that they are in fact willing to submit a claim.[70]

Participants also observed that employers, especially small businesses, may not take early resolution seriously because they lack awareness of the risks and costs involved in litigation. It was suggested that access to some legal advice at an early stage for these less well-informed employers would be likely to promote early

[65] Focus Groups: 11 November 2024, 12 November 2024, 13 November 2024, 19 November 2024 (12pm), 19 November 2024 (3pm), 20 November 2024 (12pm), 25 November 2024, 5 December 2024, 12 December 2024, 13 December 2024. Interview, 22 November 2024.

[66] Focus Group, 11 November 2024.

[67] Focus Groups: 11 November 2024, 12 November 2024, 13 November 2024, 19 November 2024 (12pm), 20 November 2024 (3pm), 5 December 2024, 10 December 2024 (9.30am), 10 December 2024 (1.30pm), 12 December 2024, 13 December 2024.

[68] Focus Groups: 11 November 2024, 20 November 2024 (12pm), 25 November 2024, 5 December 2024, 10 December 2024 (9.30am), 10 December 2024 (1.30pm).

[69] Focus Group, 19 November 2024 (3pm).

[70] Focus Groups: 11 November 2024, 19 November 2024 (12pm), 5 December 2024.

resolution success rates.[71] We suggest that this may be a role for the Employment Resolution Service which we propose to be set up under the auspices of the Fair Work Agency (see further chapter thirteen).

Another barrier to the early resolution of disputes is that an employer's insurance cover – in respect of compensation awards and legal costs – may apply only once a claim is submitted to the tribunal,[72] or at least after completion of Acas Early Conciliation.[73] In the public sector, the need for Treasury approval for a settlement was also said to be a very significant barrier to early resolution: approval could not be obtained in a timely fashion, or at all despite advice that cases should be resolved.[74] Consequently, many participants considered that there were practical reasons to commence litigation, or to take steps credibly to threaten litigation, in order to then achieve resolution.

On the other hand, some participants considered that it was better to avoid threats to litigate and legalistic language to enable settlement. If lawyers were involved, they should remain behind the scenes and focus on guiding workers through the process to enable the parties to be open to exploring productive solutions and ultimately maintaining the working relationship.[75]

A number of participants noted that workers may also be the source of difficulties in mediation, particularly where they lack trust in the process: it was observed that workplace mediation may be seen as a process favouring the employer, who retains all the power, particularly where they have paid for the mediator – perhaps because the employee is unable or unwilling to contribute to those costs. While an employer funded ombuds may not alleviate these concerns, the independence traditionally associated with an ombuds may help to build trust.

Furthermore, unrepresented employees find it difficult to assess whether they should agree to any proposed resolution.[76] This difficulty was also identified by participants who were mediators: they said that they were often asked by unrepresented employees whether they should accept an offer or not but, due to the neutrality of the mediator, were unable to advise them.[77] Unrealistic expectations of workers were another factor noted by participants, in terms of what

[71] Focus Group, 14 November 2024.

[72] Focus Group, 20 November 2024 (12pm).

[73] Focus Group, 14 November 2024.

[74] Focus Group, 20 November 2024 (12pm). In an interview with an Acas staff member (interview 16 April 2024) we were told that there was a noticeable difference in resolution rates where the employer was the civil service. They told us that the figures for resolving a standard track case (that is, an ordinary unfair dismissal claim requiring 1–2 days of hearing time) via EC was 33% for all cases, but just 13% for civil service cases and in the open track (more complex claims of discrimination and whistleblowing), it was 28% of cases but just 15% of civil service cases. This may relate to the requirement to obtain Treasury approval for settlements.

[75] Focus Group, 13 December 2024.

[76] Focus Groups: 11 November 2024, 19 November 2024 (1pm), 5 December 2024, 13 December 2024.

[77] Focus Group, 13 December 2024.

they can achieve both in mediation and from litigation. Participants repeatedly emphasised the need for early input to help employees see what the issues are, and to manage their expectations as to both the likely remedies they would obtain in litigation and the costs, time, stress and effort involved. Participants considered that managing expectations at an early stage would contribute significantly to the earlier resolution of disputes, as would giving employees access to meaningful legal advice at an early stage. Participants noted that workers are often emotionally highly engaged with the issues and do not know what they want to achieve. Without external guidance and support, this becomes a barrier to resolution.[78] Managing expectations may be a role for the Employment Resolution Service.

The issues identified in our empirical study are mirrored in the literature. For example, Bennett assessed mediation networks operating in the small and medium-sized enterprise sector. Respondents in that study identified several key drivers for introducing mediation into the organisation.[79] They were usually concerned with reducing the costs of disputes, both in terms of time and emotional distress, repairing damaged relations and ensuring that matters were not unnecessarily formalised. The main strength of mediation was identified to be facilitating questioning and discussion to change perceptions of participants. Latreille has identified similar reasons for introducing workplace mediation, focusing on cost, crisis, culture and competition. His study noted that most problems brought to mediation involve relationship problems and breakdown, stemming from absences, differences in working style and poor communication.[80] He identified the principles for success for mediation as being the voluntary and confidential nature of the mediation.

Specialist HR managers have been identified as a beneficial factor in the use of ADR: Hann, Nash and Henry identified a positive correlation between the presence of specialist HR managers in an organisation and the use of ADR by Welsh employers.[81] Moreover, their study indicates that the presence of HR managers does not prevent the use of external forms of ADR.[82] The presence of recognised trade unions in the workplace likewise increases the prevalence of ADR.[83] Unionised organisations tend to offer a greater range of access points for conflict resolution and are more ready to use early stage collaborative approaches to dispute resolution, such as mediation and the early use of Acas.[84]

[78] Focus Groups: 14 November 2024, 20 November 2024 (12pm); Interview, 22 November 2024.

[79] A Bennett, 'The role of mediation: A critical analysis of the changing nature of dispute resolution in the workplace' (2012) 41 *Industrial Law Journal* 479.

[80] P Latreille, 'Mediation: A thematic review of the Acas / CIPD Evidence' (2011) Acas Research Paper.

[81] D Hann, D Nash and E Henry, 'Workplace conflict resolution in Wales: The unexpected prevalence of alternative dispute resolution' (2019) 40 *Economic and Industrial Democracy* 776, 786–87.

[82] ibid, 797.

[83] ibid, 786–87.

[84] ibid, 797.

V. Acas Early Conciliation

A. Introduction

In 2014, compulsory early conciliation (EC) was introduced for the majority of employment claims requiring a claimant to notify Acas before the ET will accept their claim.[85] The notification may be via an online form, by letter or by phone.[86] The parties can choose whether to engage with the Acas free early conciliation service through which Acas will seek to promote a settlement between them for up to six weeks (temporarily extended to twelve weeks in November 2025).[87] This period cannot be extended, although Acas may still seek to resolve the dispute once the claim has been issued.[88] At the end of the six/twelve weeks, Acas will provide the claimant with an EC certificate, the unique number of which must be entered on the ET1 form bringing a claim before the ET. A certificate may be issued before the end of the six weeks if Acas cannot contact a prospective claimant or respondent, a party is unwilling to engage with, or withdraws from, conciliation, or the conciliator considers that there is no reasonable prospect of settlement of the dispute or part of it.[89]

The time limits for making an ET claim are effectively put 'on hold' during EC. Once the claimant notifies Acas, the running of the time limit is suspended. The running of the time limit then resumes on the day on which the claimant is deemed to receive their certificate.[90] However, if the time limit was going to expire in the period between (i) notification of Acas and (ii) one month after deemed receipt of the certificate, the claimant is given one month after receipt of the certificate to make their claim.[91]

In a handful of cases, the claimant is not required to notify Acas before making a claim but may still choose to request EC.[92] These include situations where the employer has chosen to notify Acas, in certain applications for interim relief in unfair dismissal cases, and when another person has complied with the requirement for EC in relation to the same dispute and the claimant wishes to institute proceedings on the same claim form as that other person.[93]

In Northern Ireland, the claimant is generally required to go through EC with the Labour Relations Agency (LRA). The claimant can notify the LRA by completing an

[85] Employment Tribunals Act, s18A(1) (ETA 1996).

[86] Employment Tribunals (Early Conciliation: Exemptions and Rules of Procedure) Regulations 2014/254, sch 1, rr 2(1)(a), 2(1)(b) and 3(1).

[87] Sch 1, r 6(1) (as amended).

[88] After the claimant has started an ET claim, an Acas conciliator must still attempt to promote a settlement where either (a) both parties have requested Acas conciliation, or (b) the conciliator considers that they have a reasonable prospect of successfully negotiating a settlement: ETA 1996, s 18C(1).

[89] Sch 1, rr 5(3), 7(1) and 7(2).

[90] Employment Rights Act 1996, s 207B(2), (3) (ERA 1996).

[91] ibid, s 207B(4).

[92] s 18B(2) ETA 1996.

[93] Early Conciliation Regulations 2014, reg 3(1).

online form or by phone.[94] If both parties agree to try EC then an LRA Conciliation Officer will attempt to settle the dispute for a period of one month.[95] This period can be extended by up to 14 days but an extension can be granted only once.[96] If the parties are unwilling to attempt EC, or EC is unsuccessful, the LRA will issue an EC certificate.[97] Time limits are put on hold during EC.[98] In addition, the LRA offers a free mediation service[99] and a free arbitration scheme[100] which are available upon request but they are not mandatory requirements.

B. Empirical Study Results

Participants in our focus groups overwhelmingly said that the EC process needs to be reformed. Many participants said that in practice it was just 'a tick box exercise',[101] and that employers were reluctant to take discussions through Acas seriously.[102] They observed that even at this point in the dispute, employers were still waiting to see whether employees were serious about pursuing them in litigation. Accordingly, participants emphasised that for this procedure to work, the parties had to become more committed to it.[103] One participant suggested that 'if we can upscale Acas' early conciliation, this might assist in resolving disputes out of court'.[104] Suggestions included a procedure that could become a more substantive mediation if required or could put employers under more pressure to engage meaningfully, for example by requiring them to attend in-person negotiations. Several participants suggested that employers should be under an obligation to make a concrete offer – ranging from a symbolic one-pound offer to there being a minimum threshold requiring an employer to make a substantive offer – while others were concerned that this would detract from the voluntary nature of EC.[105]

[94] Industrial Tribunals and Fair Employment Tribunal (Early Conciliation: Exemptions and Rules of Procedure) Regulations (Northern Ireland) 2020, SR 2020/2, sch 1, rr 1–2.

[95] ibid, sch 1, r 6(1).

[96] ibid, sch 1, r 6(2), (3).

[97] ibid, sch 1, r 7.

[98] See the Industrial Tribunals (1996 Order) (Application of Conciliation Provisions) Order (Northern Ireland) 2020, SR 2020/4.

[99] Labour Relations Agency, 'Mediation' (28 January 2020): www.lra.org.uk/resolving-problems/escalating-unresolved-issues/mediation.

[100] The LRA also offers a free arbitration scheme. Labour Relations Agency, 'Arbitration services' (28 January 2020): www.lra.org.uk/resolving-problems/escalating-unresolved-issues/arbitration-services.

[101] Focus Groups: 12 November 2024, 19 November 2024, 20 November 2024, 10 December 2024. The EAT held that a failure to undertake EC does not remove the employment tribunal's jurisdiction to hear the claim: *Abel Estate Agent Ltd and others v Reynolds* [2025] EAT 6.

[102] The concerns raised about Acas were mirrored with regard to the LRA.

[103] Focus Groups: 11 November 2024, 14 November 2024, 20 November 2024 (12pm), 29 November 2024.

[104] Focus Group, 11 November 2024.

[105] Focus Groups: 12 November 2024, 14 November 2024, 19 November 2024, 20 November 2024 (12pm).

Perhaps the most common concern with EC was that it was ineffective and served as a 'rubber stamp'[106] for claimants to go through before bringing their claims to the ET. Acas conciliators were often described as operating simply as a 'letter box' and that 'they just pass the message back and forth. So it all comes down to how well you can articulate it in the e-mail you pass to them'.[107] Some participants said that because the parties are not talking directly to each other, there was a missed opportunity to have a more constructive conversation.[108] Participants also said that the 'letter-box' process meant that it was only useful in disputes where the focus was on agreeing a sum of money, rather than a more nuanced settlement.[109] While participants considered that holding conversations with a neutral party could be beneficial in providing a different perspective, that would require much greater engagement by parties and the conciliator.[110]

Participants also noted that Acas conciliation is 'hit and miss … largely dependent on the conciliator that you get'.[111] Participants said that 'old fashioned'[112] conciliators, compared to the more recently appointed Acas conciliators, tended to be more proactive (which was helpful to the parties), and were perceived to be more knowledgeable and authoritative. As one focus group participant put it 'when you do get a good one and they really get it, they're worth their weight in gold'.[113] A key issue, noted by most participants, was that many conciliators lack the experience 'to be able to get stuck in and try and help the parties to an early resolution'.[114] While it was acknowledged that Acas conciliators must maintain their impartiality and cannot provide legal advice, participants said they could be more helpful in providing guidance in simple language.[115] One focus group participant considered that the LRA in Northern Ireland would refrain from giving advice but would very effectively give the parties information on parts of their claim that they 'might struggle' with, which they thought was much more helpful than the approach of Acas.[116] Another research participant, who had previously worked as an Acas conciliator, and would fall into the category of an 'old fashioned' conciliator, said that when engaging in conciliation they had tried to 'sow the seeds of doubt' with parties whose claims were unlikely to succeed and in that way, encourage the parties to resolve matters.[117]

[106] Focus Groups: 12 November 2024, 25 November 2024, 12 December 2024. If the claimant does not want to go through EC they are simply issued with the number necessary for the ET1.
[107] Focus Group, 11 November 2024.
[108] Focus Group, 12 December 2024.
[109] Focus Groups: 19 November 2024 (12pm), 5 December 2024.
[110] Focus Groups: 11 November 2024, 12 November 2024, 20 November 2024 (12pm), 29 November 2024, 10 December 2024 (1.30pm), 12 December 2024.
[111] Focus Group, 20 November 2024.
[112] Focus Group, 11 November 2024.
[113] Focus Group, 11 November 2024.
[114] Focus Group, 11 November 2024.
[115] Focus Groups: 12 November 2024, 13 November 2024, 19 November 2024 (12pm), 25 November 2024, 10 December 2024 (9.30am).
[116] Focus Group, 25 November 2024.
[117] Focus Group, 13 November 2024.

Alongside these issues, the lack of representation and legal advice for claimants was identified as a significant problem within the EC process. It was noted that where the Acas conciliator engaged with a claimant's arguments, sometimes in multiple conversations, this could give them a false impression that those arguments would succeed in court. This would, in turn, influence their decision not to agree to any resolution.[118] Participants also said that claimants felt unable to accept an offer simply because they were unable to assess the value of their claim and whether the offer was a good one or not.[119] Participants noted that unrepresented claimants often sought basic advice from Acas conciliators which they were unable to provide, which was a further barrier to resolution.[120]

A more technical issue raised by participants concerned the form that claimants are asked to complete which allows them to write only a limited amount in each box. There is no specific space to set out what resolution a claimant is seeking. An early understanding of the resolution that is sought is particularly important when that resolution is not simply monetary. This limitation, it was noted, prevents the parties from sufficiently explaining to the conciliator what the case is really about and what they are expecting to get from it.[121] Consequently, several participants considered that EC would be more productive if it took place after the claim form had been submitted to the ET because the parties would have the benefit of seeing the claim and better understanding the issues.[122]

Participants also identified problems in relation to how long it takes for a conciliator to contact parties. When we undertook the focus groups, participants said that in practice it typically takes around two weeks before a conciliator is allocated to a case, further reducing the time for EC.[123] One survey participant noted that in their experience 'by the time the conciliator contacts you, 4 weeks have already gone and you don't have much time to conciliate before litigation proceeds'. However, that timescale has been lengthening considerably. Yet, the data published by Acas presents a much shorter timeline. In 2022/23, Acas reported that they were 'able to get 70% of our cases to a conciliator within 1 day of notification compared to an average of around 5 days previously'.[124] However, in October 2024, an Acas manager informed the Scottish ET Users Group that in October 2023, there had been approximately 1,000 cases waiting to be allocated to a conciliator with a maximum waiting time of one week and that by October 2024, this had grown to 3,000 cases waiting to be allocated to a conciliator with a maximum waiting time of three weeks.[125] Acas told us that they 'do not collect data on

[118] Focus Group, 12 November 2024.

[119] Focus Groups: 14 November 2024, 19 November 2024 (12pm), 29 November 2024, 5 December 2024.

[120] Focus Groups: 13 November 2024, 10 December 2024 (9.30am).

[121] Focus Group, 20 November 2024 (12pm).

[122] Focus Group, 20 November 2024 (12pm).

[123] Focus Groups: 12 November 2024, 14 November 2024, 10 December 2024 (1.30pm).

[124] Acas, Annual Report and Accounts 2022–23 (Crown Copyright 2023) 16.

[125] See: www.judiciary.uk/wp-content/uploads/2024/11/Employment-Tribunals-Scotland-National-User-Group-minutes-October-2024.pdf.

the duration of time taken for the conciliator to first contact the claimant' after allocation. In November 2025, the time for EC was extended to 12 weeks. It is understood that this was to address the backlog of cases and delays for a conciliator to contact the parties.

The concerns raised by the participants in our survey accord with two independent studies, commissioned by Acas. First, a study examining EC in the context of disability discrimination claims found that

> [w]hile there were examples of conciliators taking a proactive approach to resolving the case, some participants felt that the conciliation service had not supported them to come to an earlier resolution. This was because they felt communication had been too slow; the conciliation process did not help parties understand each other's positions; or the service did not offer enough signposting or advice (for example, on what constitutes disability discrimination, the nature of reasonable adjustments, and to aid assessment of the strength of a claim).

In this study, both claimants and employers said conciliation needed to be more than just 'relaying messages' and that they wanted 'more of a mediation-type service'.[126]

The second study found that '[c]laimants valued the specialist advice conciliators offered around employment law because it helped them to understand the strength of their case' but, while acknowledging the need for conciliators to remain neutral,[127] 'claimants wanted conciliators to give more of an indication about the likely success of the case, and the elements needed to make the case legally viable'.[128] Participants appear to want EC to encompass a greater 'substantive role',[129] that is, 'dealing directly with the facts and details of a case; getting parties to explore issues in a critical fashion, consider the strengths and weaknesses of the claim, and looking realistically at what may be the most acceptable outcome',[130] while acknowledging that '[d]rawing a boundary between an information providing, and an advisory, role presents a constant challenge for conciliators'.[131]

Our research, together with these studies, contrast with the high levels of satisfaction reported by Acas itself. For example, in its 2015–16 Annual Report, the results of a survey were reported as finding

[126] National Centre for Social Research, 'Characteristics and Drivers of Disability Discrimination Employment Tribunal Claims' (12 September 2024): www.acas.org.uk/research-and-commentary/characteristics-and-drivers-of-disability-discrimination-employment-tribunal-claims/report.

[127] Acas, 'Early Conciliation: How the Process Works': www.acas.org.uk/early-conciliation/how-early-conciliation-works.

[128] N Rahim, H Piggott, M Davies, E Cooper and F Day, 'Acas Early Conciliation Decision-Making: Exploring the Behaviours of Claimants who neither Settle nor Proceed to an Employment Tribunal' (Acas 2017) 43.

[129] As compared with their 'reflexive role' which is concerned with building the trust of the parties and their 'informative role' which is concerned in clarifying and informing issues for the parties: G Dix, *Operating with Style: The Work of the Acas Conciliator in Individual Employment Rights Cases*: webarchive.nationalarchives.gov.uk/ukgwa/20210104113727mp_/;archive.acas.org.uk/media/336/Operating-with-Style/pdf/Operating_with_Style-accessible-version-Jan-2012.pdf, 3.

[130] ibid, 11.

[131] ibid, 10, 21 and 23–24.

> that almost 75% of employees were satisfied with Acas' conciliation after they made a tribunal claim, while more than 85% of employers said the same. Even higher levels said they would use Acas' conciliation again if in a similar situation. And more than 60% of employees and more than 45% of employers who went to tribunal said EC had helped them feel prepared for the tribunal process.[132]

In a 2019 survey, Acas reported that 82 per cent of claimant participants and 80 per cent of respondent participants were satisfied with the service provided by Acas in relation to EC and 79 per cent of claimant participants and 81 per cent of respondent participants were satisfied with post-ET1 conciliation.[133] However the survey also accords with the findings in our research including that 'conciliators were most highly rated for their explanation of the conciliation process and joint-lowest for helping participants to understand the strengths and weaknesses of the potential claim and outlining employment law as it applied to their problem'. This latter issue was identified by Acas as something that 'could be an area for improvement among conciliators moving forward'.

In terms of the conciliators' personal attributes, they were rated by users 'least well for helping participants decide whether to settle their case without undue influence'.[134] As to post-ET1 conciliation, Acas conciliators were similarly rated lowest by users for 'helping you understand the strengths and weaknesses of this potential claim'.[135] Perhaps to address this, Acas underwent a restructure sometime between 2020 and 2022 and the roles of collective conciliator and senior adviser were separated out to help to differentiate between staff undertaking a problem-solving role compared with an advisory, training role.[136]

Other challenges identified by participants in our research are also discussed by Acas in a number of their annual reports[137] which set out various steps it has taken to improve its conciliation services: improving their guidance and digital content so that parties can consider 'whether a notification is the right thing for them at the time';[138] changing the online form so that Acas conciliators know more about the dispute at an earlier stage[139] enabling the 'gathering [of] relevant

[132] Acas, Annual Report and Accounts 2015–16 (Crown Copyright 2016) 16.

[133] K Pedley, M Clemence, R Writer-Davies and D Spielman, 'Evaluation of Acas Individual Conciliation 2019: Evaluations of Early Conciliation and Conciliation in Employment Tribunal Applications' (September 2020): www.acas.org.uk/sites/default/files/inline-files/IC-evaluation-2019-Final-accessible.pdf, 63 and 102.

[134] ibid, 12–13 and 49–50.

[135] ibid, 16 and 99.

[136] D Hann, P Latreille, D Nash and R Saundry, 'Custodians of contemporary pluralism? Acas' evolving role in addressing conflict during a time of economic and regulatory flux' [2023] *Industrial Relations* 1, 15 and 17.

[137] Acas, Annual Report and Accounts 2015–16 (Crown Copyright 2016); Acas, Annual Report and Accounts 2016–17 (Crown Copyright 2017); Acas, Annual Report and Accounts 2017–18 (Crown Copyright 2018); Acas, Annual Report and Accounts 2018–19 (Crown Copyright 2019); Acas, Annual Report and Accounts 2019–20 (Crown Copyright 2020); Acas, Annual Report and Accounts 2020–21 (Crown Copyright 2021); Acas, Annual Report and Accounts 2021–22 (Crown Copyright 2022); Acas, Annual Report and Accounts 2022–23 (Crown Copyright 2023); Acas, Annual Report and Accounts 2023–24 (Crown Copyright 2024).

[138] Acas, Annual Report and Accounts 2023–24 (Crown Copyright 2024) 16 and 30.

[139] ibid.

information quickly';[140] and automating the distribution of cases to its conciliators 'speeding up the start of the conciliation'.[141] Acas also notes that they have invested in staff learning and development.[142]

C. Statistics

The Acas Annual Reports set out the success rates for EC, indicating a successful process. However, those statistics are optimistic and appear to suggest a greater success rate than can necessarily be accorded just to the work of Acas.

Table 4.1 Summary of Acas Key Performance Indicators, 2015–25[143]

Year	Early Conciliation Notifications	Early Conciliation notifications which result in a conciliated settlement	Early Conciliation notifications which result in a conciliated settlement or other positive income	Approximately how many retain?	ET1s received for conciliation	ET1 cases resulted in a conciliated settlement	ET1 cases 'positively resolved' following Acas conciliation	Resolution of collectivedisputes
2024–25	124,546	11%	38%	77,218	43,189	49.8%	79%	93%
2023–24	104,884	13%	39%	63,980	33,501	49.8%	78%	94%
2022–23	105,754	13%	37%	66,626	32,058	49.5%	77%	91%
2021–22	90,811	13%	36%	58,120	31,198	53%	77%	94%
2020–21	114,533	13%	31%	79,028	35,274	58%	79%	92%
2019–20	138,837	16%	26%	102,740	40,978	59%	80%	95%
2018–19	132,711	20%	32%	90,244	36,531	55%	74%	88%
2017–18	109,364	22%	34%	72,181	26,012	58%	n/a	92%
2016–17	92,251	24%	38%	57,196	18,647	55%	n/a	92%
2015–16	92,172	22%	38%	57,147	20,074	53%	n/a	88%

[140] Acas, Annual Report and Accounts 2022–23 (Crown Copyright 2023) 16.

[141] Acas, Annual Report and Accounts 2023–24 (Crown Copyright 2024) 30. In our interview with staff at Acas, we were told that there was a considerable delay in new ET digital infrastructure which meant that it could not connect with Acas such that Acas received ET1s as a pdf and they had to be manually typed into the Acas system. Resolution of this problem resulted in swifter allocation of conciliators.

[142] Acas, Annual Report and Accounts 2023–24 (Crown Copyright 2024) 31.

[143] This data was collated from Acas Annual Reports. Figures in column five were calculated by the authors.

The percentage of EC notifications resulting in a conciliated settlement, that is, via a COT3, have ranged from 11 per cent to 24 per cent but was just 13 per cent in 2023 and 11 per cent in 2024 (column 3 of Table 4.1). Despite this the 2024–25 Annual Report says '9 out of 10 potential claims notified to Acas were resolved without requiring a hearing in the employment tribunal. This is a strong outcome that has been achieved in the face of rising and more complex demand'.[144] This was clarified as arising because it looks 'at the full journey from Early Conciliation notification to hearing outcome at the end of the Tribunal process' and because Acas is involved throughout, all outcomes that do not involve judicial adjudication are included in the 90 per cent figure.

Once a claim is submitted to the tribunal then the settlement rates – by a COT3 – sit between 50 per cent and 59 per cent (column 7 of Table 4.1).[145] Nevertheless, the recent annual report refers to 72 per cent as 'the proportion of disputes we resolve at an early stage'.[146] However, this includes all cases that are settled or withdrawn.[147] To reach the 79 per cent figure that is used showing the '% of employment tribunal cases which are positively resolved following Acas conciliation' for the 'out-turn' on the Key Performance Indicators[148] it seems that the figure must include cases that were struck out by the tribunal. However, it is somewhat unclear exactly how this figure is reached. Nevertheless, when the measure used is of cases being 'resolved' then the percentages are impressive but the role of Acas within that is unclear: the statistics in Table 4.1 make the point.

Nevertheless, it is notable that a much higher percentage of conciliated settlements were achieved after a claim had been submitted than before. We were told in an interview that a small team of experienced conciliators were now dedicated to the post-ET1 settlement work to try to improve the success rates further which may explain some of the statistics.[149] In addition, this may support the view of the participants in our study that parties are more open to settlement once litigation is looming and there is greater clarity about the nature of the claims.

Moreover, the potential contribution of Acas in resolving disputes must be acknowledged. It is most apparent in the number of cases that are not resolved pre-litigation but do not proceed to a tribunal submission. The data shows that in the last three years, around half the disputes that are not resolved are also not submitted as a claim.[150] It may be that Acas' role as an information provider has had some influence on claimants' decision-making in these cases. In their 2019 study, Acas reported that 44 per cent of claimants who participated in EC and

[144] Acas, Annual Report and Accounts 2024–25 (Crown Copyright 2025) 16.

[145] This reflects a change in the key performance indicators used by Acas: Acas, Annual Report and Accounts 2018–19 (Crown Copyright 2019) 29; Acas, Annual Report and Accounts 2022–23 (Crown Copyright 2023) 19.

[146] ibid, 17.

[147] ibid, 50.

[148] ibid, 15.

[149] Interview, 30 April 2024.

[150] See: Table 4.1 above, by comparing the figures under 'Approximately how many remain' to the figures under 'ET1s received for conciliation'.

either reached a COT3 or private settlement or otherwise did not go on to submit a tribunal claim said that 'Acas was a factor' in this decision.[151] In 2019, the figure was 61 per cent of claimants who had submitted a claim but did not go on to a full hearing.[152]

Consequently, according to the 2024/25 Annual Report, out of 'approx 117,000 cases led by claimant' and eligible for early conciliation, only 'around 39,000' were submitted as a claim and '10,000 require judicial time such as progressing to a full hearing, there being a default judgment or a strikeout'.[153]

The LRA in Northern Ireland also produces statistics in relation to its Early Conciliation Service. It reported a settlement rate of 26 per cent of EC notifications and 34 per cent of 'all case types (including tribunal cases)' in 2024/25,[154] up from 25 per cent and 28 per cent respectively in 2023/24.[155]

VI. Other Pre-Action Issues

A. Time Limits

For most claims in the ET, the time limit for making the claim is three months from the act giving rise to the dispute.[156] For example, in a claim for unauthorised deductions from wages, time starts to run from the date of payment of the wages from which the deduction was made.[157] In a claim concerning the right to daily rest under the Working Time Regulations 1998, time starts to run from the date when the right to daily rest should have been permitted.[158] In most unfair dismissal claims, time starts to run from the effective date of termination.[159] Time limits are not put on hold while a claimant goes through an internal disciplinary or grievance procedure with the respondent, but they are put on hold while the parties go through EC.

In certain circumstances, time may be extended by the ET. The usual test is (1) whether it was 'not reasonably practicable' for the claimant to present a claim before the end of three months, and (2) the claimant actually presented the claim within such further period as the ET considers reasonable.[160] For

[151] Pedley et al (n 133) 75.
[152] ibid, 112.
[153] Acas, Annual Report and Accounts 2024–25 (Crown Copyright 2025) 32.
[154] See: www.lra.org.uk/sites/default/files/2025-08/Annual%20Report%20and%20Accounts%202024-2025%20-%20FINAL.pdf.
[155] See: www.lra.org.uk/sites/default/files/2024-07/Annual%20Report%20and%20Accounts%20for%202023-24%20-%20published%20version.pdf.
[156] These are significantly shorter than claims in the civil courts which are generally six years, with personal injury claims generally having to be brought within 3 years.
[157] s 23(2) ERA 1996.
[158] Working Time Regulations 1998, reg 30(2).
[159] s 111(2) ERA 1996.
[160] See, eg, s 111(2)(b) ERA 1996.

discrimination claims, the test is more generous: the ET can extend time for such other period as it thinks 'just and equitable'.[161] A 'just and equitable' test also applies to claims for statutory redundancy payments.[162] Although going through an internal disciplinary or grievance procedure does not 'stop the clock' on the time limits, the fact that a delay in applying to the employment tribunal was caused by the claimant's reasonable attempts to pursue an internal appeal with their employer may be a relevant factor for the ET to decide whether to extend time.[163]

Participants in our study identified time limits as a significant barrier to early resolution. They said that it is time-intensive properly to investigate matters through a grievance process which means that workers often do not view this as capable of addressing their concerns in time. If they wait for the grievance process to be completed, their time for submitting a claim is reduced and this restricts their ability to try to resolve matters before bringing a claim. Some participants said that an employer may be tempted to drag out the process to reduce an employee's time to submit a claim and that some employers tactically make the grievance decision just a few days before limitation expires, or just after it expires, so that employees are left with no time to consider their position. One participant described this as a 'fantastic tactic to time out a claimant'.[164]

Participants overwhelmingly considered that the limitation period of three months – at the time of our study – was too short. Since the early stages of workplace disputes were perceived to be a valuable window of opportunity to resolve matters before they escalate, participants considered that this window should be extended to give the parties the time they realistically need to resolve matters informally. We were told that the short time limit pushes workers into submitting a claim to protect their position which escalates disputes. If the parties had more time, it was argued, then more disputes could be resolved by allowing the parties to continue their conversations seeking to address them informally and avoiding them intensifying in the litigation process.[165] It was also said that the short limitation period meant that claim forms were often rushed, resulting in less focused, poorly drafted documents. It was felt that with a longer limitation period, claims would become clearer and more focused.[166]

Accordingly, many participants suggested extending the current limitation periods, especially for more complex issues. However, there was no consensus as to what the limitation period should be. It was broadly considered that the

[161] Equality Act 2010, s.123(1)(b) (EqA 2010).
[162] s 164(2)(c) ERA 1996.
[163] *Marks & Spencer plc v Williams-Ryan* [2005] EWCA Civ 470.
[164] Focus Group, 11 November 2024.
[165] Focus Groups: 11 November 2024, 12 November 2024, 14 November 2024, 19 November 2024 (12pm), 19 November 2024 (3pm), 20 November 2024 (3pm), 10 December 2024 (9.30am).
[166] Focus Group, 12 November 2024.

six-month time limit in the Employment Rights Act 2025 was about right,[167] but a number of participants considered that other time periods would be better, including suggestions of up to 12 months.[168] However, while most were keen on longer limitation periods, there were some participants who were concerned that any extension of the time limits would mean that the whole process would be even more delayed, with hearings taking place even longer after events with justice being further delayed, in an already very long tribunal process.[169]

In addition, most participants considered that the six-week 'pause' in limitation for EC was insufficient: they said that there is a need to 'give Acas more time to actually deal with these cases'.[170] This is especially so given the time that participants reported that it takes for a conciliator to contact the parties. Some of our participants argued that even having the full six weeks is insufficient because the conciliation process entails 'a psychological process' 'which takes time'.[171] Consequently, several participants advocated a longer period for EC.[172]

B. Acas Arbitration Scheme

Since 2001 Acas has operated an arbitration scheme for unfair dismissal claims. It was intended to be faster, cheaper, private and more informal than the tribunal.[173] However, the uptake of the service has been very limited[174] and there have been a number of criticisms of it, including its limited scope requiring a claim to be solely concerned with unfair dismissal, the voluntary nature of it, and the requirement for parties to agree through a COT3 to use the scheme. Moreover, the scheme offers more limited remedies compared with a tribunal hearing, a less robust decision-making process and limited grounds for challenging an arbitrator's award.[175] Some commentators have raised concerns about whether it meets the

[167] To be inserted as s 27BH Employment Rights Act 1996. See also the DBT Impact Assessment which notes that a longer limitation period will give employees more time to properly build their case and raise the required funds, thus potentially improving the strength of the claims submitted and the quality of the pleadings, and promoting conciliation: Department for Business and Trade, *Final Stage Impact Assessment: Employment Tribunals – Time Limits* (4 March 2025).

[168] Survey participants; Focus Groups: 19 November 2024 (12pm), 10 December 2024 (1.30pm).

[169] Focus Groups: 19 November 2024 (12pm), 10 December 2024 (1.30pm).

[170] Focus Group, 10 December 2024.

[171] Focus Group, 10 December 2024.

[172] Focus Groups: 14 November 2024, 10 December 2024 (1.30pm).

[173] J Earnshaw and S Hardy, 'Assessing an Arbitral Route for Unfair Dismissal' (2001) 30 *Industrial Law Journal* 289, 294.

[174] P Dupont, E Kirk, M McDermont and B Anderson, *Promoting Access to Injustice? Alternative Dispute Resolution and Employment Relations in the UK* (October 2018) 18: bpb-eu-w2.wpmucdn.com/blogs.bristol.ac.uk/dist/e/505/files/2019/01/Promoting-access-to-injustice-2dm3koi.pdf. See also: S Corby, *Arbitration in collective disputes: A useful tool in the toolbox* (Acas 2015).

[175] See: www.elaweb.org.uk/sites/default/files/docs/Working%20Paper%20No%205%20-%20The%20Acas%20Arbitration%20Scheme.pdf.

obligations of a fair trial under Article 6 of the European Convention on Human Rights and whether arbitrators have an obligation to abide by the substantive law on unfair dismissal.[176]

C. Pre-Action Disclosure

In contrast to many other civil cases, which we discuss in chapter five, there is no pre-action protocol for ET cases. While a claimant could write to their employer asking them to retain documents or make a subject access request under section 45 Data Protection Act 2018, there is no specific process under the employment tribunal rules. Concerns were expressed about data access requests because they were seen as being used tactically and imposing significant costs, especially in the public sector.

At one time there was a statutory procedure for asking questions of an employer by way of a questionnaire in relation to a discrimination claim,[177] but this has now been repealed and replaced with Acas guidance.[178] In contrast to Great Britain, the statutory procedure for discrimination questionnaires is still applicable in Northern Ireland.[179] The Equality and Human Rights Commission has suggested that the questionnaire process should be re-established.[180]

Participants in our focus groups were generally positive about discrimination questionnaires because they considered that the additional information provided meant that the litigation was more efficient because they allowed claimants to understand the position early on, shedding light, on '[w]hat was in the mind of the employer when decisions are being made at quite an early stage'.[181] The increased uncertainty arising from the removal of these questionnaires meant that claimants tended to be over-inclusive in their claims.

VII. Conclusions

There is near unanimity that grievance procedures do not work. They entrench disputes and make matters adversarial rather than resolving problems. HR professionals were thought to be (rightly) concerned with compliance with the law – and particularly perceived that they had to follow every detail of the Acas guidance in relation to grievances and disciplinary matters – but this prevented more creative

[176] Earnshaw and Hardy (n 173).
[177] s 138 EqA 2010.
[178] Acas, 'Questions about discrimination at work': www.acas.org.uk/asking-and-answering-questions-about-discrimination.
[179] See, eg, the Disability Discrimination (Questions and Replies) Order (Northern Ireland) 2007/470.
[180] See: www.equalityhumanrights.com/equality-law-call-evidence-our-response.
[181] Focus Group, 10 December 2024.

and informal means of addressing issues. Workplace mediation is seen as a possible solution, but too few employers pursue it. EC is hit and miss. The statistics tell a story of considerable success by Acas in resolving disputes before litigation, but the reality may be more complex. Often the success of EC depends on whether the conciliator is prepared to be more than a post box and that is becoming less frequent. Often, there is too little time to make progress in negotiations before a claim has to be issued: the three-month time limit is too short. Fundamentally, the current system is not working. It incentivises adversarial processes and procedure-driven decision-making, rather than supporting individuals to focus on resolving disputes at the earliest possible opportunity. We turn to consider other parts of the UK landscape and what we might learn from their approach to pre-litigation resolution.

5

Looking Across the UK Landscape for Methods which Might Encourage Early Settlement

I. Introduction

Employment tribunals were always intended to be a forum of last resort – at least in less complex claims – and that required early resolution of disputes. This is not happening. Our empirical work and the public statistics tell us that what is needed to prevent disputes entering litigation is flexible, informal resolution in the workplace. Where that is unsuccessful then there needs to be some form of independent support for dispute resolution such as a mediator. Once independent support is provided, the mode of dispute resolution has to include some element of evaluation and advice in relation to the merits of the claims involved. 'Reality testing' – of the likelihood of success of a claim and the amount of any compensation – becomes an important element that is needed to achieve resolution.

The question is therefore what this would look like in practice and how it might work. To address this, we explore research from the NHS Aneurin Bevan University Health Board that evaluates the impact of changing HR practice so that disciplinary investigations happen only as a matter of 'last resort'. The results are impressive, with a significant reduction in formal processes and substantial cost savings. Another study, in a different Trust in England, estimated a saving of £270,000 in one year for legal and associated costs by moving from a blame culture to a restorative justice model where, again, formal processes were pursued as a last resort. We consider what this would mean for the current emphasis on pursuing a grievance process and the procedural fairness requirement in unfair dismissal claims (section II).

From there, we cast the net a little wider. We consider the role of ombuds, with a highly successful record of mediation (albeit in the small number of cases where it is used) and effective use of investigatory powers (section III). We also consider more technical solutions. Employment disputes are harmful: to the workers, the managers dealing with issues, and the organisation as a whole. In discrimination law, the impact of discrimination is expressly recognised in injury to feelings awards and sometimes in separate awards for psychiatric injury. Given the human impact of litigation, we look to the personal injury and clinical negligence fields to consider how disputes are resolved before litigation using Pre-Action Protocols (PAPs). While we conclude that PAPs are less appropriate for employment disputes in the tribunal, they may still offer some ideas as to how to limit employment disputes proceeding to litigation (section IV).

So we turn to another jurisdiction which we think has the most to teach us: family law. Many employment disputes are highly emotional, with behaviour driven by deeply unconscious factors which may hinder resolution. There are clear parallels between the breakdown of an employment relationship and the complexities of a couple divorcing. Family law practitioners are well used to mediating disputes but since 2024 there has been a renewed focus on non-court dispute resolution with changes to the procedural rules to support and encourage early resolution (section V). Practitioners indicate that the family law, mediation-focused approach has proved not only highly successful in resolving disputes without going to court but also in providing innovative solutions to domestic issues which might not be in the judicial domain, such as creative solutions to childcare arrangements.

Thus, we consider the elements of the procedural requirements of PAPs in personal injury law and the emphasis in family law on early mediation to explore what might be used in an employment dispute model. The key appears to be informality and flexibility; informality in the process to enable participants properly to engage with each other without being tied up in procedural knots, and flexibility as to the method through which resolution is sought so that it fits well with the particular issues and participants involved in the dispute, alongside a 'legal backbone' which enables the court to reject procedural challenges in favour of substantive engagement (section VI).

We begin by considering the experiments conducted by parts of the NHS in trying to avoid cases going to employment tribunals.

II. The Health Service Experience

A. Work by the Aneurin Bevan University Health Board

With the original focus on the employment tribunal being a forum of last resort, and the concerns of the participants in our study about grievance processes pushing both sides into adversarial and entrenched positions, we explored cases where employers had experimented with different approaches. We were particularly impressed by the work done by the Aneurin Bevan University Health Board, Wales. They had identified that significant harm was being done not only to people who were taken through a disciplinary process but also to those running the process and the organisation more broadly.[1] They studied the outcomes of employee

[1] A Cooper, D Behrens, S Jones, A Neal, A Jones and W Hyll, 'Understanding the Impact of Employee Investigations on Those Who Lead Them: A Case Study from NHS Wales' (2025) 15(6) *Administrative Sciences* 2. See also A Neal et al, 'The impact of poorly applied human resources policies on individuals and organisations' [2023] *British Journal of Healthcare Management* 112.

relations investigations over a period of 15 months and established that over 50 per cent of them led to no sanctions being applied. At the same time there had been an increase in the number of staff accessing the employee well-being service because they were undergoing an investigation process. Consequently, the organisation made a commitment to make employee (disciplinary) investigations the 'last resort' for a period of 13 months (June 2022 to June 2023).[2] The 'last resort' is described as an approach

> which seeks to challenge and change the decision-making and behaviour of those responsible for commissioning, leading and supporting investigations by (i) helping them recognise the potential harm inflicted on various stakeholders during an investigation; (ii) reducing the overuse of the employee investigation process by exploring alternative options; and (iii) improving the investigation process itself.[3]

In practical terms, this meant work with senior leadership, HR and well-being teams to introduce the new approach via training events, coaching and communication.

The results of the pilot were extremely positive:

> [A] statistically significant reduction … in the mean number of [disciplinary] cases per month from 4.19 cases during the baseline period (January 2018 to February 2020) to an average of 1.23 cases during the intervention period (June 2022 to June 2023) – a reduction of 70.6% per annum, representing a reduction in the related avoidable employee harm ($U = 38$, $p < 0.001$).[4]

The team estimated that 3,307.5 sickness days had been avoided as a result, with organisational savings of £738,133. These savings arose primarily from direct savings in relation to backfilling posts and the cost of medical treatment for employees but also £151,200 related to internal administration.[5] These savings did not include any legal or court-related costs, which the Trust found difficult to identify as directly connected to this initiative because they had had relatively few cases that had gone all the way to employment tribunals in the past.

That there would be a cost saving seems self-evident. Indeed, other research in 2021 estimated that the costs involved in formal processes across the UK would amount to at least £2 billion. Saundry and Urwin do the calculations as follows:

> We estimate that there are an average of 374,760 formal grievances each year. The average cost in management time of a formal grievance is estimated at £951, giving a total cost across the economy of £356 million. In addition, there are an estimated 1.7 million

[2] A Cooper, K Teoh, R Madine, A Neal, A Jones, A Hussain and D Behrens, 'The last resort: reducing avoidable employee harm by improving the application of the disciplinary policy and process' (2024) 15 *Frontiers in Psychology* 1.

[3] ibid, 4.

[4] ibid, 7.

[5] ibid, 8.

> formal disciplinary cases in UK organisations each year. The estimated average cost of each disciplinary case is approximately £1,141 – resulting in an economy-wide total cost of £2 billion.[6]

There would also be savings in avoiding the Acas early conciliation procedure and employment tribunal litigation.[7] The impact on staff morale and productivity was significant[8] but difficult to quantify.

B. Other NHS Trust Studies

Two other studies have found a significant reduction in the volume of grievance and disciplinary proceedings by changing the approach to dealing with internal conflict. In the East Lancashire Hospitals NHS Trust, the culture in the organisation had been problematic, with widespread conflict. A new approach was taken in 2019 with investment in workplace mediation and the introduction of an Early Resolution Policy. This Policy replaced existing grievance and bullying and harassment policies and, while not preventing an employee from making a formal complaint, ensured that other forms of resolution were considered. Moreover, it 'does not replace disciplinary policy and procedure or those related to managing performance or attendance. However, in respect of these issues the Trust makes it clear that there should be a "greater focus" on informal remedy'.[9] There was also a 'cultural shift away from allocating blame towards a focus on outcomes and resolution'.[10]

Between January 2019 and July 2022, 223 cases were referred to informal resolution. By the time of the analysis, 188 had been concluded with just 22 per cent of cases progressing to a formal procedure.[11] It was found that the shift away from formal procedures resulted in a reduction in formal HR casework with issues being resolved earlier and HR and trade unions working together more effectively to try to resolve issues.[12]

In Mersey Care a 'restorative justice' model was introduced, moving from 'investigations of supposed offenders to restorative conversations between all stakeholders in the incident', and focusing on forward-looking accountability,

[6] R Saundry and P Urwin, 'Estimating the costs of workplace conflict': www.acas.org.uk/research-and-commentary/estimating-the-costs-of-workplace-conflict, 2 and 13.

[7] Saundry and Urwin estimated that an average of 428,000 employees are dismissed each year, costing organisations an estimated £13.1 billion and 136,249 early conciliation notices costing an estimated £282 million each year in management time and a further £264 million on legal fees: ibid, 13.

[8] Interview, 29 April 2025.

[9] R Saundry, G Wibberley, A Wright and A Hollinrake, 'Mediation and early resolution in East Lancashire Hospitals NHS Trust': www.acas.org.uk/research-and-commentary/early-resolution-in-east-lancashire-hospitals-NHS-trust, 2.

[10] ibid.

[11] ibid, 21.

[12] ibid, 22.

rather than punitive backward-looking questions.[13] It was also found that there was not only a significant reduction in formal proceedings but also considerable cost savings, including savings relating to fewer suspensions and lower sickness absence. They also estimated that there was

> a reduction in legal costs by £270,000 from 2016/17 to 2017/18, where previously legal costs were actually increasing. These included all expenditure on solicitors' fees across the organisation and corporate negligence costs. Similarly, termination costs were significantly reduced (by about £700,000), exclusive of Mutually Agreed Resignation Schemes costs.[14]

C. The Implications for the Reform of Employment Dispute Resolution

The team at the Aneurin Bevan University Health Board had identified that the organisation's policies and the need to adhere to the Acas Code of Practice on Disciplinary and Grievance Procedures was a significant driver for the formalisation of conflict: 'For many organizations, the potential threat of an employment tribunal has become a key driver of strict procedural compliance. However, this legal focus can overshadow the well-being and needs of the employee'.[15] This is often exacerbated by a skills deficit for managers who do not know how best to resolve issues which, according to Saundry and Cooper, 'creates a dynamic whereby many managers will seek to avoid conflict altogether'. However, they note that 'problems are then allowed to escalate, at which point many managers seek the cover of rigid procedural adherence'. They also note that there is a tendency to stress the potential for costly litigation if managers fail to stick to procedure. They also find evidence that managers worry about the threat of employment tribunal action when deciding how to handle disciplinary issues: 'This can be exacerbated by HR advice and training, which often focusses on risk management rather than resolution'.[16]

This description of a 'rush to process' reflects research in 2016 noting that

> a lack of faith in the ability of operational managers led HR practitioners to formalise 'informal' aspects of policy and procedure. Union respondents argued that managers had less discretion to deal with difficult issues and that HR involvement was more, rather than less, evident than it had been in the past. Managers in SMEs were generally

[13] M Kaur, R de Boer, A Oates, J Rafferty and S Dekker, 'Restorative Just Culture: A Study of the Practical and Economic Effects of Implementing Restorative Justice in an NHS Trust' (2019) 273(3) *Matec Web of Conferences* 01007, 1–2.

[14] ibid, 8.

[15] Cooper et al, 'Understanding the Impact of Employee Investigations' (n 1) 3.

[16] R Saundry and A Cooper, 'The impact on investigators: the harm that can be caused to line managers and others involved in disciplinary investigations' in A Cooper and A Neal (eds), *Under Investigation: Transforming Disciplinary Practice in the Workplace* (BUP 2025) 27.

> dependent on advice from employment lawyers or external HR consultants once conflict had escalated beyond a certain point. Overall, responses to conflict were still dominated by procedural and legal compliance.[17]

The Welsh experience does not mean that disciplinary investigations and hearings are avoided altogether. Rather, the emphasis is on a 'compassionate culture'. They say that '[i]t does not imply overlooking inappropriate behaviour or mistakes. It means responding to them in a way that acknowledges the complexity of each situation and finds resolutions that benefit both individual and organization'.[18] Fundamentally, it requires 'investigators … to think and operate beyond a rigid and literal interpretation of the disciplinary policy itself', taking into account factors that the policy and the Acas Code are unlikely to cover but 'understanding and using the[se factors] to inform and support practice could make all the difference to the outcome of an investigation – for both employees and employer'.[19]

The emphasis on an internal process that sees formal procedures as a last resort clearly yields significant benefits organisationally and appears to reduce the number of matters that progress beyond the workplace. This is not just something that works in the public sector. Liddle has identified similar success in emphasising early resolution rather than a process different approach[20] and an Employment Lawyers Association report notes similar success in many organisations.[21]

The difficulty, at present, is that an employee must pursue a formal grievance before starting a claim or risk a reduction in their damages if they subsequently win their claim before the tribunal. This is a legacy of the requirements of the Employment Act 2002 and the Employment Act 2002 (Dispute Resolution) Regulations 2004, repealed in 2009, which made it mandatory to bring a grievance before, for example, a claim for constructive unfair dismissal could be brought. If, however, the purpose is to encourage internal resolution of disputes, we would suggest that a more logical requirement would be that a person has sought to resolve their dispute internally and informally rather than prescribing that a grievance process is needed which puts the parties on an adversarial footing at an early stage.

Likewise, while it is right and proper that procedures should be followed before a person is dismissed, the rigid adherence to a formal process – necessitated by the requirement of procedural fairness – may be counterproductive. Greater education as to the benefits of prior, informal resolution is clearly required and the successful implementation of a focus on formal process being the last resort may

[17] R Saundry, D Adam, I Ashman, C Forde, G Wibberley and S Wright, 'Managing Individual conflict in the contemporary British workplace': www.acas.org.uk/research-and-commentary/managing-individual-conflict) 3.

[18] M West and R Windsor, 'Creating compassionate cultures: how a compassionate culture leads to the reduction and better management of employee investigations' in A Cooper and A Neal (eds), *Under Investigation: Transforming Disciplinary Practice in the Workplace* (BUP 2025) 72–73.

[19] A Cooper et al, 'The disciplinary policy and beyond: steps to improve the management of employee investigations' in A Cooper and A Neal (eds), *Under Investigation: Transforming Disciplinary Practice in the Workplace* (BUP 2025) 146.

[20] D Liddle, *Managing Conflict: A Practical Guide to Resolution in the Workplace* (Kogan Page 2023).

[21] See: www.elaweb.org.uk/content/ela-report-adr-and-employment-disputes, November 2017.

act as a useful model. Moreover, the Acas Code needs to be much clearer that the disciplinary process is one of last resort and that employers should take informal steps to resolve a dispute before engaging in any formal process. A change in the Acas Code would also allow tribunals to emphasise this when considering procedural fairness in claims of unfair dismissal.

Internal resolution will not, however, successfully resolve all issues and it is necessary to consider other approaches to dealing with disputes that cannot be resolved within the organisation. We begin by looking at the ombuds schemes as a method of involving a skilled external body.

III. Ombuds Schemes

A. The Types of Ombuds Schemes

At the heart of all ombuds schemes is dispute resolution. In the UK there are currently 21 official ombuds schemes which meet the formal ombuds criteria: independence of the Ombud from those whom the Ombud has the power to investigate; effectiveness; fairness; openness and transparency and public accountability. They also have to publish their service standards and report against them.[22] Some of the ombuds schemes were created by Parliament via legislation, giving them compulsory jurisdiction over a certain sector; some schemes are not statutory but are underpinned by legislation, in the sense that legislation required a certain sector to be covered by an ombud, but without creating the ombud scheme itself; and some are voluntary ombud schemes set up in a specific sector.[23]

All ombuds schemes have the power to investigate and make decisions on complaints (such as recommendations to apologise, to change processes or procedures, or to pay compensation for distress and inconvenience). In addition to providing redress for individuals, ombuds can also identify any systemic issues and provide feedback to help improve services and complaint handling (see further chapter twelve). There are different ombud schemes covering different sectors in the UK, and different ombud schemes have different powers.[24]

[22] The Ombudsman Association currently includes 55 organisations in its membership: the 21 official ombud schemes, but also additional complaint-handling schemes and organisations ('other complaint handling bodies') and associate members (who are interested in and support the objects of the Association and have significant relevant expertise): Ombudsman Association, 'Join the Ombudsman Association': www.ombudsmanassociation.org/about-us/join-ombudsman-association.

[23] Ombudsman Association, 'What is an Ombudsman': www.ombudsmanassociation.org/what-ombudsman.

[24] Ombudsman Association, 'A Guide to Ombudsman Offices in the UK': www.ombudsmanassociation.org/sites/default/files/2024-10/A%20Guide%20to%20Ombudsman%20Offices%20in%20UK%20%28Oct24%29.pdf.

B. Ombuds and Dispute Resolution

i. Overview

Ombuds schemes offer some positive potential as a mechanism for early-stage, informal and perhaps 'hands-on' dispute resolution, and so it is worth considering whether there are features or processes that might assist in the employment dispute resolution context. As explained by the Ombudsman Association – the membership body for ombud schemes and other complaint handling bodies – '[o]mbudsman schemes are a form of "inquisitorial adjudication" and there are significant benefits of an ombudsman over other "simple" forms of adjudication or mediation. Ombudsman schemes … take an inquisitorial approach when investigating, seeking further information and evidence when necessary'.[25] In that sense, the way these schemes handle dispute resolution procedures might be a valuable arrangement to learn from for the employment context. Indeed, our empirical study suggests that there might be advantages to increasing the inquisitorial function of employment judges, especially for unrepresented claimants.

Take the case of the Parliamentary and Health Service Ombudsman (PHSO), set up by Parliament to provide an independent complaints handling service for complaints that have not been resolved by the UK government departments and agencies, other public organisations, and the NHS in England. The service is free and open to everyone. The PHSO performs two statutory roles: of the Parliamentary Commissioner for Administration (the Parliamentary Ombudsman),[26] and of the Health Service Commissioner for England (Health Service Ombudsman).[27]

Before contacting the PHSO, the complainant must first complain to the organisation directly and go through its internal complaints process. If dissatisfied with the response, the complainant can then escalate the matter by submitting a complaint to the PHSO (for NHS complaints, people can contact the PHSO directly, while for government departments and other public service complaints, there is usually a need to ask their MP to bring their complaint to the PHSO). The PHSO reviews whether the complaint is eligible, whether an investigation is

[25] Ombudsman Association, 'What is an Ombudsman' (n 23).

[26] Parliamentary Commissioner Act 1967. Under s (1), the Commissioner is empowered to investigate 'any action taken by or on behalf of a government department or other authority to which this Act applies, being action taken in the exercise of administrative functions of that department or authority'.

[27] Health Service Commissioners Act 1993. Under s 3(1), the Commissioner is empowered to investigate a complaint made 'by or on behalf of a person that he has sustained injustice or hardship in consequence of – (a) a failure in a service provided by a health service body, (b) a failure of such a body to provide a service which it was a function of the body to provide, or (c) maladministration connected with any other action taken by or on behalf of such a body'.

warranted, and whether mediation might be the right option for the complaint. The PHSO has a team that facilitates mediation, which can take place instead of or before any investigation.[28]

ii. Mediation

As noted above, the PHSO has a mediation service for suitable complaints. The PHSO's dispute resolution team acts as an independent facilitator, helping complainants and organisations hold meetings to reach a mutually agreed resolution to a complaint. Their approach to dispute resolution includes several features that are especially pertinent to our current study and the broader employment context. First, it is informal, efficient and quick: 'we do not need files, documentation and evidence from the parties to move forward. This means less administrative work for both parties compared to our usual process'.[29] Second, it emphasises maintaining ongoing relationships between the parties: it goes 'beyond bringing closure to complaints. It can help repair damaged relationships and allow the parties involved to work well together again. This is particularly important when parties need to continue to communicate, for example in a doctor/patient relationship'.[30]

The mediation service employs standard mediation techniques. In their facilitated meetings, they start by listening to both parties individually, to understand their perspectives and find out what they would like to achieve from the process (these sessions usually take up to an hour). Then they hold a joint meeting (which typically lasts between 1.5 and 3.5 hours) where the caseworker helps both parties talk to each other constructively about the complaint and look at options for resolution. In this meeting, they encourage both parties to consider the complaint from a different perspective; they help the parties involved explore how they can support and assist one another in resolving the complaint; and finally, they help each party think about creative and constructive solutions. If the parties agree on a resolution then the case is closed, and if they cannot agree the PHSO will make their own decision about whether to conduct a detailed investigation instead.[31] We note that the approach taken in these mediation meetings aligns with the feedback we received from focus group participants, who emphasised the need for a more constructive and creative approach to problem-solving, resorting to more confrontational methods

[28] For a detailed overview of the PHSO complaint procedure, see: PHSO, 'How We Deal with Complaints': www.ombudsman.org.uk/making-complaint/how-we-deal-complaints. The adjudicative role of Ombuds is discussed in ch 12.

[29] PHSO, 'Dispute Resolution at PHSO': www.ombudsman.org.uk/sites/default/files/Early_Dispute_Resolution_Process_Leaflet_2.pdf, 1–2.

[30] ibid.

[31] ibid, 2, 4.

only when such efforts fail. We suggest that there are lessons here for the mediation function we propose for the Employment Resolution Service (chapter thirteen).

However, the PHSO caseworker, when facilitating dispute resolution, does not offer an opinion on the issues raised in the complaint or make any judgements about either party. This approach differs from their standard investigation process, where they assess the complaint and form a view based on the evidence available.[32] In our study, much of the input we have received suggests that, in the employment dispute resolution context, having a more evaluative type of mediation would be highly valuable, especially where either of the parties are unrepresented and where there is a greater power imbalance.

C. Evaluation

i. Success Rate

To what extent are the PHSO's dispute resolution services effective in resolving complaints? Looking at the data in the annual reports and accounts on the performance of the PHSO in relation to complaints they have received in the past five years,[33] we see that its mediation services resolved only a few dozen complaints out of thousands in each of these years.[34] On the other hand, out of the cases where mediation did take place, the success rate was actually high. From 2024 to 2025, for example, they facilitated only 59 mediations (while the number of new complaints received that year was 38,045), but out of these 59 sessions, they managed to reach a resolution in 58 cases.[35] Similarly, from 2023 to 2024, the PHSO facilitated 75 joint mediation meetings, and 72 of those cases were fully resolved.[36]

[32] ibid, 1, 4.

[33] PHSO, *The Ombudsman's Annual report and accounts 2024 to 2025* (PHSO 2025): www.ombudsman.org.uk/sites/default/files/2025-07/the_ombudsman_s_annual_report_and_accounts_2024_to_2025.pdf, 34–35.

[34] The Public Administration and Constitutional Affairs Committee, appointed by the House of Commons to examine the PHSO reports, found that one of the reasons for this lack of usage of mediation services is a 'cultural barrier to mediation'. In their report where they scrutinise the PHSO's report from 2022 to 2023, they noted: 'The PHSO stressed that the cultural attitudes of stakeholders, notably in the NHS, were a barrier to increasing the number of cases resolved through mediation. The PHSO should outline how it is working with stakeholders to place a stronger emphasis on mediation in the Complaint Standards for the NHS and for Government': House of Commons Public Administration and Constitutional Affairs Committee, 'Parliamentary and Health Service Ombudsman Scrutiny 2022–23: Third Report of Session 2023–24' (February 2024): committees.parliament.uk/publications/43595/documents/216592/default/, 12.

[35] PHSO, *The Ombudsman's Annual report and accounts 2024 to 2025* (n 33) 40.

[36] PHSO, *The Ombudsman's Annual Report and Accounts 2023 to 2024* (PHSO 2024): www.ombudsman.org.uk/sites/default/files/Ombudsmans_Annual_Report_2023_2024.pdf, 43.

Table 5.1 Statistics relating to PHSO complaints[37]

Year	2020–21	2021–22	2022–23	2023–24	2024–25
New complaints accepted	24,842	36,248	35,103	36,886	38,045
Complaints carried forward to next year	5,251	4,885	4,303	4,257	4,854
Decided following initial checks	8,689	29,213	27,492	28,075	28,311
Resolved by mediation	14	29	74	72	58
Decided following primary investigation	3,864	6,760	7,484	8,140	8,363
Decided following detailed investigation	557	612	612	695	722
Total complaint decisions	23,124	36,614	35,662	36,982	37,454

ii. Calls to Introduce a New Public Service Ombudsman

Alongside its advantages, there are criticisms of the current system: that multiple ombuds schemes in England constitute a barrier to justice, and accordingly that there is a need to establish a single Public Services Ombudsman – bringing together the PHSO, the Local Government and Social Care Ombudsman and the Housing Ombudsman. The rationale is that a single Public Services Ombudsman would save money, improve the effectiveness and efficiency of public services, improve access to justice, be fairer across the four nations of the UK, allow the UK to keep up with other modern democracies, and strengthen the scrutiny and transparency of public services.[38] The previous government conducted a public consultation on the matter and in 2016 published its draft Public Service Ombudsman Bill.[39] Although the Bill did not pass, the PHSO is currently promoting the establishment of a single Public Services Ombudsman and working with the government and Parliament to explore legislative opportunities to take forward this reform.[40]

[37] Data was collated from the PHSO Annual reports (nn 33 and 36).

[38] PHSO, 'Ombudsman Reform: Improving Access to Justice': www.ombudsman.org.uk/making-complaint/information-mps/our-role-and-relationship-parliament/ombudsman-reform-improving-access-justice.

[39] Draft Public Service Ombudsman Bill (December 2016): assets.publishing.service.gov.uk/media/5a802d80e5274a2e87db84e8/draft_public_service_ombudsman_bill_print_version_december_2016.pdf.

[40] 'Ombudsman Reform: Improving Access to Justice' (n 38).

The Law Society[41] has also emphasised the need for 'more joined up ombudsman services' to benefit access to justice, as part of its final report on its 21st Century Justice project, where it explored, more broadly, different options to expand access to civil justice. They proposed an outline of practical reforms intended to 'level the playing field for those of us seeking justice and enable more people to access legal advice'.[42] The report explains that 'Ombuds can play a key role in ensuring greater access to justice, as they are free to access, they can use a range of techniques to resolve different issues, and they are designed to be simple to use for a layperson'. Specifically, they note, the 'ombuds sector has the potential to act as a gold standard for out-of-court dispute resolution, adopting different dispute resolution techniques to fit the circumstances and seeking a fair outcome for all parties'.[43] However, the report concluded that the 'UK's [current] ombuds landscape was a "mess" where overlaps are common and gaps ubiquitous'.[44] This 'fragmented landscape' results in a situation where 'it is not always clear which ombudsman someone should turn to for help', making it 'difficult for people already facing an uphill struggle for redress and justice', leading to 'claimant fatigue' whereby people 'can get a bit lost and disillusioned' and may 'feel like [they] complain at one level, get rejected, so go up to the next level and eventually get to an ombuds'.[45]

Our survey showed that claimants in the employment system also described a process filled with numerous hurdles and a recurring sense that their concerns are not being taken seriously: there is a clear need for a single entry point to the system from which individuals can then be signposted. It is for this reason that we propose the establishment of the Employment Resolution Service, possibly as part of the new Fair Work Agency, to ensure a single entry point for claimants who cannot have their legal disputes resolved informally in the workplace (see further chapter thirteen).

More broadly, the Law Society report states that

> [t]he ombuds landscape in England and Wales needs to be reformed and rationalised by amalgamating services in the same sector, enhancing enforcement and investigation powers, and improving access for SMEs to ombuds services. This could reduce burdens on the courts by resolving issues effectively at an earlier stage, before disputes are brought to court, as well as improving people's experiences of this public service and ensuring decision-makers are held to account when things go wrong.[46]

Again, this resonates well with the need in the employment context to find ways to better address disputes informally and early on, and the need to filter

[41] The Law Society, '21st Century Justice: Final Report' (June 2025): www.lawsociety.org.uk/campaigns/justice-and-rule-of-law/21st-century-justice, 2.

[42] ibid.

[43] ibid.

[44] Citing Adam Sampson, a former Legal Ombudsman.

[45] The Law Society, '21st Century Justice: Final Report' (n 41) 2.

[46] ibid.

certain cases before they enter the system. Furthermore, the report makes other recommendations to enhance the enforcement and investigatory powers of ombudsman, which we discuss in chapter thirteen.[47]

But what happens if cases are destined for the courts? Is there a way of encouraging settlement? This brings us to the question of Pre-Action Protocols.

IV. Pre-Action Protocols in Personal Injury Litigation

A. What Are They?

The Pre-Action Protocols (PAPs) were introduced as part of the Woolf reforms in 1999, and guide the parties on 'what must be done, in relation to a claim to which it applies, before court proceedings are issued'.[48] The Protocols are intended to promote a 'culture of settlement', by setting out a procedural framework for information exchange and negotiations in the pre-litigation stage.[49] Their aims are

1. to encourage an early exchange of sufficient information between the parties so that they are able to understand each other's position,[50] and ultimately to avoid litigation by achieving a settlement – in particular by drawing on alternative dispute resolution, or,
2. when litigation cannot be avoided (which should be a matter of last resort)[51] to enable them at least to narrow the issues in dispute before proceedings are commenced and support the proportionate and efficient management of proceedings.[52]

[47] ibid.

[48] Pre-Action Protocols: www.justice.gov.uk/courts/procedure-rules/civil/standard-directions/general/pre-action-protocols.

[49] S Roberts, '"Listing Concentrates the Mind": The English Civil Court as an Arena for Structured Negotiation' (2009) 29 *Oxford Journal of Legal Studies* 457, 458. See also: J Jolowicz, 'Civil litigation: what's it for?' (2008) 67 *Cambridge Law Journal* 508, 515–16.

[50] The Pre-Action Protocol for the Resolution of Clinical Disputes, for example, says that '[i]t is important that each party to a clinical dispute has sufficient information and understanding of the other's perspective and case to be able to investigate a claim efficiently and, where appropriate, to resolve it. This Protocol encourages a cards-on-the-table approach when something has gone wrong with a claimant's treatment or the claimant is dissatisfied with that treatment and/or the outcome': Pre-Action Protocol for the Resolution of Clinical Disputes, s 1.3: www.justice.gov.uk/courts/procedure-rules/civil/protocol/prot_rcd.

[51] See, eg: Pre-Action Protocol for Resolution of Package Travel Claims: www.justice.gov.uk/courts/procedure-rules/civil/protocol/pre-action-protocol-for-resolution-of-package-travel-claims, s 14.1 (other PAPs have similar provisions).

[52] See, eg, Pre-Action Protocol for Resolution of Package Travel Claims (n 51) s 3.1 (and all other Protocols have similar provisions). Another example is the Pre-Action Protocol for the Resolution of Clinical Disputes (n 50) s 2.2, which adds to its list of objectives that, when litigation cannot be avoided, it aims 'to discourage the prolonged pursuit of unmeritorious claims and the prolonged defence of meritorious claims'.

In practice, PAPs pressure the parties into a period where 'co-operative communication and attempts are being made to settle the case by negotiation', with the filing of the claim occurring only if these fail. In that sense, '"filing" is most accurately seen as signalling the conclusion of a dispute process, rather than its initiation'.[53]

The aim behind PAPs, particularly their emphasis on transparency and, in the case of the Pre-Action Protocol for the Resolution of Clinical Disputes, is a 'cards on the table' approach,[54] making them an interesting model to consider for the purposes of encouraging settlement of employment tribunal disputes.[55] There are specific PAPs for different types of civil claims.[56] For present purposes we examine the PAP for personal injury claims as an example; many of its provisions are broadly replicated in the other Protocols. This PAP provides a structured set of guidelines that 'the court would normally expect prospective parties to follow prior to the commencement of proceedings';[57] sanctions may be imposed by the court if the guidelines are not followed.[58]

B. How Do They Work?

The Practice Direction on Pre-Action Conduct and Protocols,[59] which provides overall guidance, highlights the requirement for 'Proportionality':

> [a] pre-action protocol … must not be used by a party as a tactical device to secure an unfair advantage over another party. Only reasonable and proportionate steps should be taken by the parties to identify, narrow and resolve the legal, factual or expert issues.[60]

[53] Roberts (n 49) 463.

[54] The Pre-Action Protocol for Disease and Illness Claims, explicitly states as part of its objectives, under the heading of 'openness', 'to encourage early communication of the perceived problem between the parties or their insurers; to encourage employees to voice any concerns or worries about possible work related illness as soon as practicable; to encourage employers to develop systems of early reporting and investigation of suspected occupational health problems': Pre-Action Protocol for Disease and Illness Claims, s 3.2: www.justice.gov.uk/courts/procedure-rules/civil/protocol/prot_dis.

[55] PAPs apply to employment disputes in the county and High Courts; the distinction we are drawing is with disputes in the employment tribunal.

[56] Pre-Action Protocols: www.justice.gov.uk/courts/procedure-rules/civil/standard-directions/general/pre-action-protocols. There is also the Practice Direction on Pre-Action Conduct and Protocols, which addresses what is expected in disputes where no Pre-action Protocol applies: Practice Direction – Pre-Action Conduct and Protocols: www.justice.gov.uk/courts/procedure-rules/civil/rules/pd_pre-action_conduct.

[57] Pre-Action Protocol for Personal Injury Claims, s 1.4.1: www.justice.gov.uk/courts/procedure-rules/civil/protocol/prot_pic.

[58] Pre-Action Protocol for Personal Injury Claims (n 57) s 1.4.2, 1.5.

[59] Practice Direction on Pre-Action Conduct and Protocols (n 56) which addresses what is expected in disputes where no Pre-action Protocol applies.

[60] ibid, s 4.

Similarly, '[t]he costs incurred in complying with a pre-action protocol … should be proportionate'[61] and when following the Practice Direction Protocol, 'compliance should be proportionate'.[62] If the dispute proceeds to litigation, the expectation of the court is that the parties will have 'complied in substance' with the Practice Direction, and the court 'is not likely to be concerned with minor or technical infringements'.[63] This emphasis on proportionality[64] and overall reasonable conduct corresponds with the duties of cooperation and mutual trust and confidence which underpin the employment relationship.

The Pre-Action Protocol for Personal Injury Claims is primarily designed for claims which are likely to be allocated to the 'fast track' by the court,[65] that is, for claims which are worth between £10,000 and £25,000 and are expected to last no more than one day.[66] However, the approach of the Protocol is equally relevant for higher value claims and its 'spirit' should still be followed for claims which may be allocated to the intermediate track or multi-track.[67] We return to the issue of tracking in chapter nine.

The Protocol ensures that before court proceedings are issued, the claimant may receive support and early access to medical treatment or rehabilitation but also ensures that at this very early stage the parties meaningfully and promptly communicate about the claim and exchange relevant information. It provides the parties with the opportunity to conduct pre-action negotiations, ultimately enabling the parties to avoid litigation by reaching a settlement of the dispute.[68] Moreover, this Protocol was introduced to establish 'standards for the efficient conduct of

[61] ibid, s 5.

[62] ibid, s 6.

[63] ibid, s 13. Similarly, the Pre-Action Protocol for the Construction and Engineering Disputes also uses the following wording: 'If proceedings are commenced, the Court will be able to treat the standards set in this Protocol as the normal reasonable and proportionate approach to pre-action conduct. It is likely to be only in exceptional circumstances, such as a flagrant or very significant disregard for the terms of this Protocol, that the Court will impose cost consequences on a party for non-compliance with this Protocol': s 4.1: www.justice.gov.uk/courts/procedure-rules/civil/protocol/prot_ced. Moreover, the Pre-Action Protocol for Disease and Illness Claims (n 54) states that the court 'will not be concerned with minor infringements' and that '[o]ne minor breach will not exempt the "innocent" party from following the protocol': s 1.5. And, the Pre-Action Protocol for Professional Negligence adds in this regard (in relation to its described timetable and in requesting and providing information) that 'in the event that the protocol does not specifically address a problem, the parties should comply with the spirit of the protocol by acting reasonably': s 3.1: www.justice.gov.uk/courts/procedure-rules/civil/protocol/prot_neg.

[64] The emphasis on reasonable and proportionate conduct can be found throughout all protocols. Another example is the Pre-Action Protocol for Debt Claims which states as one of its aims to: 'encourage the parties to act in a reasonable and proportionate manner in all dealings with one another (for example, avoiding running up costs which do not bear a reasonable relationship to the sums in issue)': s 2.1: www.justice.gov.uk/documents/debt-pap.pdf.

[65] Pre-Action Protocol for Personal Injury Claims (n 57) s 1.1.1.

[66] HM Courts & Tribunals Service, 'The Fast Track and the Multi-Track in the Civil Courts': assets.publishing.service.gov.uk/media/5b4c7cd9ed915d438916e155/ex305-eng.pdf.

[67] Pre-Action Protocol for Personal Injury Claims (n 57) s 1.1.2.

[68] ibid, ss 1.4.1, 2.1.

pre-action litigation', to improve early communication between claimant lawyers and insurance companies, so that cases can be settled more quickly, cheaply and fairly, addressing the 'habit of issuing first, talking later'.[69] It can be equated in that sense to the evidence from our study, where claimants feel they need to submit their claim to show their seriousness to get a meaningful response.

In terms of the Protocol's requirements, the first step is sending a letter of notification, informing the defendant and/or the insurer that a claim is likely to be made, but before a detailed Letter of Claim is produced. The notification will include information that is available to assist with determining issues of liability, but also suitability of the early provision of medical treatment or other rehabilitative measures.[70] When claimants are able, they must send a detailed Letter of Claim. The information that should be included is described in a template annexed to the Protocol, and it is expected that the level of detail provided should be sufficient to assess liability and enable the defendant to estimate the likely size and heads of the claim.[71] This represents a 'substantial departure from the short, uninformative letters before action' that claimant solicitors used to send prior to the Protocol.[72] The defendant has 21 days to respond dealing with preliminary matters; there is an annexed template for the suggested content of such a letter.[73]

The Protocol establishes that:

> Letters of Claim and Response are not intended to have the same formal status as a statement of case in proceedings. It would not be consistent with the spirit of the Protocol for a party to 'take a point' on this in the proceedings, provided that there was no obvious intention by the party who changed their position to mislead the other party.[74]

This is an important feature of the Protocol supporting pre-litigation early resolution and addressing parties' 'generalised fear' of committing themselves to something that might be held against them at a later date.[75]

After their initial response, the defendant has three months to investigate the claim and produce a Letter of Response, after which it must say if it admits liability, and if it does not, to outline its version of events. An admission made at this stage may be binding on that party in the litigation.[76] At this stage the early disclosure of documents takes place, and the Protocol includes an annex specifying documents

[69] The Law Society Gazette, 'The New Pre-Action Protocol for Personal Injury Claims' (23 October 1998): www.lawgazette.co.uk/news/the-new-pre-action-protocol-for-personal-injury-claims-/20843.article.

[70] Pre-Action Protocol for Personal Injury Claims (n 57) ss 3.1, 3.2, 4.1.

[71] ibid, ss 5.1–5.4.

[72] The New Pre-Action Protocol for Personal Injury Claims (n 69).

[73] Pre-Action Protocol for Personal Injury Claims (n 57) ss 6.1–6.2.

[74] ibid, ss 5.7. Similarly, the Pre-Action Protocol for Professional Negligence (n 63) adds in this respect that if the Letter of Claim or Letter of Response differ materially from the Statement of Case or the Defence, respectively, in subsequent court proceedings, the court may decide, in its discretion, to impose sanctions: ss 6.3, 9.2.2.

[75] The New Pre-Action Protocol for Personal Injury Claims (n 69).

[76] Pre-Action Protocol for Personal Injury Claims (n 57) ss 6.3–6.6.

that are likely to be relevant for the claim. The aim here 'is not to encourage "fishing expeditions" by the claimant, but to promote an early exchange of relevant information to help in clarifying or resolving issues in dispute'.[77] The procedure for obtaining and disclosing expert reports is also outlined.[78]

Of particular relevance for the purposes of this book, the Protocol has a section on 'Alternative Dispute Resolution', stressing that '[l]itigation should be a last resort', and that 'the parties should consider whether negotiation or some other form of Alternative Dispute Resolution ("ADR") might enable them to resolve their dispute without commencing proceedings'. The Protocol specifies that the parties should consider resolving the dispute through, among other things, discussions and negotiation[79] ('which may or may not include making Part 36 Offers[80] or providing an explanation and/or apology'), mediation, arbitration and early neutral evaluation. The parties may be required to provide evidence that ADR has been considered, and an 'unreasonable refusal to consider ADR will be taken into account by the court when deciding who bears the costs of the proceedings'.[81] Moreover, the Pre-Action Protocol for Disease and Illness Claims adds that '[t]he Civil Procedure Rules Part 36 enable claimants and defendants to make formal offers to settle before proceedings are started. Parties should consider making such an offer, since to do so often leads to settlement'.[82] The connection between a failure to consider and attempt ADR, and cost consequences is helpful in incentivising parties to use ADR and a similar provision might help to address our finding that employers often do not take early resolution discussions seriously until litigation commences.

Finally, if an early resolution has not been achieved pursuant to the PAP, the Protocol requires a 'stocktake' exercise, where

> each party should undertake a review of its own positions and the strengths and weaknesses of its case. The parties should then together consider the evidence and the arguments in order to see whether litigation can be avoided or, if that is not possible, for the issues between the parties to be narrowed before proceedings are issued.

[77] ibid, ss 7.1.1– 7.1.3.

[78] ibid, ss 7.2–7.12.

[79] The Pre-Action Protocol for Claims for Damages in Relation to the Physical State of Commercial Property at Termination of a Tenancy even specifies, under the headline of 'negotiations' that '[t]he landlord and tenant and/or their respective surveyors are encouraged to meet before the tenant is required to respond to the Quantified Demand and should generally meet within 28 days after the tenant sends the Response. The meetings will be without-prejudice and the parties should seek to agree as many of the items in dispute as possible': s 7.1: www.justice.gov.uk/courts/procedure-rules/civil/protocol/pre-action-protocol-for-claims-for-damages-in-relation-to-the-physical-state-of-commercial-property-at-termination-of-a-tenancy-the-dilapidations-protocol. This requirement fits well with our empirical data which has emphasised the value of having an in-person meeting early in the dispute as a catalyst for its resolution.

[80] Pt 36 provides a regime whereby the failure of a party to 'beat' an offer made by the other party sounds in costs. This is discussed further in ch 11: www.justice.gov.uk/courts/procedure-rules/civil/rules/part36.

[81] Pre-Action Protocol for Personal Injury Claims (n 57) s 9. The Pre-Action Protocol for Disease and Illness Claims (n 54) adds in this regard that 'claims should not be issued prematurely when a settlement is still actively being explored': s 2A.1.

[82] Pre-Action Protocol for Disease and Illness Claims (n 54) s 10.1.

The Protocols Practice Direction explicitly states that the parties 'should continue to consider the possibility of reaching a settlement at all times'.[83] This resonates with our research in which participants said that there should be touchstone points for ADR to be considered throughout the employment tribunal process. Further, many participants pointed to the need to reduce the long list of issues in employment disputes and the stocktake procedure in the Protocol promoting the narrowing of the issues before court proceedings are started might be of assistance. It is for this reason that we propose that employment tribunals should have the option of referring case back to the Employment Resolution Service at any time. We also think that case management should be guided by the proportionality principle both in terms of the number and nature of the claims and also in terms of the paperwork. This proportionality principle should be enshrined in statute.

C. Evaluation

Given the aims of the PAPs in promoting a culture of settlement, have they worked in practice? Early studies by the Lord Chancellor's Department concluded that '[a]necdotal evidence suggests that pre-action protocols are working well to promote settlement before issue and to reduce the number of ill-founded claims',[84] and that '[e]vidence suggests that pre-action protocols are working well to promote settlement and a culture of openness and co-operation'.[85] A study commissioned by the Law Society and the Civil Justice Council in the early 2000s examined interviewees' perceptions on the impact of the Woolf reforms. It found that '[t]here was a strong sense that claims were now easier to settle and respondents reported a greater incidence of settlement', and that this might 'underlie a shift towards a settlement culture'. The increased incidence of settlement was attributed 'to the "cards on the table" culture embodied in the protocol and, more specifically, the claimant Part 36 offer'.[86] More recent studies have also found that the PAPs contributed to reduced litigation, and 'produced a more cooperative environment'.[87]

[83] Practice Direction on Pre-Action Conduct and Protocols (n 56) s 9.

[84] Lord Chancellor's Department, 'Emerging Findings: An Early Evaluation of the Civil Justice Reforms' (March 2001): webarchive.nationalarchives.gov.uk/ukgwa/+/http://www.dca.gov.uk/civil/emerge/emerge.htm.

[85] Lord Chancellor's Department, 'Further Findings: A Continuing Evaluation of the Civil Justice Reforms' (August 2002): webarchive.nationalarchives.gov.uk/ukgwa/+/http://www.dca.gov.uk/civil/reform/ffreform.htm.

[86] T Goriely, R Moorhead and P Abrams 'More Civil Justice? The Impact of the Woolf reforms on Pre-Action Behaviour', Research Study 43, The Law Society and Civil Justice Council (2002) 262, 273: orca.cardiff.ac.uk/id/eprint/44483/1/557.pdf.

[87] P Morgan, 'Conflicts between Jurisdiction and Procedure: Pre-Action Civil Procedure and Jurisdiction – A Poor Fit' (2011) 2 *Lloyd's Maritime and Commercial Law Quarterly* 275, 277, fn 23. See also: C Konstantinou, 'Pre-Action Protocols 14 Years on: Have they Been Proven to be Conducive to Settlement?' (2012): papers.ssrn.com/sol3/papers.cfm?abstract_id=2175448; M Young, 'The Clinical Disputes Pre-Action Protocol – Is it Working? A Claimant's Solicitor's Perspective' (2021) 7 *Clinical Risk* 43, 45.

However, others have criticised the PAPs for adding to costs and for the extended procedure without necessarily justifying the benefits. For example, Andrews said that 'in a large and complicated dispute the parties will be engaged in compliance with these requirements for many months'.[88] He concluded that:

> It is difficult to make a clear empirical assessment of the benefits conferred by the system of pre-action protocols. The values of instilling a greater prominence for settlement and ADR, as well as promoting more disclosure of information and documents, have to be weighed against the palpable increase in cost in ensuring compliance with the protocols. Sir Rupert Jackson … recommended that the general pre action provisions should not apply at all to Commercial or Chancery litigation.[89]

Zander has also argued that the Woolf reforms have led to an increase in costs, and specifically led to 'front-loading of costs', due to the early preparation of cases, early exchange of information between the parties, and more 'cards on the table' at an earlier stage. This increase, he argued, does not justify the added benefits:

> Pre-CPR, the preparation of the average case that went to trial would tend to take place at a late stage, which Lord Woolf thought was a problem. The trouble is that the front-loading of costs applies not just to the tiny minority of cases that go to trial but equally to the overwhelming majority – well over 90% – that have always settled. In my view this obvious point was never properly grasped by Lord Woolf and, insofar as it was recognised, it was brushed aside with the assertion that in cases that settled, the settlement would be based on a fuller appreciation of the facts. This may be true – but no one can say what difference that fuller appreciation of the facts makes to the terms of the settlement – in the sense of giving the claimant a better or worse result and at what cost to the paying party. 'Early better appreciation of the facts' is of little value if it adds significantly to the costs and makes little or no difference to the terms of settlement. Even if it affects the outcome, it may do so at a disproportionate cost.[90]

Concern has also been expressed about the level of voluntariness or compulsion in ADR under the PAPs. For example, De Girolamo and Underhill say that

> issues such as whether cost sanctions should be applied for the refusal to consider ADR process (including what amounts to 'reasonable refusal'), whether litigants can be compelled to engage in ADR and whether a court has the power to order such engagement despite the lack of consent of the parties, have all dominated the ADR discourse almost since the CPR's inception.[91]

Those in favour of greater use of ADR have discussed the need to better promote and incentivise parties to resolve disputes in the pre-action period, and accordingly

[88] N Andrews, *Andrews on Civil Processes: Court Proceedings* (Intersentia 2013) 66.

[89] ibid, 67.

[90] M Zander, 'Zander on Woolf: More Harm than Good? Professor Michael Zander QC Reflects on 10 Years of the Woolf Reforms' (12 March 2009): www.newlawjournal.co.uk/docs/default-source/article_files/nlj200-archive_procedure-practice_zander_15-22-april-202295b229f5-bb19-49c0-9cd3-977cd4d1eaff.pdf?sfvrsn=afef97db_1.

[91] D De Girolamo and D Spenser Underhill, 'Alternative Dispute Resolution and the Civil Courts: A Very British Type of Justice – The Legacy of the Woolf Reforms in 2022' (2022) 4 *Amicus Curiae* 129, 130.

have highlighted the potential value of establishing mandatory requirements to get the parties to meaningfully engage in dispute resolution.[92] One study, for example, critically evaluated the way the courts use the discretion granted to them by the Civil Procedure Rules to make adverse costs orders against a party which, although successful in their claim or defence, is found to have unreasonably refused to engage in ADR. Ahmed found that in these circumstances, the full range of these adverse costs orders were not fully utilised by courts. In particular, Ahmed found that while courts appear more comfortable in making adverse cost orders that restrict or deprive the successful party's recovery of its costs, courts have been reluctant to oblige the successful party to reimburse some of the unsuccessful party's costs. He concluded that

> there is a need for a change in judicial attitudes towards compulsory mediation, more effective utilisation of the overriding objective and greater use by the courts of their costs powers when dealing with ADR within the civil justice system.[93]

Hodges notes that Briggs LJ reported the perception of the Civil Mediation Council that ADR was broadly satisfactory for high value claims, but that there was a substantial proportion of claims of moderate value where mediation is insufficiently used, and a particular shortfall in the potential penetration of mediation in relation to personal injury and clinical negligence claims.[94] More recently, De Girolamo and Underhill have concluded that there is a 'growing case for and renewed interest in some form of compulsory ADR'.[95]

However, suggestions that the PAPS should be made more coercive raise difficulties both in terms of their compliance with the right to a fair trial,[96] and that it would be counterproductive to require parties or pressurise them through sanctions to use ADR.[97] It was noted in this regard that when mediation is unsuccessful, ADR unnecessarily increases the costs for the parties, who will have to pay both the ADR and the litigation costs. Moreover, from a justice point of view, '[t]here is a price to pay in terms of substantive justice for early settlement', as compared with a court procedure.[98] Therefore, while the PAPs have been criticised for not being effective because they are not compulsory, they have also been criticised for being

[92] See, eg, V McCloud, 'Pre-Action Protocols and Pre-Action Dispute Resolution Processes: Horizons Near and Far' (2023) 4 *Amicus Curiae* 344.

[93] M Ahmed, 'Bridging the Gap between Alternative Dispute Resolution and Robust Adverse Costs Orders' (2015) 66 *Northern Ireland Legal Quarterly* 71, 92.

[94] C Hodges, *Delivering Dispute Resolution: A Holistic Review of Models in England and Wales* (Hart Publishing 2019) 181.

[95] De Girolamo and Underhill (n 91) 145.

[96] On the debate over the compulsion of ADR and its compliance with Article 6 of the European Convention on Human Rights, see: McCloud (n 92) 350–55.

[97] Civil Justice Council, *Review of Pre-Action Protocols: Interim Report* (November 2021) 10: www.judiciary.uk/wp-content/uploads/2021/11/CJC-PAP-Interim-Report.pdf.

[98] H Genn, 'What is Civil Justice for? Reform, ADR, and Access to Justice' (2012) 24 *Yale Journal of Law & the Humanities* 397, 405. De Girolamo and Underhill (n 91), on the other hand, argue that 'Justice is not confined to the vindication of the legal merits of a claim; it is also found in settlement reachable by the parties through an active engagement with each other … Settlement, whether or not a compromise, can be a just outcome as is an adjudicated outcome': 148.

coercive: as part of a review of the Pre-Action Protocols, 2020–21, the Civil Justice Council's Interim Report, noted that

> a number of ADR lawyers and academics have forcefully argued that the encouragement of ADR under the current PAPs [Pre-Action Protocols] is a form of de facto compulsion. For example, under the Practice Direction – Pre-action Conduct (PD–PAC) the court is expressly empowered to treat an unreasonable refusal to use a form of ADR, or failure to respond at all to an invitation to do so, as non-compliance with the PAP, which it must take into account when making case management directions or costs orders, and which enlivens its jurisdiction to impose a sanction or order a stay.[99]

So, while there are potential merits in increasing the pressures and incentives on the parties to engage meaningfully in pre-action settlement, these, if not designed properly, carry the risk of coming with a substantial cost. We have been aware of these risks and have taken them into account when preparing our recommendations in chapter thirteen, recommendations which have been significantly informed by the experiences of non-court dispute resolution in family law, another jurisdiction where emotions can run high.

V. Family Law and Non-Court Dispute Resolution

A. Introduction

So far we have considered ways of keeping cases out of any formal dispute mechanism at all, using other fora to resolve disputes, such as an ombud, as well as more technical ways of encouraging settlements, such as PAPs. We turn now to consider the example of family law dispute resolution which we think is one of the most productive examples of how employment cases can avoid reaching the courts. As noted in chapter three, we think there are remarkable similarities between many family law and employment law cases: both involve the breakdown of personal relationships, often in emotionally charged situations. We were surprised by the number of our interviewees who drew a similar parallel. So, in this section we examine family law and non-court resolution where mediation and non-court resolution has been developing over the last two decades, now further encouraged by changes made in 2024 to the Family Procedure Rules, placing greater emphasis on non-court resolution of disputes relating to private law children and financial remedy arrangements. George et al say that 'the family justice system prides itself on its conciliatory approach to family disputes. Relatively few families therefore find themselves in the family court'.[100] The data

[99] *Review of Pre-Action Protocols: Interim Report* (n 97) 12.
[100] R George, S Thompson and J Miles, *Family Law: Text, Cases, and Materials*, 5th edn (Oxford University Press 2023) 22.

supports this: in a 2022 survey of 2,489 separated parents, only around a quarter had used the family court.[101]

So how has this shift towards a 'conciliatory approach' occurred? Rule 1.4(1) of the Family Procedure Rules 2010 (FPR 2010) provides for active case management which includes 'encouraging parties to use a non-court dispute resolution procedure if the court considers that appropriate and facilitating the use of such procedure';[102] and 'helping the parties to settle the whole or part of the case'.[103] The definition of non-court dispute resolution (NCDR) was amended in 2024 to make it deliberately broad, namely 'methods of resolving a dispute other than through the court process, including but not limited to mediation, arbitration, evaluation by a neutral third party (such as a private Financial Dispute Resolution process) and collaborative law'.[104] In practice, interviewees told us that NCDR is primarily focused on mediation – and some criticised the Ministry of Justice for being too mediation-focused to the exclusion of other forms of NCDR[105] – but the FPR does allow for a variety of dispute resolution mechanisms.

Further, different forms of NCDR can be interwoven: an interviewee told us that early neutral evaluation or arbitration can be 'a way of trying to get individuals past an impasse on a particular [issue]'. The interviewee said

> there might be 10 issues and it might be that … we can agree on 8 out of the 10. But then we've got two that they're really struggling with. And so what I would always suggest is … [to] allow someone else to make that decision or we can get an early neutral evaluation on those issues and then come back into mediation.[106]

The strong culture in family law of seeking to resolve disputes away from the courts may have developed because of the realities of limited finances so that legal costs need to be kept to a minimum, or where children are involved and 'they've got to co-parent [for a long time ahead] … so I think there is a shared realisation that this is bigger than the two of them, and they have a commitment to try and work this out for [the] children's sake'.[107] Nevertheless, the development of that culture appears to have taken some time and a number of different initiatives have been taken to achieve it: 'it's been a really, really slow burn'.[108] We consider two particular issues relevant for employment disputes: the use of early mediation in disputes and the introduction of, and recent increased emphasis on, the requirement to attend a Mediation Information and Assessment meeting before making a court application.

[101] K Dabhi, T Anand and T Tu, *Survey of Separated Parents*, DWP Ad Hoc Research Report No 1015 (2022) section 5.3: www.gov.uk/government/publications/survey-of-separated-parents/survey-of-separated-parents#support-for-separated-families-1.

[102] Family Procedure Rules 2010, r 1.4(2)(f) (FPR 2010).

[103] r 1.4(2)(g) FPR 2010.

[104] r 2.3(1) FPR 2010.

[105] Interview, 21 July 2025.

[106] Interview, 12 December 2024.

[107] Interview, 14 July 2025.

[108] Interview, 21 July 2025.

B. Early Mediation

As noted above, participants in our interviews told us that the majority of family matters do not get litigated at all. The statistics support this: in 2024 only 26 per cent of applications relating to financial remedies in divorce were contested. Of the disposals relating to financial remedies, 69.5 per cent were uncontested, 8.7 per cent were initially contested and then uncontested and 21.75 per cent were contested.[109] That was partly because solicitors 'send an awful lot of cases off to mediation'[110] and because couples seek to resolve matters themselves or go to mediation directly. One participant said that only about 10 per cent of their case load involved litigation. Much of this mediation precedes any formal engagement with the family law system.

The popularity of mediation was attributed to the profile that it has been given by the government so that people know that it exists and how to access it. Moreover, there is now a scheme whereby the government provides a £500 voucher to use on mediation to avoid accessing the court system. This was said to have made a significant difference,[111] although some argued that the voucher should be available for use for other forms of NCDR rather than being restricted to mediation.[112] Other participants emphasised that people

> don't want things to be really horrible … most people are conflict averse. They don't want to be going through that stress [of litigation]. And … most people are willing to have a conversation about it, if they think that the other person is going to listen to them and engage'.[113]

Moreover, mediation enabled parties to deal with matters that the courts would not address and reach solutions that were more creative than could be achieved through the court process.

Practically, the key to encouraging people to engage in mediation was said to be to have someone who could really enthuse about its benefits:

> The way you get people to engage is [for them] to meet somebody who talks to them about what this looks like, what it involves, how actually great it is both financially and because you have the opportunity to be really creative in mediation … to bring in other people to help you.[114]

The emphasis on creativity was also important because it enabled a range of matters to be covered which might not have been addressed had the case gone to court. The cost of mediation was also important because although mediation is not cheap, it was the cheapest option, particularly compared with litigating the issues.

[109] Family Court Statistics Quarterly, January to March 2025: www.gov.uk/government/statistics/family-court-statistics-quarterly-january-to-march-2025 table 14.
[110] Interview, 9 July 2025.
[111] Interviews: 9 July 2025, 17 July 2025 and 21 July 2025.
[112] Interview, 21 July 2025.
[113] Interview, 14 July 2025.
[114] Interview, 14 July 2025.

Lawyers are not excluded from the mediation process. Many solicitors are also mediators. Lawyers generally do not attend the mediation itself, but parties often have received some legal advice before the mediation. Once an agreement is reached at mediation, the parties will usually return to their solicitor for help to draw up the final court order. This allows the solicitor to check that an appropriate resolution has been reached and is one that the court will agree to order. The agreed order will then go before the court to be made. We were told that this was not now just a rubber-stamping exercise. Rather, it was seen as an important step, particularly where there is a power imbalance between the couple, to ensure that any settlement was appropriate.

The types of mediation in operation in family law have expanded considerably beyond the traditional facilitative mediation. While that still takes place, and was seen as appropriate for some couples, we were told that even traditional facilitative mediation will include an element of 'some guidance about what is realistic, what … other people in your situation may have thought about … and [may] want to consider what a court may or may not approve'.[115] Hybrid mediation – with an expressly evaluative element – may be more useful in other disputes where there are specific issues on which the parties need a clearer steer on their relative merits.

Some interviewees were particularly enthusiastic about mediation that drew in a family consultant or therapist: 'It's some sort of magic … They have the ability to help hold the emotional bit, so that people can bring their rational … decision making brain to the process … They help to manage the dynamic of the emotional fallout'.[116] More bluntly, one interviewee said that 'you can't separate the facts from the relationships and the feelings … if you're asking people to reach an outcome between them, then … it's a bit mad to think you … can't pay any attention to what's actually going on'.[117]

An alternative to this was to ensure that the lawyers involved in a mediation were 'trauma informed' in their approach because 'people still rely on their lawyers to provide for their emotional needs'. This required lawyers to adapt their approach to enable their clients to hear their advice and engage in the mediation process without their emotional responses overwhelming them.[118]

There were more mixed views of collaborative mediation in which lawyers talk to their clients, about the merits and demerits of the issues being discussed, in front of the other party and their lawyer. We were told by one participant that

[115] Interview, 9 July 2025.
[116] Interview, 14 July 2025.
[117] Interview, 24 July 2025. See also: LexisNexis Family Law, *Anxieties and Defences in Mediation: A case study with tentative answers* (10 September 2023).
[118] Interview, 17 July 2025 (2).

> it's quite magical, you can imagine [Parties are] not hearing the answer's black or the answer's white in their own lawyer's room. They're hearing it in the room together. So they understand that there's a difference of opinion. They understand much more clearly that if a judge has to decide, the judge could take either view. But the likelihood is it's somewhere between them.[119]

By contrast, other participants told us that it was very costly because if the negotiations break down then the parties have to change lawyers.[120]

We were told that having different forms of mediation allowed solicitors to signpost their clients to the appropriate form for them and for the dispute that needed to be resolved. It was important not to have a 'one size fits all' approach but a process that allowed for different approaches to be used in different circumstances. Solicitors also had to be aware of the fact that mediation was only likely to be successful if the parties were both ready for it. One interviewee referred to Kübler-Ross' different stages of grief (see Box 5.1):[121] if the parties were at different stages then mediation may not work.

Box 5.1 Five Stages of Grief

Elisabeth Kübler-Ross, a pioneering psychiatrist in the field of death and dying studies, developed the 'five stages of grief' model, which describes the stages through which people may cope with the dying process. Initially, this model was introduced in her 1969 book, *On Death and Dying*,[122] describing how terminally ill patients gradually accept the reality of their own impending death. This influential work has since been developed as a framework on how people cope and come to terms with grief more generally, including those experiencing bereavement[123] but also other serious life events such as divorce.

The five stages – denial and isolation, anger, bargaining, depression, and acceptance – are 'tools to help us frame and identify what we may be feeling. But they are not stops on some linear timeline in grief. Not everyone goes through all of them or goes in a prescribed order'.[124] In the ***denial stage***, people tend to be 'paralyzed with shock or blanketed with numbness'. A person who is dying might be in disbelief, denying their terminal illness; and for someone grieving, they might be in symbolic denial, where the new reality is just too hard to comprehend.[125] Once people recover from this initial denial, often feelings of ***anger*** surface, and these can be reflected in numerous ways, including

[119] Interview, 14 July 2025.
[120] Interview, 11 July 2025.
[121] Interview, 14 July 2025 (2).
[122] E Kübler-Ross, *On Death and Dying* (Macmillan Publishing Co 1969).
[123] eg, in her last book: E Kübler-Ross and D Kessler, *On Grief and Grieving: Finding the Meaning of Grief Through the Five Stages of Loss* (Simon & Schuster 2005).
[124] ibid, 7.
[125] ibid, 8.

towards the loved one who has died, towards oneself, doctors, or the situation more broadly.[126] The ***bargaining*** stage involves attempts to somehow alter or postpone the reality of the loss, with people exploring different 'what if' and 'if only' scenarios around the death.[127] Once they accept the inevitable, people in the ***depression*** stage start focusing on the present and experience deep grief and sadness.[128] This might take years, but eventually people may experience a process of ***acceptance***. This acceptance, however, is 'not a final stage with an end point'; it is reflected by 'bits and pieces of acceptance' about the new reality, recognising it is permanent, and gradually learning to live with it.[129]

C. Mediation Information and Assessment Meeting

There was already a requirement, via section 10(1) Children and Families Act 2014, that 'a person must attend a family mediation information and assessment meeting' (a MIAM requirement) in most private law proceedings relating to children[130] and most proceedings for a financial remedy.[131] The changes in 2024 served to place greater weight on these requirements such that an independent mediator must 'sign off whether [parties] have engaged in NCDR before the proceedings, but also the lawyers of the clients … have to do a form M5 where they actually give a detailed explanation as to why they're not in NCDR'.[132] Alternatively, the applicant must set out their claim that an exemption from a MIAM applies.[133] Any claim for an exemption will be examined by the court once proceedings are issued[134] and the court may direct the parties to attend a MIAM, or adjourn to enable a MIAM to take place, if they find that the exemption has not been validly claimed or is no longer applicable.[135] Once the MIAM requirement has been complied with, there are further means by which the court can encourage NCDR which we discuss in chapter ten.

Rule 3.9(1) requires that a MIAM is conducted by an authorised family mediator, that is, a fully accredited mediator on the Family Mediation Council register.[136]

[126] ibid, 11–14.
[127] ibid, 17–20.
[128] ibid, 20.
[129] ibid, 24–27.
[130] r 3.6 FPR 2010. See also FPR 2010 Practice Direction 3A (PD3A) para 12. Various exemptions operate including relating to domestic abuse (r 3.8(1)(a) FPR 2010), child protection concerns (r 3.8(1)(b) FPR 2010), and in urgent situations with a risk to the physical safety of participants (r 3.8(1)(c) FPR 2010).
[131] See PD3A, para 13.
[132] Interview, 12 December 2024.
[133] r 3.7 FPR 2010.
[134] PD3A, para 7.
[135] r 3.10(2) FPR 2010. See also *NA v LA* [2024] EWFC 113, [2024] 3 FCR 391.
[136] r 3.1 FPR 2010. Family Mediation Council, 'Guidance for all family mediators on initial mediation meetings, MIAMs and the signing of court forms': www.familymediationcouncil.org.uk/miams-guidance-pccs/.

The requirements for accreditation are stringent.[137] Rule 3.9(2) provides that during a MIAM, the mediator must:

(a) provide information about the principles, process and different models of mediation, and information about other methods of non-court dispute resolution;
(b) consider and explain the potential benefits of mediation and other methods of non-court dispute resolution as a means of resolving the dispute;
(c) assess whether there has been, or is a risk of, domestic abuse;
(d) assess whether there has been, or is a risk of, harm by a prospective party to a child that would be a subject of the application;
(e) indicate to those attending the MIAM which form, or forms, of non-court dispute resolution may be most suitable as a means of resolving the dispute, and why; and
(f) where sub-paragraph (e) applies, provide information to those attending the MIAM about how to proceed with the form, or forms, of non-court dispute resolution in question.

In theory, the MIAM is only an exercise in providing information and it has been suggested that it would be more effective if it incorporated some explanation of 'what a "normal" arrangement for either the children or finances might look like … and could include some basic legal advice'.[138] It is heavily focused on mediation rather than other forms of NCDR[139] and it has been suggested that a MIAM should be replaced by a general advice appointment, so that individuals could be signposted to a range of NCDR options, including mediation.[140]

However, the statistics show that the increased emphasis on MIAMs, and limiting the use of the exemptions,[141] is changing the trajectory of mediations: from January to March 2025, the volume of MIAMs increased by 7 per cent compared with the previous year and family mediation starts increased by 30 per cent. Total outcomes increased by 3 per cent, of which 58 per cent were successful

[137] Family Mediation Council, 'Becoming a Mediator': www.familymediationcouncil.org.uk/becoming-a-family-mediator/. Family Mediation Council, 'FMC Manual Professional Standards and Self-Regulatory Framework' (September 2024): www.familymediationcouncil.org.uk/wp-content/uploads/2024/09/FMC-Manual-of-Professonal-Standards-Regulatory-Framework-v1.5-September-2024.pdf. The requirements to become a mediator have been criticised by J Reid, 'The arduous journey to becoming an accredited family mediator' *Law Society Gazette* (30 January 2025).

[138] Sir Andrew McFarlane, 'Relaunching Family Mediation' (28 September 2022): www.judiciary.uk/speech-by-the-president-of-the-family-division-relaunching-family-mediation/.

[139] This was criticised by the Children and Families Act 2014 Committee: *Children and Families Act 2014: A failure of implementation* (HL 2022–23, 100) para 140.

[140] Children and Families Act 2014 Committee, *Children and Families Act 2014*, para 141.

[141] Previously statistics showed only 35% of applicants to the family court attended a MIAM: Children and Families Act 2014 Committee, *Children and Families Act 2014*, para 130. Consequently, concerns were raised that MIAM requirement was 'honoured more in the breach than the observance' by inappropriate reliance on the exemptions: McFarlane (n 138).

agreements. Nevertheless, the statistics are still only sitting at around half the level they were before changes were made in April 2013 removing legal aid for most divorce cases.[142]

Figure 5.1 Family mediation assessments, starts and agreements, April to June 2011 to January to March 2025[143]

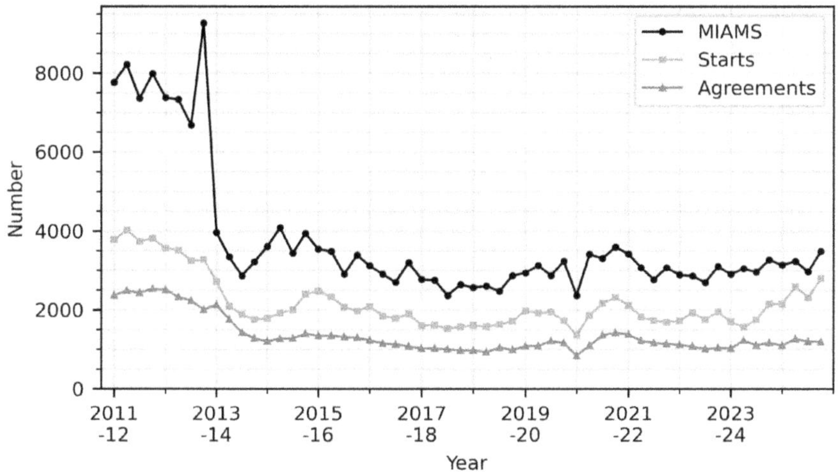

In 2020, the Family Solutions Group reported that the MIAM meeting itself is generally regarded as helpful.[144] However, our participants thought that MIAMs have not really changed things because sensible solicitors referred matters to mediation in any event.[145] Others were less critical and said that initially

> people did just see it as an additional hurdle and a tick box exercise … [but now] certainly the way I talk about a MIAM is it's a good opportunity to see if [NCDR] would work for you and you know whether the other person engages … I feel like it's probably too late at that point … [but] if it's a solicitor who hasn't already … done the discussion with them, it is an opportunity for them to actually sell [NCDR] to the client and divert them from litigation. So I suppose for those clients that would be an absolute benefit.[146]

However, MIAM, as currently practised, is not a magic wand. One interviewee said that 'there's just not been proper and consistent enforcement' by the courts at

[142] Via the Legal Aid, Sentencing and Punishment of Offenders Act 2012.
[143] Created by the authors using data from: www.gov.uk/government/statistics/legal-aid-statistics-quarterly-january-to-march-2025/legal-aid-statistics-england-and-wales-bulletin-jan-to-mar-2025#civil-legal-aid.
[144] Report of the Family Solutions Group, '"What about me?" Reframing Support for Families following Parental Separation' (12 November 2020) 82, para 307.
[145] Interview, 11 July 2025.
[146] Interview, 9 July 2025.

the 'gatekeeping stage'.[147] One particular issue is that Respondents are not required to attend a MIAM.[148] The PAP provides that in financial remedy proceedings respondents are 'expected' to attend unless there is a good reason not to,[149] and in relation to private law proceedings relating to children they are 'strongly encouraged and expected' to attend.[150] There have been calls for presidential guidance stating the expectation that they attend or for judges to adjourn and direct attendance or to use costs sanctions for non-attendance.[151] One participant noted that more recently the courts were 'buckling down' on the requirements and sending parties back to consider NCDR if they had not done so before making their application to court.[152] This was considered to be helpful: in employment disputes, the ability of the tribunal to send cases back for consideration of NCDR may be particularly productive.

The major issue with the MIAM was that it 'is too late. You know what we would say is … in an ideal world, you need people seeking some professional help as early as possible and getting to mediation or something else before they become too entrenched'.[153] In this, there are clear parallels with workplace disputes: everyone agrees that the sooner people engage in trying to resolve disputes, perhaps with outside assistance, the better.

D. Interim Conclusions

Family law has much to offer to employment dispute resolution. It acknowledges the complex emotional dynamics in the relationship that has broken down whether in a form that means the parties never have to engage with each other again (akin to the termination of an employment relationship) or where there may be an ongoing relationship because of the need to co-parent (akin to where the claimant remains in employment and a way forward has to be found). The legal system has adapted to address these emotional aspects of the dispute by offering, encouraging and in some circumstances, cajoling people to seek to resolve their disputes outside court. A suite of NCDR options are available to parties so that different approaches can be used according to the particular

[147] Interview, 21 July 2025.

[148] This has been heavily criticised. See, eg, J Edwards, 'Closer collaboration between the judicial and mediation communities Part 1: Mediation/MIAMs – how they work in practice' [2016] *Family Law* 1168, 1170; McFarlane (n 138); and Report of the Family Solutions Group (n 144) 82, para 307.

[149] Pre-application Protocol: financial remedy proceedings (Annex to PD9A) para 8.

[150] Pre-application Protocol: private law proceedings relating to children (Annex 2 to PD12B) para 19.

[151] Children and Families Act 2014 Committee, *Children and Families Act 2014*, 139, para 10. See also J Edwards who argues for greater collaboration between local judges and mediators: 'Closer collaboration between the judicial and mediation communities Part 2: The legal framework and working more closely together in practice' [2016] *Family Law* 1281.

[152] Interview, 11 July 2025 (2).

[153] Interview, 21 July 2025.

needs of those in the dispute, with the aim that this is achieved as early in the process as possible.

VI. Conclusions

Two specific issues can be identified from our survey of the broader UK landscape in respect of how cases can be resolved without going to courts/tribunals. First, that adopting an approach of formal processes being the 'last resort' can be transformative for organisations. Many HR professionals are concerned to ensure that their organisation complies with the Acas Code and Guidance which inevitably proceduralises matters at a very early stage. Furthermore, the Acas Code itself does not give sufficient emphasis to the fact that formal processes should not be the first port of call. The Code needs to be amended to make that far more clear and directional. There needs to be greater support for employers in using informal means of resolving disputes. While the PAPs are a helpful model of encouraging early information sharing, we would be concerned that their procedural focus might mean that once again the emphasis on resolution is lost.

Second, where disputes cannot be resolved within the workplace, much can be learnt from the family law context. Early mediation can pay dividends. It requires a cultural shift for the lawyers in the field so that they pay greater attention to the emotional factors involved in a dispute. Lawyers need to recognise that 'Mediation can make clients feel vulnerable and unsupported at a time when a huge amount is expected of them. They are expected to be civilised, conciliatory and compromising at a time when they can have feelings of betrayal, loss, grief, and mistrust'.[154] However, they also need to place much greater emphasis and importance on seeking to resolve disputes earlier and to make the conditions right for the parties to talk constructively.

Many lawyers already take that approach, but it is not embedded within the employment law culture or in the structure of the dispute resolution system. We would propose that early resolution takes a central position in the system. It needs to be embedded into the structure of dispute resolution so that it cannot be seen as an optional extra or a tick-box exercise. The form of that early resolution must inevitably depend on the type of dispute with the opportunity to use a variety of specific techniques according to the circumstances of a case.

[154] C Plews, *A Psychodynamic Model for Family Mediation*, LexisNexis Family Law (20 January 2022): www.familylaw.co.uk/news_and_comment/a-psychodynamic-model-for-family-mediation.

6

Looking Internationally: Lessons for Reform of Employment Dispute Resolution from Other Jurisdictions

I. Introduction

The previous chapter looked at examples drawn from other domestic contexts and jurisdictions – the NHS, ombuds, pre-action protocols in personal injury claims and family law – for features that could be built into a revised system of employment dispute resolution. What they all have in common is that Alternative Dispute Resolution (ADR), and especially mediation, is built into the system to avoid as many cases as possible going to the courts.

We turn now to consider examples of employment dispute resolution in other jurisdictions which might help us identify what a whole system model would look like, focusing on systems where research participants had indicated that we might have something to learn. Therefore, we briefly consider the Singapore model, which has a strong emphasis on mediation but also has some features which are culturally specific, making it less suitable for direct translation to the UK (section II). We move on to explore the processes in Australia and New Zealand, both of which are highly successful in the early resolution of disputes. Practitioners are very positive about much of the work by the bodies involved in dealing with lower level, less complex disputes. We think that there is much to learn from these two jurisdictions (sections III and IV).

II. Singapore and the Tripartite Alliance for Dispute Management

A. How the System Works

A key aspect of the Employment Claims Tribunal (ECT) in Singapore, established by the Employment Claims Act 2016 (ECA 2016), is that lawyers are not permitted to appear before it. Nor are they allowed to attend the mediation process before the Tripartite Alliance for Dispute Management (TADM) that must be undertaken before a claim to the ECT is brought.[1] However, an employee who is a trade union member in a unionised workplace can be represented by an officer of the trade union.[2] There is a small fee for the mediation,[3] but otherwise costs are limited by the refusal to permit lawyers to attend. Many employers are advised by lawyers in advance of both mediation and tribunal hearings. Once employers realise they have to conduct the mediation and the hearing personally before the ECT, including cross examination, 'suddenly all the fire they had in their belly [to fight the case] is now quelled'.[4]

The ECT's jurisdiction is relatively limited compared with the UK employment tribunals because of the restricted number of employment rights in Singaporean law. Their jurisdiction includes salary claims and matters of wrongful dismissal.[5] However, employees still bring claims which tribunals have no jurisdiction to hear such as claiming for a discretionary bonus. One interviewee said:

> I know even the tribunal magistrate knows that that's not something that can be … awarded … because it is purely discretionary, but yet the employer has to sit through the entire process, go through mediation, go through the case conferences, go through the hearing and only after judgment is given would … the … claim be dismissed.[6]

Consequently, he said that employers 'pay … an overly generous sum' to a claimant 'because they don't want to waste resources fighting it out'.[7] This is particularly so because the maximum amount that an employee can claim before the ECT is $20,000 (about £11,500) or $30,000 (about £17,000) if they are assisted by a trade union.[8]

Mediation with the TADM is mandatory before bringing a claim before the ECT, except where the mediator is satisfied that there is no reasonable prospect of settling the dispute through mediation.[9] A mediation request must be made within one year for salary-related claims, unless the employee is no longer employed by the organisation when the request must be submitted within six months of their last day of work. For wrongful dismissal claims, the time limit is one month from the date of dismissal.[10] The mediation process itself is swift: in 2024, the

[1] Employment Claims Act 2016, s 3(1) and s 5(1) (ECA 2016). See also Tripartite Alliance for Dispute Management, 'About Us': www.tal.sg/tadm/about.

[2] Reg 12 and sch 1, Employment Claims Regulations 2017. There are also special rules for parties under 18 and parties who are unable to represent themselves because of 'illiteracy or infirmity'.

[3] The fee is $10 if the mediation request does not exceed $10,000; otherwise the fee is $20: reg 7, Employment Claims Regulations 2017.

[4] Interview, 4 July 2025.

[5] By virtue of the Employment (Amendment) Act 2018. Workplace Fairness legislation is being enacted, which would create legal rights against certain forms of discrimination in the workplace, enforced through the ECT: Tripartite Committee on Workplace Fairness, *Building Fairer & More Harmonious Workplaces: Tripartite Committee on Workplace Fairness Final Report*: www.mom.gov.sg/-/media/mom/documents/press-releases/2023/tripartite-committee-on-workplace-fairness-final-report.pdf.

[6] Interview, 4 July 2025.

[7] Interview, 4 July 2025.

[8] Regs 6(b) and 17 Employment Claims Regulations 2017.

[9] s 4(2) ECA 2016.

[10] s 3(2) ECA 2016. Pregnant employees are given two months.

TADM concluded[11] 87 per cent of salary claims within two months[12] and 86 per cent of wrongful dismissal claims within two months.[13]

Mediation is evaluative with the mediator providing 'reality testing for parties' which was seen as a positive approach because 'employment disputes … [are] highly emotive … someone lost their job. They're feeling very emotional about it and it's good that a neutral third party comes in to talk about [it] to tell them where their case stands'.[14] There may be two or three mediation sessions and these can be face to face, online and via email. The process usually takes about two weeks.

If a claim is unresolved after mediation, the mediator must issue a 'claim referral certificate' and refer the case to the ECT.[15] A case conference will be held by the ECT[16] where the tribunal magistrate is 'quite hands on in controlling which witnesses and which documents are produced' and will seek to encourage settlement.[17] Thereafter the case will usually be heard by the ECT – presided over by a tribunal magistrate who must be legally qualified[18] – within a couple of weeks.[19] Between January and August 2022, the median duration to process and conclude ECT cases was five weeks for salary claims and seven weeks for wrongful dismissal.[20] Very few ECT cases were appealed.[21]

B. Evaluation

The success rate for mediation with the TADM is impressive. In 2024, over 80 per cent of the 11,685 employment claims lodged with the Ministry of

[11] A claim is 'concluded' if it is either resolved or referred to the ECT.

[12] Ministry of Manpower, *Employment Standards Report 2024*: www.mom.gov.sg/-/media/mom/documents/press-releases/2025/0730-annex-employment-standards-report-2024.pdf, 8.

[13] ibid, 10.

[14] Interview, 4 July 2025.

[15] s 6 ECA 2016.

[16] There are alternative routes available to trade union members but their use is relatively limited. An employee who is a union member in a non-unionised workplace can apply for mediation through the Tripartite Mediation Framework: Industrial Relations Act 1960, Pt 4A. This operates instead of TADM mediation. If a settlement is not reached, then the claim can proceed to the ECT: O Loh, *Industrial Relations in Singapore: Practice and Perspective* (World Scientific 2018) 279. An employee who is a union member in a unionised workplace can apply for conciliation with the Ministry of Manpower. If a settlement is not reached, they can then apply to the Industrial Arbitration Court: Industrial Relations Act 1960, Pt 5. This Court, established by the Industrial Relations Act 1960, has expertise in resolving collective disputes. Statistics from the Ministry of Manpower suggest that these alternative routes for trade union members are infrequently used. The Ministry of Manpower conciliates around 100 trade disputes per year: Ministry of Manpower, 'Table: Labour Relations 2023: Table E.8': stats.mom.gov.sg/Pages/Labour-Relations-Tables2023.aspx. Around 20 trade disputes are filed with the Industrial Arbitration Court per year: Table E.13. An employee who is a trade union member can instead choose to claim through the ordinary route of the TADM and the ECT.

[17] Interview, 4 July 2025.

[18] s 9(2) ECA 2016; s 2(1) Legal Profession Act 1966; Legal Profession (Qualified Persons) Rules.

[19] Interview, 4 July 2025.

[20] Singapore Parl Debates 20 October 2022, vol 95, sitting 72.

[21] Between January 2021 and November 2023, 74 appeals were filed with the Employment Claims Tribunals for permission to appeal to the High Court. Permission was granted in only four cases: Singapore Parl Debates 10 January 2024, vol 95, sitting 119.

Manpower and the TADM were resolved at the TADM stage.[22] Between January 2021 and November 2023, only 3,110 claims were unresolved after mediation and so were filed at the ECT.[23] The majority of these 3,110 claims were resolved at the case management conference, and only around 30 per cent were fixed for a hearing.[24]

Our interviewees emphasised the strong cultural perspective underpinning the system as a whole: the preservation of ongoing relationships in spite of conflict.[25] Mediation is a modern expression of this historic value and is seen as complementary to, rather than lesser than, adjudication.[26] One interviewee reflected on the 'cultural consensus' to subjugate individual rights to the broader economic aims of the country as a whole which, by necessity, results in a strongly consensus-driven process.[27] This is also reflected in the report relating to the proposed Workplace Fairness (anti-discrimination) legislation, which says that a key aim is to '[p]reserve workplace harmony and maintain a non-litigious workplace culture, with mediation as the preferred approach to resolving disputes' and remedies focusing on educating employers on correct practices and mending the employment relationship where possible.[28] It emphasises that adjudication at the ECT should be a 'last resort'.[29]

However, there is a lacuna in protection for 'white collar' workers. The TADM and ECT work well for lower value claims, which are generally made by workers who are not in the 'Professional, managerial and executive' category of worker. Once someone earns over $4,500 per month (c £2,600) they do not have as many employment rights in Singaporean law (such as limits on working hours) and in any event, the limit in the ECT means that it is not worth their while pursuing a claim. For very high earners, they would have to pursue their claims – for matters such as bonuses, stock options – in the civil courts with all the costs consequences that flow. However, 'white collar' workers are stuck: they cannot afford to bring a civil court case but the ECT process is not worthwhile. So they are increasingly bringing a claim before the ECT and seeking reinstatement as leverage for a settlement above the ECT limit. It was recognised that the system was less successful at protecting their rights.[30]

The Singaporean system is of interest for us in the UK because it indicates that these sorts of quick, resolution-focused processes with an evaluative dimension, work well for lower level or lower value disputes. However, while there is a

[22] Ministry of Manpower, *Employment Standards Report 2024* (n 12) 4.

[23] Ministry of Manpower, *Written Answer to PQ on Breakdown of claims filed at Employment Claims Tribunal from 2021 to 2023* (2024): www.mom.gov.sg/newsroom/parliament-questions-and-replies/2024/0110-written-answer-to-pq-on-breakdown-of-claims-filed-at-ect-from-2021-to-2023.

[24] ibid.

[25] D Anderson, 'The Evolving Concept of Access to Justice in Singapore's Mediation Movement' (2020) 16 *International Journal of Law in Context* 128, 131.

[26] ibid, 133.

[27] Interview, 4 July 2025 (2).

[28] Tripartite Committee on Workplace Fairness, *Final Report* (n 5) 6.

[29] ibid, 8.

[30] Interview, 4 July 2025 (2).

clear cultural aspect to the Singaporean process, it still represents an interesting model utilising speed and a lack of lawyers to achieve resolution in claims of limited financial value. We look now to Australia whose Fair Work Commission has a somewhat broader remit but appears to retain an important focus on speedy resolution.

III. Australia and the Fair Work Commission

A. Jurisdiction

The Fair Work Commission (FWC) has jurisdiction to determine disputes relating to a large number of employment matters under the Fair Work Act, including basic employment standards and independent contractor disputes.[31] It is primarily concerned with unfair dismissals.[32] Claims before the FWC are capped at six months' salary or a set figure whichever is lower, but in practice compensation is usually for about six to eight weeks of the individual's remuneration.[33] In 2014, the FWC was also given jurisdiction to make 'stop bullying' orders[34] and in 2021 to make 'stop' orders in relation to sexual harassment at work.[35] Both of these orders can be made only where the victim remains employed. Initially the orders were preventive rather than remedial, punitive or compensatory.[36] However, in 2023 the FWC was given jurisdiction to address sexual harassment more generally. The FWC now has the power to deal with sexual harassment disputes, regarding both past and future harm, through 'conciliation, mediation, making a recommendation or expressing an opinion'.[37] Where the matter is not resolved, 'the dispute may

[31] Fair Work Act 2009, s 576. See also: Fair Work Commission, *Issues We Help With*: www.fwc.gov.au/issues-we-help; Fair Work Commission, *Benchbook: General Protections* (July 2024): www.fwc.gov.au/documents/benchbooks/general-protections-benchbook.pdf. Federal anti-discrimination law is overseen by the Australian Human Rights Commission which has the power to investigate and conciliate complaints about discrimination and breaches of human rights. On the interplay between Australian anti-discrimination law and labour law, see generally B Gaze and A Chapman, 'The Human Right to Non-discrimination as a Legitimate Part of Workplace Law: Towards Substantive Equality at Work in Australia?' (2013) 29 *International Journal of Comparative Labour Law and Industrial Relations* 355; A Chapman, B Gaze and A Orifici, 'Substantive equality at work: Still elusive under Australia's Fair Work Act' (2017) 30 *Australian Journal of Labour Law* 214.

[32] Fair Work Commission, *Annual Report: Access to Justice 2023–24* (Commonwealth of Australia 2024) 23.

[33] Interview, 11 June 2025.

[34] Pt 6-4B Fair Work Act 2009. See also Fair Work Commission, *Benchbook: Orders to Stop Bullying* (June 2023) 14: www.fwc.gov.au/documents/benchbooks/stop-bullying-benchbook.pdf.

[35] Pt 6-4B Fair Work Act 2009.

[36] Fair Work Commission, *Benchbook: Orders to Stop Sexual Harassment: Transitional Arrangements* (March 2023) 15–16: www.fwc.gov.au/documents/benchbooks/orders-to-stop-sexual-harassment-transitional-benchbook.pdf.

[37] Pt 3-5A Fair Work Act 2009. See also Fair Work Commission, *Benchbook: Sexual Harassment Disputes* (1 October 2024) 23–24: www.fwc.gov.au/documents/benchbooks/sexual-harassment-disputes-benchbook.pdf.

proceed to consent arbitration in the Commission or to court, by a sexual harassment court application'.[38] Stop bullying orders remain preventative only. However, as several interviewees noted, in reality, when a stop order is sought, the discussions in mediation often turn to an exit agreement because 'no one wants to work in a toxic workplace … they just simply cannot tolerate the workplace a moment longer. And so the best thing you can do is to have a conversation about what [does] … the next stage look like'.[39]

B. Process

The FWC process is speedy and highly efficient: 40,190 people lodged an application with the Commission from 2023 to 2024 of which 39,196 matters were finalised in the same year.[40] That year, 50 per cent of all matters were finalised within five weeks, 82 per cent within eight weeks, 90 per cent within 12 weeks, and 96 per cent within 16 weeks.[41] Such timeliness is 'unheard of' for any court or tribunal.[42] Van Gramberg and others note that 'in practice, relatively few people in Australia seek recourse in the courts. The advantage of utilising the Commission is that it is a public service, which does not charge fees. Moreover, it can settle cases more quickly and less formally than the courts'.[43]

An application to the Commission must be made within 21 days of the dismissal taking effect.[44] Although the time limit may be extended, it requires truly exceptional circumstances.[45] A fee must be paid unless the claimant is in serious hardship.[46] It is $89.70 for an unfair dismissal matter (about £43). There is extensive information available to parties on the FWC website and from helpline staff in order to 'get people to self-triage out if it's not the right fit'.[47] From 2023 to 2024, the FWC website had 20.08 million visits, and its helpline handled 124,489 calls.[48] There are detailed FWC 'bench books' to provide guidance to litigants on the law and procedure, alongside extensive online resources.

[38] ibid.

[39] Interview, 11 June 2025.

[40] Fair Work Commission, *Annual Report: Access to Justice 2023–24* (n 32) 24.

[41] ibid, 41. The report states: '[t]imeliness performance results are measured as the time elapsed from the date of lodgement to the date that the finalisation result is entered on the electronic case management file'.

[42] J Catanzariti AM, 'A Reflection on Life and Work as a Vice President of the Fair Work Commission' (2024) 66 *Journal of Industrial Relations* 774, 775.

[43] B Van Gramberg et al, 'Conflict Management in Australia' in W Roche, P Teague and A Colvin et al (eds), *The Oxford Handbook of Conflict Management in Organizations* (Oxford University Press 2014). Though this is not without its critics regarding whether deserving claimants obtain reinstatement or compensation, or whether unmeritorious claims are likely to be rejected entirely: A Stewart, 'Fair Work Australia: The Commission Reborn?' (2011) 53 *Journal of Industrial Relations* 563, 572.

[44] Fair Work Act 2009, s 394(2).

[45] ibid, s 394(3).

[46] ibid, s 395(1).

[47] Interview, 30 June 2025.

[48] Fair Work Commission, *Annual Report: Access to Justice 2023–24* (n 32) 22.

Applications to the FWC can be made online, by email or by post.[49] If the complaint relates to sexual harassment, the applicant will be phoned by staff within the specialist sexual harassment unit, usually on the same day as they apply as part of their 'trauma-informed' approach. In these cases, the employer will also be contacted by phone in advance of the application being sent over to them. In all cases, the employer is required to complete a form outlining their response to the application and, in a dismissal matter, reasons for the dismissal.

The application is then passed to a staff conciliator for a phone (or sometimes video) conciliation[50] lasting a maximum of 90 minutes.[51] Conciliators play a 'more activist role than would a mediator in assisting the parties to resolve an unfair dismissal application',[52] such as 'reality testing'. They are considered to be highly 'interventionist'[53] and highly skilled in helping employers and employees resolve workplace disputes.[54] When phone conciliation was introduced the success rate of conciliation rose to 81 per cent of cases.[55] The FWC website indicates that 75 per cent of unfair dismissal cases are resolved at conciliation.[56]

If the matter does not settle, the application is immediately listed for a preliminary hearing before a Commissioner who will use that meeting to encourage settlement. One interviewee said that he would explain to parties that he was not there to determine a factual or legal dispute but was there to 'facilitate a conversation and to see whether or not I can assist the parties to resolve [the dispute]'. This would be addressed in a 90-minute hearing because 'if I can't get people to agree in 90 minutes, they're not going to agree … so there's no point … flogging a dead horse'.[57] Another interviewee said 'you're not playing for sheep stations [i.e. you're not playing a high stakes game] …. It took a while for me to realise that … what you're really doing is helping people who are in transition from … one job to

[49] Fair Work Commission, 'Apply Now': www.fwc.gov.au/apply-or-lodge/apply-now.

[50] In a 2009–10 survey, the majority of employees and employers considered that phone conciliations for unfair dismissals worked well: J Acton, 'Fair Work Australia: An Accessible, Independent Umpire for Employment Matters' (2011) 53 *Journal of Industrial Relations* 578, 590–91. Some practitioners have argued that the dynamics of face-to-face conciliation meetings are lost over the phone: A Forsyth, 'Workplace Conflict Resolution in Australia: The Dominance of the Public Dispute Resolution Framework and the Limited Role of ADR' (2012) 23 *International Journal of Human Resources Management* 476, 482–83.

[51] This has raised concerns about the FWC 'churning' through as many conciliations in as little time as possible: A See, M Barry and D Peetz, 'The Australian Unfair Dismissal Regime: Exploring How Applications for Unfair Dismissal Remedy Resolve' (2022) 35 *Australian Journal of Labour Law* 27, 46.

[52] Acton cited in Forsyth (n 50) 482.

[53] J Hamberger, 'Workplace Dispute Resolution Procedures in Australia' (PhD thesis, Macquarie University 2015) 158. See also T MacDermott and J Riley, 'Alternative Dispute Resolution and Individual Workplace Rights: The Evolving Role of Fair Work Australia' (2011) 53 *Journal of Industrial Relations* 718, 729.

[54] Van Gramberg et al (n 43) 434.

[55] Forsyth (n 50) 488.

[56] Fair Work Commission, *The process for unfair dismissal claims*: www.fwc.gov.au/job-loss-or-dismissal/unfair-dismissal/process-unfair-dismissal-claims.

[57] Interview, 1 May 2025.

another. They don't want to be in transition. Everyone hates it … But your role is to try and [support them] in that movement'.[58]

Another interviewee highlighted that most Commissioners have substantial experience in the field and were able to be 'no nonsense', taking a very practical approach to issues if they do not make a difference to resolving the dispute.

Where settlement is not achieved in the preliminary hearing, then there will be a hearing to determine the claim, almost invariably by way of arbitration, before a different Commissioner.[59]

C. Evaluation

A number of our interviewees acknowledged that the FWC was providing 'rough justice'[60] but emphasised that 'the purpose of the tribunal is to resolve as quickly as possible and informally as possible disputes in workplaces, not gaze at its own naval to develop the law. I mean, we're not here for ourselves. We're here for the parties'.[61] This emphasis appears particularly apt for simple low value claims. The FWC is not used for complex matters, or for many discrimination claims. That distinction is a strength, and the differentiation of process according to complexity appears to be a key part of the structure that is used. Another key feature was the calibre of the mediators: they were all people with long-standing experience of employment law and practice.

This idea of different approaches or tracks dealing with different types of claims has helped shape our thinking about our proposals for reform in the UK (see chapter thirteen).

IV. New Zealand and its System of Mediation

A. Process

The employment dispute resolution process in New Zealand was established with mediation as the 'pinnacle' of dispute resolution, rather than the Supreme Court.[62] The aim was to have a mediation service that was 'free, fast and fair'.[63] There is

[58] Interview, 11 June 2025.

[59] The FWC may determine disputes via mediation, conciliation, by making a recommendation or expressing an opinion, or by arbitration (including by making any orders it considers appropriate): s 595 Fair Work Act 2009. However, 'In practice, the Commission seeks to settle all such claims by conciliation, but where this fails, it invokes arbitration': Van Gramberg et al (n 43) 434.

[60] Interview, 11 February 2025.

[61] Interview, 1 May 2025.

[62] Interview, 9 July 2025.

[63] M Wilson, Speech in New Zealand Parliament on the Third Reading of the Employment Relations Act (15 August 2000) 586 NZPD 940.

an 'expectation' that 'everyone who had … a personal grievance or … an individual employment dispute would have to do mediation first'.[64] This is embedded in section 3 Employment Relations Act 2000 which provides:

> The object of this Act is –
>
> (a) to build productive employment relationships through the promotion of good faith in all aspects of the employment environment and of the employment relationship –
>
> …
>
> (v) by promoting mediation as the primary problem-solving mechanism other than for enforcing employment standards; and
>
> (vi) by reducing the need for judicial intervention.

The language of employment disputes in New Zealand is important: the Employment Relations Act 2000 refers to an 'employment relationship problem', rather than to a claim. An employment relationship problem is defined broadly, including 'a personal grievance, a dispute, and any other problem relating to or arising out of an employment relationship'.[65] The Supreme Court has emphasised the 'relational approach' of the 2000 Act and that 'employment is more than a market transaction theoretically conducted at arm's length between individuals with equal bargaining power. The result is that while the employment agreement remains very important, it is the employment relationship that is the real focus under the current Act'.[66] This feeds into the emphasis on dispute resolution rather than adjudication.

Mediation is available through the Mediation Service, set up as part of the Ministry of Business, Innovation and Employment. When a person contacts the Mediation Service, they will be given advice about addressing the issues themselves directly with their employer. Alternatively, they may apply to access the early resolution phone service, which is particularly useful where it is a very straightforward matter such as non-payment of the minimum wage. The website suggests that the phone service can be used for a large number of matters.[67] In interviews we were told different things: one person told us that it is aimed at dealing with only the simplest matters;[68] another told us how effective it was for all matters including sexual harassment issues because it enabled parties to resolve matters without being in the same room.[69] Having said that, it appears that it has been used to address a volume of matters that would otherwise have become claims: between January 2022 and June 2022 it dealt with 1,299 employment relationship

[64] Interview, 8 July 2025.
[65] Employment Relations Act 2000, s 5.
[66] *FMV v TZB* [2021] NZSC 102, [46].
[67] See: www.employment.govt.nz/resolving-problems/how-to-resolve-problems/early-resolution.
[68] Interview, 8 July 2025.
[69] Interview, 23 July 2025.

problems.[70] One interviewee told us that the phone service was particularly encouraged where both parties were not represented because 'that's a signal that [the dispute is] not entrenched'.[71]

Where issues cannot be resolved directly by the individual, and they are not resolved by the phone service or the individual chooses to access the mediation service, then they will be allocated a mediation session. An offer of a mediation session will be made by the service within five or six weeks and there is then significant flexibility as to when the session is held. Generally, it is held within two or three weeks of the offer of mediation although at present it is entirely dependent on when the parties are available. One interviewee noted that this was becoming unsustainable for the service because the economic downturn has resulted in an increase in redundancies and higher demand for mediations.[72]

Mediations are undertaken by salaried mediators who are all experienced in employment issues. Mediations are usually held over a three-hour session. They may be in person or online, although since Covid-19 they have been online. The legislation provides that it is recognised that 'the person who provides mediation services can manage any mediation process actively'.[73] Moreover, the guidance produced by the Mediation Service states that mediators will support parties to achieve a resolution and that they will 'provide an assessment of the risks if the problem is not resolved and proceeds further'.[74] An interviewee described it as providing a 'robust risk assessment'. Research by Morris suggests that mediators 'use a variety of styles within any given mediation and also from mediation to mediation. This fluid approach is one of the strengths of this statutory regime, but it does breach the theoretical foundations of some mediation styles'.[75] Moreover, in interviews with Morris, he said: 'Many mediators stressed that they use different styles in different circumstances and that all mediators should be familiar with the full range'.[76]

Some commentators have raised concerns that 'mediation was more akin to an exit settlement negotiation when the employment relationship had ended' than a mediation with a variety of possible outcomes.[77] The statistics support that view: about 60 per cent of applicants to the service are still in employment when they make their application but about 80 per cent are not employed at the end of mediation.[78]

[70] E Rasmussen and D Anderson, 'The changing face of public dispute resolution in New Zealand' (2023) 54 *Industrial Relations* 341, 352.

[71] Interview, 23 July 2025.

[72] Interview, 23 July 2025.

[73] Employment Relations Act 2000, s 143(da).

[74] See: www.employment.govt.nz/resolving-problems/how-to-resolve-problems/mediation.

[75] G Morris, 'Eclecticism versus Purity: Mediation Styles Used in New Zealand Employment Disputes' (2015) 33 *Conflict Resolution Quarterly* 203, 209.

[76] ibid, 217.

[77] Rasmussen and Anderson (n 70) 346 and 352.

[78] Interview, 23 July 2025.

Parties may be represented in the mediation and one interviewee estimated that about 70 per cent of parties are represented.[79] The success rates for mediation are impressive: in 2023/24, a total of 18,915 employment dispute resolutions were delivered, including 4,580 mediations and 2,454 early resolutions.[80] A settlement rate of 67 per cent was recorded in relation to the mediations. There were 12,266 records of settlement received over the year with 94 per cent completed in five days.

There is no obligation to go through mediation before lodging a claim before the Employment Relations Authority (the Authority) but it is strongly encouraged. Section 159 Employment Relations Act 2000 provides that when a matter comes before the Authority for determination, the Authority

> (a) must … first consider whether an attempt has been made to resolve the matter by the use of mediation; and
> (b) must direct that mediation or further mediation, as the case may require, be used before the Authority investigates the matter unless there are specified circumstances, and
> (c) must, in the course of investigating any matter, consider from time to time, as the Authority thinks fit, whether to direct the parties to use mediation.

The circumstances where mediation will not be directed are when mediation will not 'contribute constructively to resolving the matter', is not in the public interest, will undermine the urgent or interim nature of the proceedings, or will be otherwise impractical or inappropriate in the circumstances. If mediation is directed then parties are obliged to comply and 'attempt in good faith to reach an agreed settlement of their differences'.

Where mediation has not been attempted, the Authority will usually refer a case back to mediation. Even where parties have previously attempted mediation, 'if there's been a problem with the mediation' or 'it's been online mediation', or 'if one party or other hasn't been represented … has had a change of representation, or … has had a change of heart' then the Authority will also refer the case back to mediation.[81]

If a case cannot be resolved by mediation, then the Authority will hold an investigation meeting and then issue a determination of the dispute. We consider the adjudicative function of the Authority further in chapter nine.

B. Evaluation

There is very little literature that criticises the New Zealand approach. However, Dolder raises concerns that the 'political agenda' encouraging mediation may have

[79] Interview, 8 July 2025.
[80] Ministry of Business, Innovation and Employment, *Annual Report 2023/24* (Crown Copyright 2024) 23.
[81] Interview, 9 July 2025.

resulted in mediators becoming 'susceptible to procedural pressure to become dealmakers protected by a cloak of confidentiality – a far cry from the neutral facilitators they were intended to be'.[82] In 2011 Lafferty and May identified a lack of knowledge about dispute resolution 'concentrated among the low paid, new workers, part-timers, non-union members and those without a formal contract – that is, the most vulnerable members of the workforce'.[83] They raised concerns about the individualisation of disputes when union involvement might be more successful.

However, Judge Beck, a judge in the Employment Court, was positive about mediation and how accessible it is to parties who are not represented. He noted that this is particularly important in the New Zealand context because 'the overwhelming number of [Kiwi businesses] are small businesses. This is defined as organisations with fewer than 20 employees. There are approximately 530,000 small businesses in New Zealand representing 97 per cent of all organisations; they contribute to 29 per cent of the country's employment'.[84]

In terms of the mediation process, it is notable that representation is permitted and does not appear to present difficulties in achieving resolution of disputes. Once again, the disputes are generally at the less complex end of the spectrum and are primarily focused on a financial resolution of a dismissal claim. Speed is of the essence. The use of experienced professionals as mediators appears to be a significant part of the reason for its success.

V. Conclusions

These international examples are instructive in four respects.

First, the single access point in New Zealand is particularly attractive. Having one body with whom individuals interact would simplify matters considerably, particularly if that body could provide them with information and basic advice and thereafter triage the issues into the correct route. Given the significant number of litigants in person in the UK employment tribunal system, that early advice and triage would be invaluable. Moreover, cases could be more efficiently directed to the body which could assist with the resolution of the issues. This may be the Fair Work Agency for the enforcement of some rights. It may be into particular forms of dispute resolution. An early triage system would enable claims to be

[82] C Dolder, 'The contribution of mediation to workplace justice' (2004) 33 *Industrial Law Journal* 320, 329.

[83] G Lafferty and R May, 'Legislation, mediation and unions: New Zealand's Employment Relations Act 2000' (2011) Industrial Relations Centre, Victoria University of Wellington research paper: www.wgtn.ac.nz/som/research/dhc-publtns/DHCLegislationMediation.pdf, 5.

[84] Judge K Beck, 'Employment Institutions and their contribution to better work stories' paper presented to Auckland University Employment Law Class, May 2021: www.courtsofnz.govt.nz/publications/speeches-and-papers/employment-institutions-and-their-contribution-to-better-work-stories.

filtered into the appropriate non-court dispute resolution mechanism whereby the particular method used depended on the circumstances and complexity of the case. For example, phone-based conciliation may be appropriate for more straightforward claims but a more substantial mediation service may be more appropriate for potential complex discrimination or whistleblowing claims.

Second, all three systems considered in this chapter are based on speedy resolution. There is a significant value to disputes being resolved swiftly so that people do not become entrenched.

Third, mediation is mandatory, or where it is not strictly mandatory the subsequent adjudicative tribunal will refer the parties back to mediation where it has not taken place. This means that mediation – or other non-court dispute resolution – is front and centre of the process; it is the 'pinnacle' of the system, rather than an optional extra. We were particularly attracted by the statutory underpinning for this approach in section 3 of New Zealand's Employment Relations Act 2000.

Fourth, the mediation approach that is used by all three models is 'evaluative', 'reality testing', 'interventionist' and 'practical', conducted by experienced professionals. The sense we got was that the systems all worked because mediators operated in a fundamentally different way from being a 'post box'. This was a key criticism of Acas early conciliation by the participants in our empirical study and it is striking that the opposite model is used in all three countries with great success. Equally, the use of trauma-informed mediation was important in Australia when dealing with sexual harassment. That is of note to ensure that the emotional aspects of the dispute are recognised and addressed.

A detailed analysis of recommendations going forward is addressed in chapter thirteen.

PART III

The Tribunal Litigation Process

In Part II of this book we looked at the burdens on the system caused by the increased volume and complexity of cases, and whether it is possible to consider alternative approaches to resolving disputes before starting litigation, mainly through alternative dispute resolution (ADR). In Part III of the book, we look more closely at the litigation process itself to identify how it can be made more efficient and effective for all participants, including those who are representing themselves. In chapter seven we describe the current system and, drawing from our participant data and academic literature, we consider the issues with the current system. In chapters eight and nine we look at other jurisdictions in the UK and elsewhere to see if there are lessons which can be learned.

We note, in particular, that the forms that parties use to make and respond to a claim are the same irrespective of the type of claim that is brought.[1] The substantive section of the form is an open-ended text box requiring the claimant to set out their claims. This often results in a lengthy narrative that may or may not identify legal claims requiring considerable case management to ensure that the parties and the tribunal understand the specific case that they are addressing. To date the use of generative AI has exacerbated the problem, enabling litigants in person to write lengthy forms covering every possible claim. However, we also think that a dedicated AI package might provide the solution.

The process by which parties go from making a claim and response to having a final hearing is long and laborious. Although the process is intended to help all claimants, including litigants in person, our research overwhelmingly found that employment tribunal procedures are not really accessible to litigants in person, partly because the processes are complex and partly because the vocabulary used is not understood by litigants in person – what is a 'bundle' and what is 'disclosure'? In addition, litigants in person often become deeply and emotionally involved in the dispute. This 'emotional baggage' makes it difficult for them to engage objectively and within the constraints of the process that must be followed. Consequently, the efficiency of the process suffers.

Administrative systems are very stretched in the tribunal system, with our focus group participants identifying significant difficulties in trying to communicate with staff to be informed of case management decisions. Additional resources – particularly administrative resources but also judicial resources – would make

[1] See: assets.publishing.service.gov.uk/media/65bcbd214a666f000d1747ba/ET1_0224.pdf.

an enormous difference. Although cases are 'tracked' (short, standard or open),[2] they are all addressed in essentially the same way. There are, however, significant regional differences in how bundles and witness statements are dealt with. We discuss the current issues in chapter seven.

Thinking beyond the need for further financial resources, we argue in this part of the book that there is a need for a new approach to the claim and response forms. We have considered a number of different options that are utilised both in other civil court jurisdictions in the UK and other countries. Specifically, we explore the different claim forms in civil litigation and family court disputes. We have considered an AI model that appears to be particularly effective at producing a timeline and identifying the legal claims within a narrative. We also examine the forms that are used to start employment claims in Australia, New Zealand, Canada and the Republic of Ireland (chapter eight).

We argue that the ET1 and ET3 forms need to be radically remodelled. The forms need to ask clear, specific questions that depend on the answers that have previously been given. Legal terminology needs to be avoided and simple language used. There should be a focus from the outset on the remedy that is sought, with specific questions being asked so that a schedule of loss can be produced automatically. Parties should be asked to upload certain documents according to the claims made. An AI model, such as that used by Valla, should be carefully evaluated as an alternative with seemingly significant possibilities.

Moving on to the hearing itself, we have considered the use of track allocations and the different procedural rules that flow from that tracking in personal injury claims. We argue that there needs to be an acceptance that high value, complex claims, usually involving discrimination and whistleblowing, are essentially the same as a high court trial in terms of the volume and complexity of evidence. Therefore, cases should be tracked and for the most complex cases, there should be similarly strict procedural rules (chapter nine). These cases require careful, detailed determination such that a lengthy written judgment will usually be appropriate.

However, the most straightforward and low value claims do not need this level of procedural control and we recommend that a very much simplified process should be used, as it is in Australia and New Zealand (chapter nine). This should allow parties – if they have been unable to resolve matters at the short phone mediation session recommended in Part II – to appear before a single judge within a matter of weeks for a short online hearing to consider the issues with a ruling through an *ex tempore* judgment. This would fit with the original objectives of tribunals to deliver quick, cheap accessible justice. The need to avoid technicalities should be expressly prescribed.

The cases in the middle are more difficult because there will inevitably be more documentation, and a greater need to hear from more witnesses. There may be cases where their value is limited but they remain highly complex. Equally, they

[2] See further ch 7.

may be of lower value and lesser complexity. However, we argue that limits should be applied. Drawing on the family court rules, we argue that there should be clear and specific rules delineating what evidence should be disclosed and included in a bundle and there should be limits on the length of bundles and of witness statements (chapter nine). There should be a general power for the tribunal to extend those limits where appropriate but the usual process should be contained and restricted. Extensions should be the exception.

Moreover, we agree with the participants in our research that there should be strong case management of these claims, including limiting the number of issues that can be addressed: judges should be given the power to restrict claims to a certain number of issues. However, this should be provided for alongside an ability for parties to opt into a higher track if they want all of their issues to be addressed: this would necessitate a more formal structure to deal with a multitude of issues. Equally, as in personal injury claims, parties may opt into a lower track by limiting their claims.

Alongside these changes to the control of evidence and case management, and to adjudication, we consider that there needs to be easy access to alternative methods of resolution throughout the process. Currently there are a number of different options which are discussed in chapter ten, but there are tight controls on when they can be accessed, primarily because of resourcing. We recommend a model of non-court dispute resolution similar to that found in the family courts, with mandatory early neutral evaluation in the most complex cases, either within the tribunal system or accessed privately by the parties.

Recommendations

We therefore make the following recommendations:

1. The ET1 and ET3 forms should be remodelled. Questions should avoid legal labels, use simple language and be specific and precise. Previous answers should determine the questions that are asked next so that they are dependent on the claims that are brought. Answer boxes should be restricted to a certain number of words to help parties remain focused on key issues. Specific questions about remedy should be asked so that a schedule of loss is produced at the outset. Parties should be asked to upload certain documents according to the claims made.
2. An AI model to convert a narrative into a timeline of events and specific legal claims should be carefully evaluated.
3. There should be an increase in the current £25,000 limit on the contractual jurisdiction in employment tribunals to £100,000.
4. There should be statements, enshrined in statute, that tribunals, especially in the less complex cases, are intended to be quick, cheap and accessible

fora as well as a statutory presumption that tribunals should be the last resort.

5. Cases should be allocated to one of three tracks by a legal officer. Non-court dispute resolution should be actively encouraged on every track.
   a. Track 1 should deal with claims for less than six months' earnings. This track would deal with matters informally, with little additional documentation than that lodged with the claim and response forms and would be heard online before a judge for no more than three hours.
   b. Track 2 would deal with claims for more than six months' earnings and less than two years' earnings. Standard directions should be given with strict limits on the number of pages for a bundle and the length of witness statements. Track 2 cases should be subject to rigorous case management whereby the judge can require parties to pick their best five or ten points, or to limit the case so that it can be heard within a maximum of five days. Strike outs and deposit orders should be more readily used. A half day early neutral evaluation hearing should be listed before a judge after exchange of witness statements. The judgment should be given orally, with parties required to pay for a transcript of the judgment if they seek it.
   c. Track 3 would deal with claims for more than two years' earnings or where the claimant chooses to bring their claim under this regime. These claims should, where possible, be case managed by the same judge throughout the life of the case. Directions should be made with sanctions for non-compliance. Mandatory touch points should operate throughout the litigation process when parties and the tribunal are required to consider non court dispute resolution. Mediation – including transformative mediation – should be encouraged, together with private early neutral evaluation (ENE) hearings. After witness statement exchange, a one-day ENE hearing should be held, unless a private ENE has been conducted. Orders for disclosure, bundles and witness statements should follow the Civil Procedure Rules with limits determined by the judge case managing the claim. These claims should be heard by experienced judges with the appropriate ticket and a written judgment should be produced.
6. Claims involving ten or more claimants should usually be managed as Track 3 cases. Specific rules should be developed to manage these claims including rules about the selection of test claimants and addressing disclosure proportionately.

7

The Litigation Process in the Employment Tribunal System

I. Introduction

In this chapter we look at the litigation process as it now stands and the problems with it. The major concerns for participants in our study were the delays in the system, variations in approach to case management across different tribunal regions, and a perception of many unmeritorious claims blocking the system. Another issue was the difficulty that litigants, particularly those without legal representation, had in expressing their claims as legal claims, rather than as a lengthy narrative of the wrongs that they perceived had been done to them. So how can the wide variety of type of claim – in terms of complexity, importance and value – be managed appropriately?

We therefore explore how the litigation process operates from the initial steps of making and responding to a claim (section II) through the case management process (section III), dealing with unmeritorious claims (section IV), interim applications and preliminary hearings (section V), preparations for the final hearing (section VI) and the final hearing itself (section VII).

II. Initial Steps in Making and Responding to a Claim

A. Making a Claim

A claimant must make a claim using the form ET1. Rule 12(1) of the Employment Tribunal Procedure Rules 2024 (ET Procedure Rules 2024) specifies the required contents of the form, including information such as each party's name and address and the Acas early conciliation certificate number.[1] Two or more claimants can use

[1] Employment Tribunal Procedure Rules 2024, SI 2024/1155, r 12(1) (ET Procedure Rules 2024).

the same ET1 if their claims give rise to common or related issues of fact or law, or it is otherwise reasonable.[2]

In England and Wales and Scotland, the substantive questions about the claim are at question 8 which starts with a multiple-choice question (see fig 7.1):

Figure 7.1 ET1 claim form[3]

8.1* Please indicate the type of claim you are making by ticking one or more of the boxes below.

- ☐ I was unfairly dismissed (including constructive dismissal)
- ☐ I was discriminated against on the grounds of:
  - ☐ age
  - ☐ race (including colour, nationality, and ethnic or national origins)
  - ☐ gender reassignment
  - ☐ disability
  - ☐ pregnancy or maternity
  - ☐ marriage or civil partnership
  - ☐ sexual orientation
  - ☐ sex (including equal pay)
  - ☐ religion or belief
- ☐ I am making a whistleblowing claim including dismissal or any other unfair treatment after whistleblowing
- ☐ I am claiming a redundancy payment
- ☐ I am owed
  - ☐ notice pay
  - ☐ holiday pay
  - ☐ arrears of pay
  - ☐ other payments
- ☐ I am making another type of claim which the Employment Tribunal can deal with.
  (Please state the nature of the claim. Examples are provided in the Guidance.)

The claimant is then asked, at 8.2, to 'set out the background and details of your claim in the space below'. In complex claims, a separate Particulars of Complaint document is often attached and referred to instead. The Employment Appeal Tribunal (EAT) has warned parties against drafting 'narrative style' particulars that read like a witness statement.[4]

Section 9 asks the individual what they want if their claim is successful (see fig 7.2).

[2] r 11(1) ET Procedure Rules 2024.
[3] See: assets.publishing.service.gov.uk/media/65bcbd214a666f000d1747ba/ET1_0224.pdf.
[4] *C v D* (2019) UKEAT/0132/19.

Figure 7.2 Question relating to remedy on ET1

9 What do you want if your claim is successful?

9.1 Please tick the relevant box(es) to say what you want if your claim is successful:

☐ If claiming unfair dismissal, to get your old job back and compensation (reinstatement)

☐ If claiming unfair dismissal, to get another job with the same employer or associated employer and compensation (re-engagement)

☐ Compensation only

☐ If claiming discrimination, a recommendation (see Guidance).

9.2 What compensation or remedy are you seeking?

If you are claiming financial compensation please give as much detail as you can about how much you are claiming and how you have calculated this sum. (Please note any figure stated below will be viewed as helpful information but it will not restrict what you can claim and you will be permitted to revise the sum claimed later. See the Guidance for further information about how you can calculate compensation). **If you are seeking any other remedy from the Tribunal which you have not already identified please also state this below.**

The official guidance document is fairly limited.[5] It notes that a claim cannot be accepted unless names, addresses and the Acas early conciliation certificate number are provided. It states that a claimant 'must also give sufficient details of your claim so that the tribunal and respondent can understand what your claim is about'. The section dealing with question 8 simply tells a claimant to 'tick the appropriate box or boxes to say what you are complaining about' and to 'give the background and details of your complaint'. There is then more specific guidance for common claims, such as unfair dismissal which says:

> Please use the box provided to explain the background to the dismissal and give any other information you think would be helpful to use. If you disagree with the reason the respondent gave for dismissing you, please say what you think the reason was. You should describe the events which led up to your dismissal and describe how the dismissal took place, including dates, times and the people involved. If you are claiming that the respondent's actions led you to resign and leave your job (constructive dismissal), please explain in detail the circumstances surrounding this.

The guidance on discrimination sets out the different protected characteristics, explains that it covers 'all areas of employment' and asks the claimant to

> describe the incidents which you believe amounted to discrimination, the dates of these incidents and the people who were involved. Explain in what way you believe you were discriminated against. If you are complaining about discrimination when you applied for a job, please say what job you were applying for. If you are complaining about more than one type of discrimination, please provide separate details of the act (or acts) of

[5] See: www.gov.uk/government/publications/making-a-claim-to-an-employment-tribunal-t420/making-a-claim-to-an-employment-tribunal-t420.

discrimination. You should describe how you have been affected by the events you are complaining about. If you are unable to give the dates of all the incidents you are complaining about, you must at least give the date of the last incident or tell us if the discrimination is ongoing.

There are some small differences with the ET1 in Northern Ireland. The question about details of the claim being made is found at question 9 (see fig 7.3).

Figure 7.3 ET1 form in Northern Ireland[6]

9 Details of your claim

9.1 Please indicate the type of claim you are making by ticking all the boxes which apply to your claim

I was unfairly dismissed (including constructive dismissal) ☐

I was discriminated against on the grounds of:

If you select religious belief/political opinion, we will regard your complaint as a matter for the Fair Employment Tribunal which deals with unlawful discrimination on these grounds.

Age		Disability		Equal Pay	
Part-time working		Race		Religious belief/ political opinion	
Sex		Sexual Orientation		Whistleblowing	

I am claiming a redundancy payment ☐

I am owed

Arrears of pay	£	Breach of contract	£	Holiday pay	£
Notice pay	£	Other *(please specify)*			£

I am making another type of claim which the Employment Tribunal can deal with ☐

Please state the nature of the claim

9.2 If you are complaining about discrimination

Please give the date(s) on which the matter about which you are complaining happened. Where discrimination occurred on a number of occasions give the most recent date when it happened. If you wish to give additional dates you can include this at 9.4 below. Please also indicate if the discrimination is ongoing.

Date ☐☐ / ☐☐ / ☐☐☐☐ Ongoing ☐

9.3 You only need to answer this question if you are complaining about discrimination on the grounds of religious belief/ political opinion.

When did you first know of the matter about which you are complaining? ☐☐ / ☐☐ / ☐☐☐☐

9.4* It is important that you provide us with details to support the complaints you have selected at 9.1.

Details should include:

A description of the act(s) complained of

When the act(s) took place

The names of the people involved

Why you believe the action was unlawful

Why you believe you are entitled to claim for payment that you say is owed

The amount of any payment you believe is owed

If you are complaining about discrimination in recruitment - what job did you apply for

If you are complaining about discrimination by way of victimisation, the type of discrimination that you are relying on e.g. sex, race, disability etc

[6] See: www.employmenttribunalsni.co.uk/files/employmenttribunalsni/media-files/ET1-Claim-Form-Jan-2020.pdf.

Question 9.2, which applies only to discrimination claims, requires the most recent date of discrimination to be given, rather than this being something that must be given in the free-text box. Question 9.4 provides a list of specific details that should be provided in the free-text box, which is very similar to the information in the England and Wales and Scotland guidance document. It may be that the level of specificity in 9.2, and the detail being on the face of the form in 9.4, is more helpful to claimants.

Once the form is completed, it must be submitted to the tribunal in accordance with any Practice Direction.[7] There are three main methods for submitting ET1:

(1) online, using either –
  (a) an online form;[8]
  (b) the MyHMCTS platform, if the claimant is represented; or
  (c) the CitizenUI platform, if the claimant is a litigant in person;
(2) by post; or
(3) in person at designated regional tribunal offices.[9]

If the claimant is professionally represented and the representative is going to submit online, the MyHMCTS platform must be used.[10] The ET1 cannot simply be sent by email.[11]

Upon receipt, the tribunal will check various matters and decide if the ET1 should be accepted or rejected. For example, staff will check whether the correct form has been used with the correct information;[12] whether the claim is outside the ET's jurisdiction;[13] and whether the claim cannot sensibly be responded to or is otherwise an abuse of process.[14] If the tribunal rejects the ET1, it will send a notice of rejection to the claimant.[15] The claimant can apply to the tribunal to reconsider its rejection within 14 days.[16]

A number of participants in our research suggested that the ET1 form needed to be restructured so that it is more conducive to focusing on what the claim is and what the claimant seeks to achieve through the claim. We were told that the current blank box invites irrelevant information. It was suggested that more

[7] r 83(2) ET Procedure Rules 2024. The Scottish Practice Direction has various differences that are noted below but as regards submission of the ET1, there are no material differences.

[8] See: www.employmenttribunals.service.gov.uk.

[9] Practice Direction (England & Wales) – Presentation of Claims (2 March 2020) para 4.

[10] Courts and Tribunals Judiciary, Letter from Judge Susan Walker and Judge Barry Clarke (10 May 2024). The MyHMCTS and CitizenUI platforms are being rolled out in Scotland but are not available in Northern Ireland.

[11] r 83(1)(c) ET Procedure Rules 2024.

[12] ibid, r 12(1).

[13] ibid, r 13(1)(a).

[14] ibid, r 13(1)(b).

[15] ibid r 12(2) and 13(5).

[16] ibid, r 14.i.

focused questions could be used to guide claimants more clearly, including being more specific about the remedy they wanted.[17]

Participants also suggested that the form should be more upfront about the level of detail that was required, with clearer questions asking claimants to specify what happened, by whom, when and why it happened. Participants said that greater detail on the form could help to reduce the need for further and better particulars, or lengthy preliminary hearings trying to understand the claims.[18] It was suggested that one way of achieving this was to create a 'smart' electronic ET1 form, using flowcharts where relevant questions appeared based on the answers or choices ticked by the claimant in previous answers.[19] We consider this further in chapter eight.

Participants recognised that the level of legal costs were a significant barrier to litigants obtaining good advice to help them to produce clear and focused ET1s. They said that litigants in person often struggled to be objective and to detach their emotions about their situation from the facts. They tended to overemphasise the motives they perceived to be at play, rather than the specific legal requirements that had to be shown for a claim. Given how complex the law is and the specialised knowledge that is required, participants said that litigants in person struggled to articulate their claims. Often it was noted that litigants in person overcomplicate their claims or fail properly to articulate them and it was a real challenge to deal with claims, particularly where they are not necessarily weak but are simply badly pleaded.[20]

Some participants suggested that a schedule of loss should also be provided with the ET1 and evidence of what the claimant had done to mitigate their loss.[21] However, other participants said that claimants were unlikely to have sufficient information at this early stage to be able to prepare these documents.[22] It was also suggested 'smart' templates could be used where claimants would be required to fill in only specific fields of information and the schedule would be calculated automatically from that information. It was suggested that this would be particularly helpful for litigants in person who struggle to know what compensation they can claim or how to calculate it.[23]

In addition to the issues relating to the ET1, participants also reported that it takes around two to three months to process a claim. Participants said that the delay in processing a claim, and particularly in having a claim assigned with a case number, prevented the parties from taking any action to progress the proceedings. Consequently, claimants cannot make any requests of the tribunal

[17] Focus Groups: 25 November 2024, 29 November 2024, 10 December 2024 (1.30pm).
[18] Focus Groups: 12 November 2024, 20 November 2024 (12pm).
[19] Focus Groups: 20 November 2024 (3pm), 25 November 2024.
[20] Focus Groups: 12 November 2024, 25 November 2024.
[21] Focus Groups: 10 December 2024 (1.30pm), 25 November 2024.
[22] Focus Group, 10 December 2024 (1.30pm).
[23] Focus Group, 25 November 2024.

during this period including updating their contact details. This is particularly challenging in group litigation where claimants are then prevented from making a request to withdraw members of the group claim who do not wish to proceed. Furthermore, participants said that, while service of the claim on the respondent was awaited, it made it difficult to have discussions between the parties about resolution without knowing the claim number or the details of the claim. They said that having these long periods of inaction was hugely unproductive and the longer the adversarial process continued the more the dispute intensified.[24]

B. Responding to a Claim

If the tribunal accepts the ET1, it will send a copy to the respondent, together with a blank ET3 form[25] on which the respondent must respond. The ET3 contains a number of boxes, and space for the respondent to set out its Grounds of Resistance. The substantive question is 6.1 which asks the respondent to tick yes or no to the question 'Do you contest all or part of the claim?' And then 'If Yes, please set out the facts which you rely on to contest the claim'. The Northern Ireland ET3 has more user-friendly language: 'If Yes, please set out the facts which you intend to rely on to defend the claim'.[26] The respondent must respond to each allegation made by the claimant in the ET1,[27] and should set out their own positive case on the facts in issue.[28]

There is no guidance document for England and Wales and Scotland about how to complete the ET3. The Northern Ireland guidance says that respondents who are defending the claim should

> explain the grounds on which you are resisting the claim. If the claim is about more than one issue, you will need to respond to each issue. Please explain what points you disagree with and give information to support your argument. If your organisation dismissed the claimant, explain the procedure you followed before the actual dismissal and give full reasons why you dismissed the claimant. If the claim is about discrimination, please provide a response to each of the statements made by the claimant and describe the action you took when the claimant raised the matter with you. Give full reasons if you disagree that your organisation owes the claimant money or if you

[24] Focus Groups: 19 November 2024 (12pm), 20 November 2024 (12pm), 10 December 2024 (9.30am), 10 December 2024 (1.30pm).

[25] ET Procedure Rules 2024, r 16(1): assets.publishing.service.gov.uk/media/65bcbec74a666f00101747b6/ET3_0224.pdf.

[26] See: www.employmenttribunalsni.co.uk/files/employmenttribunalsni/media-files/ET3-Response-Form-Jan-2020.pdf at question 8.2.

[27] r 18(1)(b)(iii) ET Procedure Rules 2024.

[28] *C v D* UKEAT/0132/19, [12].

disagree with the amount the claimant expects. At this stage you should not send any documents to support your response.

The respondent is usually required to reply within 28 days of the date that the tribunal sent the ET1 to the respondent.[29] However, the respondent can apply to the tribunal for an extension of time if necessary.[30]

If the respondent fails to use the ET3 form,[31] fails to provide the required information,[32] or lodges their response after the deadline has expired,[33] the tribunal will reject the ET3. The tribunal will then send a notice of rejection to the respondent.[34] The respondent can apply for reconsideration of the rejection within 14 days of the date of notice of the rejection.[35]

If the respondent fails to reply in time or does not contest the case, then Rule 22 of the ET Procedure Rules 2024, supplemented by Presidential Guidance,[36] applies and the following process takes place:

(a) The claimant does not generally need to make an application.
(b) The employment judge reviews all the material presently available. If they require more information, they might request further information from the parties.
(c) The employment judge must then decide whether to –
    (i) issue a judgment in full for all claims and remedy;
    (ii) issue a judgment in full for all liability issues and schedule a remedy hearing;
    (iii) issue a judgment in part; or
    (iv) arrange a final hearing for outstanding parts of the claim and make case management orders.

If the Employment Tribunal (ET) arranges a final hearing for all or part of the claim, the respondent is entitled to receive notice of the hearing. However, their entitlement to participate in the hearing may be limited.

Participants noted that it is not necessarily only claimants who act in person but also some respondents. Many of the same difficulties in completing the forms and articulating the issues then arise with respondents failing to be sufficiently specific about why they are defending the claim. In chapter eight we look at how claims are lodged in the civil and family courts to draw lessons from those jurisdictions.

[29] r 17(1) ET Procedure Rules 2024.
[30] ibid, r 21.
[31] ibid, r 18(1)(a).
[32] ibid, r 18(1)(b).
[33] ibid, r 19(1).
[34] ibid, rr 18(2) and 19(3).
[35] ibid, r 20.
[36] Presidential Guidance (England & Wales) – Rule 21 Judgments.

III. Case Management Processes

A. The Sift Stage

If the ET accepts the ET3, it will send a copy of the response to all other parties[37] and then proceed to the sift stage. During this stage, the tribunal must consider all the documents it has received to confirm whether there are arguable complaints and defences that are within its jurisdiction. For this purpose, a judge can order a party to provide further information.[38] They may also propose judicial mediation or another form of Alternative Dispute Resolution (ADR), though in practice it appears to be rare for this to be proposed at this early stage.[39] If the judge considers either that the tribunal lacks jurisdiction to consider the claim, or that the claim or response, or part thereof, has no reasonable prospect of success, the tribunal will send a note to the parties explaining its view and ordering that the claim or response will be dismissed on a specified date, unless the tribunal receives written explanations as to why the claim or response should not be dismissed. If the tribunal does not receive written representations before the specified date, the claim or response, or part thereof, stands dismissed without further order. If the tribunal does receive written representations in time, the judge must either permit the claim to proceed or fix a hearing to decide whether the claim should proceed. If the claim is permitted to proceed, the tribunal must make a case management order.[40] If the response is dismissed, then Rule 22 of the ET Procedure Rules 2024 applies and the respondent is treated as if they failed to make a response within the required time limit.[41]

Once the ET1 has been accepted, it will be allocated to the short track, the standard track, or the open track.

B. Tracks for Different Cases

The tracks are a matter of internal administrative practice; they are not governed by the tribunal's rules of procedure.[42] Track allocation influences the case management orders that are made (see Table 7.1).

[37] r 23 ET Procedure Rules 2024.
[38] ibid, r 27(1).
[39] ibid, r 27(2).
[40] ibid, rr 28 and 29.
[41] ibid, r 29(6).
[42] Although they are occasionally mentioned in Presidential Guidance.

Table 7.1 Use of track allocation in the employment tribunal[43]

Allocation	**Short track**	**Standard track**	**Open track**
Typical claims	Unpaid wages, notice pay, redundancy pay	Ordinary unfair dismissal claims	Discrimination and whistleblowing claims
Typical hearing length	1-2 hours	1-2 days	2 days or longer
Typical case management orders	Case management orders are probably unnecessary	Standard case management orders are made on receipt of the claim. The parties may apply for a case management preliminary hearing if they want different orders.	A case management preliminary hearing is listed at the sift stage. Parties are asked to complete a case management agenda at least seven days before the hearing.
When is the final hearing typically listed?	Final hearing listed on receipt of the claim	Final hearing listed on receipt of the claim. If the judicial sift reveals complexity, the listing may be revisited.	Some regions list the final hearing on receipt of the claim; other regions wait until the case management hearing.

Participants in our research suggested that the current use of different tracks could be developed so that each track was dealt with substantially differently; at present the only real difference between the tracks is that open cases go to a case management hearing. Participants considered that different judges and different administrative staff could be assigned to different tracks so that there was greater use of specialist judges for the more complex cases.[44] Some participants raised concerns that while pay and wages claims may appear to be simple, they may be more significant for a business than appears at first sight. They noted that a dispute about a small amount of money in one case might apply more broadly across the business and have significant costs implications.[45] Such a case may not then be suitable for a low value track and flexibility is needed in the system to enable such a case to be addressed on a different track.

[43] Material collated by authors from: I Smith et al, *Harvey on Industrial Relations and Employment Law* (Issue 320, LexisNexis 2024) Division PI, para 300.01; IDS Employment Law Handbooks, Volume 10 – Practice and Procedure I: Employment Tribunals (Sweet & Maxwell, 2025) paras 4.76 and 12.18–12.24.

[44] Focus Group, 10 December 2024 (1.30pm).

[45] Focus Groups: 25 November 2024, 10 December 2024 (9.30am).

Various participants also said that there needed to be a separate track for large-scale multiple claims, that is, group litigation. It was suggested that 'group claim hubs' could be established where group claims could be sent for processing, case management and hearings to enable administrative staff to be utilised who have particular experience in dealing with the greater complexities that arise.[46]

More significantly, participants also suggested not just that there was a need for different tracks but also there was a need for different adjudication (and enforcement approaches)[47] to be taken in relation to different types of claim.[48] Hodges has taken a similar view:

> [D]ifferent tracks, involving different approaches, may be productive for different case types. Initial, independent, expert and authoritative evaluation may be all that is necessary for the more straightforward claim types, such as those involving money (deductions, NMW and some equal pay cases), or many breach of contract cases. The challenge in some more complex types is how to avoid the need to prepare, explain, evaluate and determine differences between expert views, such as in some age discrimination or working conditions cases. If the expertise is with a panel rather than with a single judge, would that take care of the vast majority of cases, save that the panel could have the discretion to call on experts on particular issues in some cases? In relation to cases involving extended narratives (eg. unfair dismissal and discrimination) oral hearings would be more likely to be an efficient way of obtaining and evaluating the evidence and of providing an opportunity for the parties to engage and perhaps settle. The solution may be to provide an opportunity to permit venting of emotions, ideally at an early stage, before feelings become aggravated and entrenched, and without taking an extended period of time for too many people. How employers react when faced with emotional grievances may be a critical determinant. That consideration suggests the need for a mediation-ticketed case handler or judge to be available.[49]

We return to the issue of managing emotions in the context of employment disputes in our consideration of mediation in chapter ten. We consider the issue of a more robust system of tracking in chapter nine.

C. Standard Case Management

The tribunal's case management powers are wide and can be exercised on its own initiative, or on the application of a party at any stage during proceedings.[50] Part 6 of the ET Procedure Rules 2024 contains a number of important case management

[46] Focus Group, 10 December 2024 (1.30pm).

[47] This is addressed further in ch 12.

[48] Focus Groups: 20 November 2024 (12pm), 29 November 2024, 10 December 2024 (1.30pm).

[49] C Hodges, *Delivering Dispute Resolution: A Holistic Review of Models in England and Wales* (Hart Publishing 2019) 508.

[50] r 31(1) ET Procedure Rules 2024.

powers, including all general case management,[51] postponements,[52] third-party disclosure orders,[53] requiring witnesses to attend a hearing,[54] adding, substituting, or removing parties,[55] striking out all or part of a claim or response,[56] making unless orders,[57] and making deposit orders.[58]

The tribunal can vary, suspend, or set aside earlier case management orders where this is necessary in the interests of justice.[59] The tribunal's discretion to exercise its case management powers is primarily guided by the overriding objective in Rule 3(1) of the ET Procedure Rules 2024, namely 'to enable the Tribunal to deal with cases fairly and justly'. This is explained further in Rule 3(2) as

> so far as practicable –
>
> (a) ensuring that the parties are on an equal footing,
> (b) dealing with cases in ways which are proportionate to the complexity and importance of the issues,
> (c) avoiding unnecessary formality and seeking flexibility in the proceedings,
> (d) avoiding delay, so far as compatible with proper consideration of the issues, and
> (e) saving expense.

In addition, the tribunal is required, wherever practicable and appropriate, to encourage the use of Acas, judicial or other mediation, or other forms of ADR, in accordance with Rule 4. Presidential Guidance on case management is also relevant.[60]

Rule 7(1) now creates a broad power for the Senior President of Tribunals to authorise tribunal staff to carry out 'functions of a judicial nature' including making case management orders. If a member of staff makes a decision, rather than a judge, a party has 14 days from the date on which the tribunal sent notice of its decision to apply for the decision to be considered afresh by an employment judge.[61] This has been deployed to good effect by the use of Legal Officers, which is considered at section III.D below.

The main concern of participants in our research was the variation in case management approaches across regions. It was noted that in London the final hearing is only scheduled after witness statements have been exchanged.[62]

[51] ibid, r 30.
[52] ibid, r 32.
[53] ibid, r 33.
[54] ibid, r 34.
[55] ibid, r 35.
[56] ibid, r 38.
[57] ibid, r 39.
[58] ibid, r 40.
[59] ibid, r 30(3).
[60] Presidential Guidance (England & Wales) – General Case Management (22 January 2018). This only extends to England and Wales; there is no equivalent in Scotland. However, there is a specific Practice Direction in relation to sisting a case (stay of proceedings) to allow for mediation: Employment Tribunals (Scotland) Practice Direction No 2: Sist for Mediation (14 December 2006).
[61] r 7(2) ET Procedure Rules 2024.
[62] Focus Group, 13 November 2024.

In Northern Ireland there are no automatic directions for case management, but directions are bespoke as agreed with the parties.[63] Participants viewed these examples positively because it prevented available judicial slots being taken up by hearings that would not in fact take place. Similarly, many participants were very positive about how robustly Bristol deals with case management orders.[64] An unfavourable comparison was made with Watford which was reported as struggling with a significant backlog of work,[65] resulting in regular communications being sent out on a Sunday.[66] However, the differences between regions was looked on unfavourably. One participant said 'I feel it's unfair … that it depends on the region your case is in whether you get a robustly dealt with case management hearing and set of orders and very strict deadlines'.[67] Another participant said 'judges are … so insanely different, like who you have could absolutely make or break your case'.[68] Participants pointed to the need for consistency in approach by identifying best practices and applying them across the board.[69]

It was suggested that a centralised administrative body could be established to deal with all ongoing case management decisions. However, other participants were concerned that having a 'faceless' national system would lead to a loss of personal accountability vis-a-vis the parties when managing cases.[70] We were told that in Wales the parties receive a checklist after a case management hearing with the tasks and deadlines set out which participants found particularly helpful.[71] Another suggestion was increased digitisation and particularly the possibility of having an online system where parties could see a calendar or schedule of the next steps, the dates by when papers were required as well as being able to access online templates that were relevant to those steps. Similarly, it was suggested that it would be helpful if parties could see updates in an online system about applications they had made, or whether a party had complied so that they would not need to contact the tribunal to find out the position.[72]

D. Legal Officers

Legal officers, a recent innovation, are currently employed across the various employment tribunal regions. We were told that they play a key role in triaging correspondence for judges and responding to anything that does not require a

[63] Focus Group, 25 November 2024.
[64] Focus Groups: 12 November 2024, 25 November 2024.
[65] Focus Groups: 20 November 2024 (12pm), 10 December 2024 (9.30am).
[66] Focus Group, 11 November 2024.
[67] Focus Group, 25 November 2024.
[68] Focus Group, 25 November 2024.
[69] Focus Groups: 11 November 2024, 12 November 2024, 20 November 2024 (12pm).
[70] Focus Group, 11 November 2024.
[71] Focus Group, 25 November 2024.
[72] Focus Group, 20 November 2024 (3pm).

judicial decision. It was estimated that they could deal with between 75 and 80 per cent of correspondence that the tribunal receives. This would significantly reduce judicial time, but there are insufficient of them to do this at present. We were told that for legal officers to make a real difference to the system there needed to be about three times as many as there are currently but that recruitment and resources were a real challenge. The administrative structure means that the tribunal judges do not manage them; they are an HM Courts & Tribunals Service (HMCTS) resource. They are paid as HMCTS staff and there is limited career progression.

In addition to the usual work of legal officers, a pilot scheme has been running in Scotland whereby legal officers intervene in some simple money claims to clarify what is in dispute and to ensure the parties have the right information before a hearing. Simple money claims include claims for unpaid wages, redundancy and holiday pay. The extent of the pilot has been expanded over time.[73] This intervention has been successful in enabling claims to be resolved without the need for a hearing, with between 75 and 80 per cent of claims within its scope resolving. Furthermore, where there has been a hearing, it has often been shorter because the legal officer has helped to clarify and narrow the issues in dispute before the hearing. Consequently, in Scotland, fast-track claims are not listed for a final hearing on receipt of the ET1 but are listed for hearing only on receipt of the ET3, after intervention by legal officers.[74] Legal officers do not mediate in these claims but there is no reason why they could not be trained to provide limited, low-level mediation to parties.

We consider that this pilot is significant in showing the possibilities for simple claims to be resolved expeditiously with limited input from the tribunal system and there are clear parallels between the work of the legal officers here and the process that operates in Australia and New Zealand, discussed in chapter six and chapter nine.

Moreover, legal officer resource appears to have real untapped potential: their roles could be significantly reimagined and developed so that legal officers could take on many more duties, proactively managing cases and developing relationships with parties (particularly in multiple claims) with the ability to raise queries with judges where required. Arguably, the role of legal officer could become a stepping stone towards becoming a fee paid judge.

IV. Dealing with Unmeritorious Claims

Participants in our study perceived that there was a high volume of unmeritorious claims. Tribunals already have powers to deal with these either via striking out (section A) or through a deposit order (section B).

[73] Minutes of the Employment Tribunals (Scotland) National User Group Meeting (26 March 2024) 4.
[74] Minutes of the Employment Tribunals (Scotland) National User Group Meeting (2 October 2024) 3–4.

A. Striking Out Claims

Rule 38 of the Employment Tribunal Procedure Rules 2024 provides that:

> (1) The Tribunal may, on its own initiative or on the application of a party, strike out all or part of a claim, response or reply on any of the following grounds –
>
> (a) that it … has no reasonable prospect of success;
>
> …
>
> (2) A claim, response or reply may not be struck out unless the party advancing it has been given a reasonable opportunity to make representations, either in writing or, if requested by the party, at a hearing.

The tribunal can determine a strike out application at a preliminary hearing[75] and if it does, then it must be held in public.[76]

Before determining a strike out application, the tribunal must consider what the claims and issues are. It is not possible to decide if a claim has reasonable prospects of success if the tribunal does not know what the claim is.[77] If the claim would have reasonable prospects of success if it had been properly pleaded, the tribunal should consider the possibility of an amendment (subject to the usual test of whether an amendment is permitted).[78] The tribunal should consider the possibility that a litigant in person has applied the wrong 'legal label' to a factual claim that, if properly pleaded, would be arguable.[79]

Having understood the claims and issues, the tribunal may strike out a claim if it is obvious that, taking the facts at their highest in favour of the claimant, 'the claim simply could not succeed on the legal basis on which it has been put forward'.[80] One example of this might be a discrimination claim where there is a time bar to the tribunal's jurisdiction, and the claimant advances no evidence to show that it would be just and equitable to extend time.[81] Another example is where a pleaded discrimination case offers nothing more than an assertion of a difference of treatment and a difference of a protected characteristic.[82]

Rule 38(1) of the ET Procedure Rules 2024 permits the tribunal to strike out 'all or part' of a claim. However, tribunals may be reluctant to strike out some but not all allegations within a claim if the allegations are all closely connected.[83]

When considering a strike out application that depends to some extent on disputed facts, 'what is important is the particular nature and scope of the factual

[75] r 52(1)(c) ET Procedure Rules 2024.
[76] ibid, r 54(2).
[77] *Cox v Adecco* [2021] ICR 1307, [28](5).
[78] ibid, [28](9).
[79] ibid, [31].
[80] *Romanowska v Aspirations Care Ltd* UKEAT/0015/14, [1].
[81] *Chandhok v Tirkey* [2015] ICR 527, [20].
[82] ibid.
[83] *Dossen v Headcount Resources Ltd* UKEAT/0483/12.

dispute in question'.[84] When there is no 'crucial core of disputed facts',[85] a strike out may be appropriate.[86] However, where there is 'a crucial core of disputed facts in this case that is not susceptible to determination otherwise than by hearing and evaluating the evidence' then 'it would only be in an exceptional case' that the claim would be struck out'.[87]

The case law suggests two narrow exceptions to this general rule. First, a claim can be struck out where 'the facts sought to be established by the claimant were totally and inexplicably inconsistent with the undisputed contemporaneous documentation'.[88] Second, a claim can be struck out where (1) the underlying allegations are fanciful or inherently implausible and (2) there is an absence of evidence to support these allegations.[89]

The tribunal must be particularly cautious about striking out discrimination claims 'except in the most obvious and plainest cases' because they are 'generally fact-sensitive, and their proper determination is always vital in our pluralistic society'.[90] A similarly cautious approach is required in whistleblowing cases.[91] Where the 'central facts are in dispute' in an unfair dismissal claim, then it will usually require to be determined after a hearing.[92]

The strike out power is intended to have its principal use at a pre-hearing.[93] It is possible to strike out a claim during a hearing, but this would be 'very exceptional indeed, to the point of the instances of it being vanishingly small'.[94]

Once the tribunal has concluded that a claim has no reasonable prospect of success, rule 38 provides that the tribunal has a discretion whether to strike out the claim. It is an error of law if a tribunal fails to consider whether it should exercise this discretion in favour of not striking out the claim.[95] Relevant factors include the stage of the proceedings, the tribunal's power to direct further and better particulars, and whether the strike out was on the application of the respondent or not.[96] It should be considered in the context of the overriding objective in Rule 3(1), namely 'to enable the Tribunal to deal with cases fairly and justly'.[97]

[84] *Ezsias v North Glamorgan NHS Trust* [2007] ICR 1126, [27].

[85] Adopting the language of Maurice Kay LJ in *Ezsias v North Glamorgan NHS Trust* [2007] ICR 1126, [29].

[86] See, eg, *Kaur v Leeds Teaching Hospitals NHS Trust* [2019] ICR 1.

[87] ibid [29]. See similarly, *Cox v Adecco* [2021] ICR 1307, [28].

[88] *Ezsias v North Glamorgan NHS Trust* [2007] ICR 1126, [29]. See also *Mechkarov v Citibank* [2016] ICR 1121, [14](4) and *Tayside Public Transport Company Ltd v Reilly* [2012] IRLR 755, [30].

[89] *Ahir v British Airways plc* [2017] EWCA Civ 1392.

[90] *Anyanwu v South Bank Students' Union* [2001] IRLR 305, [24]. See also *Logo v Payone GmbH* [2024] EAT 9 and the five principles set out by Mitting J in *Mechkarov v Citibank* [2016] ICR 1121, [14].

[91] *Ezsias v North Glamorgan NHS Trust* [2007] ICR 1126, [30] and [32].

[92] *Tayside Public Transport Company Ltd v Reilly* [2012] IRLR 755, [30]. See also *Romanowska v Aspirations Care Ltd* UKEAT/0015/14, [15].

[93] *Williams v Real Care Agency Ltd* UKEATS/0051/11, [19].

[94] ibid, [21].

[95] *Hasan v Tesco Stores Ltd* UKEAT/0098/16, [17]–[18].

[96] ibid, [18].

[97] *Mallon v Aecom Ltd* [2021] ICR 1151, [13].

B. Deposit Orders

Rule 40 of the Employment Tribunal Procedure Rules 2024 provides that where a claim, response or reply has 'little reasonable prospect of success' an order may be made requiring the party to pay a deposit 'not exceeding £1000 as a condition of continuing to advance that allegation or argument'. The party's ability to pay must be considered. Where the deposit is not paid by the specified date then the tribunal must strike out the allegation or argument. Moreover, where the final hearing determines that the specific allegation or argument fails 'for substantially the reasons given in the deposit order' then the party must be treated as having acted unreasonably for costs purposes and the deposit must be paid to the other party.

The purpose of a deposit order is 'to identify at an early stage claims with little prospect of success and to discourage the pursuit of those claims', it is 'emphatically not … to make it difficult to access justice or to effect a strike out through the back door'.[98] As in strike out applications, the tribunal must 'properly identify' and 'characterise' the party's case.[99] They cannot be used as a 'shortcut substitute' for case management orders such as requiring further particulars.[100]

The 'little reasonable prospect of success' standard is less rigorous than the test for a strike out.[101] 'Little' reasonable prospect of success is plainly less onerous than no reasonable prospect of success but it is more than an argument being 'likely' to fail.[102] The tribunal may conclude that a party has little reasonable prospect of establishing the facts that are essential to their case, provided that it has a proper basis for doing so.[103] The tribunal should avoid undertaking a mini trial because the application for a deposit order is a 'summary assessment intended to avoid cost and delay'.[104] The tribunal should take the claimant's case at its highest.[105] The tribunal may consider previous litigation when deciding if an argument has little reasonable prospect of success.[106]

Once a tribunal has concluded that a claim or allegation has little reasonable prospect of success, then the decision as to whether to make a deposit order is 'a matter of discretion and does not follow automatically'. The power should be

[98] *Hemdan v Ishmail* [2017] ICR 486, [10].

[99] *Tree v South East Coastal Ambulance Service* UKEAT/0043/17, [39].

[100] ibid. See also the nine principles set out in *Amber v West Yorkshire Fire and Rescue Service* [2024] EAT 146, [26].

[101] *Van Rensburg v Royal Borough of Kingston-Upon-Thames* UKEAT/0096/07, [27]. See also *Ahir v British Airways plc* [2017] EWCA Civ 1392, [16].

[102] *Blitz v Vectone Group Holdings Ltd* UKEAT/0306/09, [21].

[103] *Van Rensburg v Royal Borough of Kingston-Upon-Thames* UKEAT/0096/07, [23] and [27]. See also *Wright v Nipponkoa Insurance (Europe) Ltd* UKEAT/0113/14, [33]–[34].

[104] *Hemdan v Ishmail* [2017] ICR 486, [13].

[105] *Linton v The Athelstan Trust* [2024] EAT 14, [59] and *Garcia v The Leadership Factor* [2022] EAT 19, [67]. Query whether HHJ Beard was suggesting something less than this or whether he was simply suggesting that the case must also be examined 'through the prism of reality': *Amber v West Yorkshire Fire and Rescue Service* [2024] EAT 146, [28].

[106] *Addison Lee v Afshar* [2024] EAT 114, [64]–[65] (Griffiths J).

exercised in accordance with the overriding objective (that the tribunal deal with cases 'fairly and justly').[107] Relevant factors include the need for case management, the need for parties to focus on the real issues in the case, the extent to which costs are likely to be saved, and the extent to which the case is likely to be allocated a fair share of limited tribunal resources.[108]

C. Empirical Research Findings

As noted above, there was a widespread perception among participants in our research that the system is overloaded with weak and unmeritorious claims. This significantly increases the overall burden on the system and on the parties, as well as increasing costs. Many participants said that there should be better filtering of cases and a greater use of strike out and deposit orders which participants said were utilised too little.[109] Participants said that cases where a person lacked the required continuity of service or were out of time should be rejected from the outset, without requiring a formal strike out application.[110] Some participants suggested that cases that were obviously appropriate to be struck out could be decided by legal officers, rather than judges.[111] However, other participants said that this was too risky because some claims that appear to be weak, are subsequently successful, which can be the case particularly with litigants in person who might have a valid claim but have failed to explain it properly.[112]

Participants considered that deposit orders were a helpful middle ground because they are a less harsh alternative that does not completely block claimants from pursuing their case.[113] However, these were perceived as being rarely used, particularly when discrimination is claimed.[114] Moreover, participants noted that even where a deposit is ordered, the sums that are required to be paid are too low to deter a party from pursuing a weak claim. They said that orders should be made more frequently and for greater sums.[115] Others were concerned about the effect on access to justice, particularly for low-paid workers.[116] Participants also said that deposits should be used more vigorously against respondents.[117]

[107] *Hemdan v Ishmail* [2017] ICR 486, [15].
[108] ibid.
[109] Focus Groups: 11 November 2024, 12 November 2024, 13 November 2024, 19 November 2024 (12pm), 19 November 2024 (3pm), 25 November 2024.
[110] Focus Group, 25 November 2024.
[111] Focus Group, 25 November 2024.
[112] Focus Groups: 20 November 2024 (12pm), 10 December 2024 (1.30pm).
[113] Focus Groups: 11 November 2024, 12 November 2024.
[114] Focus Groups: 12 November 2024, 10 December 2024 (1.30pm).
[115] Focus Groups: 11 November 2024, 12 November 2024, 20 November 2024 (12pm), 20 November 2024 (3pm), 25 November 2024.
[116] Focus Groups: 12 November 2024, 14 November 2024.
[117] Focus Groups: 25 November 2024, 10 December 2024 (9.30am).

Relatedly, even where it would be inappropriate to strike out an entire claim or impose a deposit order in relation to the claim, participants said that there was a need for greater focus on removing weak allegations from cases where there was a long list of issues, including a large number of weak (often discrimination or whistleblowing) allegations. Participants said that once these allegations are included in the list of issues at the case management stage then they tend to stick and have to be dealt with throughout the litigation. Participants said that this complicates the litigation and increases costs. They said that judges should be more robust in the early case management stages, performing a more rigorous assessment of the pleadings, providing parties with less leeway about whether an allegation was weak and seeking to limit or narrow the list of issues.[118] It was suggested that judges should be allowed to require claimants to focus claims on the actual issues that are in play or to impose orders identifying the lead claim or claims, perhaps leaving room to reassess the validity of the other issues at a later stage in the process. Another suggestion was that judges should require claimants to 'pick their best five' claims or that the ET1 form should have space only for a certain number of issues, rather than an unlimited text box, to try to encourage parties to limit the issues.[119]

Another significant issue raised by participants was the lack of availability of legal advice. Many participants said that they thought that if litigants in person received advice before submitting their ET1, it would significantly reduce the number of weak claims that are submitted.[120] Some participants suggested that basic legal advice should be provided free to parties[121] and this should be encouraged by the tribunals[122] or even be a precondition to making a claim.[123] Most participants recognised, however, that the restoration of legal aid was unlikely to happen, despite the likely benefits to the public purse outweighing the financial cost of providing legal aid.[124] Other participants doubted that providing legal advice would be effective because many claimants submit a claim despite having received negative legal advice.[125]

The literature also identifies issues with the lack of legal advice. For example, Kirk says:

> Problems with 'weak' cases are at least partially attributable to the lack of availability of free, quality legal advice, and the weakness of employment rights that many vulnerable, low-paid workers attempt to cling to. The decline of unions has led to the degradation of work and conditions, meaning that increasingly vulnerable workers have more

[118] Focus Groups: 11 November 2024, 12 November 2024, 13 November 2024, 19 November 2024 (12pm), 10 December 2024 (1.30pm).
[119] Focus Group, 13 November 2024.
[120] Focus Groups: 11 November 2024, 12 November 2024, 13 November 2024.
[121] Focus Group, 19 November 2024 (12pm).
[122] Focus Group, 29 November 2024.
[123] Focus Group, 10 December 2024 (9.30am).
[124] Focus Group, 20 November 2024 (12pm).
[125] Focus Group, 10 December 2024 (9.30am).

> to complain about, but less capacity to do so. At the same time, less and less support is available via legal aid and CABx [citizens' advice] are struggling to cope with the demand for employment advice (let alone representation).[126]

Others note the lack of places for workers to turn to for advice.[127]

Some participants raised concerns that poor legal representation could be worse than no legal representation. They reported on situations where they felt that the lawyers in a case had convinced claimants to pursue weak claims or to try to (over-)expand the nature and value of the claims.[128] It was suggested that there was a difference in approach between practitioners in Scotland, where the community is smaller and close-knit, compared with London where lawyers may never or rarely be against each other in a subsequent case so there is less need for interpersonal accountability and collegiality.[129]

Participants said that there was a broader issue concerned with legal education of the public. There were a number of facets to this. First, some claimants had unrealistic expectations – arising from online content, social media and news reports – about the kinds of claims that could be made and the level of compensation awarded.[130] Second, there appears to be a perception that bringing a tribunal claim is simple and swift. As one focus group participant said,

> your average claimant thinks 'I just fill in this form and then I'll probably, I don't know, have half an hour chat with the judge and … that will be it', and it's only when you get to case management … you can see the penny dropping where they're realising what they've taken on.[131]

Third, there is a lack of understanding about the specific claims and what is required for them: victimisation is a good example whereby many people will say that they have been victimised in the layperson's sense of the word of being treated badly, but they have not been subjected to victimisation under the Equality Act 2010 which requires them to have done a protected act and been subjected to a detriment because of that act. Participants stressed the need for there to be much better information available about what rights people have, the limited scale of remedies and the challenges of the litigation process.[132]

When discussing unmeritorious claims with judges, frustration was expressed about the perception of the numbers of unmeritorious claims and the perception of

[126] E Kirk, 'The "problem" with the employment tribunal system: Reform, rhetoric and realities for the clients of citizens' advice bureaux' (2017) 32 *Work, Employment and Society* 975.

[127] See, eg, J Holgate, J Keles and A Pollert, 'Union decline, minority ethnic workers and employment advice in local communities' (2009) 38 *Industrial Law Journal* 412 and C Barnard, A Ludlow and S Fraser Butlin, 'Beyond Employment Tribunals: Enforcement of Employment Rights by EU-8 Migrant Workers' (2018) 47 *Industrial Law Journal* 226.

[128] Focus Group, 12 November 2024.

[129] Focus Group, 29 November 2024.

[130] Focus Groups: 14 November 2024, 20 November 2024 (12pm), 20 November 2024 (3pm), 10 December 2024 (9.30am).

[131] Focus Group, 25 November 2024.

[132] Focus Groups: 13 November 2024, 19 November 2024 (12pm), 25 November 2024, 10 December 2024 (1.30pm).

a failure to strike more of them out. In relation to the former, the judges said that the main difficulty related to claimants being precise in their pleadings rather than the claims lacking merits per se. With regard to striking out, they pointed to the fact that the EAT had repeatedly said that claims should not be struck out if there is a factual dispute that goes to the heart of the issues, which was usually the case. Thus, they said that while they might want to strike out more claims or to require claimants to limit the issues, they were bound by the authorities and if they did, then their decisions would simply be appealed which would be of no benefit to the parties.

In order to explore these two points, we considered the success rates in the employment tribunal. These are limited to the cases dealt with via the Reform case management tool. In 2023/24, 40 per cent of jurisdictional complaints[133] are recorded as being Acas conciliated and 19 per cent are withdrawn. Two per cent are recorded as dismissed at a preliminary hearing and 7 per cent are struck out (not at a hearing). Just 3 per cent of all jurisdictional complaints brought are successful at hearing and 5 per cent are unsuccessful at hearing. However, this equates to 37.5 per cent of jurisdictional complaints that reach a hearing succeeding.[134] In 2024/25, 30 per cent of jurisdictional complaints are recorded as being Acas conciliated and 26 per cent are withdrawn. One per cent are recorded as dismissed at a preliminary hearing and 4 per cent are struck out (not at a hearing). Five per cent of the total complaints that are brought are recorded as successful at hearing and 4 per cent are unsuccessful at hearing (equating to 55.5 per cent of complaints that reach a hearing succeeding).[135] Therefore when considering the success and failure rates of cases that reach a hearing, alongside the strike out rates, it might be argued that there should be a greater use of the strike out process.

While there are a reasonable percentage of complaints that are struck out or dismissed at a preliminary hearing, the figures relating to success and lack of success at a hearing are not entirely clear. Although it is noted that the mean jurisdictional complaints per claim was 2.6 in 2024/25 and 2.3 in 2023/24, as noted in chapter one, a jurisdictional complaint may encompass a large number of different elements and allegations. It appears that provided that one allegation is successful – irrespective of how many allegations are made within a jurisdictional complaint – then the jurisdictional complaint is marked as successful at the final hearing. This means that a claim might encompass several jurisdictional complaints which might each encompass different causes of action within the complaint and different allegations within those causes of action many of which are unsuccessful, but the jurisdictional complaint is still within the 'successful' data.

We also reviewed the decisions of the EAT from 1 January 2020 to 31 December 2024 that concerned strike outs and deposit orders.[136] There

[133] A claim may contain a number of different jurisdictional complaints, on which see ch 1.

[134] The remaining 23% is made up of: 16% dismissed on withdrawal, 1% default judgment, 1% rule 27 dismissal, 1% discontinued and 4% other.

[135] Ministry of Justice Tribunal Statistics Quarterly, Main Tables, July to September 2025.

[136] Using the government website for EAT decisions, we searched for 'strike out' producing 193 cases between 1 January 2020 and 1 January 2025. 83 were appeals against strike outs; appeals against

were relatively few such appeals. This may reflect the hesitancy of judges to strike out and order deposits. However, in relation to appeals against both strike outs and deposit orders, the success rate was over 60 per cent.[137] Therefore, this supports the tribunal judges' views that greater use of strike out orders may not survive EAT scrutiny.

V. Interim Applications and Preliminary Hearings

A. Interim Applications

A party can make an application to the tribunal for a case management order, either at a hearing or in writing.[138] Online platforms for applications are being rolled out across the regions. A copy of the application must be sent to all other parties[139] with a notification that they should send any objections to the tribunal as soon as possible.[140] Presidential Guidance states that a party should make any application 'as early as possible'.[141] The tribunal will then deal with the application in writing, or order that should be considered at a preliminary or final hearing.[142]

Where the application relates to the postponement of a hearing, it must be made 'as soon as possible after the need for a postponement becomes known'[143] and where the application is made less than seven days before the hearing date, then the tribunal's power to order a postponement is more restricted.[144]

The delays in dealing with interim applications was a significant issue for many participants in our empirical study. Participants noted that the delays meant that by the time interim orders were made or an application to extend a deadline was considered, the time had already passed and it had become irrelevant. This was particularly problematic where the application was to postpone a hearing because until a judicial decision is made, they were required to continue to prepare for the hearing incurring significant costs.[145] One focus group participant said that 'in England … everything, goes into a black hole … you can't make any proactive interventions with the tribunal because you just don't have any confidence that it's

a refusal to strike out a claim were not included. We searched for 'deposit' producing 123 cases between 1 January 2019 and 1 January 2025 (an additional year was included to increase the sample size). 18 were appeals against the imposition of deposit orders; appeals against a refusal to make a deposit order were not included.

[137] Out of 83 appeals against strike out, 53 succeeded (64%) and 11 out of 18 appeals against deposit orders succeeded (61%).

[138] r 31(1) ET Procedure Rules 2024.

[139] ibid, r 90(1).

[140] ibid, r 31(2).

[141] Presidential Guidance (England & Wales) – General Case Management (n 60) para 13.

[142] r 31(3) ET Procedure Rules 2024.

[143] ibid, r 32(1).

[144] ibid, r 32(2) and (3).

[145] Focus Groups: 11 November 2024, 10 December 2024 (9.30am).

going to get looked at or responded to in time'.[146] Moreover, the delay in the tribunal responding to an application in respect of a breach of a case management order meant that there was little incentive to comply with the order in the first place.[147]

Participants in our study repeatedly pointed to the need for there to be more administrative support within the tribunal system so that phones and emails could be answered more rapidly. Numerous participants reflected on the significant difficulty they faced when trying to contact the tribunal service.[148] One survey participant recalled that

> 'a trainee called an ET last year and held on for circa 3 hours until the call was answered. When asked why it had taken so long, the tribunal clerk who answered burst into tears and said she was under massive stress and didn't know if she could cope. Sadly, that example typifies the situation.

Many regions have moved to a centralised number for phone calls raising concerns amongst participants that a 'call centre' approach is being taken with people answering calls that they are unable to deal with.

There appears to be more administrative support in Scotland – as well as significantly greater legal officer resource – where the difficulties in contacting the tribunal were reported to be less acute and case management processes were reported to be much smoother.[149]

In our empirical research, a number of participants suggested that there needed to be an increase in specialisation of the employment judges, and that administrative staff/legal officers should be trained to deal with, and then be assigned to manage, particular types of case.[150] There was considerable enthusiasm for each case having a designated judge and administrative team member or legal officer so that they were better equipped to answer queries and there was greater accountability for ensuring that the process moved forward. This, it was felt, would improve efficiency in the system.[151] Many participants considered that there was greater scope to use legal officers to make simple case management decisions and to deal with applications.[152] However, some participants were concerned that such a shift might give rise to a variable quality of decisions.[153]

Other participants suggested that there needed to be more prioritisation within tribunals. In Wales judges ask parties to write in the subject heading a brief description of what the email is about, and this allows judges to split their inboxes more effectively. Participants said that this had led to significantly quicker responses.[154]

[146] Focus Group, 29 November 2024.
[147] Survey participant.
[148] Focus Groups: 12 November 2024, 25 November 2024, 29 November 2024, 10 December 2024 (9.30am).
[149] Focus Group, 29 November 2024.
[150] Focus Groups: 10 December 2024 (9.30am), 10 December 2024 (1.30pm).
[151] Focus Group, 25 November 2024.
[152] Focus Groups: 12 November 2024, 25 November 2024, 10 December 2024 (1.30pm).
[153] Focus Group, 13 November 2024.
[154] Focus Group, 25 November 2024.

Other participants suggested that time-sensitive emails could be titled as 'urgent' and that these should accordingly be treated with priority.[155]

B. Preliminary Hearings

The tribunal has a wide discretion whether to hold a preliminary hearing. A party may also apply for a preliminary hearing.[156] The parties must be given reasonable notice of the date, and at least 14 days for a substantive, as opposed to case management, preliminary hearing.[157]

In Northern Ireland, all cases are subject to active case management and a preliminary hearing will invariably be held – online if the parties are represented – to identify the issues and to see if the dispute can be resolved.

Many preliminary hearings deal with case management. The tribunal will usually send the parties a case management agenda[158] that they are encouraged to try to agree and submit in advance.[159] Nevertheless, significant time may be spent identifying the issues in a claim so that a list of issues can be produced. However, even where a list of issues has been agreed, the employment tribunal at the final hearing may be required to depart from it where it is in the interests of justice, including where a pleaded claim has been omitted from the list but not abandoned, and where a claim has not been pleaded but fairness requires it to be considered.[160]

In Northern Ireland, the employment judge may ask for a member of the Labour Relations Agency (LRA) to sit in on the hearing so that they can hear the judge's views on what the issues are. The judge will then often encourage the parties to engage with the LRA again to seek to resolve the dispute.

Thereafter a case management order will be made, setting the timetable to trial. Within that timetable, a further preliminary hearing may be required to determine any preliminary issues, that is, 'any substantive issue which may determine the complaint or the Tribunal's jurisdiction',[161] consider whether a claim or response should be struck out, in full or in part, or whether a deposit order should be made.[162] The preliminary hearing may also be used to explore the possibility of settlement or ADR although this generally involves scheduling a date for judicial

[155] Focus Group, 19 November 2024 (3pm).

[156] r 53(1) ET Procedure Rules 2024.

[157] ibid, r 53(2).

[158] Presidential Guidance (England & Wales) – General Case Management (n 60) para 23.

[159] Courts and Tribunals Judiciary, Agenda for Case Management (England & Wales): www.judiciary.uk/wp-content/uploads/2024/11/Agenda-for-Case-Management-England-Wales-English-PDF-version-2.pdf.

[160] *Moustache v Chelsea and Westminster Hospital NHS Foundation Trust* [2025] EWCA Civ 185.

[161] r 52(3) ET Procedure Rules 2024. This is often concerned with time limits or whether someone is disabled within the Equality Act 2010.

[162] r 52(1) ET Procedure Rules 2024.

mediation if the parties are so inclined, rather than any discussion of resolution at the hearing.

Participants in our research said that litigants in person particularly struggled with tribunal procedures and the need to engage objectively with the issues. A number of participants noted the difficulties for individuals when trying to articulate their claims as legal claims, particularly where the law is complex, rather than an expression of everything that had happened to them. Some participants said that litigants in person have a tendency to exaggerate or overcomplicate their claims, but most said that the fundamental problem was that litigants in person failed properly to articulate their claims in legal terms. Attempts to clarify claims in advance of a preliminary hearing were often difficult because of a lack of trust and this meant that case management hearings to agree a list of issues could be very challenging and lengthy, increasing the costs of the other party.[163] The lack of legal representation was another difficulty and several participants suggested that an arrangement comparable to a 'duty solicitor' in housing possession cases might be helpful to support a claimant to identify the issues in their case with greater clarity.[164] However, other participants said that providing such limited legal advice given the time constraints prior to a hearing was unlikely to assist and the tribunal was fundamentally different from the specific circumstances of the housing possession lists in court where individuals face eviction or repossession and the issues involved are urgent and limited.[165]

Other participants noted that there are significant differences in the workloads across different regions, with London and the South-East being particularly overloaded. This means that it may take a year in the south of England to be listed for a preliminary hearing but much less if it is listed in the north of England.[166] Other participants felt that in some regions preliminary hearings were listed too quickly, requiring parties to attend hearings when they were still trying to resolve the matter.[167] This was perhaps a side effect of the short three-month limitation period applying at the time of our research.

Participants also noted that even where preliminary hearings were listed quite quickly, the final hearing was then not listed for a long time thereafter. This caused considerable 'front-loading' of the costs and the stress involved in the litigation.[168] Despite the long wait for the substantive hearing, some participants noted that the case management order required the preparation for the case to be done swiftly and then there was often a long hiatus before the hearing itself. Again, this

[163] Focus Groups: 11 November 2024, 12 November 2024, 20 November 2024 (12pm), 10 December 2024 (1.30pm).

[164] Focus Groups: 11 November 2024, 13 November 2024. 19 November 2024 (12pm), 20 November 2024 (12pm), 25 November 2024, 29 November 2024, 5 December 2024, 10 December 2024 (1.30pm).

[165] Focus Groups: 13 November 2024, 10 December 2024 (9.30am).

[166] Focus Groups: 11 November 2024, 12 November 2024, 20 November 2024 (12pm), 25 November 2024, 13 December 2024.

[167] Focus Group, 25 November 2024.

[168] Focus Group, 13 November 2024.

front-loaded costs and participants felt that there was little scope to pause directions while mediation or ADR was attempted because they could not communicate with the tribunal to get directions amended.[169]

The response to online preliminary hearings was mostly positive as a means of saving considerable time and money for parties.[170] However, some concerns were raised that this meant that there was less opportunity for parties to meet and perhaps resolve matters.[171]

VI. Preparations for a Final Hearing

A. Disclosure

The ET Procedure Rules 2004 do not impose a general duty of disclosure on parties. However, in England and Wales, the tribunal will routinely order disclosure by the parties using its general case management power in Rule 30.[172] The ET can also order disclosure by third parties.[173] The England and Wales Presidential Guidance on case management identifies documents that usually must be disclosed because they are relevant to the issues the ET has to decide, including a contract of employment, notes of a disciplinary interview, a resignation or dismissal letter, and materials such as emails, text messages and relevant social media content.[174] This guidance states that disclosure should start and be completed 'as soon as possible'. The case management order will usually set out when disclosure must be completed by.[175] In addition, the claimant will be required to produce a Schedule of Loss setting out the sums they are claiming with relevant supporting evidence, such as documents relating to searching for a new job.[176]

In Scotland, parties are expected to comply with the timetable set down in the Practice Direction, rather than having it determined on a case-by-case basis. Where a party is legally represented, their representative must provide a list of the documents on which the party intends to rely to the other parties at least 14 days before a hearing. In individual cases, the tribunal may decide to impose a more onerous timetable.[177]

[169] Focus Groups: 12 November 2024, 19 November 2024 (3pm), 25 November 2024.
[170] Focus Groups: 13 November 2024, 29 November 2024, 10 December 2024 (9.30am).
[171] Focus Group, 25 November 2024.
[172] *Sarnoff v YZ* [2021] EWCA Civ 26.
[173] r 33 ET Procedure Rules 2024.
[174] Presidential Guidance (England & Wales) – General Case Management (n 60) Guidance Note 2, para 7.
[175] ibid para 10.
[176] Presidential Guidance (England & Wales) – General Case Management (n 60) Guidance Note 6, paras 10–15.
[177] Employment Tribunals (Scotland) Practice Direction No 1: Intimation of List of Documents 14 days before a Hearing (14 December 2006).

Once the documents have been disclosed between the parties, they must agree which of them will go into the hearing bundle. This should be only the documents that (a) are relevant to the issues in the proceedings and (b) are mentioned in witness statements or will be used in cross-examination.[178] Usually the respondent prepares the hearing bundle.[179] Disputes about the contents of the bundle may result in an application to the tribunal.

In Northern Ireland, the standard case management directions require the parties to 'serve any Notices for Discovery and/or Additional Information' and thereafter 'to exchange all relevant documents with each other' by a set date. The directions specify that 'this includes any documents, emails, letters, texts, messages, hand-written notes, diary entries, electronic messages, and video or audio recordings that are within their possession, control or custody, which are relevant to the issues before the tribunal'.

B. Witness Statements

In England and Wales, witness statements are also usually ordered to be prepared and exchanged simultaneously.[180] Unless ordered otherwise, the exchange of witness statements should take place no later than two weeks before the hearing.[181]

In Northern Ireland, witness statements are usually exchanged sequentially, with the Respondent serving their statements four to six weeks after the claimant. Where witness statements address issues outwith the agreed list of issues, a preliminary hearing may be held to address what should be removed from the statements.

In England and Wales, the witness statement will stand as the witness's evidence in chief.[182] The Guidance reminds litigants that the statement should be 'in a logical order' and 'as full as possible'.[183] In the South-West region, word limits are routinely applied to witness statements.

No procedural guidance is available in relation to Northern Ireland.[184] However, the practice is the same as in England and Wales.

[178] Presidential Guidance (England & Wales) – General Case Management (n 60) Guidance Note 2, para 13.

[179] ibid, para 14.

[180] Presidential Guidance (England & Wales) – General Case Management (n 60) Guidance Note 3, para 10. However, the guidance recognises that, in some cases, it is more efficient for the claimant to provide their witness statements to the respondent first to enable the respondent to know the case they have to answer: para 22.

[181] ibid, para 23.

[182] r 43(1) ET Procedure Rules 2024.

[183] Presidential Guidance (England & Wales) – General Case Management (n 60) Guidance Note 3.

[184] See: www.employmenttribunalsni.co.uk/process.

In contrast, in Scotland, the presumption is that evidence in chief will be given orally, without the use of a witness statement.[185] Nevertheless, in Scotland the tribunal may order, of its own motion or on the application of a party, that evidence in chief can be given by a witness statement.[186] A party that wishes to apply for an order permitting witness statements must make their application as early in the proceedings as possible.[187] Relevant factors include the views of the parties and whether the interests of justice would be equally well or better served by an order that the parties should produce an agreed statement of facts. There are detailed rules in the Practice Direction about ensuring that any witness statement is as succinct as possible and contains only evidence as to matters of fact that need to be proved during the hearing.[188] Witness statements must include a statement of truth in a prescribed form, which must be signed and dated.[189] Where a witness statement is prepared with the assistance of a professional representative, there must also be a confirmation in a prescribed form, which must be signed and dated by the representative.[190] Importantly, the standard direction on the exchange of witness statements is that witnesses for a party are not permitted to see the witness statements of any other witnesses for the same party prior to giving their evidence and no witness can see the statement for the other party until they have finalised and signed their own witness statement.[191]

The tribunal may order any person in Great Britain to attend a hearing to give evidence, produce documents, or provide information.[192]

C. Page Limits

Page limits on a hearing bundle, and word limits on witness statements may be imposed.[193] This is a regular practice in the South-West region. Page and word limits are routinely imposed in Northern Ireland. For bundles they are usually 300–500 pages. Witness statements are usually restricted to 5,000 words for each witness statement, although some latitude is given to claimants.

In our research, the majority of participants said that page limits were a positive step. It was said that currently parties disclose too many documents, the

[185] Employment Tribunals (Scotland) Practice Direction in connection with the use of witness statements (3 August 2022) para 6.
[186] ibid, para 7.
[187] ibid, para 10.
[188] ibid, paras 17–18.
[189] ibid, para 29.
[190] ibid, para 30.
[191] ibid, para 24.
[192] r 34(1) ET Procedure Rules 2024.
[193] The EAT rejected an appeal to the imposition of a 350-page limit on the hearing bundle and 5,000 words in a witness statement, noting that it is within the power of the ET to regulate the volume of evidence in a full hearing, and that limits can promote a fair trial by focusing the parties on the relevant issues and evidence: *Miron v Adecco* UKEAT/0409/20, [43] and [64].

vast majority of which are not relevant.[194] There were particular challenges now in relation to digital disclosure.[195] Page limits were thought to be particularly helpful when dealing with litigants in person who were often unable to be objective about what was relevant, whether in relation to disclosure or witness statements, and who did not trust the representative on the other side, making it difficult to manage the compilation of the bundle and keep the litigation within bounds.[196] As one participant said, 'you kick and scream and you hate the word limit, but it is so good, and it just focuses everyone and your client, whether it's respondent or claimant, to the actual legal issues'.[197] Moreover, it also had the effect of limiting the length of the hearings compared with other regions which, according to a focus group participant, allow 'a parade of witnesses' significantly increasing the parties' costs.[198]

However, the main concern for participants was the inconsistencies across the country. Participants noted that they generally worked to represent clients across all regions but the inconsistencies in approach made it more difficult and costly.[199] Many people suggested that there was a need for a streamlined and consistent approach to case management, particularly in relation to bundle page-limits and word limits on witness statements.[200] In chapter nine we consider whether lessons can be learned from the High Court and from the Family Procedure Rules as to how to improve the current system.

VII. Final Hearing

A. Conduct of the Final Hearing

The tribunal must give the parties at least 14 days' notice of the date of a final hearing.[201] If the tribunal schedules a final hearing before the respondent has presented their ET3, the date must be at least 14 days after the deadline for presenting the ET3.[202] A significant concern for the participants in our research was the lengthy delays before a final hearing is held, and the frequency of last minute cancellations of those hearings. This unnecessarily increases the legal costs of the parties because all the preparation for the hearing has been done, with the costs incurred, but must be repeated when the hearing is relisted,

[194] Focus Groups: 12 November 2024, 20 November 2024.
[195] Focus Groups: 20 November 2024, 25 November 2024.
[196] Focus Groups: 13 November 2024, 25 November 2024.
[197] Focus Group, 12 November 2024.
[198] Focus Group, 12 November 2024.
[199] Focus Groups: 11 November 2024, 12 November 2024.
[200] Focus Groups: 11 November 2024, 12 November 2024, 25 November 2024.
[201] r 56(1) ET Procedure Rules 2024.
[202] ibid, r 56(2).

particularly where that new hearing is a long way in the future.[203] Moreover, the delays were noted to cause considerable stress for all the parties.[204]

If a party fails to attend a hearing, the tribunal must consider any information which is available to it, after any enquiries that may be practicable, about the reasons for the party's absence. Having considered this, the tribunal may dismiss the claim or proceed with the hearing in the absence of that party,[205] or may adjourn or postpone the hearing.[206]

At the final hearing, the tribunal has a broad discretion to regulate its own procedure, guided by the factors in Rule 41, and must:

(a) conduct any hearing in the manner it considers fair;
(b) have regard to the overriding objective; and
(c) seek to avoid undue formality and may itself question the parties or any witnesses in order to clarify the issues or elicit evidence.

Time limits for presenting evidence, questioning witnesses and making submissions may be imposed, but in practice this is used relatively rarely.[207] As noted above, in England and Wales and Northern Ireland, a witness statement will be 'taken as read', that is, simply confirmed as accurate orally and any supplementary questions put before cross-examination. However, in Scotland, even if a witness statement has been produced, the tribunal may order that the statement will be read aloud, in addition to permitting any supplementary evidence in chief. One reason for allowing a party, particularly an unrepresented claimant, to read out their statement is to enable them to 'feel they have had their say'.[208] The practice in Scotland is that all witnesses (other than the parties) remain outside the hearing room until they are called to give evidence. The tribunal will give permission to make an exception to this practice only in exceptional circumstances.[209] The tribunal can use special measures in similar ways to the criminal courts, such as allowing witnesses to give evidence behind a screen or via a pre-recorded video.[210] In *Duffy v George*, the Court of Appeal considered that tribunals should hold case management preliminary hearings to discuss how to deal with sexual harassment cases where the claimant is fearful of being cross-examined by the alleged harasser.[211]

[203] Focus Groups: 11 November 2024, 12 November 2024, 19 November 2024 (12pm), 20 November 2024 (12pm), 25 November 2024, 10 December 2024 (9.30am).
[204] Focus Group, 19 November 2024 (12pm).
[205] r 47 ET Procedure Rules 2024.
[206] ibid, r 30(1).
[207] ibid, r 45.
[208] Employment Tribunals (Scotland) Presidential Guidance in connection with the preparation and use of witness statements (3 August 2022) paras 14–15.
[209] ibid, para 11. The practice was noted by the EAT in *E & O Laboratories v Miller* UKEATS/0007/19/SS, [3].
[210] Presidential Guidance (England & Wales) – Vulnerable Parties and Witnesses (22 April 2020) especially paras 15 and 22.
[211] *Duffy v George* [2013] EWCA Civ 908.

Hearings may be online, provided that it is just and equitable and that those attending are able to hear what the tribunal hears and, so far as practicable, see any witness as seen by the tribunal.[212]

Final hearings are heard by an employment judge who may sit with two non-legal members. Non-legal members previously sat on all cases but now only sit on whistleblowing and discrimination cases or where there is a particular need for industrial experience.[213] In Northern Ireland, non-legal members are always used.

In England and Wales, it is not unusual to have a liability hearing and then only proceed to a later remedy hearing if relevant. However, in Scotland and Northern Ireland, the starting point is that the tribunal will deal with liability and remedy at the same hearing. Split hearings are rare.[214]

It is striking that in our research, despite all the criticism of delays and process, there was little or no criticism of the judges themselves and the fairness of proceedings. Some participants said that employment judges should be more inquisitorial, to promote access to justice for litigants in person and to steer the procedure more productively. Others said that although judges had greater inquisitorial powers than the courts, they often refrained from using them and should be encouraged to 'step into the arena' more.[215] But this view was not universally shared. Some participants said that judges were already taking enough of a role, by spending time explaining and clarifying matters for litigants in person. They were concerned by a more interventionist approach, particularly where there was insufficient structure and training to implement a proper inquisitorial process.[216] They considered that litigants in person today 'get a lot of indulgence from the judge' and 'that's slightly unfair on the respondent', who is already facing more difficulties in handling the unqualified litigant in person.[217] Other participants suggested that different adjudication and enforcement measures were needed for different types of claim, for example they said that wages and monetary claims could be addressed better via a non-tribunal enforcement mechanism.[218]

B. Decisions and Reasons

After a hearing, the tribunal will either announce its decision orally at the hearing, or reserve the decision to be sent out in writing.[219] If the tribunal announces its

[212] r 46 ET Procedure Rules 204.

[213] See further ch 1 in relation to the benefits of lay members and issues relating to non-specialists being appointed as employment judges.

[214] An example of misunderstandings that may arise from the difference can be found in *Gordon v J & D Pierce (Contracts) Ltd* UKEATS/0010/20/SS.

[215] Focus Groups: 12 November 2024, 13 November 2024, 19 November 2024 (12pm).

[216] Focus Groups: 13 November 2024, 20 November 2024 (12pm), 29 November 2024.

[217] Focus Group, 11 November 2024.

[218] Focus Groups: 20 November 2024 (12pm), 29 November 2024, 10 December 2024 (1.30pm).

[219] r 59(1) ET Procedure Rules 2024.

decision orally, a written record of the decision will be sent out later,[220] and written reasons may be requested within 14 days of the sending of the written record of the decision.[221] There is no fee for the provision of written reasons and they may be requested by either party, whether or not they lost.

VIII. Conclusions

Participants in our research expressed considerable dissatisfaction with the tribunal system as currently structured. There was near unanimity that the forms used to bring and respond to claims are not working: parties need much more help to formulate their claims in the terms required by the legislation. We consider this issue in more detail in chapter eight. Thereafter, the process that is used in the tribunals is very broad and flexible. The difficulties highlighted within our research are that it lacks consistency across the different geographical reasons and there is insufficient differentiation between different types of case. There was significant support for stronger case management of cases – including limiting the issues that could be litigated – and the restriction of documentary and witness evidence, in proportion to the value and complexity of the case. There was a recognition that different cases need different approaches, both in terms of case management and administratively.

There is a strong perception of a large number of unmeritorious claims blocking up the system. This is not the view of the judiciary, nor do the statistics particularly support this. A good percentage of claims are struck out either without a hearing or at a preliminary hearing and the percentages of success and lack of success at a final hearing are about the same. However, it is unclear how 'success' is defined: if it only requires success in relation to one allegation – irrespective of the number of claims and allegations made – then the statistics may be misleading. Nevertheless, the major issue appears to be how claims are identified at the outset to ensure that only relevant claims are brought rather than the system being full of unmeritorious claims per se.

We turn now to consider alternative approaches to pleading requirements and dealing with unmeritorious claims.

[220] ibid, r 59(2).
[221] ibid, r 60(4).

8

Starting Claims and Dealing with Problem Pleadings

I. Introduction

In the last chapter we looked at the litigation process in the employment tribunal (ET) system. We considered some of the blockages in the system, as identified by our research participants, including unmeritorious cases and how claims are pleaded. It was particularly noted that many litigants in person now use AI, such as ChatGPT, to help draft their claims which has led to significantly longer claims covering a large number of legal issues, some of which are not legally relevant. Our findings therefore pointed to the need for the ET1 and ET3 forms to be re-thought, recognising the limited understanding most lay people have about what must be established for a legal claim to succeed. This was also considered to be key to dealing with the perceived volume of unmeritorious claims; many are badly pleaded, requiring very considerable judicial resources to identify the issues and claims within the morass of information produced, rather than necessarily being weak per se.

Many of the issues that have been raised about the operation of the tribunal system might have at least a partial solution in technology: a different way of producing a claim form and schedule of loss, an online means of seeing what is required on a claim and whether applications have been considered, and more effective identification of decisions that need to be made urgently. Therefore, in this chapter, we consider how a case must be pleaded in civil cases, particularly personal injury claims, and family cases, and whether lessons can be learned from that. We also consider whether AI might have a role to play to help rather than hinder the process (section II). We then look internationally and consider the claim forms used for the purpose of presenting claims in four other jurisdictions: Australia, New Zealand, Canada and the Republic of Ireland (section III). We consider the strengths and weaknesses of these different claim forms and what can be learned from the different approaches. We also examine how to address badly pleaded and unmeritorious cases (section IV). We argue that concerns about how unmeritorious claims are dealt with are in fact less of a concern; the real issue is how to ensure that claims are properly pleaded. We therefore make recommendations as to how the claim form should be changed to add clarity to claims brought.

II. Pleading Requirements

We begin by considering the very practical matter of pleading cases. We noted the criticisms of the ET1 and ET3 forms in chapter seven. In this section we consider how a case must be pleaded in other civil cases, particularly personal injury claims, and in family cases where we think the relevant forms provide a better model than the ET1 and ET3 because they use more specific questions. We also consider whether AI might help in improving the quality of pleadings.

A. Civil Court Pleadings

In the civil court, a case is started with the lodging of a claim form together with particulars of claim. This, together with the defence and any reply, 'should enable the court and the parties to identify and define the real issues in dispute, they are not evidence at trial'.[1] The particulars of claim must be contained in or served with the claim form.[2] When the particulars of claim are served, they must be accompanied by a form for defending or admitting the claim or acknowledging service of it.[3] The claim form itself must contain a concise statement of the nature of the claim, specify the remedy sought, contain a statement of value where the claim is for money and a statement of the interest sought, and set out any other matters required by a relevant Practice Direction (PD).[4] In personal injury claims, the claimant's date of birth and brief details of the claimant's injuries must be set out. The report of a medical practitioner who the claimant relies on must also be provided, together with a schedule of loss.[5] The claim form must be verified by a statement of truth.[6] Further, the particulars of claim must set out 'a concise statement of the facts on which the claimant relies' as well as whether the claimant is seeking interest, aggravated damages, exemplary damages and/or provisional damages.[7]

With regard to the particulars of claim and the contents of the defence, the Civil Procedure Rules (CPR) 'offer little guidance on drafting statements of case and contain no precedents or specimens'.[8] The White Book notes that specimen forms have been prescribed for possession claims, and useful guidance is 'regularly set out in the Chancery Guide, the King's Bench Guide and the Commercial Court guide'.[9] However there is nothing equivalent for personal injury claims. Nevertheless, a key principle is that '[s]tatements of case must be concise. They must plead only material facts, meaning those necessary for the purpose of

[1] *Kimathi v The Foreign and Commonwealth Office* [2018] EWHC 2066, [35]. See also Lord Justice Coulson (ed), *Civil Procedure: The White Book Service* (Vol 1, Sweet & Maxwell 2025) (White Book 2025).
[2] Civil Procedure Rules, r 7.4 (CPR).
[3] ibid, r 7.8.
[4] ibid, r 16.2.
[5] Practice Direction 16, para 4.
[6] r 22.1 CPR.
[7] ibid, r 16.4.
[8] White Book 2025, Pt 16.
[9] White Book 2025, 478.

formulating a cause of action or defence, and not background facts or evidence. Still less should they contain arguments, reasons or rhetoric'.[10] Only in exceptional cases should Particulars of Claim exceed 25 pages.[11]

The defence 'must deal with every allegation in the particulars of claim', specifying which allegations are denied, which are admitted and which allegations the defendant is unable to admit or deny but which the claimant is required to prove.[12] If an allegation is denied, then the defendant must set out their reasons for doing so and 'if they intend to put forward a different version of events from that given by the claimant, they must state their own version'.[13] There is a 'positive duty' for a defendant to admit or deny the allegations,[14] so as to prevent 'a stonewalling defence full of indiscriminate non-admissions'.[15] The defence must also be verified by a statement of truth.[16] In personal injury claims, the defendant must state whether they agree, dispute or have no knowledge of the matters in the medical report provided by the claimant and give reasons for any dispute. The same position is required of the schedule of loss.[17]

There is a balance to be struck between concision and pleading sufficient detail. The fact that a claim or issue has not been pleaded does not preclude a summary judgment application on such 'claim or issue' as the claim relies on.[18] Where a claim should obviously have been pleaded, the court may go straight to an 'unless order'[19] obliging a proper pleading to be produced.[20] If both sides have come to court ready to deal with an issue and it would be unjust not to address it, even though it has not been pleaded, the court may determine it.[21] More usually, if an issue is raised late and parties are not in a position to deal with it the court may adjourn the trial with costs consequences for the party who failed to plead the relevant issue.

This formality of process is appropriate for claims where parties are represented but may be a significant stumbling-block to unrepresented litigants and may therefore not be appropriate for many employment claims.

B. Family Court Pleadings

The Family Procedure Rules 2010[22] (FPR 2010) say very little about what is required when pleading a case. The rules simply require a person to complete the correct form and provide the information on that form.[23] For example, Form D8 is for a

[10] Leggatt J, as he then was, in *Tchenguiz v Grant Thornton UK LLP* [2015] EWHC 405, [1].
[11] PD16, para 1.3.
[12] r 16.5 CPR.
[13] ibid, r 16.5.
[14] White Book 2025, 489.
[15] Henderson LJ, *SPI North Ltd v Swiss Post International (UK) Ltd* [2019] EWCA Civ 7, [48].
[16] r 22.1 CPR.
[17] PD16, para 11.
[18] *Mishcon de Reya LLP v RJI (Middle East) Ltd* [2020] EWHC 1670.
[19] This says that unless a party performs an obligation by a specified date, they will be penalised by the sanction set out in the order: CPR, r 3.1(3).
[20] White Book 2025, 478.
[21] White Book 2025, 479.
[22] Family Procedure Rules 2010 SI 2010/2955 (FPR 2010).
[23] rr 5.1–5.3 FPR 2010.

request for a divorce or to dissolve a civil partnership; Form A is for giving notice of an intention to proceed with an application for a financial order; and Form D50H is for alteration of a maintenance agreement. The forms provide an explanation of what is being asked before providing limited space boxes or tick-box options to complete. A more detailed form is required where a financial order is sought consequent upon divorce or dissolution of a civil partnership. The form is, once again, self-explanatory with specific boxes for the answers to very precise questions. There is very little legal jargon; it is in user-friendly language. Section 4 provides boxes for more narrative and in box 4.4 'bad behaviour or conduct of the other party' must be set out. However, the form makes it clear that this 'will only be taken into account in very exceptional circumstances' when considering the division of assets.[24] If allegations are pursued in this regard, then they must be specified, must explain how they meet the threshold required and what the financial impact of the conduct is.[25]

Looking at the forms, we consider that they are straightforward to complete and most people would be able to understand what information needs to be provided and what documents must be attached, albeit it is a little difficult to navigate the website to identify the relevant form. The financial remedy form is particularly clear because of the precision of the questions that are asked and the boxes that are provided for the answers. This is especially important given the number of litigants in person who use the family courts and the degree of specificity in the forms provides a helpful model that could be used in employment claims. In addition, the family court forms do not use legal labels which is helpful for litigants in person. We think there is much to be gained from amending the ET1 and ET3 to something in line with the simplicity of the family court forms.

C. Using Artificial Intelligence

Issues with difficulty of pleading prompted us to consider whether AI might have a role. We were aware of practitioners raising concerns about an increased use of some AI models that were generic in their approach, resulting in lengthy and ever more complicated ET1s and ET3s.[26] However, we considered that a specialist AI model might be more productive.

We spoke with the founder and other team members at Valla, a company working to use AI to help claimants formulate and understand their claims. Valla provides a variety of services to clients including a case management tool allowing them to produce a chronology with documents attached and templates for grievance letters and ET1s. Of most interest to us is their assessment tool.

[24] See: assets.publishing.service.gov.uk/media/63c132468fa8f516ac0d5a6d/Form_E_0123_save.pdf.

[25] *Tsvetkov v Khayrova* [2023] EWFC 130 and 131.

[26] Material is being produced by employment tribunal judges to support litigants in person including YouTube videos about the process and what should go in a claim form. Dissemination of this information online will have the additional benefit of influencing the AI algorithms which may also help to improve them.

We were told that Valla's ambition is to 'clean up claims before the ET'. The key was 'claim identification'. The company was started because of a belief that there was a real need for something inexpensive to help people understand what claims they had before they tried to present them in the ET1. Initially Valla used a decision tree approach to identifying claims by asking clients questions that arose from their earlier answers. This is still used to create their ET1 form but a 'peace of mind' check by a human is also provided where the claims are often reduced and refined through discussion. They found that the main stumbling-block was a lack of understanding of what particular terms meant. Even when natural language is used, a decision tree still relies on a person 'recognising the language'. A recent survey that Valla conducted through YouGov showed that most participants did not understand the terms 'discrimination' or 'disability' in the legal context. However refined they made the decision tree process, Valla found it remained inaccurate. In addition, people using Valla were 'anxious to include everything' but did 'not really know what to include'. Therefore, Valla had 'built an assessment tool to identify claims' and this generative AI tool performed considerably better than decision trees.

For £149, a client can upload documents to the Valla system and the AI tool will build a timeline of legally relevant points. The documents are usually a grievance letter and response or disciplinary letter and hearing notes or they may be notes written by the client. In addition to the timeline, the AI tool will set out a list of claims that it thinks the client has. Then the client will have a one-hour call with a 'coach', many of whom are legally qualified, to discuss those claims. The transcript of the call is put through the AI model again and the claims identified are refined. A report is written for the client. The coach will review the report and may refine it further. The report sets out what claims the client has, the merits of them, the likely remedy, and the next steps the client should take.

The team said that many of their coaches had been sceptical about how accurate the AI tool would be in identifying the claimants' claims but they had discovered that in 88 per cent of cases, the AI tool's assessment of which claims exist following its analysis of the transcript accords with the claims that are presented in the final report after human analysis. The team's experience is that it is substantially more accurate than the claims identified by clients using a decision tree model.

AI is also being used by Felix Steffek and his team to predict the outcomes in employment tribunal cases. As they note:

> Employment tribunals play a critical role in resolving disputes between employers and employees, yet the volume and complexity of cases create challenges for timely and consistent resolution. Predicting case outcomes through advanced AI can enhance access to justice, streamline legal processes and help stakeholders make better-informed decisions.[27]

[27] Holli Sargeant and Felix Steffek, 'Benchmarking Case Outcome Prediction for the UK Employment Tribunal: The CLC-UKET Dataset', Oxford Law Blogs: blogs.law.ox.ac.uk/oblb/blog-post/2025/01/benchmarking-case-outcome-prediction-uk-employment-tribunal-clc-uket-dataset. This provides a succinct summary; there are links to their papers in the blog.

However, 'publicly accessible, comprehensive datasets are rare, particularly those that offer standardised annotations of legal decisions'. They have therefore created their own dataset 'providing an extensive, curated collection of UKET cases, annotated and organised to enhance predictability and transparency within employment dispute resolution'.[28] They anticipate that in the future this will be 80–90 per cent accurate. If this is correct, it would help claimants gain, with some legal help, an idea of the strength of their claim and its potential outcome.

In an ideal world, everybody who is contemplating bringing a claim to the ET would have good access to legal advice to discuss the issues, identify potential claims and receive a view on the merits of, and likely remedies for, those claims. However, there is not the funding for legal aid to be reinstated (though there is an interesting argument whether early legal help funding would reduce the costs to the tribunal system sufficiently that it would at least not cost more than it does currently). We are aware of significant problems with AI including 'hallucinations' when AI is asked about case law. However, it appears that the model being used by Valla may be of interest going forward as a means of drawing together a simple timeline of events out of a large volume of documentation and of better identifying claims that an individual may have.

While caution is required, there may be real opportunities in using AI to help people where early legal advice is unavailable. Our participants suggested better use of decision trees to guide people through the ET1 (and ET3) forms and to help them focus on precisely what their claims are. We think that this would go some way to helping claims to be more specific and focused. However, there is an underlying difficulty – as identified by Valla – that decision trees require a level of understanding of core legal concepts that many people lack. A good generative AI model may go some way to fill that gap.

III. Application Forms in Other Jurisdictions

The forms used in other UK jurisdictions provide some help in thinking about what a different claim form might look like. However, we decided to cast the net

[28] They explain 'Through an iterative approach to prompt design, we optimized the LLM's performance for annotating the following details: (1) facts, (2) claims, (3) references to legal statutes, (4) references to precedents, (5) general case outcomes, (6) general case outcomes labelled as "claimant wins", "claimant loses", "claimant partly wins", and "other", (7) detailed orders and remedies and (8) reasons'. In this prediction task, 'given a set of case facts and claims, the model generates an outcome label that falls into one of four categories: "claimant wins", "claimant loses", "claimant partly wins" or "other"'. To establish a baseline for model performance, 'human predictions were collected by providing experts access to the same facts and claims without the actual case outcomes'.

more widely to see whether there are lessons to be learned from other jurisdictions. Given the advantages of the Australian and New Zealand systems identified in chapter six, we start by considering the claim forms used there (section III.A and III.B). We then look beyond them to Canada (section III.C) and the Republic of Ireland (section III.D).

A. Australia

The website for the Fair Work Commission (FWC) contains over a hundred forms. They each address different types of claim or response or application during the FWC process. The forms are named using language that is mostly likely to be comprehensible to a layperson. There are some that use technical language. The three claim forms that are of most interest to us are: the F2 Form for unfair dismissal, the F8 form for 'general protections' claims involving dismissal, and the F8C form for 'general protections' claims not involving dismissal.[29] 'Unfair dismissal' claims are available to employees who have completed a 'minimum employment period'[30] and will usually succeed where the dismissal was 'harsh, unjust or unreasonable', and was not a 'genuine redundancy'.[31] 'General protections' claims usually relate to 'adverse action' taken by an employer against a worker for a 'prohibited reason'. These prohibited reasons include discrimination,[32] exercise of workplace rights,[33] and union/industrial activities.[34]

After questions about personal details, representation and dates of employment and dismissal, the first free-text question of the F2 Unfair Dismissal form asks simply 'what outcome are you seeking by lodging this application?'[35] This is of interest in light of the focus by the FWC on resolving disputes at an early stage: the requirement to specify the remedy sought as the first substantive question emphasises the forward-looking nature of the exercise. We think this is particularly helpful.

The next questions explore the reason for the dismissal (see Figure 8.1).

[29] The forms were updated in November 2025. The forms we are referring to predate the amendments that were made at that time.

[30] Fair Work Act 2009, s 382.

[31] ibid, s 385.

[32] ibid, s 351.

[33] ibid, s 340.

[34] ibid, s 346.

[35] For the new form see: www.fwc.gov.au/documents/forms/form_f2.pdf. The old form is no longer available online.

Figure 8.1 Excerpt from (previous) F2 Unfair Dismissal form[36]

3. Dismissal

3.1 What were the reasons for the dismissal, if any, given by the employer?

Using numbered paragraphs, specify the reason(s), if any, given by the employer for your dismissal. Attach any letter of dismissal and/or separation certificate given to you by the employer. Note that the Commission will send copies of any documents you provide to the employer. Attach extra pages if necessary.

3.2 Why was the dismissal unfair?

Using numbered paragraphs, describe the relevant facts and circumstances and specify why you say the dismissal was unfair. This should include:

- your response to any reasons for dismissal given by the employer
- whether you were counselled or warned by the employer of any deficiencies in your performance or conduct and the circumstances of each counselling session or warning
- why you believe the dismissal was unfair.

Although limited explanatory instructions are provided at each stage, the questions asked are reasonably straightforward. Because the form is asking only about unfair dismissal the bullet points under the questions provide a reasonable indication of what is required. Moreover, the request for documents to be attached once again focuses the applicant on the essential issues in their claim. There are no further substantive questions: the next two pages contain only space for signatures and questions about payment and information sharing.

Form F8 – dealing with general protections involving dismissal[37] – asks about remedies as its first substantive question. Thereafter, the following questions ask about the 'alleged contravention' (Figure 8.2).

Figure 8.2 Question relating to 'alleged contravention'[38]

3. Alleged contravention

3.1 Describe the actions of the employer, including any reasons given for your dismissal, that have led you to make this application.

Using numbered paragraphs, describe the relevant facts and circumstances. Specify the reason(s), if any, given by the employer for your dismissal. Attach any letter of dismissal and/or separation certificate given to you by the employer. Note that the Commission will send copies of any documents you provide to the employer. Attach extra pages if necessary.

[36] ibid.

[37] For the new form see: www.fwc.gov.au/documents/forms/form_f8.pdf. The old form is no longer available online.

[38] ibid.

Figure 8.3 Excerpt from Form F8 dealing with general protections involving dismissal

3.2 Do you allege that you were dismissed in contravention of the general protections provisions in Part 3-1 of the *Fair Work Act 2009*?

You can only make a general protections application involving dismissal if you have been dismissed and you allege your dismissal was in contravention of the general protections provisions in Part 3-1 of the Fair Work Act 2009.

☐ Yes [Go to question 3.3]

☐ No [You cannot make this application. See page ii of this form for more information]

3.3 Which section(s) of the *Fair Work Act 2009* did the employer contravene when they dismissed you?

You should only make a general protections dismissal application if your employer dismissed you **because** you have the protections described in one or more sections of the Fair Work Act 2009 listed below. See the General Protections Benchbook for information.

Division 3 – Workplace rights

☐ section 340 Protection

☐ section 343 Coercion

Division 4 – Industrial activities

☐ section 346 Protection

☐ section 348 Coercion

Division 5 – Other protections

☐ section 351 Discrimination - select the attribute as set out in section 351(1):

☐	Race	☐	Colour
☐	Sex	☐	Sexual orientation
☐	Breastfeeding	☐	Gender identity
☐	Intersex status	☐	Age
☐	Physical or mental disability	☐	Marital status
☐	Family or carer's responsibilities	☐	Subjection to family and domestic violence
☐	Pregnancy	☐	Religion
☐	Political opinion	☐	National extraction or social origin

☐ section 352 Temporary absence – illness or injury

Division 6 – Sham arrangements

☐ section 358 Dismissing to engage as an independent contractor

☐ section 359B Dismissing to engage as a casual employee

The language of 'alleged contravention' is not very user-friendly, although the following wording of Q3.1 is easier to understand. Helpfully, applicants are asked to provide relevant documents. However, the lengthy free-form text box is less focused than the unfair dismissal form. Question 3.2 asks the applicant to confirm that they are alleging there has been a dismissal in contravention of the 'general protections' and Q3.3 asks the applicant, as a multiple-choice question, to select which of the protections the employer contravened (see fig. 8.3).

The final question is Q3.4, which gives an empty text box and asks, 'Explain how the actions you have described in Q3.1 have contravened the section(s) of the *Fair Work Act 2009* you identified in question 3.3'.

The approach is therefore similar to the ET1, using a tick-box approach to the type of claim, and then providing an opportunity to explain in free-text. There is a higher level of specificity on the Australian Form F8 because, on the ET1, all of these headings would be covered by 'unfair dismissal' and 'discrimination', whereas the F8 has separate space, for example, for 'industrial activities'. More helpfully, the form separates out the question of 'what happened' at Q3.1, from the question of, essentially, 'why was it unlawful' at Q3.4. It seems likely that this would enable applicants to provide greater clarity about their claim.

Form F8C – general protections application not involving dismissal[39] – is materially the same as Form F8. Q3.1 asks the applicant to describe the employer's actions, and Q3.2 then provides a similar list of tick boxes (albeit the list of options differs slightly), asking which section of the Fair Work Act the employer contravened. Q3.3 asks the applicant to explain how the employer's conduct contravened the protection in question.

The use of different forms for different types of claim has significant advantages because the forms can then be more closely tailored to the claim that is being brought, but this raises difficulties for people in locating and determining the correct form to use, and poses problems where claims concern multiple different types of claim. It is also helpful that the form asks for certain basic documents to be attached. However, the forms for the FWC still use specific legal terminology and provide lengthy free-text boxes that could result in a lack of focus on the required detail.

B. New Zealand

Before making an application to the Employment Relations Authority, most applicants will have been through mediation with the Mediation Service. There are three different forms to request online mediation depending on the nature of the problem being raised: a work-related problem, collective bargaining, and lockout/strike notice. The work-related problem form asks for basic details and then asks the applicant if they have raised the problem internally, if their employer is willing to mediate, how long they have been employed for, and whether they remain

[39] For the new form see: www.fwc.gov.au/documents/forms/form_f8c.pdf.

employed. They are then simply asked to set out the 'Nature of the problem'. There is no further explanation. Documents may be attached to the request for mediation. While this allows an applicant to explain in narrative form the issues they are facing, we do not think this level of generality is particularly helpful as a model.

If mediation is unsuccessful, then the applicant may apply to the Employment Relations Authority.[40] The form that is used to make an application provides space for the personal details of the applicant and respondent, and then asks three substantive questions, each followed by a few lines for free-text:

1. The problem or matter that I wish the Authority to resolve is: [state details fully, fairly and clearly];
2. The facts that have given rise to the problem or matter are: [state details fully, fairly, and clearly];
3. I would like the problem or matter to be resolved in the following way: [state details fully, fairly and clearly].

There are then questions about willingness to mediate, attaching evidence, and the prescribed fee. The website says that the applicant should also upload certain documents: 'your employment agreement (if you have one); payslips from your employer (if you have these); any correspondence (for example, letters and emails) between you and the respondent; and notes from any meetings you have had about the problem'.[41] This form is very similar to the ET1 with limited specificity and extended free-text space. The division between the problem/matter to be resolved and the facts that have given rise to it is unlikely to be helpful: it is unclear what should go into which box.

Discrimination complaints must first be made to the Human Rights Commission, which will try to resolve them through mediation.[42] The form for these complaints asks for the personal details of the applicant and respondent and then provides a tick-box list to specify the grounds of discrimination: age, race, disability, etc. A free-text box is provided after each of the following substantive questions:

- When did this happen? Day/month/year, or a date range.
- What happened? Please summarise the key point: what happened, where did it happen, who was involved?
- How has this affected you?
- Have you tried sorting out your complaint another way? For example, have you talked to the person, gone to your employer or complained to another agency?
- What outcomes are you seeking?

While there is a little more specificity than the equivalent questions in the ET1, the commentary requested is relatively limited. As this is an application for mediation then this may explain the more narrative style of the request.

[40] See: www.era.govt.nz/about-us/forms (Form 1).
[41] See: www.era.govt.nz/resolution-process/lodge-your-application.
[42] See: tikatangata.org.nz/resources-and-support/make-a-complaint.

Where mediation is unsuccessful then the complainant may bring a claim before the Human Rights Review Tribunal.[43] Parts 1 and 2 of the relevant form deal with the personal details of the parties. Part 3 requires the complainant to specify the provisions of the Human Rights Act 1993 they 'consider to have been contravened' providing a free-text box to do so. Once again, the legal terminology is notable, and we consider this unhelpful. Part 4 then seeks to establish the details of the case (Figure 8.4).

Figure 8.4 New Zealand form for discrimination (Part 4)[44]

Part 4: Facts of the case

What do you say the defendant has done or not done (or the defendants have done or not done) that contravened the provisions of the Human Rights Act 1993 in your case?

State briefly and clearly the facts giving rise to your claim such as:

- When (date and time) did this happen?
- Where did this happen?
- Who was involved?
- What have the consequences been for you as a result of the alleged infringement?

Please state each allegation in a separate numbered paragraph.

1.

2.

Part 5 asks which orders are sought, again in numbered paragraphs (Figure 8.5).

Figure 8.5 New Zealand form for discrimination (Part 5)[45]

Part 5: What order(s) do you want the Tribunal to make?

With reference to sections 92I to 92W of the Human Rights Act 1993, please state the particular orders that you want the Tribunal to make. If you are claiming a sum of money, specify the amount and show how this amount was reached. If you need additional space, please attach a separate sheet of paper.

Take further notice that at a date and time to be fixed by the Chairperson of the Human Rights Review Tribunal you (the plaintiff) will ask the Tribunal to make the following orders:

1.

2.

[43] See: www.justice.govt.nz/assets/Documents/Forms/Statement-of-Claim-HRA-v0.1.pdf.
[44] ibid.
[45] ibid.

It is perhaps helpful to have the numbered paragraph structure and specific bullet point questions in Part 4 but the form is very similar to the ET1.

In conclusion, since neither the Australian nor the New Zealand forms entirely meet the needs of a closely tailored approach to which questions are asked and greater specificity in those questions to elicit more precise answers, we looked to Canada and Ireland to consider the content of their application forms.

C. Canada

In Canada, several of the provincial jurisdictions use application forms that are very similar to the ET1 in that they provide large text boxes allowing for extensive free-form answers to general questions.[46] However, we found an impressive specificity in the 'monetary complaints' form applying to the Federal Labour Program.[47] There are different forms for 'monetary and non-monetary' complaints and for 'unjust dismissals'. After asking for the personal information of the applicant and the employer, Section C deals with monetary complaints and requires claimants to tick the relevant boxes (from a selection of 13, such as 'unpaid wages' or 'overtime pay'), and then complete the next three columns: period covered from, period covered to and estimated amount.

The specificity and simplicity is attractive and likely to make things easier for a litigant in person, and for a respondent in understanding what a monetary claim is about. By using separate forms for dismissal claims and separating out the monetary from the non-monetary elements, this allows for greater focus in the following questions.

Where a claim is brought to the Canada Industrial Relations Board in relation to Health and Safety Reprisals, a different approach is taken. After the basic questions of personal details, the form asks a series of very specific questions dealing with the particular elements of the claim that must be proved.

[46] See, eg, the Ontario Human Rights Tribunal application: tribunalsontario.ca/hrto/forms-and-filing/, although the detail provided in the guidance is impressive and by giving practical examples, it is user-friendly: tribunalsontario.ca/documents/hrto/Guides/Applicants%20Guide.html. See also the British Colombia Employment Standards Branch Complaint Form: www2.gov.bc.ca/assets/gov/employment-business-and-economic-development/employment-standards-workplace-safety/employment-standards/forms/complaint_form.pdf and the British Colombia Human Rights Tribunal form: www.bchrt.bc.ca/app/uploads/sites/876/2024/07/form-1.1-print.pdf.

[47] See: catalogue.servicecanada.gc.ca/content/EForms/en/Detail.html?Form=LAB1189.

Figure 8.6 Claim form for applications to the Canada Industrial Relations Board re Health and Safety Reprisals: details of claim[48]

- Did you refuse to perform what you believe was unsafe work?

  ☐ No

  ☐ Yes – Please explain:

- If you refused to perform what you believe was unsafe work, did you raise this with your supervisor?

  ☐ No

  ☐ Yes – Please explain:

- Did you raise this issue as an individual employee or as part of your duties as an occupational health and safety representative?

- When did you first raise your health and safety issue?

- With whom did you raise your health and safety issue? Please check all that apply.

  ☐ Supervisor: ______

  ☐ Health and safety representative: ______

  ☐ Employer representative: ______

  ☐ Other–Please specify: ______

The form then asks about how the complaint was handled and about disciplinary action that was taken, again using a series of specific questions (fig 8.7).

[48] See: cirb-ccri.gc.ca/en/resources/section-147-reprisal-complaint-canada. The form is reproduced in part.

Figure 8.7 Claim form for applications to the Canada Industrial Relations Board re Health and Safety Reprisals: action in consequence[49]

How was your complaint handled? Please check all that apply. Attach all relevant documents.

- ☐ The complaint was referred to a workplace committee, a health and safety representative, or someone else authorized to receive such complaints.
- ☐ The complaint was investigated.
- ☐ The complaint was investigated and an investigation report was prepared.
- ☐ The complaint was referred to a health and safety officer of the Labour Program.
- ☐ The health and safety officer rendered a decision about the complaint.
- ☐ The decision of the health and safety officer was appealed.
- ☐ The appeals officer rendered a decision.
- ☐ Other–Please specify:

II–Disciplinary Action

Do you believe that your employer disciplined you or retaliated against you for raising your health and safety issue?

☐ Yes ☐ No

If yes, please respond to the following questions, and attach all relevant documents.

- ☐ If your employment was terminated–Date of dismissal or termination:
- ☐ If you were laid off–Date of layoff:
- ☐ If you were suspended–Date of suspension:

  Length of suspension:
- ☐ If you were demoted–Date of demotion:

If your working conditions were changed, when and how did this occur?

If your wages were affected, when and how did this occur?

Other–Please specify

- Why do you believe the disciplinary action imposed against you is because you raised a health and safety issue?

[49] ibid. The form is reproduced in part.

After a series of questions that are specific to unionised employees, Section III asks applicants to:

> Provide a chronology of the facts and events in support of your complaint. Include details such as the dates on which events occurred, the date you reported your health and safety concerns to the employer or took other actions. Include the names of the employer and health and safety officials involved and the names of any witnesses.
>
> Please mention and attach any relevant documents that you are filing in support of your complaint. Number or assign a letter to each document (e.g., A, B, C). Examples of relevant documents include: documents related to the reported issue, workplace health and safety committee minutes, investigation report or the decision of the Minister, a Labour Canada officer or appeals officer. If certain documents are not in your possession, please mention this and explain why.
>
> You may use additional pages if necessary. Please print clearly and number the pages.

The series of short free-text questions in Part II is an effective way of gathering all the necessary information in a way that litigants in person can engage with. This approach is possible because this form is specific to health and safety concerns, so the questions asked will be of relevance to all complaints using this form. The combination of the short free-text answers and the request for a detailed chronology may result in repetition and perhaps confusion. However, the requirement to provide documents at the outset, together with the guidance about numbering them and examples of what should be provided, is very helpful.

D. Republic of Ireland

The Workplace Relations Commission e-Complaint Form requires applicants to complete each section of the form before they can access the next section.[50] After requesting basic details, the form takes the complainant to the 'General Complaint area' where they can create one or more 'specific complaints'. Documentation can also be uploaded to support each specific complaint. Once the complainant clicks 'create', they may select the type of complaint from a drop-down menu, and a range of sub-types are then available as a tick-box selection. Below is the example from the 'user guide', in which a complaint as to 'pay' has been selected (see Fig 8.8).

[50] Helpfully, the user guide provides screenshots of each section: www.workplacerelations.ie/en/publications_forms/wrc-ecomplaint-portal-user-guide.pdf.

Figure 8.8 Example from the Irish 'user guide' where a complaint as to 'pay' has been selected[51]

My complaint falls under (Please select from the drop down list below):

Pay

My complaint more specifically falls under: *

- I do not receive the National Minimum Rate of Pay
- I am not given compensation for working on a Sunday
- I do not get a payslip
- My payslip does not show the gross wages payable and/or the amount of any deductions
- My employer has made an unlawful deduction from my wages and/or tips or gratuities
- My employer has not paid me or has paid me less than the amount due to me
- My employer pays me by a method other than that legally prescribed
- My employer is not keeping statutory employment records
- I did not receive my paid holiday/annual leave entitlement
- I have not received my Public Holiday entitlements
- I did not receive the appropriate payment in lieu of notice of termination of my employment
- I did not receive a statement of my average hourly rate of pay
- I do not receive the minimum rates(s) of pay set out in an Employment Regulation Order (ERO)
- I do not receive the minimum rate(s) of pay set out in a Sectoral Employment Orders (SEO)
- My employer has not paid me my paid sick leave

Further questions may still be asked after this point, though the user guide notes that not all of these will be mandatory. If, for example, the complainant selects 'Pay', and then 'I do not receive the National Minimum Rate of Pay', they will be given the option to enter a 'pay reference period', and the most recent date of underpayment, as well as to state whether they have obtained a statement from their employer regarding their rate of pay for the reference period. For some complaint types, the complainant will then be able to choose between 'adjudication' and 'inspection' as the means of resolution. Finally, they will be asked (optionally) to provide details of their pay where relevant, and whether they would be willing to undergo mediation.

[51] ibid.

There is an impressive level of granularity in these forms, asking the complainant for specific information depending on the nature of the claim. This achieves the same result as having different forms for different types of claim and increases the chances that all the relevant information will be provided, particularly by those with no legal expertise. This granularity is facilitated by the electronic nature of the form. Trying to compose a branching decision tree to encompass all the possible selections by the complainant would be impossible on paper, and, in any case, hugely unwieldy for a litigant to use.

E. Interim Conclusions

There are varying approaches to claim forms across the different jurisdictions we reviewed. We think that the most useful forms are those with a good degree of granularity where applicants are asked only questions that are relevant to the claims that they are making. In this regard, the Irish Workplace Relations Commission e-form is particularly effective. However, it still uses technical legal terminology and requires applicants to know what kind of claim they are seeking to bring. We also commend the Australian form asking about the remedy sought as the first question. This ensures that the focus is on the resolution of the dispute.

IV. Badly Pleaded and Unmeritorious Claims

Our emphasis on improving the quality of the claim forms is intended to help address another theme that emerged from our empirical research: a concern about the tribunals' reluctance to strike out unmeritorious claims. So we have considered and compared the approach to striking out claims in the civil courts. However, the approach is broadly similar to that found in the employment tribunals (section IV.A). Therefore, we cast our net more widely to consider whether a permission mechanism might help limit claims that are unlikely to succeed and we have explored how permission applications work in judicial review claims (section IV.B). We are unconvinced that this would help because of the fact-sensitive nature of most employment tribunal claims.

A. Comparing Strike Outs in Employment Tribunals and Civil Courts

A criticism of participants in our research was that tribunals should be more ready to strike out claims that were hopeless. We have considered the approach to strike out applications in the civil courts to see whether there is a significant divergence in approach and whether the employment tribunals are being more lenient than the civil courts.

In the civil courts a claim may be struck out where the 'statement of case discloses no reasonable grounds for bringing or defending the claim'[52] as opposed to the employment tribunal rules which require that the claim has 'no reasonable prospect of success'.[53] This difference in wording does not appear to cause a significantly different approach.

First, when faced with incoherent pleadings, while the employment tribunal is required to consider in reasonable detail what the claims and issues are[54] and the possibility of amendment;[55] the civil courts take a stricter approach. Cases 'which are incoherent and make no sense' are given as an example of a case that is appropriate for strike out.[56] In *Ashraf v Lester Dominic Solicitors*, Smith J held that an 'unreasonably vague and incoherent' statement of case which is 'likely to obstruct the just disposal of the case' can be struck out (although Smith J indicated that this could be a strike out on the ground of abuse of process).[57] However, where there is a reason to believe that an amendment could cure a defect in a statement of case, the court will normally refrain from striking out the statement of case until the court has given the party the opportunity to amend it.[58]

Second, when dealing with a claim that cannot succeed in law, the tribunal can strike such a claim out,[59] as can the civil courts where a case contains 'a coherent set of facts but those facts, even if true, do not disclose any legally recognisable claim against the defendant'.[60]

Third, where a claim depends on disputed facts, then the tribunal will generally not strike the claim out.[61] The civil courts mostly take a similar stance: in *Bridgeman v McAlpine Brown*, Hale LJ held that '[t]he essence of a strike out is that one does not look at the evidence on the claim'.[62] On the facts, a strike out was inappropriate because there 'was a serious live issue of fact of the sort that ought properly to be determined by hearing oral evidence from all involved'.[63] Moreover, the case law also states 'there is nothing wrong in the practice of bringing an application under both Part 3 and Part 24 on the basis that the claim is factually hopeless'.[64] This is similar to the approach of the employment tribunals. Both courts and employment tribunals are reluctant to strike out claims on disputed

[52] r 3.4(2)(a) CPR.
[53] Employment Tribunal Procedure Rules 2024, r 38.
[54] *Cox v Adecco* [2021] ICR 1307, [28](5).
[55] ibid, [28](9).
[56] PD3A, para 1.2.
[57] *Ashraf v Lester Dominic Solicitors* [2023] EWHC 2800 (Ch), [68]–[70].
[58] *Soo Kim v Young Geun Park* [2011] EWHC 1781 (QB), [40]–[41].
[59] *Romanowska v Aspirations Care Ltd* UKEAT/0015/14, [1].
[60] PD3A, para 1.2.
[61] *Ezsias v North Glamorgan NHS Trust* [2007] ICR 1126, [29]. See further ch 7.
[62] *Bridgeman v McAlpine Brown* (CA, 19 January 2000), [21].
[63] ibid, [24].
[64] *Libyan Investment Authority v King* [2020] EWCA Civ 1690, [2021] 1 WLR 2659, [57](4).

facts, but there are exceptional cases where a strike out is appropriate because the factual case is obviously wrong. The approach to discrimination claims in the civil courts is the same as that in the tribunals.[65]

Therefore, the civil courts broadly approach the question of strike out in the same way as tribunals, save in one regard. That is, the emphasis on understanding the claim and identifying the issues before making the strike out decision. That perhaps reflects the stricter approach to pleadings that is taken under the civil procedure rules and the expectation that, despite many claimants being litigants in person, those rules must be complied with.

B. Permission in Judicial Review

Given that the strike out powers are mostly used in the same way in civil litigation and in the employment tribunal (save in relation to how pleadings are analysed), we wondered whether there might be scope for a 'gateway' of permission to be used to filter cases out of the system at an early stage. We therefore looked at judicial review where permission must be obtained to bring a claim. The requirement for permission adds a further step to the litigation process but it also enables the court to have oversight at an early stage of which claims proceed.

i. The Process

Before reaching the permission stage of judicial review, the claimant is expected to exhaust all suitable alternative remedies and the parties may also undertake forms of alternative dispute resolution.[66] Thereafter, the claimant sends a letter before claim and the respondent sends a letter of response;[67] the parties prepare and serve statements of case; and then the claimant applies for permission to make a claim for judicial review. Before the application for permission takes place, the defendant will have provided an acknowledgment of service together with their summary grounds of resisting the claim.[68] This means that, when the court is deciding whether to grant permission, it will have the benefit of these summary grounds.[69]

Permission to proceed is required in every claim for judicial review.[70] The court may decide to grant permission for the claimant to rely on some, but not all,

[65] *Sivanandan v London Borough of Islington* [2005] EWHC 3213 (Admin).

[66] I Hare et al, *De Smith's Judicial Review* (Sweet & Maxwell, 2023) para 16–013.

[67] In accordance with the Pre-Action Protocol for Judicial Review, paras 14–24 (www.justice.gov.uk/courts/procedure-rules/civil/protocol/prot_jrv).

[68] r 54.8 CPR.

[69] Indeed, the purpose of the requirement to serve summary grounds is to assist the court in deciding whether to grant permission: Courts and Tribunals Judiciary, *The Administrative Court Judicial Review Guide 2024* (Admin Court Guide 2024) para 8.3.5; *R (Ministry of Defence) v Wiltshire and Swindon Coroner* [2005] EWHC 889 (Admin), [2006] 1 WLR 134, [44].

[70] r 54.4 CPR.

of their grounds for judicial review.[71] If the claimant wishes to rely on new grounds for judicial review at the final hearing, they must obtain permission to add those new grounds.[72]

The permission application will be considered on the papers.[73] Where permission is granted, then the case will go to a substantive hearing. Where it is refused, written reasons will be given[74] and the claimant may file a renewal notice within seven days of service of the court's reasons.[75] An oral permission hearing will be held to determine whether permission should be granted. The oral permission hearing is usually listed for 30 minutes, to include the judge giving their judgment.[76]

However, if the application is refused as 'totally without merit', then the case comes to an end, and the claimant has no right to seek oral reconsideration of the refusal of permission.[77] An application is totally without merit if there is 'no rational basis on which the claim could succeed'. In contrast, the judge should refuse permission, but not certify the application as totally without merit, where the claimant 'has identified a rational argument in support of his claim but where the judge is confident that, even taking the case at its highest, it is wrong'.[78] Where the claim form and grounds are too confused or inadequate to disclose a claim worthy of granting permission, but where the judge nevertheless suspects that proper presentation might disclose an arguable claim, the judge should usually refuse permission but should not certify the application as totally without merit.[79]

For permission to be granted, the court must be satisfied that the claim for judicial review is 'arguable' or has a 'realistic prospect of success'. The claim must be more than potentially arguable on a speculative basis and in the hope that the case may strengthen over time.[80] Moreover, the court must be satisfied that all alternative remedies have been used,[81] there has not been undue delay in applying for judicial review,[82] the claimant has standing ('sufficient interest in the matter') to bring the claim,[83] the outcome would have been substantially different

[71] ibid, r 54.12(1)(ii).
[72] ibid, r 54.15.
[73] Admin Court Guide 2024 (n 69) para 9.1.2.
[74] r 54.12(2) CPR.
[75] ibid, r 54.12.
[76] Admin Court Guide 2024 (n 69) para 9.5.1.
[77] r 54.12(7) CPR.
[78] *R (Wasif) v Home Secretary* [2016] EWCA Civ 82, [15].
[79] ibid, [17](5).
[80] *Sharma v Brown-Antoine* [2006] UKPC 57, [2007] 1 WLR 780, [14](4).
[81] *R (Archer) v Revenue and Customs Commissioners* [2019] EWCA Civ 1021, [89]–[93] and *R (Sivasubramaniam) v Wandsworth County Court* [2002] EWCA Civ 1738, [46]–[47].
[82] r 54.5(1) CPR.
[83] Senior Courts Act 1981, s 31(3) (SCA 1981). Although generally this should be left to the substantive hearing: *IRC v National Federation of Self-Employed and Small Businesses Ltd* [1982] AC 617, 630, in simple cases it may be addressed at the permission stage 'to prevent abuse by busybodies, cranks, and other mischief-makers' (653).

if the defendant's conduct complained of had not occurred,[84] and the claim is not premature[85] or academic.[86]

ii. Assessment

In 2024,[87] claimants lodged 2,995 judicial review cases. Of these cases, 1,098 reached the permission stage. At the paper sift stage, permission was granted in 311 cases (ie, 28 per cent of the cases that reached the permission stage); it was refused in 660 cases (60 per cent); and the case was withdrawn or the outcome is unknown in 127 cases (12 per cent).

Out of the 660 cases which were refused permission at the first stage, 102 cases went to the oral renewal stage and permission was granted in 27 cases. Thus, the total number of cases which were granted permission, either on the papers or after oral reconsideration, was 338. One hundred and fifty-five cases were classed as totally without merit.[88] Bondy and Sunkin found that the proportion of applications obtaining permission decreased from 71 per cent in 1981 to 22 per cent in 2006.[89] The claimant's failure to satisfy the judge that their claim was sufficiently arguable was the most common reason for refusing permission.[90]

In 2021, the Independent Review of Administrative Law (IRAL) found that the permission stage is a significant filter of judicial review claims.[91] For the most part, judges' refusals of permission on the papers did not lead to a high number of oral renewal hearings.[92] In addition, after permission was granted, parties often went on to settle their claims without the need for a final hearing.[93] The majority of respondents to the IRAL supported the current law on permission and considered that the permission stage is an effective filter of judicial review claims. Raising the bar for claimants, or limiting the right to request an oral renewal hearing, would risk filtering out meritorious claims. The oral renewal process was essential to ensure access to justice; and put together, the Pre-Action Protocol and the permission requirement made judicial review an efficient process for resolving many disputes without the need for formal litigation.[94]

[84] s 31, SCA 1981.

[85] *R (Gill) v Cabinet Office* [2019] EWHC 3407, [88]. See also *R (De Whalley) v Norfolk County Council* [2011] EWHC 3739, [35]; *De Smith's Judicial Review* (n 66) para 16–062.

[86] *R (Heathrow Hub Ltd) v Transport Secretary* [2020] EWCA Civ 213, [208]–[210]. See also Admin Court Guide 2024 (n 69) para 9.1.6.

[87] Ministry of Justice, *Civil Justice Statistics Quarterly: October to December 2024*, Table 2.2.

[88] ibid, Table 2.4.

[89] V Bondy and M Sunkin, *The Dynamics of Judicial Review Litigation: The resolution of public law challenges before final hearing* (Public Law Project 2009) 49–50.

[90] ibid, 53 and 58.

[91] Lord Faulks et al, *The Independent Review of Administrative Law* (CP 407, March 2021) para 4.41.

[92] ibid, para 4.74.

[93] ibid, para 4.46.

[94] ibid, para C50.

The judicial review process is very similar to the sift process in the Employment Appeal Tribunal, with an equivalent system of the papers being considered, an oral hearing where the appeal is not permitted to proceed, and a 'totally without merit' refusal which prevents an oral hearing being sought. It is clear that a permission process can be highly effective in ensuring that unmeritorious claims do not proceed, and nudging people to resolve meritorious claims away from litigation. However, while there are attractions to this approach, the difference with employment tribunal claims is that they are usually highly fact-sensitive which would not lend themselves to a permission decision. By contrast, judicial review claims tend to be more procedurally focused, and Employment Appeal Tribunal decisions are only concerned with an error of law, enabling a clearer view to be taken at an early stage of whether the claim should be permitted to proceed.

The fundamental issue in employment tribunal proceedings appears to be helping claimants to articulate their claims at an early stage, limiting them appropriately, so that a proper assessment can be made as to their merits, rather than necessarily a change to the striking out test or inserting a permission stage. This takes us back to the importance of good, clear pleadings which would be facilitated by better claim forms, as discussed in sections II and III.

C. Interim Conclusion

A concern for many participants in our research was that unmeritorious claims were clogging up the system. The approach to striking out claims is very similar as between the employment tribunal and civil litigation. We are unconvinced that a permission mechanism like that found in judicial review claims would work, given the fact-sensitive nature of employment disputes. So, how can the unmeritorious claims be dealt with? We think that many of the unmeritorious claims are, in fact, badly pleaded claims, with claimants including too many issues for fear of missing points. This takes us back to having better claim forms, discussed in sections II and III, and stronger case management to limit claims and make them more focused (discussed in chapter nine). For cases which are genuinely unmeritorious, there are already tools in the system – strike outs and deposit orders – which could be used more robustly.

V. Conclusions

We think improved claims forms will do much to help claimants both to understand what they are claiming and to focus more clearly on what they are claiming. The ET1 and ET3 forms need to use much simpler language and not require litigants in person to understand legal labels for specific claims. The forms should ask much more specific and precise questions, ideally leading to follow-up questions being asked in light of the answers given. An AI model – if it is sufficiently accurate – may be of significant interest to enable a timeline of events and particular claims to be identified from a narrative account.

Looking at other jurisdictions, it is striking how few have a claim form that contains all the elements that we think would be valuable. The Republic of Ireland form is probably the best: specific questions follow from earlier answers and there is a granularity and precision to the questions. Applicants are clearly channelled to provide only the information that is relevant to the claim that they are bringing. Other jurisdictions require applicants to bring different types of claim to different bodies and, while the split jurisdiction is likely to cause confusion, the different forms to be completed may be helpful. Further, placing the question of remedy at the start of the form is an important means of focusing the minds of applicants on what they are seeking to achieve by bringing the claim.

If pleadings are clearer and more focused, this will help with the next issue we shall consider: how different types of claim might be addressed differently and changes that might be made to the litigation process to achieve greater efficiency in the system.

9

Exploring the Landscape of the Litigation Process: Tracking, Evidence and Disclosure

I. Introduction

In the last chapter we looked at different claim forms from analogous jurisdictions in the UK and internationally and made recommendations as to how this process could be improved. We shall now consider the rest of the litigation process. We saw in chapter seven that many of our research participants felt that there needed to be greater differentiation in the management of different types of claim and greater control of the evidence through widespread use of page limits for both bundles and witness statements. We therefore suggest that there needs to be a system that treats different types of case differently, with different case management and administrative processes operating accordingly. We recognise this is the most radical of our suggestions. However, we look to see how it might work, drawing inspiration from the track allocation system used in personal injury claims, with different approaches to the management and control of evidence depending on the track (section II). Where claims are of particularly high value or significant complexity, we think that these are more akin to High Court commercial litigation and so we have explored how evidence is controlled and managed in the Commercial Court (section III).

However, many employment cases are not akin to High Court commercial litigation but are nonetheless more complex than the most straightforward claims for unpaid wages. Such cases are often brought by litigants in person. These claims need to be managed in a way that is accessible for those without representation or where legal representation may be limited. We therefore turn to consider how the family courts control and manage the litigation process in a context of high emotion and limited legal representation (section IV).

In addition, there are particular challenges in claims brought by multiple claimants, for example in relation to equal pay and holiday pay. A number of participants suggested that such claims needed to be managed separately. We therefore consider how group litigation orders operate in the civil courts (section V). This provides some assistance in thinking about managing multiple claims.

Finally, we consider how claims are dealt with in Commonwealth jurisdictions from which we think we have much to learn: Australia and New Zealand (section VI), building on our work drawing on their experiences in the pre-litigation stage in chapter six.

II. Personal Injury Claims: Track Allocations and Controlling Evidence

We think the formal use of tracks to determine how a case is managed and the length of the hearing could be transformative for the employment tribunal system. Many participants felt that there needed to be greater differentiation in the management of different types of claim than exists at present (considered in chapter seven, section III). Different track allocations are used in personal injury claims with different approaches to the management and control of evidence depending on the track.

A. Track Allocation

The use of different tracks for civil claims is described as 'a fundamental feature of the [civil procedure] rules'.[1] They apply to all cases but in this section, we will consider how they work in personal injury claims. The aim of allocating different cases to different tracks is to ensure that each case is dealt with proportionately to its size and complexity.

Once a defence has been filed, a court officer provisionally decides the track which appears to be most suitable for the claim and notifies the parties of this decision.[2] Parties are required to complete a directions questionnaire,[3] in which they may provide further information relevant to track allocation.[4] Parties must cooperate in the completion of the questionnaires and consider the appropriate track and complexity of the case.[5] The questionnaire must also provide information that is relevant to allocation and the future management of the case, such as a party's intention to seek summary judgment, to add another party, or issue an additional claim.[6] A stay to allow for the settlement of the case may be applied, either upon application by the parties or on the initiative of the court.[7] The stay will be for one month, unless extended.[8]

[1] Lord Justice Coulson (ed), *Civil Procedure: The White Book Service* (Vol 1, Sweet & Maxwell 2025) (White Book 2025).

[2] Civil Procedure Rules, r 26.4(1) (CPR).

[3] A copy of the questionnaire is provided to any unrepresented parties for them to complete.

[4] Practice Direction (PD) 26, para 3(1).

[5] ibid, para 4.

[6] White Book 2025, 768.

[7] r 26.5 CPR.

[8] ibid, r 26.5(4).

The White Book notes that while a court officer provisionally decides on track allocation, this decision remains a judicial function.[9] Allocation is confirmed only after the filing of the directions questionnaires or when giving directions, and this is done by the court, not a court officer.[10] An allocation hearing may be listed or further information sought, where required.[11]

When deciding which track a claim should be allocated to, the court must consider all the circumstances including nine matters set out in the Civil Procedure Rules (CPR):

- the financial value of the claim;
- the nature of the remedy sought;
- the likely complexity of the facts, law or evidence;
- the number of parties or likely parties;
- the value and complexity of any counterclaim or additional claim;
- the amount of oral evidence which may be required;
- the importance of the claim to persons who are not parties to the proceedings;
- the views expressed by the parties;
- and the circumstances of the parties.[12]

It is for the court to assess the financial value of a claim, disregarding any undisputed amount, claims for interest and costs, and any contributory negligence.[13] While the views of the parties are important, which track the case should be allocated to is ultimately a decision for the court.[14] However, when considering the financial value of the claim, the court is restricted by the sums claimed and even if it considers that the claim may be worth more than that figure, it cannot increase the value of the sums claimed.[15] There is thus nothing objectionable in insurers agreeing to limit the size of a claim, with the consequence that it would be placed on a lower track.[16]

The difficulty that may arise in employment disputes is that claims may be of high complexity but low financial value, particularly in some discrimination or whistleblowing claims. However, it is notable that in the personal injury context, parties can agree to limit the size of a claim and be placed on a lower track than would otherwise apply. This could also be the case for employment claims.

The court has a generally unfettered discretion to reallocate a case,[17] whether by application of the parties or on its own initiative.[18] However, where a claim has

[9] White Book 2025, 767.
[10] r 26.7 CPR.
[11] ibid, r 26.7 and PD26 paras 9 and 13.
[12] r 26.13(1)(a)–(i) CPR.
[13] ibid, r 26.13(2).
[14] PD26, para 14.
[15] White Book 2025, 779.
[16] *Khiaban v Beard* [2003] EWCA Civ 358.
[17] Or reassign a claim to a different complexity band.
[18] r 26.18 CPR.

been allocated to the intermediate track and directions have been given, then there must be 'exceptional reasons' to justify reallocating the case.[19] Again, this could also apply in employment matters.

B. The Tracks

There are four tracks that a case may be allocated to: small claims track, fast track, intermediate track and multi-track. We consider each in turn.

i. Small Claims Track

The small claims track is for claims which have a value of not more than £10,000.[20] Where the claim is for personal injuries, then the value of any claim for damages for personal injuries must be not more than £5,000 arising from a road traffic accident[21] or £1,500 in any other personal injury claim.[22] The Practice Direction provides that the track is for the most straightforward claims which do not require substantial pre-hearing preparation nor the formalities of a traditional trial.[23]

The forms that are used to start a claim on the small claims track are the same as for higher value claims. As noted in chapter eight, the Practice Direction makes it clear that in a road traffic claim including an element of personal injury then a medical report is also required from an accredited medical expert.[24] While in the small claims track there is no restriction on legal representation, many small claims are brought by litigants in person. The Practice Directions therefore provide specific information about what must be done. The rules on disclosure, experts and evidence are all disapplied.[25] In most cases, there is no preliminary hearing[26] and standard directions – perhaps with some amendment requiring parties to clarify their case – are generally used. The Standard Directions are set out in Appendix B of Practice Direction 27. In relation to disclosure, the standard direction is for parties to send copies of relevant documents to the other side before the hearing.[27] No formal requests for further information may be made under Part 18.[28] Expert evidence is limited and permission must always be obtained in advance.[29]

[19] ibid, r 26.18(2). To reassign a claim to a different complexity band, there must have been a change in circumstances that justifies reassignment: r 26.18(3) CPR.

[20] Exceptions apply to claims by a tenant of residential premises against a landlord and claims under the Renting Homes (Wales) Act 2016: CPR, r 26.9(b) and (c).

[21] In certain cases this is reduced to £1,000: CPR, r 26.10.

[22] r 26.9 CPR.

[23] PD26, para 15.

[24] PD27B, para 1.11.

[25] r 27.2 CPR.

[26] ibid, r 27.6.

[27] ibid, r 27.4(3)(i).

[28] ibid, r 27.2(3).

[29] ibid, r 27.5.

The Practice Direction provides a list of information and documentation that is required for particular types of case. In road traffic cases, where the information is available, then the list of documentation is witness statements, including from the parties; invoices and estimates for repairs; agreements and invoices for any car hire costs; the police accident report; sketch plan which should wherever possible be agreed; and photographs of the scene of the accident and of the damage.[30] For claims including personal injury a further medical report may be provided but only where it is justified for a reason set out in paragraph 1.12 of Practice Direction 27B, including where it is recommended by the first expert, further time is required for the prognosis to become clear or treatment is ongoing, or where the claimant has not recovered as expected in the original prognosis.

A small claims hearing is usually listed for between two and four hours, and never normally more than one day. The claims are almost invariably heard by district judges.[31] While a bundle and witness statements will usually be ordered, the hearing itself is relatively informal and evidence need not be taken on oath.[32] The approach of the judge will often be more interventionist than at a trial on one of the other tracks, with the judge taking the lead in asking questions of witnesses before inviting the parties to ask any additional questions.[33]

Cases can be dealt with entirely on the papers if all the parties agree,[34] and a party may, giving seven days' notice to the other side and the court, submit their case in writing instead of attending in person.[35] On 22 May 2024, a new Practice Direction established an automatic referral to the Small Claims Mediation Pilot Scheme.[36] However, personal injury claims are excluded from the scheme.[37] While the Practice Direction provides a lot of detail about what documentation is required, it is lengthy with different parts of it dealing with different scenarios, such as whether liability has been admitted. The language is also technical, referring to matters such as acknowledgement of service, a small claims notification form, a court valuation form, and the RTA (road traffic accident) small claims protocol. We anticipate that many litigants in person in the employment tribunal would find it challenging to navigate a process of this nature.

ii. The Fast Track

The fast track is generally for claims for monetary relief, which have a value of more than £10,000 and up to £25,000.[38] In addition, cases must be expected to last

[30] PD27, Appendix A.
[31] White Book 2025, 794 and PD27, para 1.
[32] r 27.8 CPR.
[33] PD27, para 4.3.
[34] r 27.10 CPR.
[35] ibid, r 27.9.
[36] PD51ZE. It was previously optional if both parties agreed: CPR, r 26.6.
[37] r 26.6(1)(a) CPR.
[38] ibid, r 26.9(5).

no longer than one day with expert evidence limited to one expert per party in relation to any expert field, and a maximum of two expert fields.[39]

Directions are given by the court when the case is allocated unless it considers it necessary to fix a case management conference.[40] These include all directions to trial and will include a trial date or a trial window:[41] 'early fixing of the trial date or trial period – and insisting upon it – has always been of the essence of the fast track'.[42] The 'typical timetable' is for trial to take place within 30 weeks of giving directions. Directions must deal with the disclosure of documents, service of witness statements, expert evidence and (an addition from 1 October 2024), 'whether to order or encourage the parties to engage in alternative dispute resolution'.[43] The standard disclosure rules apply to fast track cases as they do in the intermediate and multi-track cases.[44] However, expert evidence is usually restricted to a single joint expert, to ensure proportionality and given that the trial will usually be one day.[45] A party must apply to the court to vary the case management timetable and dates for compliance with directions cannot be varied by consent.[46] The trial bundle will be limited to documents actually required at trial, and begin with an index and case summary.[47]

iii. The Intermediate Track

The intermediate track was introduced in October 2023 as an addition to the other three tracks. It is the normal track for claims that are not suitable for either the small claims track or the fast track and, where they are for monetary relief, they have a value of up to £100,000.[48] Moreover, it must be expected that the trial will take no longer than three days, with no more than two expert witnesses per party and is either a claim brought by one claimant against no more than two defendants, or is a claim brought by no more than two claimants against one defendant.[49] The court may also allocate a claim to the intermediate track where it is 'in the interests of justice to do so'.[50] Certain claims must be allocated to the multi-track in any event including mesothelioma and asbestos-related claims and most clinical negligence claims.[51]

[39] ibid, r 26.9(6).
[40] ibid, r 28.2.
[41] ibid, r 28.2(3).
[42] White Book 2025, 862.
[43] r 28.7 CPR.
[44] Different provisions are made for noise induced hearing loss cases: CPR, r 28.9–28.11.
[45] White Book 2025, 866.
[46] r 28.3 CPR.
[47] White Book 2025, 865.
[48] r 26.9(7) CPR.
[49] ibid.
[50] r 26.9(8) CPR.
[51] ibid, r 26.9(10).

A case management conference is considered the usual approach in cases on the intermediate track, although directions may be given on paper.[52] Parties must try to agree directions and submit them or their proposals to the court at least seven days before the case management conference. If the court approves the agreed directions, or issues its own, then the case management conference will be vacated.[53] The court will 'seek to tailor its directions to the needs of the case and the steps of which it is aware that the parties have already taken', particularly under the Pre-Action Protocol.[54]

The usual rules for disclosure apply, but oral expert evidence will be limited to 'one witness per party, save where the oral evidence of a second expert for any party is reasonably required and is proportionate'.[55] Expert reports are limited to 20 pages, excluding the expert's CV and any supporting materials such as plans, photographs and academic articles. The total length of all witness statements is restricted to 30 pages per party.[56] When a case is listed, the trial date will be fixed 'on the footing' that the hearing will last one day but the directions sought by the parties may provide for a longer time estimate.[57]

iv. Complexity Bands

When a claim is allocated to the fast track or intermediate track then the court must also assign the claim to a complexity band.[58] The complexity bands provide an ascending scale of allowable costs 'commensurate with the complexity of the claim'.[59] Tables in the CPR provide the complexity bands and set out the usual type of claim found in each band.[60] The parties may agree on the complexity band; if they disagree then each party must specify which band they consider to be most appropriate and the court will determine the issue.[61]

v. The Multi-Track

The multi-track is for cases that exceed the limit for the intermediate track, that is over £100,000, or where the multi-track is the required track, such as most clinical negligence claims. A case may also be allocated to the multi-track if its value is under £100,000 but it is of sufficient complexity. Many cases, even if issued in the High Court, will be transferred to the county court for case management and trial.

[52] ibid, r 28.12 and White Book 2025, 867.
[53] ibid, r 28.13 and PD28 para 3.5 and 3.8.
[54] PD28, para 3.2.
[55] r 28.14(2) CPR.
[56] ibid, r 28.14(3).
[57] PD28, para 7.1.
[58] Unless s VIII of Pt 45 CPR applies (HMRC debt claims).
[59] r 26.14(2) CPR.
[60] ibid, r 26.15 and 26.16.
[61] ibid, r 26.14.

The Practice Direction describes the 'hallmarks' of the multi-track as 'the ability of the court to deal with cases of widely differing values and complexity, and the flexibility given to the court in the way it will manage a case in a way appropriate to its particular needs'.[62]

There is active case management by the court of cases on this track and the parties and their legal representatives are expected to cooperate in the conduct of proceedings.[63] Moreover, consideration of alternative dispute resolution (ADR) is mandatory and the court may, where appropriate, give directions encouraging or requiring the parties to attend ADR.[64]

When a case is allocated to the multi-track, the court will either issue directions for the case, setting a timetable for the required actions, or it will fix a case management conference, or both. On allocation, 'the court's first concern will be to ensure that the issues between the parties are identified and that the necessary evidence is prepared and disclosed'.[65] This is reflected in the topics that are considered at the case management conference, including 'whether the claimant has made clear the claim he is bringing, in particular the amount he is claiming, so that the other party can understand the case he has to meet'.[66]

If a case management conference is held, then the parties, or their representatives, must ensure that they are 'familiar with the case and with sufficient authority to deal with any issues that are likely to arise'.[67] As with the intermediate track, parties are required to try to agree directions which, if approved by the court, will enable the case management conference to be vacated.[68] Consideration is given to the steps that have already been taken under the Pre-Action Protocol.[69] Alternatively, the court will issue its own directions, either before or at the case management conference. If the directions are to be varied, then an application must be made.[70]

The directions need to address disclosure, witness statements and expert evidence, setting out a timetable for the steps to be taken for the preparation of the case. The court 'will scrutinise the timetable carefully and in particular will be concerned to see that any proposed date or period for the trial … is no later than is reasonably necessary'.[71]

The directions will be for a single joint expert unless there is good reason to the contrary.[72] If there are to be separate experts then simultaneous exchange will usually be ordered. In addition, directions will be given for the experts to hold a discussion and produce a statement of agreed and disputed issues.[73] Permission

[62] PD29, para 3.2.
[63] White Book 2025, 877.
[64] r 29.2(1A) CPR.
[65] PD29, para 4.3.
[66] ibid, para 5.3.
[67] r 29.3(2) CPR.
[68] ibid, r 29.4.
[69] PD29, para 4.2.
[70] r 29.5 CPR.
[71] PD29, para 4.7.
[72] ibid, para 4.
[73] ibid.

will not be given unless the expert is identified by name or field, and it can be said whether they will be giving oral evidence or their report will be relied on.[74]

A trial date or trial period will also be fixed 'as soon as practicable'.[75] This is seen as a key element in furthering the overriding objective of dealing with cases expeditiously and, taken together with active case management, it means that 'the court will manage the case at the speed and on the dates which the court thinks appropriate. Once started the court will be reluctant to let the case slow down except to facilitate the parties to reach settlement'.[76] The postponement of a trial because of non-compliance with a case management order will be regarded as 'an order of last resort'.[77]

The trial will be conducted according to the agreed timetable, unless the judge directs otherwise. The judge has considerable discretion as to the conduct of the trial, including restricting cross-examination.[78] A written judgment is usually given.

C. Interim Conclusion

We consider that differentiation between different types of case is a good thing. It allows different kinds of cases to be managed differently, according to the value and complexity of the claims involved. In 2015, the Law Society proposed that all employment cases (including those currently heard in the civil courts) could be heard in a single employment tribunal jurisdiction but that the cases should be allocated to four levels (tracks).[79] These levels were explained as follows (see Table 9.1).

Table 9.1 Law Society proposal for the tracking of ET claims[80]

Level	Approach	Types of cases
1	Document based decision making.	Simple straightforward cases, such as unpaid wages claims, where the judge can make a decision on the documents alone.
2	Judicial inquisitorial approach.	Straightforward cases, such as redundancy payments or failure to consult, that need further investigation.

(continued)

[74] White Book 2025, 882.
[75] r 29.2(3) CPR.
[76] White Book 2025, 879.
[77] PD29, para 7.
[78] r 29.9, r 32.1 and r 32.5 CPR.
[79] Law Society, 'Making employment tribunals work for all: Is it time for a single employment jurisdiction? A discussion document (September 2015) 4, para 2. See also Hodges' recommendation for better use of tracks, discussed in ch 7.
[80] ibid.

Table 9.1 ***(Continued)***

Level	Approach	Types of cases
3	Encourage early neutral evaluation and ADR.	Cases that make up the majority of claims currently heard in the ET.
4	Cases heard under civil litigation principles.	Employment disputes which are currently heard in the civil court, such as restrictive covenants. Costs will apply to some cases.

Although we are less convinced about the particular cases that are put into the particular tracks in the Law Society proposal, we think the use of tracks to differentiate claims is important. We think lower value, less complex cases can and should be managed more flexibly with less emphasis on detailed legal pleading and greater limits on the quantity of documentation and witness evidence that is permitted. However, with higher value or more complex claims, strong case management with a trial date that is not readily moved would support greater efficiencies in the system. There is also a valuable difference in the modes of adjudication moving from the more informal, oral judgment in the small claims track to a written judgment in multi-track cases. That appears to us to be a proportionate approach to the different types of claim.

That said, we should recognise that some commentators have raised concerns that the introduction of tracks and active case management has increased, rather than reduced, overall costs in civil litigation on the basis that costs have increased since the introduction of the CPR.[81] Further, it has been argued that the CPR reforms may have caused greater delays. For example, Peysner and Seneviratne say:

> In the multi-track, some judges thought that case management actually caused delay. Some judges believe that solicitors can case-manage more effectively than judges, and should be allowed to get on with it, with judicial intervention only when necessary. It was also difficult to allocate responsibility for delay. In many cases the fault lay not with solicitors or clients, but with experts not submitting reports on time. There were mixed views about the 30-week deadline for fast-track cases. Some judges thought this target was potentially damaging, and that the process should not be target-driven. On the other hand, there were those who said that many fast-track cases could be tried within 20 weeks.

However, they conclude:

> From the practitioners' point of view, there was general agreement among solicitors that timetabling was a good thing, as it moved cases on more quickly. Overall, by a combination of timetabling, the drop in litigation and effective use of listing for trial the notion that delay is an inevitable feature of our civil procedure seems to be a thing of the past.[82]

[81] J Peysner and M Seneviratne, 'The Management of Civil Cases: A Snapshot' (2006) 25 *Civil Justice Quarterly* 312, 323–24.

[82] ibid, 314.

We think that tracking may be an important way of addressing delays in the tribunal system too, with high value/complexity cases dealt with like High Court claims. We turn now to consider how high value claims in the commercial courts are addressed.

III. Evidence and Adjudication in Commercial Cases

The Commercial Court has much stricter rules than the employment tribunal in relation to evidence; there is a role for this approach in high value, complex employment litigation. Commercial Court proceedings are governed by the CPR. They permit the Court to control evidence by giving directions on the issues on which it requires evidence, the nature of the evidence required, and the way in which that evidence is to be placed before the Court.[83] Moreover, the Court may exclude evidence and restrict cross-examination where appropriate. That power extends to giving directions limiting the issues to which factual evidence may be directed, identifying the witnesses who may be called or whose evidence may be read and limiting the length or format of witness statements.[84] The Court will generally wish to exercise its power at an early stage, ideally before costs have been incurred needlessly but may still be exercised after statements have been drafted.[85] When limits are applied to how many witnesses may be called then liberty to apply is usually given so that the limits can be reconsidered if necessary.

Alongside the CPR, the Commercial Court guide 'sets out the way in which the Court normally expects business to be done' but does not override the CPR or fetter judicial discretion.[86] At an early stage in the litigation, parties are expected to produce the following documents:[87]

- **A case memorandum**. This includes a short and uncontroversial description of what the case is about and a very short and uncontroversial summary of the procedural history.[88] The purpose of the case memorandum is to assist the judge at the Case Management Conference.[89]
- **A List of Common Ground and Issues** specifying the common ground between the parties and a list of the key issues of fact and law.[90] The List is used

[83] r 32.1 CPR.

[84] ibid, r 32.3(3).

[85] *MacLennan v Morgan Sindal* [2013] EWHC 4044 (QB), [12].

[86] Courts and Tribunals Judiciary, 'Business and Property Courts of England & Wales: The Commercial Court Guide (incorporating The Admiralty Court Guide)' (revised July 2023) 13. See also Commercial Court Guide at A.1.5.

[87] Commercial Court Guide (n 86) D.2.1(b).

[88] ibid, D.4.2.

[89] ibid, D.4.1.

[90] ibid, D.5.1.

as a tool to consider what factual and expert evidence is necessary and the scope of disclosure.[91]

- **A case management bundle** containing, where they exist: (a) the claim form, (b) all statements of case, (c) the case memorandum, (d) the List of Common Ground and Issues, (e) the case management information sheets[92] and pre-trial timetable, (f) the principal orders in the case, and (g) any written agreement between the parties concerning disclosure without a list or disclosure (or inspection) in stages.[93]

A Case Management Conference will be held to approve the List of Common Ground and Issues and discuss disclosure.[94]

A. Disclosure

For most Commercial Court cases, the special disclosure regime in Practice Direction 57AD – Disclosure in the Business and Property Courts (PD57AD) applies.[95] Under PD57AD, the court expects the parties to cooperate with each other on disclosure, and that disclosure will be reasonable and proportionate.[96] Parties have a duty to act honestly and to use reasonable efforts to avoid disclosing documents that have no relevance to the Issues for Disclosure.[97] Importantly, parties will already have disclosed documents under the Pre-Action protocol[98] and have provided Initial Disclosure with their statement of case, namely the key documents on which they rely in support of the claims or defences advanced, that are necessary to enable the other parties to understand the claim or defence they have to meet.[99] The judge at the first Case Management Conference will usually determine the requirements for Extended Disclosure,[100] which may follow one of five models, ranging from a requirement to disclose 'known adverse documents'[101] but not undertake a specific search,

[91] ibid, D.2.1(c).

[92] The standard form is set out at Appendix 2 to the Guide and includes questions about the parties' disclosure proposals and evidence including the number of witnesses parties intend to call at trial.

[93] Commercial Court Guide (n 86) D.6.2.

[94] ibid, D.7.9.

[95] In other Commercial Court cases, disclosure is governed by CPR Pt 31, read together with Appendix 15 of the Commercial Court Guide (n 86) and paras E.2.1 and E.3.1.

[96] CPR PD57AD, para 2.3 and 2.4.

[97] ibid, para 3.1(5), (6).

[98] The Practice Direction on Pre-Action Conduct and Protocols still applies in the Commercial Court thus before a claim is issues, parties should have disclosed 'key documents relevant to the issues in dispute': para 6(c).

[99] CPR PD57AD, para 5.4. There is no duty to search for documents or to provide documents that are known to be in the possession of the other party already.

[100] ibid, para 6.8. Disclosure guidance may also be sought by parties rather than a formal order: PD57AD para 11.

[101] That is a document that 'contradicts or materially damages the disclosing party's contention or version of events on an issue in dispute, or supports the contention or version of events of an opposing party on an issue in dispute' that a 'party is actually aware [...] both (a) are or were previously within in its control, and (b) are adverse': CPR PD57AD, paras 2.7 and 2.8.

through to a requirement to disclose documents which are likely to support or adversely affect the party's claim or defence or that of another party, to disclose documents which may lead to a train of enquiry which may then result in the identification of other documents for disclosure and to undertake a reasonable and proportionate search.[102]

A disclosure model may apply to some or all of the issues in the case and there is no 'default' model for disclosure.[103] Where no Extended Disclosure order is made, a party must still disclose all known adverse documents within 60 days of the first case management conference.[104] Various documents must be produced identifying the disclosure points that are in issue,[105] and a review document to assist the parties to discuss and agree the ambit of Extended Disclosure.[106]

While CPR Part 31 preserves the distinction between disclosure and inspection of documents, PD57AD does not. Instead, a party discloses a document by both identifying the existence of a document and producing a copy (or stating why a copy will not be produced).[107] A bespoke regime for specific disclosure operates whereby the court may make such further orders in relation to disclosure as appropriate.[108] Adverse costs orders may follow a significant breach of a party's duties of initial disclosure[109] or an extended disclosure order.[110]

Claims that are valued at less than £1,000,000 will usually follow a simplified disclosure regime requiring more limited disclosure.[111]

B. Bundles

After disclosure has taken place, the Commercial Court Guide says that the parties should consider how much of the disclosed material should be placed before the trial judge and how it is to be introduced into evidence. Consideration must also be given to what is reasonably required by way of witness, and expert, evidence.[112]

Apart from certain specified documents, such as the pleadings, trial bundles 'should include only documents that the trial judge will be asked to read or that it

[102] CPR PD57AD, Appendix 1, para 1.12.
[103] ibid, para 8.
[104] ibid, para 9.2.
[105] ibid, para 7.1, 7.2 and 7.6.
[106] ibid, para 10.1.
[107] ibid, Appendix 1, para 1.4.
[108] ibid, para 17.
[109] ibid, para 5.13.
[110] ibid, para 20. Other sanctions include adjourning a hearing, making further disclosure conditional on a matter specified by the court and proceedings for contempt of court.
[111] ibid, Appendix 5.
[112] Commercial Court Guide (n 86) E.5.2: www.judiciary.uk/courts-and-tribunals/business-and-property-courts/commercial-court/litigating-in-the-commercial-court/commercial-court-guide/.

is expected will be shown to the Court at trial (including when witnesses are giving evidence)'.[113] The Guide also states that where a document has been included unnecessarily, a party may be required to explain its inclusion and may be penalised in costs if there is no satisfactory explanation. There are strict rules relating to the format and electronic organisation of bundles.[114] In addition, where the bundle is for a trial, or a more complex application hearing, then a core bundle containing the most important documents in the case should be provided to the court.[115]

C. Witness Statements

Witness statements must comply with the relevant Practice Direction and include only evidence as to matters of fact that need to be proved at trial by the witness and that the witness would be asked to give in evidence in chief.[116] The statement must set out only matters of fact of which the witness has personal knowledge[117] and identify which documents the witness referred to for the purposes of their evidence.[118] Witnesses are required to provide confirmation, beyond the usual statement of truth, that 'I understand that it is not my function to argue the case … or to take the court through the documents in the case' and 'This witness statement sets out only my personal knowledge and recollection, in my own words.'[119] The court has a range of sanctions it can apply for non-compliance, including striking out the witness statement, ordering that the witness statement be re-drafted, making an adverse costs order, and ordering the witness to give their evidence in chief orally.[120] There is no limit on the length of witness statements unless the case is being heard under the Shorter Trials Scheme,[121] whereby the case will be less than four days[122] and does not require extensive disclosure or involve multiple parties, or include allegations of fraud or dishonesty.[123] Where the Shorter Trial Scheme does apply, witness statements should be no longer than 25 pages unless there is a 'good reason'.[124]

[113] ibid, J.4.3 and Appendix 7.
[114] ibid, Appendix 7.
[115] ibid, Appendix 7, para 3.
[116] CPR PD57AC Practice Direction 57AC – Trial Witness Statements in the Business and Property Courts, para 3.1. The Appendix to the Practice Direction is a Statement of Best Practice for trial witness statements.
[117] CPR PD57AC, para 3.2.
[118] ibid, para 3.2.
[119] ibid, para 4.1.
[120] ibid, para 5.2.
[121] CPR PD57AB.
[122] ibid, para 2.3.
[123] ibid, para 2.2.
[124] ibid, para 2.44.

D. The Trial

Before a trial, or complex application hearing, parties must consider whether an agreed detailed narrative of uncontentious relevant facts should be prepared, set out chronologically or in a logical structure of chapters.[125] Skeleton arguments should be limited to 50 pages 'so far as possible'.[126] Judges are specifically ticketed as specialists who can sit in the Commercial Court. Judgment following a trial in the Commercial Court is generally delivered in writing following the hearing.

E. Interim Conclusion

The Commercial Court provides a useful example of detailed procedural rules that deal with high value and complex litigation in a clear and structured manner. The Court retains discretion in managing cases but the limitation and restriction of evidence to that which is relevant and necessary is clearly set out, with sanctions that can be applied for any breaches. This is helpful to consider in relation to the high value, complex litigation that often ends up in employment tribunals but is currently managed using much more informal, flexible rules. However, Commercial Court proceedings are rarely brought by litigants in person. Therefore, we turn to consider family law procedural rules, where a greater number of litigants are unrepresented to consider how a more structured format operates in that context.

IV. Controlling Evidence in Family Cases

A. Introduction

As noted above, many employment cases are not akin to High Court commercial litigation but are also more complex than the most straightforward claims for unpaid wages. Such cases are often brought by litigants in person. These claims need to be managed in a way that is accessible for those without representation or where legal representation may be limited and where emotions can run high. There are parallels here with family law (see further chapter three). The family courts are very specific with litigants about what they can and cannot rely on in evidence and how that evidence is to be presented; we think that is helpful for litigants in person and would add value to the employment tribunal process.

Family proceedings are governed by the Family Procedure Rules 2010 (FPR 2010). The FPR require the court to deal with cases in accordance with the applicable overriding objective, that is, 'to deal with cases justly, having regard

[125] Commercial Court Guide (n 86) J.6.5.
[126] ibid, J.6.3 and J.6.4.

to any welfare issues involved'[127] and to further it by 'actively managing cases'.[128] The FPR are more flexible than the CPR. For example, rule 22.1 FPR concerns the court's general powers to control evidence. It contains the usual provisions stating that the court may control evidence by giving directions on the issues on which it requires evidence, the nature of the evidence required, and the way in which that evidence is to be placed before the court. However, it also provides that '[t]he court may permit a party to adduce evidence, or to seek to rely on a document, in respect of which that party has failed to comply with the requirements of this Part'. In addition, the FPR 2010 do not contain a provision equivalent to the power in CPR rule 32.2(3), which enables the ordinary civil courts to limit the issues to which factual evidence may be directed, identify the witness who may be called, and limit the length or format of witness statements.

B. Disclosure

In family proceedings, the parties are under a general duty of full and frank disclosure. As to matters relating to children, the duty is on the parties to 'use their best endeavours: (a) to confine the issues and the evidence called to what is reasonably considered to be essential for the proper presentation of their case'.[129] In financial remedy proceedings, the duty relates to 'disclosure of all material facts to the other party and the court'.[130]

In addition, in proceedings for a financial remedy, the FPR 2010 provide a staged process of disclosure.[131] The first stage is for both parties to serve a financial statement called Form E, together with the documents that are required to be attached to it.[132] Form E is lengthy. It requires, for example, general information about the parents and children in the case, information about the family home, business interests, income earned from employment, and income earned from investments. Form E also includes a detailed list of documents that should be attached, such as a recent valuation of the matrimonial home, a recent mortgage statement, bank statements, business accounts, and the party's last three payslips from their employer.[133] Parties may then request further disclosure and

[127] Family Procedure Rules 2010 (FPR 2010) r 1.1. Rule 1.2 states that dealing with a case justly 'includes so far as is practicable – (a) ensuring that it is dealt with expeditiously and fairly; (b) dealing with the case in ways which are proportionate to the nature, importance and complexity of the issues; (c) ensuring that the parties are on an equal footing; (d) saving expense; and (e) allotting to it an appropriate share of the court's resources, while taking into account the need to allot resources to other cases'.

[128] ibid, r 1.4.

[129] *Practice Direction: Case Management* [1995] 1 WLR 332, para 4.

[130] *Livesey (formerly Jenkins) v Jenkins* [1985] AC 424, 437–38.

[131] PD21A, para 2.2 (FPR 2010).

[132] ibid, r 9.14(1).

[133] Form E: assets.publishing.service.gov.uk/media/63c132468fa8f516ac0d5a6d/Form_E_0123_save.pdf.

documents from each other via a questionnaire.[134] At the first appointment, the court is required to determine whether these requests should be answered.[135] Lord Neuberger MR described the court's involvement in disclosure in the following way:

> [w]hereas in ordinary civil proceedings the parties can normally choose what documentary evidence to tender, it is the court which controls what documents are to be disclosed and tendered by way of evidence in ancillary relief proceedings … [J]udges deciding such applications have a far greater control than they have under the CPR in normal civil proceedings, over which documents should or should not be produced in evidence.[136]

In other family proceedings, the normal order for disclosure will be for 'each party setting out, in a list or questionnaire, the documents material to the proceedings, of the existence of which that party is aware and which are or have been in that party's control'.[137]

In addition, under the court's general powers of case management, the court may 'make such order for disclosure and inspection, including specific disclosure of documents, as it thinks fit'.[138] Specific disclosure can include an order that a party must disclose documents or classes of document, carry out a search, and/or disclose any documents located as a result of that search.[139]

C. Bundles

Bundles for the court should contain 'only those documents which are relevant to the hearing and which it is necessary for the court to read or which will actually be referred to during the hearing'.[140] Munby J has referred to this as a 'double requirement': a document must be both relevant and a document that will either be read or referred to.[141] The Practice Direction provides a list of documents which must not be included in the bundle unless specifically directed by the court, including correspondence, medical records, bank statements, notes of contact visits, foster carer logs, social services files and police disclosure.[142] The Practice Direction sets out how the bundle is to be structured and divided into specific sections, the first of which are the preliminary documents. These are listed as an up-to-date case summary (limited to four A4 pages where

[134] r 9.14(5)(c) FPR 2010.
[135] ibid, r 9.15(2).
[136] *Tchenguiz v Imerman* [2010] EWCA Civ 908, [33]–[34].
[137] PD21A, para 2.1 FPR 2010. Although termed standard disclosure, it is different from that found in CPR, r.31.6.
[138] r 4.1(3)(b) FPR 2010.
[139] PD21A, para 2.4 FPR 2010.
[140] PD27A – Family Proceedings: Court Bundles, para 4.1 (FPR 2010).
[141] *Re L (A Child) (Procedure: Bundles: Translation)* [2015] EWFC 15, [20].
[142] PD27A, para 4.1 (FPR 2010).

possible), a statement of issues, a position statement by each party including a summary of the order or directions sought, an up-to-date chronology with each entry being limited, if practicable, to one sentence and cross-referenced to the relevant page(s) in the bundle, skeleton arguments, if appropriate, and an essential reading list.[143] In every case, a time estimate must be inserted at the front of the bundle specifying (i) the time estimated for judicial pre-reading, (ii) the time required for hearing all evidence and submissions, and (iii) the time estimated for preparing and delivering judgment.[144] The bundle must be no more than one A4 ring binder or lever arch file limited to 350 sheets of A4, single-sided pages.[145] Specific page limits are provided in relation to each section of the bundle. Unless the court directs otherwise, there is a limit of 10 authorities.[146]

PD27A paragraph 12.1 provides that failure to comply with the Practice Direction may result in the judge removing the case from the list, the judge putting the case further back in the list, or an adverse costs order.

D. Witness Statements

PD27A provides for a maximum page limit of 25 pages for witness statements. However, the President's Memorandum provides that witness statements must be 'as concise as possible without omitting anything of significance' and generally 'should not exceed 15 pages in length (excluding exhibits)'.[147] The Memorandum also provides guidance on the contents of statements. They must only contain evidence from the maker of the statement; be expressed in the first person using the witness's own words; not (a) quote at length from documents, (b) argue the case, (c) take the court through the documents in the case, (d) express the opinions of the witness, or (e) use rhetoric; and must identify which documents the witness referred to for the purpose of providing the evidence in the statement.[148] Where a statement does not comply with the Memorandum then the court may exclude the statement[149] or disallow the costs incurred in preparing it.[150] The Memorandum also includes a suggested template for litigants in person to write their witness statements in non-complex private law welfare cases. The use of this template is optional but strongly encouraged.[151]

[143] ibid, para 4.3.
[144] ibid, para 10.1.
[145] ibid, para 5.1.
[146] ibid, para 4.3A.1.
[147] President's Memorandum: Witness Statements President of the Family Division (10 November 2021) paras 15 and 16.
[148] ibid, paras 5, 6, 7, 11(a).
[149] r 22.1(2) FPR 2010.
[150] President's Memorandum: Witness Statements (n 147) para 17.
[151] ibid, para 18.

E. Special Rules for Financial Remedy Proceedings

There are two judicial guidance documents concerning evidence in financial remedy proceedings. One guide is for proceedings allocated to below High Court judge level; the other guide is for proceedings allocated to a High Court judge. We will address here only proceedings allocated to below High Court judge level given our focus on a procedure that a litigant in person is better able to navigate.

Most financial remedy proceedings in this context begin with a First Appointment.[152] Fourteen days before the First Appointment, the parties are required to file with the court information about properties used as a family home, housing need and borrowing capacities.[153] One day before the First Appointment, the applicant is then required to file (1) a case summary using a template document called ES1, and (2) a schedule of assets and income using a template document called ES2.[154]

Seven days before a Financial Dispute Resolution hearing, the applicant must file updated versions of ES1 and ES2, together with a chronology recording the key dates of the parties' relationship and the litigation. Parties are required to collaborate to produce these documents. The documents can note points of disagreement, but it is unacceptable for the court to receive competing asset schedules and chronologies.[155] Again, updated versions of ES1 and ES2 must be filed seven days before a final hearing. The parties are expected to collaborate on these documents as above.[156]

Position statements and skeleton arguments may be filed but there are limits on their length. The Practice Direction requires that there are no more than 20 pages.[157] However, the judicial guidance states that they should not exceed six pages for the First Appointment (including schedules); eight pages for any other interim hearing (including schedules); 12 pages for the Financial Dispute Resolution hearing (excluding certain agreed documents but including schedules); and 15 pages for the final hearing (excluding certain agreed documents but including schedules).[158] If a position statement or skeleton argument needs to exceed the limitations set out above, permission from the court should be sought and good reasons are required.[159] Costs sanctions may be applied to advocates who do not adhere to these requirements.[160]

[152] Mostyn J and HHJ Hess, 'Statement on the Efficient Conduct of Financial Remedy Hearing Proceedings in the Financial Remedies Court below High Court Judge Level' (11 January 2022) para 7.

[153] ibid, para 10.

[154] ibid, para 11.

[155] ibid, para 13.

[156] ibid, para 21.

[157] PD27A (FPR 2010).

[158] Mostyn and Hess, 'Statement on the Efficient Conduct of Financial Remedy Hearing Proceedings' (n 152) para 24.

[159] ibid, para 27.

[160] ibid, para 29.

F. Interim Conclusion

What is striking in the family court procedure rules is that they are very prescriptive in relation to what documents should – and should not – be disclosed and placed in trial bundles. The guidance is very clear about what parties need to do and by when and clear limits on witness statements are also provided. This may be particularly helpful to a litigant in person to require them to think much more carefully about the documents that they seek to rely on and help to keep the litigation within reasonable bounds. We think this will be most helpful in employment cases that are neither the most straightforward nor the most complex disputes.

Another challenge in the employment tribunals is the management of litigation where there are multiple claimants. This has been particularly significant in the employment tribunals in relation to holiday pay claims and equal pay claims. Therefore, we consider how group litigation is addressed in the civil courts.

V. Group Litigation in the Civil Courts

The CPR provides for how group litigation is to be managed, that is, multiple claims 'which give rise to common or related issues of fact or law (the "GLO issues")'.[161] A Group Litigation Order (GLO) will be made 'where there are or are likely to be a number of claims giving rise to the GLO issues'.[162] The application for the GLO may be made by either party or by the court on its own initiative.[163] It may be made before or after claims have been issued.[164] The decision about whether to make a GLO is an exercise of case management discretion and will not be lightly interfered with on appeal.[165] The GLO will direct that a group register of the claims that are being addressed should be established. In addition, it will specify the GLO issues so that it is clear which claims are within the GLO. The GLO will also specify the court that will manage the claims on the Group Register.[166] Judgments, orders and directions of the court in relation to a claim on the register will be binding on all claims within the GLO, unless the court orders otherwise.[167] Case management will usually be carried out by one judge throughout the life of the case.[168] Once a GLO has been made, every claim on the Group Register will be automatically allocated to the multi-track.

[161] r 19.21 CPR.
[162] ibid, r 19.22.
[163] PD19B, paras 3 and 4 (FPR 2010).
[164] ibid, para 3.1.
[165] *Austin v Miller Argent (South Wales) Ltd* [2011] EWCA Civ 928.
[166] r 19.22 CPR.
[167] ibid, r 19.23.
[168] PD19B (FPR 2010).

Directions given by the management court may include providing for one or more claims to proceed as test claims[169] and appointing the solicitor of one or more parties as the lead solicitor for the claimants or defendants.[170] Moreover, the directions may require GLO claimants to serve 'Group Particulars of Claim' which set out the various claims of all the claimants on the Register. They will usually contain general allegations relating to all claims and a schedule relating to each individual's claims setting out specific facts relevant to them.[171] The management court may direct that there is a trial of common issues (usually at the management court) and then a trial of individual issues (which may be at a court more convenient to the particular party).[172]

A party on the Group Register may apply to be removed from the Register, or the court may remove a claim and make directions about the claim's future management where it believes the case cannot conveniently be case managed with the other cases.[173]

The uptake of GLOs in the civil courts has been limited, perhaps because it involves 'an opt-in regime whereby each claimant must file a claim form and be entered upon the group register', rather than the opt-out systems in, for example, Ontario and Australia.[174] The problem may also be funding:

> [L]arge-scale litigation will not be brought unless there is substantial private funding or public support. As [to private funding], it would appear that the conditional fee system has not worked in this context. This seems to be attributable to the absence (in this especially risky context) of ATE [After-the-Event] legal expenses insurance to cover the claimants' risk of liability for the defendant's costs.[175]

What is of interest to us is the process that is applied once there is a GLO. The employment tribunals have seen a significant growth in multiple claims, and the issue is how they should best be managed. We consider that, as occurs at present, there is a real value in having a management court with a designated judge for such claims. We are less convinced that there should be a separate, designated

[169] This is a similar test to r 37 Employment Tribunal Procedure Rules 2024 where certain claims may be designated lead claims and others stayed (or in Scotland, sisted) where 'two or more claims give rise to common or related issues of fact or law'.

[170] r 19.24 CPR.

[171] PD19B, para 14.1 (FPR 2010).

[172] ibid para 15.1 and 15.2.

[173] r 19.25 CPR and PD19B, para 6.4 (FPR 2010).

[174] R Mulheron, 'Reform of Collective Redress in England and Wales: A Perspective of Need'. A Research Paper for submission to the Civil Justice Council of England and Wales (2008) 7: www.judiciary.uk/wp-content/uploads/JCO/Documents/CJC/Publications/Other+papers/reform-of-collective-redress.pdf.

[175] N Andrews, *Andrews on Civil Processes: Court Proceedings* (Intersentia 2013) 655. Note that the Civil Justice Council suggested that an opt-out scheme 'might equally be properly and fairly utilised in actions that seek to vindicate civil or other general rights i.e., equal pay claims; anti-discrimination claims; employment claims': 'Improving Access to Justice through Collective Actions' at: www.judiciary.uk/wp-content/uploads/JCO/Documents/CJC/Publications/CJC+papers/CJC+Improving+Access+to+Justice+through+Collective+Actions.pdf.

administrative system for multiple claims, as participants have suggested, provided that there is sufficient experienced resource in the tribunal region to which they are allocated. It may be that senior legal officers could be used to a greater degree to support the management of these claims.

The process that is used in the civil courts is not dissimilar to the process in the employment tribunals. However, there is arguably more formality and structure in the management of GLOs by virtue of the greater formality found in the CPR. Given the complexity of the litigation, we consider that multiple claims should be treated in the same way as high value, complex claims: requiring a stricter case management approach to the litigation. The clarity of the CPR process is something that we consider could be utilised very effectively in the employment tribunals.

We turn now to consider the processes used in two Commonwealth jurisdictions from which we have already gained considerable learning: Australia and New Zealand.

VI. International Comparators

A. The Australian Fair Work Commission Process

The Fair Work Commission (FWC) is required by section 577 of the Fair Work Act 2009 to perform its 'functions and exercise its powers in a manner that … is quick, informal and avoids unnecessary technicalities'. This enables Commissioners to stop parties taking overly legal points and tying the process up in knots.[176] The FWC has considerable flexibility in its approach, because it is not bound by rules of procedure or evidence,[177] although commentators argue that in practice the FWC tends to apply a set approach.[178]

Section 590 of the Fair Work Act 2009 provides that the FWC may 'inform itself in relation to any matter before it in such manner as it considers appropriate'. It may do so:

a. by requiring a person to attend before the FWC;
b. by inviting, subject to any terms and conditions determined by the FWC, oral or written submissions;
c. by requiring a person to provide copies of documents or records, or to provide any other information to the FWC;
d. by taking evidence under oath or affirmation in accordance with the regulations (if any);

[176] Interview, 30 June 2025.
[177] Fair Work Act 2009, s 591.
[178] A Stewart, 'Fair Work Australia: The Commission Reborn?' (2011) 53 *Journal of Industrial Relations* 563, 571.

e. by requiring an FWC Member, a Full Bench or Expert Panel to prepare a report;
f. by conducting inquiries;
g. by undertaking or commissioning research;
h. by conducting a conference;[179]
i. by holding a hearing.[180]

Permission is required for a person to be represented by a lawyer and is, in most cases, refused.[181] This informality is viewed positively because as a consequence there is less of 'a disincentive to parties bringing matters before [FWC] (in the way that excessive legalism has marred the US and, to a lesser extent, UK employment conflict resolution systems)'.[182] However, it adds to the workload of the FWC because litigants in person require more guidance from Members and thus increases public costs.[183] In addition, some commentators have questioned whether the lack of representation exacerbates the power imbalance between employer and employee and noted the challenges for litigants in explaining their case logically without the assistance of lawyers to act as an 'emotional sounding board' during private conferences and to take the emotion out of the hearing itself.[184] We were told that an important reason why the FWC process worked was because Members are all experienced professionals who carry considerable authority with the parties and can firmly guide them, often to a resolution.

The Member dealing with the matter may list it for a private case management conference. Further attempts may be made at that conference to resolve matters. Thereafter directions will be made. The Member will decide whether the matter should be determined at a private determinative conference or a public hearing. Conferences are less formal than hearings and are usually used where the parties are unrepresented. A hearing may change to a conference at any point in the proceedings. Parties may apply for a matter to be heard at a hearing if it has been

[179] Fair Work Act 2009, s 592.

[180] ibid, s 593.

[181] ibid, s 596 and rules 13 and 14 Fair Work Commission Rules 2024. Examples of circumstances when lawyers would be permitted were where a party did not have English as their first language or were particularly young or vulnerable: Interview, 1 May 2025. See also: www.fwc.gov.au/apply-or-lodge/legal-help-and-representation/representatives-and-rules-they-must-follow/how-we.

[182] A Forsyth, 'Workplace Conflict Resolution in Australia: The Dominance of the Public Dispute Resolution Framework and the Limited Role of ADR' (2012) 23 *International Journal of Human Resources Management* 476, 488.

[183] I Ross, 'Future Directions: Enhancing the Public Value of the Fair Work Commission' (2016) 58 *Journal of Industrial Relations* 402, 407.

[184] M Mourell and C Cameron, 'Neither Simple nor Fair – Restricting Legal Representation before Fair Work Australia' (2009) 22 *Australian Journal of Labour Law* 51, 66–70. See also A See, M Barry and D Peetz, 'The Australian Unfair Dismissal Regime: Exploring How Applications for Unfair Dismissal Remedy Resolve' (2022) 35 *Australian Journal of Labour Law* 27, 40 who found that unrepresented applicants before the FWC often had difficulty keeping their emotions under control.

listed as a conference. Unfair dismissal claims will generally be listed as a private conference.

Parties must supply documents with the original application and response forms. In addition, they will be directed to produce any other documents on which they seek to rely and witness statements from themselves and any witnesses. The Commission may direct the parties to file written outlines of submissions:[185] the requirements for them will be less onerous and more informal for conferences than for hearings.[186]

In a hearing, witnesses may not hear the evidence of other witnesses and will be asked to leave the room, whether in person or virtual.[187] At a hearing or conference, the Member will hear evidence and submissions before coming to a decision. The Member will be more active in investigating the complaints in a conference compared with a hearing. On average a determinative conference or hearing will be scheduled for between half a day and three days.[188]

A decision may be given orally or in writing at a subsequent date. Where a written decision is promulgated, it must be expressed in plain English and be easy to understand.[189]

An appeal against a decision of the FWC is heard by a 'full bench' of the FWC. They may confirm, quash or vary the decision, make a further decision, or refer the matter to another FWC Member.[190] Questions of law may be referred to the Federal Court for an opinion and thereafter, the FWC must make a decision in light of the opinion of the Federal Court.[191]

Some concerns have been raised about the division of jurisdictions between discrimination law protection and other employment rights and that this has risked the 'position of employment discrimination as a poor relation of employment law'.[192] There have also been concerns raised about fragmentation and complexity of the choice of regime to use to pursue a complaint.[193]

[185] A very user-friendly practice note is on the website, as well as various YouTube videos explaining the process: www.fwc.gov.au/hearings-decisions/practice-notes/practice-note-fair-hearings.

[186] See: www.fwc.gov.au/hearings-decisions/practice-notes/practice-note-unfair-dismissal-proceedings # listing-solely-as-a-conference.

[187] See: www.fwc.gov.au/documents/documents/consultation/online-proceedings-participants-guide-2022-08-15.pdf.

[188] See: www.fwc.gov.au/hearings-decisions/practice-notes/practice-note-fair-hearings.

[189] Fair Work Act 2009, s 601(2)–(3).

[190] ibid, s 607(3)9.

[191] ibid, s 608(4).

[192] B Gaze and A Chapman, 'The Human Right to Non-discrimination as a Legitimate Part of Workplace Law: Towards Substantive Equality at Work in Australia?' (2013) 29 *International Journal of Comparative Labour Law and Industrial Relations* 355, 356–57 and 371.

[193] T MacDermott, 'The Role of Mandatory ADR and Agency Engagement in Resolving Employment Discrimination Complaints: An Australian Perspective' (2015) 31 *International Journal of Comparative Labour Law and Industrial Relations* 27, 31. See also A Blackham, 'Why Do Employment Age Discrimination Cases Fail? An Analysis of Australian Case Law' (2020) 42 *Sydney Law Review* 1, 34.

B. New Zealand and the Employment Relations Authority

In New Zealand cases go to Employment Relations Authority (ERA). There is a three-year limitation period for claims to the ERA. However, a personal grievance – which may be the application for mediation to the mediation service or may be something separate – must be lodged within 90 days of the issue arising or coming to the employee's attention, whichever is later.[194]

If a case cannot be resolved by mediation, then the ERA will hold a brief phone meeting for case management.[195] In addition, the ERA Member may discuss 'whether other methods of resolving the problem would be helpful, such as mediation (or more mediation), making a recommendation, or dismissing the matter'. A timetable of next steps is usually produced, including what further documents must be provided.

Thereafter, an investigation meeting will be held and the ERA will then issue a determination of the dispute. However, if during an investigation meeting it appears that the matter can be resolved, attempts to do so will be made by the Member of the ERA, with the case being referred to a different Member subsequently for determination if resolution is not achieved.

Investigation meetings usually take place in the town or city where the employment took, or is taking, place.[196] The meetings are held in public, unless there is a non-publication order in place. They are inquisitorial and informal: the ERA 'look[s] into the facts of a case and make[s] decisions based on the merits of the matter, not on technicalities'.[197] Section 157 of the Employment Relations Act 2000 provides that the ERA is 'an investigative body … resolving employment relationship problems by establishing the facts and making a determination according to the substantial merits of the case, without regard to technicalities'. In carrying out its role, the ERA must:

(a) comply with the principles of natural justice; and
(b) aim to promote good faith behaviour; and
(c) support successful employment relationships; and
(d) generally further the object of this Act.

Because the ERA has an investigative role, they must 'take an active fact-finding approach where they choose what is relevant, question the various parties and their witnesses – if necessary, calling for certain documentation to be produced and even calling for people they want to hear from'.[198] The investigation meeting

[194] There is a 12-month period for claims of sexual harassment.
[195] See: www.era.govt.nz/resolution-process/case-management-conference.
[196] See: www.era.govt.nz/resolution-process/investigation-meeting.
[197] Employment Relations Authority, 'What We Do': www.era.govt.nz/about-us/what-we-do.
[198] Judge K Beck, 'Employment Institutions and their contribution to better work stories' paper presented to Auckland University Employment Law Class, May 2021: www.courtsofnz.govt.nz/publications/speeches-and-papers/employment-institutions-and-their-contribution-to-better-work-stories.

itself is very informal with people sitting around a table. Although parties may appear in person or be represented by lawyers, lay advocates, union representatives or family members, the majority of parties are represented either by lawyers or advocates.[199]

Witnesses will usually be asked to swear or affirm that the evidence they give is the truth and the ERA Member will ask them questions about their statement. Parties may cross-examine witnesses.

After hearing the evidence, the ERA Member will invite the parties to sum up their case orally, or sometimes this may be done in writing after the meeting. Usually, an oral determination is given at the hearing before providing written reasons. There is no official record kept of what takes place in an investigation meeting: this is 'designed to create a speedy and accessible dispute resolution service'.[200] The determination is legally binding.[201]

If a party wishes to challenge a determination then they must make an application to the Employment Court within 28 days. They may challenge the whole of the determination seeking a full rehearing of the claim (a *de novo* challenge) or a challenge that is limited to specific parts of the determination (a non-*de novo* challenge).[202]

A *de novo* challenge essentially restarts the entire claim before the Court: 'Everything is back up for grabs, even findings that went in the challenger's favour'.[203] This has been described as the safety net for the informal processes in the ERA.[204] A non-*de novo* challenge asks the Court to revisit an issue or issues of fact or law. Proceedings before the Employment Court are legalistic and adversarial: the processes are the same as in a civil court.[205]

The ERA's Annual Reports present impressive results in relation to the time frame for making determinations on cases received (see Table 9.2).

Table 9.2 Statistics relating to the work of the ERA[206]

Year	Applications received	Applications referred to Mediation	Number of determinations issued	Issued within 3 months	Challenges in the Employment Court
2020	2,475	1,622	539	91%	18%
2021	2,114	1,341	581	90%	17%

(continued)

[199] In 2024, for example, '50 percent of parties were represented by lawyers, 24 percent were represented by advocates and 19 percent were self-represented. There was no appearance from seven percent of parties': Employment Relations Authority, *Annual Report 2024* (Crown Copyright 2025) 4 and 15.
[200] Beck (n 198).
[201] See: www.era.govt.nz/determinations.
[202] Employment Relations Act 2000, s 179.
[203] Beck (n 198).
[204] ibid.
[205] See: www.employmentcourt.govt.nz/info-guidance/during-a-hearing/.
[206] Data collated by authors from the ERA Annual Reports: www.era.govt.nz/about-us.

Table 9.2 ***(Continued)***

Year	Applications received	Applications referred to Mediation	Number of determinations issued	Issued within 3 months	Challenges in the Employment Court
2022	1,970	1,170	689	88%	17%
2023	2,117	1,352	780	92%	17%
2024	2,745	1,624	781	95%	22%

In the past five years, the ERA has consistently finalised around 90 per cent of its cases within three months. Moreover, only 22 per cent of the ERA's determinations in 2024 were challenged by the parties in the Employment Court, which was itself an increase on previous years.[207]

VII. Conclusions

Once the claim and response have been provided, allocation of claims to different tracks that are case managed differently would enable resources to be focused differently according to the needs of the case. While tracks are currently used administratively in the employment tribunal system, we consider that there is much to be learned from the personal injury track allocation and case management process. There are those cases, much like the small claims track, that can be determined quickly with the minimum paperwork and an informal oral judgment. Other cases are akin to Commercial Court litigation and should be required to comply with similar formal procedural requirements, a formal trial process resulting in a written judgment. Cases which are neither low value or simple, nor high value or complex, should be managed through a process that is proportionate. The ability for parties to opt into a lower track by limiting their claims is also attractive.

There is much to be learned from the family court process that is both specific as to the requirements on the parties, so that litigants in person can understand easily what they should be doing, and appropriately restrictive in terms of bundle size and witness evidence. Claims brought by multiple claimants require an entirely separate track, with experienced administrative resource and a designated judge case managing the matter throughout.

The processes that are used by the FWC in Australia and the ERA in New Zealand provide useful models for how to address simple, low value claims. The emphasis, which is also provided in the statute for the FWC, on avoiding technicalities is crucial. In both countries the processes are quick, simple, efficient and accessible to unrepresented parties. We consider that there is much to be learned from them.

[207] Employment Relations Authority, *Annual Report 2024* (Crown Copyright 2025) 4, 24 and 25.

10

Alternative Dispute Resolution Once a Claim has been Issued

I. Introduction

Employment contracts are fundamentally relational (see chapter three). We think that resolving disputes away from court at the earliest opportunity is the optimum solution for most cases. However, there will be claims that are not resolved before litigation commences. In this chapter we explore the current use of alternative dispute resolution (ADR) once an employment claim has been started, and particularly the use of, and views of participants about, judicial mediation, judicial evaluation and early neutral evaluation. We also consider the pilot project in Scotland for fast-tracking money claims which has proved highly successful. These opportunities for ADR were viewed positively by our research participants and they called for greater availability of ADR throughout the employment tribunal litigation process (section II).

ADR has also been given greater prominence in the wider civil court system including the small claims mediation service which is being progressively rolled out (section III) and the changes that have been made to the Civil Procedure Rules (CPR) so that the courts may mandate the use of alternative dispute resolution (section IV). Although making ADR mandatory is controversial, we think that it is an important development in an area as emotionally fraught as employment disputes. We also explore how ongoing non-court dispute resolution (NCDR) operates in family law. We think that there is much to be learned from the ongoing availability of a suite of options throughout the litigation process, with judges being unrestrained in sending parties away to explore NCDR for particular issues (section V).

II. ADR During Litigation in Employment Disputes

A. Introduction

Discussions between parties may continue throughout the litigation process to resolve disputes outside the courts. Acas may assist in this process; the statistics for their success rates are discussed in chapter four. If Acas assist in the negotiation of a settlement, the terms of the settlement will usually be recorded in form COT3. In other cases, a settlement agreement will take the form of a private written agreement which will require the claimant to withdraw their claim[1] and for it to be dismissed upon withdrawal.[2]

In addition to parties privately seeking to resolve matters, the employment tribunal system offers a variety of judicial ADR. These vary as between England and Wales, Northern Ireland, and Scotland.

B. ADR in England and Wales

There are three main types of judicial ADR: judicial assessments, judicial mediation and dispute resolution appointments. The procedure for each is set out in the Presidential Guidance on ADR.[3] Judicial ADR takes place only when a regional employment judge (or any employment judge nominated by them) considers that it would give effect to the overriding objective to deal with cases fairly and justly[4] and the duty to promote ADR,[5] having considered the parties' views.[6] Judicial mediation has been the mechanism that has been used predominantly by the employment tribunals, but with dispute resolution appointments and judicial assessments also being used in some regions. In this section we describe the different processes. We consider the empirical research findings in section V.

i. Judicial Mediation

In judicial mediation, an employment judge facilitates discussions and negotiations between the parties with the aim of promoting settlement. The mediation is facilitative rather than evaluative although some judges will provide a limited reality check on the parties' desired outcomes. Participants in our research were particularly positive when this happened. All parties must agree to participate; it is not compulsory. Judicial mediation will typically be offered only if the final hearing is listed for three or more days and the parties have indicated a willingness to negotiate. The question of whether judicial mediation will take place is usually discussed at the case management preliminary hearing with the mediation taking place at a later date. It will be listed for one day and usually takes place by video, although it may be held in person.[7]

[1] Employment Tribunal Procedure Rules 2024, r 50 (ET Procedure Rules 2024).
[2] ibid, r 51.
[3] Presidential Guidance (England & Wales) – Alternative Dispute Resolution (7 July 2023) (ADR Presidential Guidance (E&W)).
[4] r 3 ET Procedure Rules 2024.
[5] ibid, r 4.
[6] ADR Presidential Guidance (E&W) (n 3) para 16.
[7] ibid.

The Presidential Guidance states that '[o]ver 65% of cases mediated reach a successful settlement on the day of mediation. Most cases that do not succeed on the day of the mediation are settled before the hearing as a result of the impetus created by the judicial mediation'.[8] This is also reflected in the net sitting days that are estimated to have been saved each year, ranging from just over 2,000 days to around 2,700 days each year over the last five years.

Older studies suggest that the relative success rates – compared with what would have happened in any event – are more limited. Urwin and Latreille, who studied the pilot scheme for judicial mediation, found that it made little statistical impact on resolution rates. They suggested that although it combined some of the legal and moral gravitas of adjudication with the flexibility of ADR, judicial mediation remained very similar to the conciliation functions of Acas,[9] with the limitations that this entails (considered further in chapter four).

ii. Judicial Assessment

In judicial assessment, an employment judge gives the parties a confidential evaluation of their respective prospects of success and possible remedies. All parties must agree to a judicial assessment, but it can be offered for any kind of case. It is typically offered in cases listed for a case management hearing and may take place at the end of a preliminary hearing or in a separate hearing. Judicial assessment necessarily takes place at an early stage in the process but only when the issues between the parties are clear. It will be listed for half a day or less and typically takes place by video, although it may be held in person.

iii. Dispute Resolution Appointment

A Dispute Resolution Appointment can be arranged even if the parties do not agree to it. At the appointment, an employment judge gives the parties a confidential evaluation of their respective prospects of success and possible remedies. An appointment may be offered where the final hearing is listed for six days or more, but this can vary according to region. The appointment is held four to six weeks after the date on which the parties are directed to exchange witness statements so the employment judge will have considered substantial amounts of the evidence before giving their evaluation. The appointment lasts between two and three hours. It is typically held via video but may be held in person.

[8] See: assets.publishing.service.gov.uk/media/5b05377a40f0b61f8b37aba7/t612-eng.pdf.

[9] P Urwin and P Latreille, 'Experiences of judicial mediation in employment tribunals' in W Roche, P Teague and A Colvin (eds), *The Oxford Handbook of Conflict Management in Organisations* (Oxford University Press 2014). See similarly, A Boon, P Irwin and V Karuk, 'What difference does it make? Facilitative judicial mediation of discrimination cases in employment tribunals' (2011) 40 *Industrial Law Journal* 45.

C. ADR in Northern Ireland

Judicial assessments and judicial mediation are available in the Northern Ireland tribunals.[10] However, dispute resolution appointments remain limited to England and Wales because different Presidential Guidance applies.

The Presidential Guidance for Northern Ireland says that

> an early assessment of the case by an Employment Judge [via a judicial assessment] may assist the parties in identifying what the case is really about, what is at stake, and may clarify and narrow the issues and encourage settlement. This may lead to resolution of the case by agreement between the parties before positions become entrenched and costs excessive, or may shorten and simplify the scope of hearings.[11]

The decision as to whether to offer judicial mediation is made by the Vice President of Tribunals and the rule of thumb is that it will be offered in cases listed for three days or more. Discrimination claims are noted to be particularly suitable for judicial mediation.[12] From 2024 to 2025, '73.2% of the Judicial Mediations that took place, resulted in resolution of the tribunal claim, either on the day of the Judicial Mediation or within a short period thereafter'.[13] This resulted in a net saving of 289 hearing days.

The guidance addressing when judicial assessments are offered mirrors that of England and Wales. The Presidential Guidance notes that resolution of the case does not usually happen at the judicial assessment but that it assists future resolution. At the end of the judicial assessment, the parties may be reminded of the services of the Labour Relations Agency (LRA) or offered a judicial mediation appointment.[14] Participants in our research from Northern Ireland noted that judges take a very firm approach to case management in the first preliminary hearing of all claims.[15] This often involves an element of judicial assessment. Moreover, the LRA may be invited to sit in on some preliminary hearings where it is thought that they might be able to help parties reach a settlement, particularly after there has been robust case management.

D. ADR in Scotland

The Presidential Guidance on ADR extends only to England and Wales.[16] Consequently, Scottish tribunals have no equivalent of judicial assessments or

[10] The Industrial Tribunals and Fair Employment Tribunal (Northern Ireland) Presidential Guidance: Rule 3 –Alternative Dispute Resolution (31 March 2023).

[11] ibid, Appendix 1, para 3.

[12] ibid, Appendix 3, para 4.

[13] See: www.employmenttribunalsni.co.uk/files/employmenttribunalsni/2025-07/Judicial%20Mediation%20Scheme%202024-25%20Report_0.pdf.

[14] ADR Presidential Guidance (Northern Ireland) (n 10) Appendix 1, para 27.

[15] Interview, 22 October 2025.

[16] ADR Presidential Guidance (E&W) (n 3).

dispute resolution appointments. Judicial mediation is available and cases will be identified as suitable for mediation by a judge, usually at the case management preliminary hearing. To be considered for mediation, a case must include a complaint of discrimination or unfair dismissal and normally be predicted to have a full hearing lasting at least three days. Even if a case meets these criteria, it may still be unsuitable. A case is more likely to be suitable if the claimant is still employed by the respondent or wishes to return to employment with the respondent. Where a case is suitable, parties will be asked whether they consent. If they agree, then the Vice President of Employment Tribunals (Scotland) will decide whether mediation will go ahead and will appoint a judicial mediator. A mediation case management discussion will be held shortly thereafter by phone, setting a date for mediation. The mediation will generally last one or two days.[17]

In addition, a pilot has been running since August 2023 whereby a legal officer 'intervenes' in defended money claims, for example, wages, holiday pay, notice pay and redundancy pay. An intervention involves no change in the tribunal process:

> Users involved in a defended money claim, which is considered suitable for the pilot, will be contacted by a legal officer to clarify areas of dispute in the hope that either the claim can resolve without a hearing or intervention will assist the employment judge to determine the claim effectively. For example, this might involve parties agreeing rates of pay, or amounts claimed to be outstanding. The aim is that legal officer intervention will reduce the length of any hearing and the need for adjournments.[18]

Fourteen months after the pilot started it was reported that it had gone well and between 75 and 80 per cent of claims in scope had been resolved without the need for a hearing.[19] Where a hearing was required, it was often shorter because issues had been clarified. During the pilot, its scope had been expanded to include monetary claims as part of unfair dismissal claims and this had been successful in resolving or clarifying those parts of the claim before a hearing. In October 2024, it was announced that fast-track claims would no longer be listed for a final hearing on receipt of the ET1 form but would be listed on receipt of the ET3 to give legal officers more time to intervene.

E. Empirical Research Findings

i. Support for Judicial ADR

Participants in our research emphasised the need for alternative dispute resolution to be used at as early a stage as possible to reduce the pressures on the

[17] Employment Tribunals (Scotland) Judicial Mediation: assets.publishing.service.gov.uk/media/5b05374440f0b61f72c9ec50/t611-eng.pdf.

[18] See: www.judiciary.uk/wp-content/uploads/2024/03/1-.-Scottish-National-User-Group-Minutes-October-2023.pdf.

[19] See: www.judiciary.uk/wp-content/uploads/2024/11/Employment-Tribunals-Scotland-National-User-Group-minutes-October-2024.pdf.

tribunal system and more fundamentally to enable participants to avoid the costs – including financial and emotional costs – of litigation.[20] They felt that there was scope for more and better ADR throughout the litigation process.[21]

When considering all three types of 'judicial' ADR, participants highlighted the significant value that is brought to bear by having a judge as the mediator or assessor because of the gravitas and authority they inherently hold. This was significant in managing parties' expectations: even where advice had been given to parties by their representatives, participants noted that it sometimes helped clients 'to hear it from the judge'.[22] Having a judicial mediator was also seen as particularly helpful for litigants in person who may not trust the representative for the other side, or a private mediator who had been paid for by the respondent and might be perceived as biased in their favour.[23]

Moreover, participants said that having a judge as the mediator meant that for some parties they felt that they had still had their 'day in court': having the mediation in a tribunal building, or in an online setting that had the feel of a tribunal, with a person who was a judge, albeit acting as a mediator, contributed to parties feeling they had been heard and to their willingness to settle. This was particularly noted in high conflict or emotionally charged cases.[24]

Participants emphasised the need for mediators to be able to get the parties to focus on the real issues at stake, rather than discussing what had happened in the past or technical legal issues.[25] As one participant, who was a mediator themselves, said: 'you approach them by talking about what you're actually talking about rather than everything that's gone wrong … So I think you just cut through the crap and you go to what actually everyone's talking about'.[26] Additionally, participants said that a mediator should not be 'overly facilitative'; that is, the best mediators were those who provided reality testing.[27] One participant said: 'I think it works where the judges [are] more interventionist in terms of trying to, and on both sides, give a steer around'.[28]

Lawyers also have a role to play. A number of participants said that there was a need for a more cooperative, rather than 'combative', culture to develop.[29] As noted in chapter seven, some regions (particularly Scotland) seem to have a more

[20] See further ch 4.

[21] Focus Groups: 11 November 2024, 12 November 2024, 13 November 2024, 14 November 2024, 19 November 2024 (12pm), 19 November 2024 (3pm), 20 November 2024 (12pm), 20 November 2024 (3pm), 25 November 2024, 29 November 2024, 5 December 2024, 10 December 2024 (1.30pm), 13 December 2024.

[22] Focus Groups: 11 November 2024, 12 November 2024, 13 November 2024, 20 November 2024 (12pm), 20 November 2024 (3pm), 25 November 2024, 29 November 2024, 5 December 2024, 10 December 2024 (1.30pm).

[23] Focus Groups: 11 November 2024, 12 November 2024, 19 November 2024 (12pm), 20 November 2024 (3pm), 29 November 2024, 5 December 2024.

[24] Focus Groups: 13 November 2024, 20 November 2024 (12pm), 5 December 2024.

[25] Focus Groups: 13 November 2024, 13 December 2024.

[26] Focus Group, 13 December 2024.

[27] Focus Groups: 13 November 2024, 25 November 2024, 29 November 2024.

[28] Focus Group, 10 December 2024 (1.30pm).

[29] Focus Groups: 19 November 2024 (12pm), 19 November 2024 (3pm), 25 November 2024, 5 December 2024, 13 December 2024.

cooperative environment than others. Participants said that legal representatives had an important role to play in promoting settlement by focusing parties on potential solutions.[30]

ii. Timing of ADR?

Participants were not, however, unanimous as to when during the litigation process ADR was most helpful. Some said that ADR should be available from the outset, that is, as soon as a claim is lodged.[31] However, others felt that this was too early and parties did not at that stage have sufficient information to be able to weigh the merits of the claim.

Many participants said that a realistic point in time to try ADR was after the first case management preliminary hearing when the issues have been clarified because by then the parties had sufficient information to evaluate the claims and because after the preliminary hearing significant costs are incurred.[32] Moreover 'No one's going to blink during pleadings because you don't want to kind of give that perception that you're kind of unsure of your own case or intimidated by the other [side]'.[33]

Having both the ET1 and the ET3 provides a helpful basis for the discussions for the parties because they know what the case is about (although see the discussion on how the claim forms might be improved in chapter eight) and means that a judge undertaking a judicial assessment has clearer information before them.[34] In addition, participants said that having to attend a preliminary hearing before ADR 'focuses minds' because it meant that managers in the respondent employer thought seriously about the dispute: 'people aren't really addressing their minds to it until we get to the week before the tribunal and then all of a sudden it's real'[35] and the preliminary hearing helps to 'set things in motion, which often means setting settlement conversations in motion'.[36] However other participants said that there was insufficient information at the preliminary hearing stage and having at least some key documents is important for a successful mediation.

Other participants said that conducting ADR once disclosure has been completed but before witness statement exchange meant that the parties have a clearer view of the case and can sensibly seek to resolve matters, but before

[30] Focus Groups: 11 November 2024, 25 November 2024, 29 November 2024.

[31] Focus Groups: 19 November 2024 (3pm), 25 November 2024, 5 December 2024, 10 December 2024 (9.30am).

[32] Focus Groups: 11 November 2024, 12 November 2024, 20 November 2024 (3pm).

[33] Focus Group, 25 November 2024.

[34] Focus Groups: 11 November 2024, 12 November 2024, 13 November 2024, 19 November 2024 (12pm), 19 November 2024 (3pm), 20 November 2024 (3pm), 5 December 2024.

[35] Focus Group, 25 November 2024.

[36] Focus Group, 19 November 2024 (12pm).

incurring the financial and emotional costs of preparing witness statements.[37] Some participants said that because a schedule of loss was necessary for settlement, mediation was impractical before disclosure was completed because they were often ordered to be completed at the same time. Other participants noted that in some regions the schedule of loss is ordered to be completed four to five weeks after the ET1 which helps to promote earlier settlement discussions.[38]

However, a number of participants said that waiting until after disclosure was too late: disclosure often requires significant hours of work for legal representatives which increases the costs involved. Once substantial legal costs have been incurred, it is more difficult for parties to settle.[39] Participants who were also mediators noted that in practice mediation is not about having all the documents, as the mediator's job is to focus on 'finding solutions'.[40] Moreover, it was said that the longer the process, the more entrenched the parties become, making it less likely that settlement will be achieved.[41]

A final suggested point of time for ADR was after exchange of witness statements by which time the evidence would be very clear to all parties. Particular concern was expressed about the risks of earlier judicial assessment when judges have more limited information about the case which might encourage parties to present a misleading narrative. This was compared with the position in dispute resolution appointments when judges have the witness statements and it was said that judges seem to feel more empowered to give their views on the prospects of the claims then. However, it was said that the process of preparing witness statements often entrenches parties' positions and adds to the costs.[42]

Some participants suggested that ADR should be made available throughout the tribunal litigation process, because there was no specific time that was ideal in every case.[43] It was suggested that it would be helpful to have mandatory touch points during the litigation where ADR had to be considered but that it could be available throughout the process. The advantage of having mandatory touch points was that parties would not then be concerned about appearing weak by suggesting that ADR should be considered.[44]

iii. How can Engagement with ADR be Encouraged?

Some participants said that ADR should be a mandatory precondition to litigation because getting the right people in a room, including the relevant decision-makers,

[37] Focus Groups: 11 November 2024, 10 December 2024 (9.30am), 10 December 2024 (1.30pm).
[38] Focus Group, 20 November 2024 (12pm).
[39] Focus Groups: 11 November 2024, 20 November 2024 (3pm), 25 November 2024.
[40] Focus Groups: 19 November 2024 (12pm), 13 December 2024.
[41] Focus Groups: 19 November 2024 (12pm), 25 November 2024, 5 December 2024.
[42] Focus Groups: 13 November 2024, 10 December 2024 (1.30pm).
[43] Focus Groups: 11 November 2024, 5 December 2024.
[44] Focus Group, 19 November 2024 (12pm).

in itself contributed to achieving a settlement.[45] Other participants said that it was not productive to force ADR if the parties were not interested.[46] Concerns were also raised about requiring individuals to face each other in the context of particularly sensitive or traumatic claims.[47] Another suggestion was that a failure properly to participate in mediation could result in an uplift or reduction in compensation or for a costs order to be imposed. Other participants were concerned that assessing whether someone had properly participated would be very difficult to evaluate and that it would become a tick-box exercise.[48]

Having a costs regime attached to ADR was a concern for participants, particularly in relation to claimants:

> [T]hat gets pretty scary and intimidating for claimants with perfectly good cases, but who are just, you know, tend to get very worried. There's a real access to justice problem there. And I speak mostly as a respondent lawyer, but I wouldn't feel uncomfortable about [it]. Part 36 lawyers' offers used to fill me with dread.[49]

Some participants said that having any kind of a 'stick' to enforce mediation was not conducive to an open and collaborative dialogue of the kind needed in ADR discussions.[50] Others said that there was no need to create additional incentives for mediation because the incentives to avoid litigation already exist, particularly given its high costs. Rather, they said, what was needed was better education as to the advantages of mediation and the disadvantages of litigation.[51] Participants said that the flexibility of remedies available in mediation in contrast to litigation needed to be emphasised far more with the parties. In other words, the mediation agreement could address matters that were not available as a remedy from the tribunal.[52] Moreover, parties needed to be encouraged to continue to try ADR even though Acas early conciliation had not succeeded.[53]

A number of participants said that litigants in person faced particular barriers to ADR because they lacked a trustworthy assessment of the merits of their claim and the likely remedies that they would receive. Having some form of independent assessment was essential to their understanding the value of the offers being made.[54] Participants said that unrepresented parties often seek that

[45] Focus Groups: 12 November 2024, 13 November 2024, 14 November 2024, 19 November 2024 (12pm), 20 November 2024 (12pm), 20 November 2024 (3pm), 29 November 2024.

[46] Focus Groups: 13 November 2024, 25 November 2024, 29 November 2024, 10 December 2024 (1.30pm).

[47] Focus Groups: 13 November 2024, 10 December 2024 (9.30am).

[48] Focus Groups: 11 November 2024, 12 November 2024, 13 November 2024, 20 November 2024 (12pm), 25 November 2024, 29 November 2024.

[49] Focus Group, 12 November 2024.

[50] Focus Group, 29 November 2024.

[51] Focus Groups: 11 November 2024, 14 November 2024, 19 November 2024 (12pm), 10 December 2024 (1.30pm), 13 December 2024.

[52] Focus Groups: 20 November 2024 (12pm), 13 December 2024.

[53] Focus Group, 13 December 2024.

[54] Focus Groups: 14 November 2024, 19 November 2024 (12pm), 20 November 2024 (12pm), 5 December 2024, 10 December 2024 (1.30pm).

guidance from the mediator, who is constrained in what they can say, and they said that more evaluative mediation processes would help increase the number of settlements.[55]

Other participants said that sometimes lawyers operated as a barrier to settlement because they are under pressure to meet billing targets which may influence them not to encourage their client to pursue ADR. One participant said that it is 'difficult to meet your billing target even in a [reputable] firm … if you weren't litigating at least two or three cases all the way through to hearing'.[56] This is especially true since the parties are not facing the risks of costs, which means that 'as the lawyer representing the parties, settling isn't in your financial interests in any way, shape or form'.[57] Other participants noted that some arrangements with legal expenses insurers were particularly disincentivising: some insurance policies cover all of a client's legal and litigation costs for a monthly fee which means that as long as they follow the insurers' requirements, there is no incentive to settle.[58] A more stringent costs regime would change that position.

III. Small Claims Mediation Service

So, are there examples of mediation actually being used in courts? The Small Claims Mediation Service (SCMS) operates for claims under £10,000. It is a confidential phone mediation service which lasts for one hour and is free (once a claim has been issued in court).[59] Before the service was made compulsory in certain claims, government statistics showed that 52.5 per cent of cases mediated via the SCMS resulted in a settlement, but only 19 per cent of parties utilised the service.[60] There were significant problems with resourcing the SCMS[61] as well as a lack of understanding by parties of what mediation was and how successful it could be.[62]

However, from May 2024, a two-year pilot commenced whereby specific claims are automatically referred to the SCMS, namely money claims that are allocated to the small claims track, are not road traffic claims and do not involve any claim for personal injury.[63] If a party fails to attend a mandatory mediation session then the

[55] Focus Groups: 11 November 2024, 19 November 2024 (12pm), 13 December 2024.
[56] Focus Group, 13 December 2024.
[57] Focus Group, 13 December 2024.
[58] Focus Group, 29 November 2024.
[59] See: www.gov.uk/respond-to-court-claim-for-money/mediation.
[60] See: assets.publishing.service.gov.uk/media/6582dc34fc07f3000d8d459b/carm-impact-assessment-unsigned.pdf.
[61] See: www.judiciary.uk/wp-content/uploads/2021/06/April-2021-The-Resolution-of-Small-Claims-interim-report-FINAL.pdf.
[62] See: assets.publishing.service.gov.uk/media/6582dc34fc07f3000d8d459b/carm-impact-assessment-unsigned.pdf.
[63] PD51ZE para 3. Further restrictions apply in relation to legal representation and fee remission: PD51R para 2.1(3).

court may sanction them including striking out the claim or requiring them to pay costs.[64] A further pilot was launched in July 2025 for road traffic claims that would ordinarily be allocated to the small claims track.[65]

The success of these pilots will be assessed in due course. Simply combining employment tribunal proceedings with the SCMS would not work because of the very specialist nature of employment matters and – as we address in chapter twelve – the potential need to identify systemic issues that may underlie a 'simple' claim relating to wages or the non-payment of holiday pay. However, we note that this is a further example of mediation for small claims through short, swift meetings. It is of particular note that these processes are now mandatory: requiring a party to participate, albeit not requiring them to come to a settlement.

IV. Changes to the Civil Procedure Rules

In *Churchill v Merthyr Tydfil County Borough Council*[66] the Court of Appeal had to consider whether a court can lawfully order the parties to court proceedings to engage in non-court-based dispute resolution and if so, in what circumstances. The case concerned a claim in nuisance when an internal complaints procedure operated by the local authority had not first been utilised. The Court of Appeal had previously held in *Halsey v Milton Keynes General NHS Trust*[67] that 'to oblige truly unwilling parties to refer their disputes to mediation would be to impose an unacceptable obstruction on their right of access to the court'.[68] However, the Court of Appeal in *Churchill* said the remarks in *Halsey* were obiter. In addition, the Court rejected the submission that the Supreme Court's decision in *Unison*[69] was relevant:

> *UNISON* was concerned with an impediment that prevented access to a judicial determination, not with the circumstances in which it might be considered proportionate to delay such access for a legitimate objective such as achieving resolution of the dispute by other means.[70]

Accordingly, in *Churchill* the Court of Appeal held that the courts did have the power to stay proceedings to allow for, and to order parties to participate in non-court dispute resolution (NCDR), another name for ADR, even when they did not

[64] PD51ZE, paras 7 and 8.

[65] See: www.lawgazette.co.uk/news/low-value-rta-claims-will-go-to-automatic-mediation/5124050.article.

[66] *Churchill v Merthyr Tydfil County Borough Council* [2023] EWCA Civ 1416.

[67] *Halsey v Milton Keynes General NHS Trust* [2004] EWCA Civ 576.

[68] ibid, [9].

[69] *R (on the application of Unison) (Appellant) v Lord Chancellor (Respondent)* [2017] UKSC 51.

[70] *Churchill v Merthyr Tydfil County Borough Council* [2023] EWCA Civ 1416, [44]. *UNISON* is discussed further in ch 11.

consent to do so.[71] The Court had the power to regulate its own procedure which included making an order for parties to engage in NCDR.

The Master of the Rolls, Sir Geoffrey Vos, said in *Churchill* that:

> Experience has shown that it is extremely beneficial for the parties to disputes to be able to settle their differences cheaply and quickly. Even with initially unwilling parties, mediation can often be successful. Mediation, early neutral evaluation and other means of non-court-based dispute resolution are, in general terms, cheaper and quicker than court-based solutions. Whether the court should order or facilitate any particular method of non-court-based dispute resolution in a particular case is a matter of the court's discretion, to which many factors will be relevant.[72]

The Court declined to set out a list of the factors relevant to the exercise of that discretion but noted that certain factors suggested in submissions might be relevant, including the form of ADR, whether the parties were legally advised or represented and the impact of that on the likely effectiveness of the ADR, whether it was made clear to the parties that, if they did not settle, they were free to pursue their claim or defence, the urgency of the claim and the reasonableness of the delay, the costs involved, any significant imbalance between the parties in relation to resources, bargaining power or sophistication, the reasons for not wanting to mediate, and the reasonableness of the sanction if a party declined ADR.[73]

Recognising the value of ADR, the CPR have been amended. CPR rule 1.4, dealing with the court's duty of active case management, includes 'ordering or encouraging the parties to use an ADR procedure if the court considers it appropriate and facilitating the use of such procedure'. CPR rule 3.1 which sets out the court's case management powers has had two additional powers added:

(o) order the parties to participate in ADR;
(p) take any other step or make any other order for the purpose of managing the case and furthering the overriding objective, including hearing an Early Neutral Evaluation with the aim of helping the parties settle the case.

In multi-track cases, the court now 'must consider whether to order or encourage the parties to participate in ADR'.[74] The White Book says that the court 'now has the procedural power to order parties to attend ADR and has a mandatory duty to consider imposing it'.[75]

Thus, we see the importance that is placed on ADR in the civil courts. The Court of Appeal has confirmed that a court can order ADR during litigation,

[71] ibid, [50]–[58].
[72] ibid, [59].
[73] ibid, [61] and [66].
[74] Civil Procedure Rules, r 29(1A).
[75] Lord Justice Coulson (ed), *Civil Procedure: The White Book Service* (Vol 1, Sweet & Maxwell 2025) 879 (White Book 2025).

rather than merely encourage or recommend it. We would argue that the same rules should apply in employment tribunals.

V. Non-Court Dispute Resolution in Family Law

As noted in chapter five, family law places great weight on ADR. There are four particular means within the Family Procedure Rules 2010 (FPR 2010) by which the court can encourage NCDR:

(1) Rule 3.3(1) places the court under a general duty to 'consider, at every stage in proceedings, whether non-court dispute resolution is appropriate'.
(2) Through Rule 3.3(1A) the court may require a party to file and serve a form setting out their views on using NCDR as a means of resolving the dispute.[76]
(3) Rule 3.4(1A) provides that where timetabling of proceedings allows sufficient time, 'the court should encourage parties, as it considers appropriate, to (a) obtain information and advice about, and consider using, non-court dispute resolution; and (b) undertake non-court dispute resolution'. This may be achieved by the court directing parties to obtain information,[77] encouraging parties to attend NCDR in gaps in the process or by adjourning proceedings.[78] The pre-action protocols both make it clear that before starting court proceedings, the court 'will expect parties to have attended at least one form of non-court dispute resolution', unless there is a good reason not to.[79] If the parties fail to comply, then the court may decline to commence the court timetable, may suspend the timetable and give directions to ensure that at least one form of NCDR is attempted,[80] or may order that gaps between court hearings are used for a party to comply.[81]
(4) The court may use its power to award costs to encourage NCDR. In financial remedy proceedings, the general rule is that the court will make no order as to costs.[82] However, costs may be ordered because of a party's conduct in relation to which the court 'must have regard to' any failure by a party, without good reason, to attend a MIAM or attend NCDR.[83]

[76] Form FM5, which must usually be filed and served at least seven days before the first on notice hearing and may be required before subsequent hearings: PD31A, paras 10B and 10C.
[77] Family Procedure Rules, r 3.4(2) (FPR 2010).
[78] PD3A, para 10D.
[79] Pre-application Protocol: financial remedy proceedings (Annex to PD9A), para 14.
[80] ibid, para 8, para 15.
[81] Pre-application Protocol: private law proceedings relating to children (Annex 2 to PD12B) para 26.
[82] r 28.3(5) FPR 2010.
[83] r 28.3(7) FPR 2010. In private law proceedings relating to children, the court will take into account any failure to comply with the Pre-application Protocol when deciding whether to order the payment of costs: Pre-application Protocol: private law proceedings relating to children (Annex 2 to PD12B), para 27. The Protocol also includes an expectation that parties will consider NCDR (para 17).

There is some lack of clarity about whether a court can go further and order parties to engage in NCDR: the Practice Direction says not.[84] However, following the decision in *Churchill* discussed above, Knowles J said:

> It may be thought that the decision … is of limited relevance to family proceedings. To make that assumption is unwise. The active case management powers of the CPR mirror the active case management powers in the FPR almost word for word and both the civil and the family court have a long-established right to control their own processes. The settling of cases quickly supports the accessibility, fairness and efficiency of the civil, and I emphasise, the family justice system.

She also noted that although the FPR rule changes due on 29 April 2024 did not go as far as compelling parties to proceedings to engage in NCDR, the agreement of the parties to an adjournment for that purpose will no longer be required. Instead, the family court may – where the timetabling of the proceedings allows sufficient time for these steps to be taken – 'encourage' the parties to obtain information and advice about and consider using NCDR and 'undertake non-court dispute resolution' (rule 3.4(1A) with effect from 29 April 2024). She also said that the accompanying Practice Direction 3A has been amended and makes clear that the court may also use its powers to adjourn proceedings to encourage the use of NCDR (rule 4.1). In financial remedy cases, the power to encourage even unwilling parties is reinforced by an amended rule 28.3(7) which will make the failure, without good reason, to engage in NCDR a reason to consider departing from the general starting point that there should be no order as to costs.[85]

Knowles J also noted that NCDR was 'particularly apposite for the resolution of family disputes' because litigation is 'so often corrosive of trust and scars those who may need to collaborate and co-operate in future'. As we discussed in chapter three, we consider this to be equally applicable in employment disputes. Knowles J said that

> parties to financial remedy and private law children proceedings can expect – at each stage of the proceedings-- the court to keep under active review whether non-court dispute resolution is suitable in order to resolve the proceedings.[86]

In our empirical research, a number of participants noted that there seemed to be more emphasis by the family courts on NCDR than there had been historically. One interviewee said that the ability to send things back to mediation was being used as a stick to encourage parties to resolve things without a final hearing.[87]

It is important to emphasise that the objective of family mediation is not to reconcile the relationship between ex-partners; it is to resolve disputes concerning

[84] PD31A, para 10A.
[85] *Re X (Financial Remedy: Non-Court Dispute Resolution)* [2024] EWHC 538 (Fam), [15].
[86] ibid, [16].
[87] Interview with family law practitioner, 11 July 2025 (2).

finances and children.[88] In other words, the emphasis is on forward-looking solutions to specific issues. This is not necessarily different from the position in employment disputes: there may be an ongoing employment relationship, or the forward-looking solution may relate to providing a reference to future employers. Family mediation usually takes place over a series of sessions, with the length and number of sessions varying depending on the case. Usually it takes between three and five sessions lasting one to two hours, to reach an agreement.[89] Mediation can take place online or in person.[90] The format of holding multiple mediation sessions on different days is seen as advantageous in giving the parties more 'processing time' with gaps between sessions allowing parties to obtain further information or advice, and consult with family members, friends and colleagues, making it more likely that they will change their positions.[91]

Mediation sessions cost around £130–£170 per person per hour.[92] Legal aid is available for family mediation. If one partner is eligible for legal aid, then the first mediation session will be free for both partners. The partner who is ineligible for legal aid must pay their share of any subsequent mediation sessions.[93] Separately, there is a family mediation voucher scheme through which the government will pay up to £500 per family for mediation (but not the Mediation Information Assessment Meeting (MIAM) appointment)[94] regardless of the partners' incomes, where they are a party to private law proceedings relating to children or financial remedy proceedings if they are also a party to proceedings relating to children.[95] Where parties are eligible for the voucher scheme, they will be given information about it during a MIAM.[96] The provision of legal aid and/or specific funding for mediation would be a considerable incentive for parties in employment disputes if similar provision were made.

[88] Family Mediation Council and the Ministry of Justice, 'Family mediation: Sorting out family disputes without going through court': assets.publishing.service.gov.uk/media/5a800f33ed915d74e33f834d/family-mediation-leaflet.pdf.

[89] Family Mediation Council, 'Mediation Sessions': www.familymediationcouncil.org.uk/family-mediation/mediation-meetings-sessions/.

[90] Family Mediation Council, 'Online Mediation': www.familymediationcouncil.org.uk/online-mediation/.

[91] A Sims, 'Exploring the scope of family mediation in England and Wales' in M Roberts and M Federica Moscati (eds), *Family Law Mediation: Contemporary Issues* (Bloomsbury Professional 2020) 309.

[92] Family Mediation Council, 'What Does Mediation Cost?': www.familymediationcouncil.org.uk/family-mediation/cost/.

[93] ibid.

[94] Ministry of Justice, 'Family Mediation Voucher Scheme' (26 March 2021): www.gov.uk/guidance/family-mediation-voucher-scheme.

[95] ibid and PD36V, para 1.4. As of December 2023, the scheme helped over 24,000 families to access mediation. Out of the scheme's first 7,200 users, 69% reached whole or partial agreement and did not need to go to court: Ministry of Justice, 'Supporting earlier resolution of private family law arrangements: Government response' (January 2024): assets.publishing.service.gov.uk/media/65c3518e3f6aea000dc15549/early-resolution-consultation-response.pdf.

[96] PD36V, para 5.1.

The mediator usually sees the two parties together, rather than using conventional shuttle mediation.[97] The Family Mediation Council (FMC) Code of Practice says that mediations are commonly conducted without lawyers.[98] The orthodox understanding is that family mediation is a purely facilitative process. However, Blakey's research found that, in practice, family mediators often perform some evaluative functions.[99] Family mediators aim not just to achieve a settlement, but an outcome that avoids injustice or unfairness, which requires an evaluative judgement to be made.[100] This is particularly important because the court must endorse any agreement that is made through the final order; only an agreement that is not unjust or unfair will be ordered.

Blakey also noted that mediators can go beyond providing information about the law and the legal process and into predicting court outcomes.[101] Whether mediation should be facilitative or evaluative is a contested issue. If it is purely facilitative, there is a danger that inequality of bargaining power and structural inequalities could lead to unjust outcomes because 'power rather than principle may dictate the outcome of negotiations'.[102] If it is more evaluative, there is a danger that mediation will become 'a form of informal adjudication without the safeguards of formal legal process'.[103] Roberts considers that evaluative mediation 'is primarily focused on disposing of the legal issues in dispute at the expense of those non-justiciable issues that are frequently of primary significance to the parties and which could be essential to any resolution of their dispute – such as ethical, practical, personal and communication concerns'.[104]

An alternative format for family mediation is 'hybrid' or 'integrated' mediation, where parties are accompanied by their lawyers and generally spend time in separate rooms.[105] The mediator may keep information from one party confidential from the other party.[106] Hybrid mediation is usually scheduled for a whole day, rather than over multiple days, with a view to achieving settlement at the end of that day.[107] Criticism has been levelled at this form of mediation because it reduces

[97] Family Mediation Council, 'Mediation Sessions' (n 89).

[98] Family Mediation Council, 'Code of Practice for Family Mediators' (September 2024) para 8.15.

[99] R Blakey, *Rethinking Family Mediation: The Role of the Family Mediator in Contemporary Times* (Bristol University Press 2025) 205.

[100] ibid, 207.

[101] ibid, 211.

[102] R George, S Thompson and J Miles, *Family Law: Text, Cases, and Materials*, 5th edn (Oxford University Press 2023) 27–28.

[103] ibid, 28.

[104] M Roberts, 'The meaning of power in family mediation' in M Roberts and M Federica Moscati (eds), *Family Law Mediation: Contemporary Issues* (Bloomsbury Professional 2020) 152–53.

[105] Resolution, *Hybrid Mediation:* resolution.org.uk/looking-for-help/splitting-up/your-process-options-for-divorce-and-dissolution/hybrid-mediation/.

[106] M Roberts, 'What is happening to family mediation? Part 2 Hybrid Mediation' [2022] *Family Law* 1079.

[107] Resolution, *Hybrid Mediation* (n 105).

direct interaction between parties, and the use of lawyers to communicate undermines an 'essential component' of mediation.[108]

There may also be 'child-inclusive mediation' in which the mediator meets with the child separately from their parents to ascertain the child's views on the issues. If the child consents, the mediator will pass on the child's views to the parents.[109] Hope praises the development of co-mediation, where there are two or more mediators involved, for example, a lawyer mediator together with a therapeutic mediator. Alternatively, where there are particularly complex financial matters, there could be a lawyer mediator together with an accountant mediator. She argues that co-mediators are better placed to address a power imbalance between two parties and may be better at detecting parties' verbal and non-verbal cues.[110]

There are other methods of NCDR but mediation has been the focus in family law disputes. Sir James Munby[111] told a House of Lords Select Committee that

> one of the great disasters and one of the great mistakes by government in 2013 was identifying mediation as the non-court solution … We need to encourage people to use all of these techniques, recognising that one technique may suit one case and another technique may suit another couple. The idea that one technique suits everybody and all cases is, I am afraid, simply silly.[112]

Moreover, the 'official promotion of family mediation … as the preferred default process' may result in an increase in referrals of unsuitable cases for mediation.[113] The Select Committee concluded that '[t]he Government's focus on mediation as a mechanism of reducing the court backlog, to the exclusion of all other forms of dispute resolution, is excessive'.[114]

One alternative method of NCDR that was often referred to in our interviews with family law practitioners was private financial dispute resolution (FDR) hearings. Court-based FDR is listed in every financial dispute case unless a private FDR has been conducted. They are set up during the directions hearing with parties agreeing the name of the person who will undertake the private FDR. A private FDR is usually conducted by a barrister in the barrister's chambers (as opposed to in the court). The barrister will read the papers and provide the parties with a view on the merits of the case and the without prejudice proposals of the parties. Offers are often then made and the FDR judge remains available to assist parties on any further specific points. It is essentially the same as early neutral evaluation in the tribunal system. One practitioner estimated that between 95 and 97 per cent

[108] Roberts, 'What is happening to family mediation?' (n 106) 1083. See also G Davies, Shuttle mediation: mediating on the back foot? [2013] *Family Law* 222, 223.

[109] Family Mediation Council, 'Mediation Is Not Only for Adults!': www.familymediationcouncil.org.uk/mediation-isnt-only-for-the-adults/.

[110] G Hope, 'Co-mediation – what is it and how can it help resolve disputes?' [2019] *Family Law* 1332.

[111] President of the Family Division from 2013 to 2018.

[112] Children and Families Act 2014 Committee, 'Children and Families Act 2014: A failure of implementation' (HL 2022–23, 100) para 133.

[113] Roberts, 'The meaning of power in family mediation' (n 104) 152.

[114] Children and Families Act 2014 Committee (n 112) para 139.

of cases settle at or around the time of a private FDR;[115] another estimated it was about 90 per cent.[116]

A key part of why a private FDR is successful is because

> [y]ou choose your tribunal, you've got somebody you both trust as opposed to pot luck in the courts ... you get somebody who will have read the papers and is not saying you're one of five cases ... And you can come back, to and fro.[117]

Another participant said that because the parties cooperated in the decision as to who the FDR judge will be, 'you don't get the scenario of distrusting that person'.[118] The time that was available in a private FDR, compared with a court FDR, was also identified as a key difference: previously in court FDR

> judges had time to sit down and hear the arguments and give advice and guidance ... but then over time the court system got so under pressure that court-based FDRs just became less [and] less valuable. The judges didn't have time to read the bundle in advance. They had too many on the day, they didn't have the time to really engage with the arguments.[119]

Another participant said that in a private FDR clients

> hear ... what the judge's view is. And of course, you say this is all confidential. Another judge at a final hearing might take a different view ... There are a range of possible outcomes ... [you say to the parties] I'm an experienced judge and I think most judges would take the view that that isn't going to be relevant or impact on a decision or this is going to influence an outcome and you know it can be a really helpful way of cutting through things.[120]

In addition, participants said that being in a barrister's chambers was helpful because 'The environment is more congenial because you're in somebody's chambers as opposed to a horrid courtroom. You're kept fed and watered, and [that] always sounds stupid, but it's not'.[121]

However, a concern was raised that because the fees of the FDR judge must be paid by the parties, it was only available to individuals who could afford it and therefore a participant said that 'my concern about non-court dispute resolution is that actually we're moving towards a really, really unequal' system.[122]

Family law provides a useful model of a suite of NCDR methods that may be used by parties and mandated by the courts. Mediation, taking a variety of forms, remains the predominant model but participants, once again, noted the importance of evaluative rather than merely facilitative mediation. Private FDRs – akin

[115] Interview with family law practitioner, 11 July 2025.
[116] Interview with family law practitioner, 9 July 2025.
[117] Interview with family law practitioner, 11 July 2025.
[118] Interview with family law practitioner, 11 May 2025.
[119] Interview with family law practitioner, 9 July 2025.
[120] Interview with family law practitioner, 17 July 2025.
[121] Interview with family law practitioner, 11 July 2025.
[122] Interview with family law practitioner, 14 July 2025 (2).

to early neutral evaluation – was understood to be of particular assistance when trying to resolve claims.

VI. Conclusions

Participants in our research were enthusiastic about using ADR to resolve employment disputes. Mediation, particularly led by a judge, was viewed positively when it was evaluative rather than facilitative. There was more disagreement about when ADR should be offered. In practice, we think that the timing of ADR should be case specific and it needs to be available throughout the litigation process, with touchstone points when parties should be required to consider it, but that at certain points in the journey some form of ADR should be mandatory. The Scottish pilot for small money claims and the SCMS show the potential for short sessions of mediation to resolve simple claims. Family law provides a helpful insight into the use of both mediation and early neutral evaluation in claims that are deeply emotional, with different forms of NCDR being appropriate at different times. These issues are of particular relevance to the employment tribunals and a suite of NCDR options should be available throughout the litigation process in that forum.

Having looked at ADR, in the next chapter we consider issues relating to costs and tribunal fees and whether these can be used to encourage settlement.

PART IV

Costs, Fees and Enforcement

Costs and fees are controversial and difficult issues in employment disputes; they are an almost existential issue for employment lawyers. However, fees regimes operate in both civil and family litigation which may both deal with important basic rights of the parties. Costs regimes also operate in civil litigation and to a degree in family litigation. We consider the current position in relation to costs and fees in the employment tribunal and look at how costs and fees operate in civil, family and personal injury litigation where qualified one-way costs shifting applies (chapter eleven). While fees are unlikely to be reintroduced in employment tribunals, we think they should be considered and that in certain cases, a costs regime should operate.

Once a case has been through a tribunal and the claimant has won, the next (and much under-discussed) issue concerns the question of enforcement of any award. Enforcement of employment tribunal awards has been problematic for many years. Too few successful claimants – only about half – see the money to which they are entitled, whether that arises from a tribunal award or a settlement. Claimants have to go through further hoops to try to enforce a tribunal judgment. We examine those different processes and consider how the new Fair Work Agency (FWA) might be able to make some important changes.

There is a further issue. There is no strategic consideration of individual tribunal judgments to ensure that structural, systemic issues are addressed in workplaces. We explore the work of ombuds and the use of Prevention of Future Death reports by coroners to see what might be learned from their approach in seeking to engender systemic change (chapter twelve). We think there is real scope for the FWA's role to be developed significantly to address the enforcement of awards and to monitor and track issues arising in relation to particular employers or sectors.

Recommendations

1. In Track 1 cases, no fees or costs should be payable.
2. In Track 2 cases, consideration should be given to court fees being payable, as a percentage of the value of the claim. Further, where offers made after the early neutral evaluation (ENE) hearing are not beaten, this should usually result in a costs award limited to a percentage of the value of the claim. So, for example, if an offer is made of £20k which is rejected

but the tribunal subsequently awards only £15k, then the costs award would be eg 10% of the £15k (ie £1500).

3. In Track 3 cases, a court fee, as a percentage of the value of the sum claimed, should be payable. A full costs regime should operate on an issue basis, including provisions equivalent to Part 36.
4. The FWA should be properly resourced to enable them to enforce tribunal awards and COT3 settlement payments, and impose a penalty for non-payment.
5. Tribunal awards should have the same status as county court judgments and be enforceable accordingly. Tribunals should have the power to require parties to confirm to them that awards have been paid, with the possibility of imposing a penalty where they are not.
6. Proper data should be collected as to the types of claims that are successful, and where awards are not paid, to enable the FWA to investigate and/or advise and support particular employers or those operating in particular sectors.

11

Costs and Tribunal Fees

I. Introduction

Fees and costs orders are controversial subjects in the employment tribunal system. Costs orders are rare in the tribunal: the starting point is that costs will not be awarded. The requirement to pay fees across all cases applied from July 2013 until found unlawful in 2017. During that period, the number of cases in the tribunal system plummeted and it was primarily low value, straightforward claims that disappeared. The Conservative government under Rishi Sunak commenced consultation on whether fees should be introduced but these proposals did not proceed.[1] Media reports indicated that the Labour government was also thinking about reintroducing fees,[2] but then decided not to.[3] In this chapter we consider the issue of costs (section II) and fees (section III).

The tribunal system is, in fact, unusual in being both a no fees and also a primarily costs-free jurisdiction. Some suggest that the current system must change to help address the backlog of cases in the tribunal system. Therefore, we look to how costs are dealt with in ordinary civil courts and in family cases. One suggestion from our empirical research was the introduction of Qualified One-Way Costs Shifting (QOCS), currently used in personal injury claims, to be applied in employment cases. We have considered what this involves and some of the critiques of QOCS. However, we are doubtful that they would work. By contrast, we do think serious consideration should be given to introducing a costs regime in the most complex (Track 3) cases, equivalent to that found in the civil courts (section III).

We also examine the use of tribunal fees, especially in light of the judgment of the Supreme Court in *Unison*,[4] and the views of participants in our research about fees. We have considered the fees that are payable in the civil courts and family courts, and the scope for remission of fees in those jurisdictions. We think that a

[1] See: www.gov.uk/government/consultations/introducing-fees-in-the-employment-tribunals-and-the-employment-appeal-tribunal/introducing-fees-in-the-employment-tribunals-and-the-employment-appeal-tribunal.

[2] See: www.theguardian.com/money/2025/oct/01/labour-considering-charging-workers-for-employment-tribunal-claims-sources-say.

[3] See: www.theguardian.com/money/2025/oct/08/david-lammy-rules-out-charging-workers-for-employment-tribunal-claims.

[4] *R (on the application of Unison) v Lord Chancellor* [2017] UKSC 51.

fee system should be considered, particularly in the complex 'Track 3' cases, as is the case for ordinary civil claims (section III).

II. Costs

A. Costs in the Employment Tribunal

The starting point is that employment tribunals do not order one party to pay the costs of another party to a claim.[5] Costs are the exception not the rule.[6] However, the tribunal must consider making a costs order where:

(a) a party (or that party's representative) has acted vexatiously, abusively, disruptively or otherwise unreasonably in either the bringing of the proceedings, or part of it, or the way that the proceedings, or part of it, have been conducted,
(b) any claim, response or reply had no reasonable prospect of success, or
(c) a hearing has been postponed or adjourned on the application of a party made less than 7 days before the date on which that hearing begins.[7]

A tribunal may also make a costs order where a party 'has been in breach of any order, rule or practice direction or where a hearing has been postponed or adjourned'.[8] If one of these limbs is established then the tribunal must consider whether to exercise its discretion to make an order, which will include consideration of the party's ability to pay any order, and then consider the amount payable and the form of the order.

It is relevant, but not determinative, whether an application for strike out and/or deposit order was made prior to the final hearing and whether a costs warning letter has been sent to the claimant.[9] Where a deposit order has previously been ordered, and the tribunal decided the specific allegation or argument against the 'depositor' for substantially the same reasons given in the deposit order, that party will be treated as having acted unreasonably in pursuing their claim, unless the contrary is shown.[10] Nonetheless, the tribunal must still consider whether to exercise its discretion to make a costs order.[11] The deposit will be set off against the amount of any costs order.[12]

Costs can be awarded only where a party has been represented by a legal representative, or a representative who charges for representation, in relation to

[5] Presidential Guidance (England & Wales) – General Case Management (22 January 2018) Guidance Note 7, para 1.
[6] ibid, para 10.8. See also, eg, *Gee v Shell UK Ltd* [2002] EWCA Civ 1479.
[7] Employment Tribunal Rules of Procedure 2024 SI 2024/1155, r 74(2).
[8] ibid, r 74(3).
[9] *Vaughan v London Borough of Lewisham* [2013] IRLR 713 and *Rogers v Dorothy Barley School* (UKEAT/0013/12).
[10] Employment Tribunal Rules of Procedure 2024 (n 7) r 40(7).
[11] *Oni v Unison* (UKEAT/0370/14).
[12] Employment Tribunal Rules of Procedure 2024 (n 7) r 40(8).

costs that have actually been incurred.[13] Where costs are assessed summarily in the tribunal, they will be limited to £20,000.[14] Alternatively, a costs order may be made in the tribunal for costs to be subject to detailed assessment in the county court where there is no limit on the amount of costs.[15] In Northern Ireland, costs are usually capped at £10,000.[16]

Where a person has not paid for representation, a preparation time order may be made.[17] The hours of preparation are determined according to information from the party and the tribunal's own assessment of 'what it considers to be a reasonable and proportionate amount of time' to spend on the preparatory work.[18] This is then multiplied by an hourly rate of £44.[19]

The tribunal may make a costs order on its own initiative or on the application of a party.[20] A party can apply for a costs order at any stage up to 28 days after the date on which the final judgment was sent to the parties.[21]

In addition, a wasted costs order may be made against a representative (rather than the party) where costs have been incurred 'as a result of any improper, unreasonable or negligent act or omission' by the representative or 'which, in the light of any such act or omission occurring after they were incurred, the tribunal considers it unreasonable to expect that party to pay'.[22]

Participants in our research discussed the impact of the use of costs orders in limiting how many weak claims are submitted. Many participants considered that the current regime was insufficiently robust and that there should be greater use of costs to deter claimants from bringing hopeless claims.[23] This was linked to the use of deposit orders which were noted to be set at too low an amount and resulted in claimants 'having nothing to lose' in trying to bring a claim.[24] Participants also said that facing a costs risk would deter respondents from pursuing hopeless defences or artificially complicating claims for tactical reasons.[25] However, other participants said that claimants are already deterred from bringing claims and that costs warning letters are frequently sent by employers, intimidating workers who have valid and meritorious claims from pursuing litigation. They said that the threat was particularly effective in

[13] ibid, r 72.
[14] ibid, r 76(1)(a).
[15] ibid, r 76(1)(b).
[16] Industrial Tribunals and Fair Employment Tribunal Rules of Procedure 2000, r 75(1).
[17] Employment Tribunal Rules of Procedure 2024 (n 7) r 73(2).
[18] ibid, r 77(1).
[19] ibid, r 77(2).
[20] ibid, r 74(1).
[21] ibid, r 75(1).
[22] ibid, r 78(1).
[23] Focus Groups: 11 November 2024, 12 November 2024, 13 November 2024, 20 November 2024 (3pm), 25 November 2024; Survey answers.
[24] Focus Groups: 11 November 2024, 12 November 2024, 13 November 2024, 19 November 2024 (12pm), 20 November 2024 (12pm), 20 November 2024 (3pm), 25 November 2024, 10 December 2024 (1.30pm); Survey answers.
[25] Focus Groups: 19 November 2024 (12pm), 25 November 2024, 10 December 2024 (9.30am); Survey answers.

lower value claims, for example, for holiday pay and wages.[26] Participants were concerned that extending the costs regime would result in significant impediments to workers' access to justice. Some participants therefore said that the employment tribunal system should remain a no costs environment.[27] Another suggestion was that a different approach to costs was needed according to the type of claim.[28] We share this view.

Other participants viewed a costs regime as an opportunity to enable better legal representation for claimants because, by allowing the winning side to recover costs, it would facilitate the use of conditional fee agreements (CFAs) by lawyers and increase the likelihood that a claimant would be represented. A costs regime that facilitated a claimant having legal representation by way of a CFA would particularly help those workers who are precarious and vulnerable, who have a valid claim but lack the personal funds to pay for lawyers. This would improve the efficiency of the whole system. One of the advantages of this approach was that, in practice, it would promote access to representation for those workers with strong claims because the lawyers will evaluate the strength of the claim before agreeing to take a case on under a CFA. This would also therefore operate as a further mechanism to filter out weak claims.[29]

Participants remained concerned about the risk of workers having to pay an employer's costs. After-the-Event insurance, used in CFAs in personal injury claims, might be an option.[30] Alternatively, participants said that a 'qualified one-way costs shifting' (QOCS) regime might mitigate the disadvantages. QOCS are discussed below (section II.D) but in essence claimants do not pay the respondent's costs unless the respondent establishes fundamental dishonesty by the claimant. Participants said that this would be appropriate because, in the context of employment law, there is an inherent inequality of power relationships and financial capacity between the parties. They said that a QOCS regime would 'level the playing field'.[31] Moreover, participants said that it would promote early settlements by discouraging respondents from seeking to drag out cases to increase the financial burden on the claimant.[32]

However, a significant number of participants were concerned about the use of QOCS because of the burden this would place on employers, particularly small or medium-sized businesses. Respondents would face a situation where they paid their own legal costs irrespective of whether they won the case:[33] 'That's invidious

[26] Focus Groups: 13 November 2024, 14 November 2024, 20 November 2024 (12pm); Survey answers.

[27] Focus Groups: 11 November 2024, 13 November 2024; Survey answers.

[28] Survey answers.

[29] Focus Groups: 11 November 2024, 19 November 2024 (3pm), 20 November 2024 (12pm), 20 November 2024 (3pm), 29 November 2024, 10 December 2024 (1.30pm); Survey answers.

[30] Focus Group, 11 November 2024.

[31] Focus Group, 11 November 2024; Survey answers.

[32] Focus Group, 29 November 2024; Survey answers.

[33] Focus Groups: 12 November 2024, 19 November 2024 (12pm), 10 December 2024 (1.30pm).

because as soon as an employee stands up and says I've got an employment claim, you know that you're going to have to start spending money on it regardless'.[34]

Furthermore, participants said that they thought that a QOCS regime would increase the number of unmeritorious claims because workers stood to gain from winning a case but would face no costs consequences if they lost.[35] One way to mitigate these concerns would be to introduce the equivalent of Part 36 offers at the same time (discussed further in section II.B.iii), so that a party who rejected a settlement offer that they did not subsequently beat would be liable in costs.[36]

We turn now to consider costs in civil litigation, exploring the usual rules that apply, how costs operate depending on the track that a case is allocated to, the impact of Part 36 offers and the special rules that apply to litigants in person.

B. Costs in Ordinary Civil Cases

i. The Basic Rule

Under the Civil Procedure Rules (CPR) rule 44.2(1), the court has discretion as to (a) whether costs are payable by one party to another; (b) the amount of those costs; and (c) when they are to be paid. Costs are the costs 'of and incidental to' legal proceedings,[37] that is those payable by a client to their legal representative[38] and disbursements. A party is not entitled to receive an award of costs that exceeds their liability to their own solicitor.[39]

If the court decides to make an order about costs, the general rule is that the unsuccessful party will be ordered to pay the costs of the successful party, that is, 'costs follow the event'.[40] However, the court may make a different order including: that a party pay only a proportion of another party's costs, a stated amount of another party's costs, costs from or until a certain date or relating to particular steps taken in or a part of the proceedings.[41]

When deciding what costs order to make, the court will 'have regard to all the circumstances',[42] including the conduct of the parties, whether a party has succeeded on part of its case, even if that party has not been wholly successful; and any admissible offer to settle made by a party which is drawn to the court's attention, and which is not an offer to which costs consequences under Part 36 apply.[43]

[34] Focus Group, 13 November 2024.
[35] Focus Groups: 11 November 2024, 19 November 2024 (12pm), 20 November 2024 (12pm), 25 November 2024.
[36] Focus Group, 11 November 2024; Survey answers.
[37] Senior Courts Act 1981, s 51(1).
[38] Civil Procedure Rules, r 44.1(2)(a)(iii) (CPR).
[39] *Gundry v Sainsbury* [1910] 1 KB 645.
[40] r 44.2(2)(a) CPR.
[41] ibid, r 44.2(6).
[42] ibid, r 44.2(4).
[43] Also known as a *Calderbank* offer.

Conduct of the parties for these purposes includes whether it was reasonable for a party to 'raise, pursue or contest a particular allegation or issue', whether a claimant has 'exaggerated its claim', how the proceedings have been conducted, and 'whether a party failed to comply with an order for alternative dispute resolution, or unreasonably failed to engage in alternative dispute resolution'.[44]

Costs may be payable on the standard basis or on the indemnity basis, as determined by the court.[45] Costs awarded on the standard basis are those costs reasonably incurred and reasonable in amount[46] and must be proportionate to the matters in issue.[47] The court will resolve any doubt about the reasonableness and proportionality of costs in favour of the paying party.[48] Costs awarded on the indemnity basis must be reasonably incurred and reasonable in amount[49] but there is no requirement of proportionality and the court will resolve any doubt about the reasonableness of costs in favour of the receiving party.[50] Ordering costs on the indemnity basis may be appropriate where '[t]here is something in the conduct of the action or the circumstances of the case which takes the case out of the norm in a way which justifies an order for indemnity costs'.[51]

Unless a claim is being dealt with on a track that has fixed costs (see below), the court will either assess costs summarily or by detailed assessment.[52] In a summary assessment, the court determines the amount of costs payable at the end of a hearing[53] in a 'rough and ready' way.[54] The general rule is that a summary assessment should be carried out at the end of a fast-track trial, and at the conclusion of any other hearing which has lasted only one day.[55] Detailed assessment is carried out by a costs officer[56] at a later date, although the court may order it to take place immediately.[57]

ii. Controlling Costs on the Four Tracks

Costs are addressed differently according to the track to which the claim has been allocated (see chapter seven).

[44] r 44.2(5) CPR.
[45] ibid, r 44.3(1). Subject to specific limits relating to the track the case was allocated to: see section II.B.
[46] ibid, r 44.3(1).
[47] ibid, r 44.3(2)(a).
[48] ibid, r 44.3(2)(b).
[49] ibid, r 44.3(1).
[50] ibid, r 44.3(3).
[51] *Excelsior Commercial and Industrial Holdings v Salisbury Hamer Aspden & Johnson* [2002] EWCA Civ 879, [2002] CP Rep 67, [39]. For example, a dishonest claim: *Esure Services v Quarcoo* [2009] EWCA Civ 595, [25].
[52] ibid, r 44.6(1).
[53] CPR PD44, para 9.2.
[54] A Zuckerman et al, *Zuckerman on Civil Procedure: Principles of Practice* (Sweet & Maxwell, 2021) para 28.144.
[55] CPR PD44, para 9.2.
[56] r 44.6(1)(b) CPR.
[57] ibid, r 47.1.

Costs on the small claims track are tightly limited. CPR rule 27.14(2) provides that the court may only award costs for:

(a) fixed costs attributable to issuing the claim;
(b) in claims for an injunction or specific performance, a sum for legal advice and assistance up to £260;[58]
(c) court fees;
(d) expenses which a party or witness reasonably incurred in travelling to and from a hearing or staying away from home for a hearing;
(e) loss of earnings or loss of leave by a party or witness due to attending a hearing or staying away from home for a hearing, up to £95 per person per day (see PD27A para 7.3(1));
(f) experts' fees up to £750 per expert (see PD27A para 7.3(2));
(g) further costs as the court may assess by the summary procedure when a party has behaved unreasonably;
(h) certain fixed costs in Road Traffic Accident cases or Employers' Liability and Public Liability Claims;
(i) in an appeal, the cost of any approved transcript reasonably incurred.

Costs for a legal representative may only be awarded if a party has behaved unreasonably.[59]

A fixed costs regime applies to the fast track,[60] whereby the amount of the costs that are payable are limited by the rules: the court cannot award more or less than the rules allow,[61] unless the parties have expressly agreed that the fixed costs regime should not apply.[62] The court still has discretion as to whether costs are payable, when they are to be paid, and whether to make a percentage costs order.[63]

The amount of fixed costs (and disbursements) are defined by the rules and depend on the stage reached in the litigation, the complexity band assigned to the case, and the value of the claim.[64]

On the intermediate track, fixed costs also apply.[65] However, the successful party is generally entitled to any disbursement which has been reasonably incurred.[66]

Costs on the multi-track are generally controlled through the costs management process, which usually proceeds alongside the case management process.[67] The stages of costs management are:

- The parties are required to file and exchange costs budgets. Litigants in person are exempt from this requirement.[68] Costs budgets are set out on a standard

[58] CPR PD27A, para 7.2.
[59] r 27.14(2)(g) CPR. See also White Book 2025, para 27.0.2(iii).
[60] r 28.8 CPR.
[61] ibid, r 45.1(3).
[62] ibid, r 45.1(3).
[63] ibid, r 45.1(2).
[64] ibid, r 45.44 and r 45.59 and PD45 Table 12.
[65] r 45.60 CPR and PD45 Table 14.
[66] r 45.60 CPR.
[67] ibid, r 3.12– r 3.18.
[68] ibid, r 3.13(1).

form called Precedent H. The parties record their past costs ('incurred costs') and estimated future costs ('budgeted costs') for various stages of the litigation.

- The parties should discuss and attempt to agree each other's budgets. They then file a budget discussion report at least 7 days before the first case management conference.[69]
- Once costs budgets have been exchanged, the court will make a costs management order, unless it is satisfied that the litigation can be conducted justly and at proportionate cost without one.[70] In a costs management order:
  - (a) the court records the extent to which budgeted and incurred costs are agreed;[71]
  - (b) where there is disagreement on budgeted costs, the court approves budgeted costs[72] by deciding if they are reasonable and proportionate;[73]
  - (c) the court does not approve incurred costs but may record any comments it has about incurred costs.[74]
- In making case management decisions, the court will have regard to the parties' costs budgets.[75] Where a costs management order has been made, the court will thereafter control the parties' budgets in respect of recoverable costs.[76]
- If significant developments in the litigation warrant it, a party must revise its budgeted costs upwards or downwards. The court may then approve, vary, or disallow the party's proposals.[77]
- The recoverable costs of the costs management process itself are very limited.[78]

Where a costs management order was made, then, when the court is assessing costs on the standard basis at the end of a case, the court will not depart from a party's last approved or agreed costs budget, unless there is a good reason to do so. The court will also take into account any comments a judge had previously recorded about incurred costs.[79] Where a costs management order was not made, then, in deciding whether costs are reasonable and proportionate, the court will have regard to the receiving party's last approved or agreed costs budget.[80] A bill of costs exceeding the last costs budget by 20 per cent may be evidence of unreasonable or disproportionate costs, unless there is a satisfactory explanation for the increase.[81]

[69] ibid, r 3.13(2).
[70] ibid, r 3.15(2).
[71] ibid, r 3.15(2)(a), (c).
[72] ibid, r 3.15(2)(b).
[73] CPR PD3D, para 12.
[74] r 3.15(4) CPR.
[75] ibid, r 3.17(1).
[76] ibid, r 3.15(3).
[77] ibid, r 3.15A.
[78] See, r 3.15(5) CPR.
[79] ibid, r 3.18.
[80] ibid, r 44.4(3)(h). See also PD44.
[81] CPR PD44, para 3.5–3.7.

If costs are assessed on the indemnity basis, costs budgets and costs management orders are not a constraint on the amount that can be awarded.[82] Guideline Hourly Rates are published setting out the hourly rates that will be awarded for particular grades of solicitor in different geographical locations.[83]

iii. Cost Impact of Part 36 Offers

CPR Part 36 is a self-contained procedural code for making settlement offers.[84] Valid Part 36 offers must be made in a certain form. This includes a requirement (in most cases) for the offeror to specify a 'relevant period' within which the offeror will be liable for the offeree's costs if the offer is accepted.[85] If a Part 36 offer is accepted within the relevant period then the claimant is entitled to the costs of the proceedings up to the date of acceptance.[86] There is no discretion for the court. Costs are assessed on the standard basis, unless the parties agree or the fixed costs regime applies.[87] Where a Part 36 offer is accepted after the end of the relevant period, liability for costs must be determined by the court unless the parties have agreed on costs. The court must, unless it considers it unjust, order that the claimant will be awarded costs up to the end of the relevant period and the offeree will pay the offeror's costs from the end of the relevant period to the date of acceptance.[88]

If a claimant does not accept a defendant's Part 36 offer and then fails to 'beat' the offer at trial, the claimant is usually entitled to their costs up to the end of the relevant period. Thereafter, the court must, unless it considers it unjust, order that the defendant is entitled to their costs from the end of the relevant period, and interest on those costs.[89] If a defendant did not accept a claimant's Part 36 offer and the claimant then 'matched or beat' the offer at trial, the court must, unless it considers it unjust, order that the claimant is entitled to costs on the indemnity basis from the end of the relevant period plus interest on those costs at a rate not exceeding 10 per cent above base rate.[90]

iv. Special Rules for Litigants in Person

The maximum amount a litigant in person can be awarded in costs (except in the case of a disbursement) is two-thirds of the amount which would have been allowed if the litigant in person had been represented by a legal representative.[91] Under CPR rule 46.5(3), litigants in person can be awarded costs for work and

[82] *Burgess v Lejonvarn* [2020] EWCA Civ 114, [93].
[83] See: www.gov.uk/guidance/solicitors-guideline-hourly-rates.
[84] r 36.1 CPR.
[85] Usually 21 days; r 36.5(1)(c) CPR.
[86] r 36.13(1) CPR.
[87] ibid, r 36.13(3).
[88] ibid, r 36.13(4), (5).
[89] ibid, r 36.17(3).
[90] ibid, r 36.17(4)(b), (c).
[91] ibid, r 46.5(2).

disbursements which would have been allowed if the work had been done by a legal representative, payments reasonably made by the litigant in person for legal services relating to the proceedings, and the costs of obtaining expert assistance in assessing the costs claim. The amount of costs payable to a litigant in person for an item of work will be either:

(a) where the litigant can prove financial loss, the amount that the litigant can prove to have been lost for time reasonably spent on doing the work; or
(b) where the litigant cannot prove financial loss an amount for the time reasonably spent on doing the work at a rate of £19 per hour.[92]

The civil court costs rules provide a useful example of how a costs regime can operate differently according to the track to which the claim is allocated, with a more rigorous costs regime applying to more complex or high value claims. A full costs regime may have the advantage of enabling litigants in person to access representation via CFAs.

A jurisdiction where there are many litigants in person is family law; we turn now to consider the costs rules that apply there.

C. Costs in Family Cases

The costs rules in family cases are found in both the Family Procedure Rules 2010[93] (FPR 2010) and the CPR.[94] Three different costs regimes apply in the family court and the Family Division of the High Court:[95]

(1) the 'clean sheet' starting point, which is the default regime under the FPR 2010; it applies to proceedings about children and some financial remedy proceedings; and
(2) the 'no order as to costs' starting point, which applies to most but not all financial remedy proceedings; and
(3) the 'costs follow the event' starting point, which applies to a limited number of cases heard in the Family Division of the High Court.

Under section 51(1) Senior Courts Act 1981, the costs of proceedings in the family court and the Family Division of the High Court are in the discretion of the Court. This is reflected in FPR 2010 rule 28.1, which provides that the court 'may at any

[92] r 46.5(4) CPR and PD46 para 3.4.

[93] Family Procedure Rules 2010 SI 2010/2955 (FPR 2010).

[94] CPR Pt 44 applies to family proceedings, apart from rules 44.2(2), 44.2(3), 44.10(2) and 44.10(3): FPR 2010 r 28.2(1). However, CPR rules 44.2(1), 44.2(4) and 44.2(5) do not apply to certain financial remedy proceedings: FPR 2010, r 28.3(2). CPR, r 45.8 and CPR Pts 46 and 47 apply with modifications to family proceedings: FPR 2010, r 28.2(1).

[95] See F Wilkinson and S Hunton, *Costs in Family Proceedings* (Bloomsbury Professional 2020) para 1.23.

time make such order as to costs as it thinks just'. The general rule in civil litigation that costs follow the event is disapplied.[96]

In 'clean sheet' cases, FPR 2010 do not provide a replacement starting point on costs. Therefore, there is no presumption and no general rule about whether to make a costs order. Costs are simply discretionary. This is the position in family proceedings concerning children,[97] and some financial remedy cases, such as interim orders and orders for the maintenance of a child.[98] Costs orders should be made only in rare circumstances because the child should be regarded as the only 'winner' in the proceedings. There are inquisitorial features of the proceedings and treating one parent as the 'winner' may reduce cooperation between the parents and the resources available to look after the child.[99] Costs may be ordered where the conduct of one party has been reprehensible, or a party's stance has been outside the band of what is reasonable.[100]

In final financial remedy cases relating to divorce, nullity and judicial separation, the general rule is 'no order as to costs', that is, 'the court will not make an order requiring one party to pay the costs of another party'.[101] However, the court may make a costs order 'at any stage of the proceedings where it considers it appropriate to do so because of the conduct of a party in relation to the proceedings (whether before or during them)'.[102] The court takes a 'broad view of conduct' and will generally conclude that to 'refuse openly to negotiate reasonably and responsibly will amount to conduct' for which a costs order will be considered. Other factors include a failure, without good reason, to attend a Mediation Information and Assessment Meeting or other non-court dispute resolution, any failure to comply with the FPR 2010 or a court order, open offers to settle,[103] whether it was reasonable for a party to raise, pursue, or contest a particular allegation or issue, the manner in which matters have been pursued and 'any other aspect of a party's conduct' in the proceedings that is considered relevant and had a financial effect on the parties.[104]

There are some disputes which can be heard in the Family Division of the High Court, but which will not be governed by the FPR 2010 when heard in the Family Division.[105] In those cases, the general CPR costs rules apply,[106] with the starting point that costs follow the event.[107]

[96] r 28.2(1) FPR 2010.
[97] Wilkinson and Hunton (n 95) para 2.01.
[98] ibid, para 3.08.
[99] *Re S (A Child)* [2015] UKSC 20.
[100] ibid, [26].
[101] r 28.2(1) and r 28.3(4)(b) and (5) FPR 2010.
[102] ibid, r 28.3(6).
[103] Excluding *Calderbank* offers: FPR, r 28.3(8); PD28A, para 4.3.
[104] r 28.3(6) and (7) FPR 2010.
[105] This includes disputes concerning the Inheritance (Provision for Family and Dependants) Act 1975, the Protection from Harassment Act 1997, and the Trusts of Land and Appointment of Trustees Act 1996.
[106] Wilkinson and Hunton (n 95) paras 1.17–1.18.
[107] r 44.2(2) CPR.

The emphasis on non-court dispute resolution, discussed in chapter five, is evident in the costs regime and we think may be of relevance in employment disputes: a failure to engage with dispute resolution processes has consequences for parties in terms of their costs and the family courts recognise this in being willing to make costs orders in those circumstances.

D. Costs in Personal Injury Cases and QOCS

i. How does the QOCS Regime Work?

As noted above, some research participants suggested that we consider the costs regime in personal injury cases and specifically the qualified one-way costs shifting (QOCS) regime which may affect the ability of a defendant to enforce a costs order against a claimant by applying the same principles as those that apply in ordinary civil cases (see section II.A).[108]

The QOCS regime applies to personal injury proceedings[109] and protects 'claimants' against the enforcement of costs orders: this includes a person bringing a claim, a defendant bringing a counter-claim, and a person bringing a claim for contribution under Part 20.[110] The effect of QOCS is that

> orders for costs made against a claimant may be enforced without the permission of the court but only to the extent that the aggregate amount in money terms of such orders does not exceed the aggregate amount in money terms of any orders for, or agreements to pay or settle a claim for, damages, costs and interest made in favour of the claimant.[111]

Therefore, if a claimant loses at trial and is awarded no damages, the defendant cannot recover any costs from the claimant. If a claimant is awarded damages at trial but faces an adverse costs order because, for example, they have failed to beat a Part 36 offer, the defendant can enforce that costs order only up to the amount of money that the claimant was awarded in damages, interest and costs.

There are four exceptions to QOCS. First, costs orders can be enforced fully if proceedings are struck out under CPR rule 3.4(2)(a) or (b).[112] The court's permission is not required.[113]

[108] ibid, r 44.13–44.17.
[109] Specifically, proceedings which include a claim for damages for personal injuries, under the Fatal Accidents Act 1976, or which arise out of death or personal injury and survives for the benefit of an estate by virtue of s 1(1) of the Law Reform (Miscellaneous Provisions) Act 1934: CPR, r 44.13(1).
[110] r 44.13(2) CPR.
[111] ibid, r 44.14(1).
[112] See further ch 8. A party's failure to comply with a rule, Practice Direction, or court order may result in strike out under CPR r 3.4(2), but this will not constitute a ground for losing QOCS protection.
[113] r 44.15 CPR.

Second, costs orders can be enforced fully where the court finds the claim to be fundamentally dishonest on the balance of probabilities.[114] Fundamental dishonesty goes to the root of either the whole claim or a substantial/important part of it.[115] The claimant must be given adequate warning of, and a proper opportunity to deal with, the possibility of a finding of fundamental dishonesty.[116] The court's permission is required to enforce a costs order.[117]

Third, costs orders can be enforced to the extent the court considers just where a claim is brought for the financial benefit of a person other than the claimant or certain dependants under the Fatal Accidents Act 1976.[118] The court's permission is required.[119]

Fourth, costs can be enforced to the extent the court considers just where the personal injury claim is combined with a non-PI claim, such as a road traffic accident where there may be personal injuries and damage to the vehicle. If the proceedings 'can fairly be described in the round as a personal injury case', then the court will usually exercise its discretion to reach a similar outcome to full QOCS protection.[120] The court's permission is required to enforce the order.[121]

ii. Academic and Practitioner Views on QOCS

Jackson LJ recommended the introduction of QOCS for personal injury cases in his final report on civil litigation costs (Jackson Report) as part of his overall aim to reduce disproportionate costs in civil litigation and promote access to justice.[122] He said that, in personal injury cases, the inclusion of a lawyer's success fee and after-the-event insurance premiums were 'the major contributor to disproportionate costs'.[123] Jackson LJ recommended that success fees and After the Event (ATE) insurance premiums should cease to be recoverable from unsuccessful defendants.[124] However, he recognised that there were sound policy reasons for providing costs protection to claimants in personal injury cases: a person with 'a meritorious claim for damages for personal injuries should be able to bring that claim, without being deterred by the risk of

[114] Concerns have been raised that the loss of QOCS protection creates an incentive for defendants to make unfounded allegations of fundamental dishonesty: J Miller, 'QOCS Not Recovering Well' (2018) 168 (7808) *New Law Journal* 5 and K Walden-Smith, 'Fundamental Dishonesty: A Double-Edged Sword?' (2021) 171 (7928) *New Law Journal* 17.

[115] *Howlett v Davies* [2017] EWCA Civ 1696, [16].

[116] ibid, [31].

[117] r 44.16(1) CPR.

[118] PD 44, para 12.2 gives examples of such claims including subrogated claims and claims for credit hire.

[119] r 44.16(2)(a) CPR.

[120] *Brown v Commissioner of Police* [2019] EWCA Civ 1724, [56]–[59].

[121] r 44.16(2)(b) CPR.

[122] R Jackson, *Review of Civil Litigation Costs: Final Report* (December 2009) xvii, para 2.6 and xvi, para 1.1.

[123] ibid, xvi, para 2.1.

[124] ibid, xvi, para 2.2.

adverse costs'.[125] Thus, he said that the 'only practicable way' to achieve this was through QOCS. Indeed, he said that QOCS may be 'appropriate on grounds of social policy, where the parties are in an asymmetric relationship'.[126]

The formulation of QOCS recommended by Jackson LJ was not implemented by the government because of concerns about a lack of certainty for claimants as to when they would be protected from an adverse costs order.[127] Concerns were also raised that QOCS would increase speculative or frivolous claims and that it was unfair on defendants.[128] There has been considerable satellite litigation as to the formulation of QOCS,[129] resulting in amendments to the CPR including allowing defendants to enforce costs orders out of settlement agreement payments.[130]

Higgins argues that QOCS is not a matter of corrective justice because a litigant who advances an arguable case that merits resolution at trial, but who ultimately loses at trial, does not commit any wrong against their opponent.[131] However, it is a matter of distributive justice because there is nothing wrong in principle in requiring parties in an asymmetrical relationship to make asymmetrical contributions to the costs of resolving disputes between them.[132] In cases where QOCS apply, and costs do not shift to the claimant, Higgins says that the burden of funding civil litigation can justly be spread across users, potential users, lawyers, insurers and commercial funders.[133]

Views are mixed as to whether QOCS have achieved their objectives. In 2013, Higgins predicted that, in contrast to Jackson LJ's views, QOCS would not inevitably reduce the costs of personal injury litigation because claimants might still obtain ATE insurance because of the risk of losing protection via Part 36 offers and because introducing QOCS may increase the total number of personal injury claimants, thus increasing defendants' total spend on litigation.[134] Higgins argues that the best way to reduce litigation costs is instead to adopt the German system of fixing the amount of recoverable costs in advance by reference to the value of the dispute.[135]

[125] ibid, xvii, para 2.7.

[126] ibid, 89, para 5.11.

[127] Ministry of Justice, *Reforming Civil Litigation Funding and Costs in England and Wales–Implementation of Lord Justice Jackson's Recommendations: The Government Response* (Cm 8041, 2011) paras 163–64.

[128] ibid, para 166.

[129] eg, *Cartwright v Venduct Engineering* [2018] EWCA Civ 1654 and *Ho v Adelekun* [2021] UKSC 43. See also: D Bailey-Vella, 'Watching the QOCS' (2023) 173 (8014) *New Law Journal* 20.

[130] This has been much criticised, see for example: S Hayman and T Jenkinson, 'Claimants: Caught in a Trap?' (2023) 173(8021) *New Law Journal* 12 and E Reyes, 'Counting the Costs' *Law Society Gazette* (28 April 2023).

[131] A Higgins, 'A Defence of Qualified One Way Cost Shifting' (2013) 32 *Civil Justice Quarterly* 198, 206–07.

[132] ibid 208.

[133] ibid 211.

[134] ibid 199.

[135] ibid 204–05.

However, in 2018 Jackson LJ concluded that the reforms ending recoverable ATE premiums and introducing QOCS 'have been a success … Ending recoverable ATE premiums and introducing QOCS for PI cases has substantially reduced the cost of litigation, thereby promoting access to justice'.[136] By contrast, the Law Society said, also in 2018, that it had not seen any evidence of more cases being settled since the introduction of QOCS, particularly in high value claims.[137]

Academics and practitioners have continued to call for a broader scope for QOCS.[138] Tom Hickman KC says that 'the most important issue in public law' is that the majority of the population cannot in practice bring a judicial review claim, because of the potential for adverse costs orders if the claim is unsuccessful. He therefore argues for a version of QOCS in judicial review cases. The default rule would be that defendants cannot recover their costs against unsuccessful claimants. This would be qualified by allowing a sum to be recovered that represents a reasonable amount for the claimant to pay, having regard to their ability to pay. There would also be recovery for abusive claims and unreasonable conduct. The defendant would be required to apply for a qualification to the default rule at an early stage in the proceedings, and the application would be determined at the permission stage.[139] Fordham and Boyd argue that there is nothing unfair in requiring the state to absorb the cost of judicial reviews that pass the permission stage but are ultimately unsuccessful. This is because the scrutiny of the state provided by judicial review is in the public interest, even where the judicial review is ultimately unsuccessful.[140]

We think that QOCS are likely to be problematic in employment disputes. Employers do not have relevant insurance to cover both their own fees and a claimant's fees. The use of the fundamental dishonesty test has also been difficult in practice in personal injury claims, resulting in extensive litigation. We recognise that there are some attractions to the QOCS regime, but we do not think that it would be appropriate in the employment sphere: it places the respondent at too great a disadvantage and we are unconvinced of its efficacy in limiting unmeritorious claims. While we consider that there is a role for costs in employment disputes, we do not think that QOCS is the answer.

E. Interim Conclusions

Rules on costs are complex and do not speak to the need for quick justice. For simple, Track 1 claims[141] there should be no costs orders. However, as we have

[136] R Jackson, 'Was It All Worth It?' (2018) 34 *Journal of Professional Negligence* 61, 65.
[137] Miller (n 114).
[138] Jackson, 'Was It All Worth It?' (n 136) 65.
[139] Tom Hickman, 'Public Law's Disgrace' UK Constitutional Law Blog (9 February 2017): ukconstitutionallaw.org/2017/02/09/tom-hickman-public-laws-disgrace/.
[140] M Fordham and J Boyd, 'Rethinking Costs in Judicial Review' [2009] *Judicial Review* 306, 307, para 8.
[141] See ch 9.

seen, a substantial number of cases before an employment tribunal are high value and complex claims. For Track 3 cases, we consider that a costs regime should be put in place, equivalent to that found in the civil courts. This would have the added advantage of facilitating parties to obtain legal representation via conditional fee agreements (with suitable ATE insurance) which would support the needs of the parties and the system in navigating this litigation. Moreover, it would open the door to a regime equivalent to Part 36 to support and encourage parties to resolve their disputes outside of the tribunal.

For cases on Track 2 we think that a limited costs regime should be used. We consider that these claims should not generally be subject to costs. However, where offers made after the proposed early neutral evaluation hearing are not beaten, this should be a basis for the judge to consider making a costs award. This would have the dual benefit of enabling claimants to bring claims without the fear of costs consequences but also encouraging settlement once a clear indication has been provided as to the merits and value of their claim. The level of the costs payable could be calibrated so that they are a proportion of the sums claimed, thereby encouraging parties to carefully consider what the value of their claim really is while ensuring access to justice. So, if an offer is made of £20,000 which is rejected by the claimant and the tribunal subsequently awards only £15,000, a costs award could be made as a percentage (eg 10%) of the final amount awarded (ie £1500).

We turn now to look at the controversial question of fees.

III. Fees

A. Tribunal Fees

No court fees are charged by either the employment tribunal or the Employment Appeal Tribunal. This principle dates to the founding of the tribunals in the 1960s where the idea was that access to tribunals should be quick and cheap. For employment lawyers this understanding is part of their DNA. Therefore, the introduction of fees by the Coalition government in July 2013 came as a profound shock, especially when done in such an unthinking way. Fees were introduced to address the volume of cases being lodged with employment tribunals and were payable in all cases, unless the claimant qualified for fee remission.[142] An issue fee and a hearing fee were payable. The level of fee depended on the subject matter of the claim (designated as Type A or Type B) and the number of claimants. Type B claims included unfair dismissal claims, equal pay claims and discrimination claims. The fees were significant: £160 issue fee and £230 hearing fee for a Type A claim; £250 issue fee and £950 hearing fee for Type B claims. By contrast with the civil court fees, the tribunal fees bore 'no direct relation to the amount sought' and could

[142] Fees were introduced by the Employment Tribunals and the Employment Appeal Tribunal Fees Order 2013 SI 2013/1893 (Fees Order), under the powers given to the Lord Chancellor by s 42(1) Tribunals, Courts and Enforcement Act 2007.

'therefore be expected to act as a deterrent to claims for small amounts and non-monetary claims'.[143] As can be seen by comparing these fees with the fees in the civil courts (see section III.B), they are well above the highest fees for small claims in the county court.

Fee remission was available to those claimants who had disposable capital and gross monthly income of less than a specified amount. Monthly income included a partner's income. Partial remission was available whereby for every £10 of gross monthly income above the specified amount, the claimant would pay £5 towards the fee. If a claimant was successful before the employment tribunal, the respondent could be ordered to pay the fee.

After fees were introduced, the number of claims fell dramatically. The fall was particularly significant in relation to lower value claims, such as claims for unpaid wages and unpaid annual leave or in claims in which a financial remedy was not sought, such as relating to the entitlement to breaks.[144]

The fees regime was challenged in the *Unison* case and was declared unlawful by the Supreme Court.[145] There was no dispute that the purposes underlying the Fees Order were legitimate: fees paid by litigants can reasonably be considered a justifiable way of making resources available for the justice system and measures that deter the bringing of frivolous and vexatious cases can increase the efficiency of the system. Nevertheless, the fees regime was unlawful because there was found to be a real risk that people would effectively be prevented from having access to justice and the degree of intrusion on the right to access to justice was greater than was justified by the objectives the measure was intended to serve.[146] The Supreme Court noted that the available statistics following the introduction of fees showed there was 'no basis for concluding that only stronger cases are being litigated'[147] as well as noting that 'some employers were delaying negotiations to see whether the claimant would be prepared to pay the fee'.[148] The fees were unaffordable for some people; they rendered it 'futile or irrational' to bring certain (low value) claims; and 'only half of the claimants who succeed in obtaining an award receive payment in full, and around a third of them receive nothing at all' because of failures in the enforcement of awards (see further Chapter 12).[149]

The Supreme Court emphasised that the 'constitutional right of access to the courts is inherent in the rule of law', it is not 'merely a public service like any other, that the courts and tribunals are providers of services to the "users" who appear before them, and that the provision of those services is of value only to the users themselves'. Rather, at the heart of the rule of law is the

[143] *R (on the application of Unison) v Lord Chancellor* [2017] UKSC 51, [20].
[144] ibid, [40].
[145] ibid.
[146] ibid, [96].
[147] ibid, [57].
[148] ibid, [59].
[149] ibid, [96].

> idea that society is governed by law … Courts exist in order to ensure that the laws made by Parliament, and the common law created by the courts themselves, are applied and enforced … In order for the courts to perform that role, people must in principle have unimpeded access to them. Without such access, laws are liable to become a dead letter, the work done by Parliament may be rendered nugatory, and the democratic election of Members of Parliament may become a meaningless charade.[150]

The Supreme Court said that people and businesses 'need to know … that they will be able to enforce their rights if they have to do so, and … that if they fail to meet their obligations, there is likely to be a remedy against them'.[151] While recognising the importance of the resolution of employment disputes by negotiation or mediation, the Supreme Court said that

> those procedures can only work fairly and properly if they are backed up by the knowledge on both sides that a fair and just system of adjudication will be available if they fail. Otherwise the party in the stronger bargaining position will always prevail.[152]

Likewise, it was observed that, in so far as the fees have the 'practical effect' of making it unaffordable for people to exercise their rights or 'of rendering the bringing of claims to enforce such rights a futile or irrational exercise, it must be regarded as rendering those rights nugatory'.[153] As a result, the Fees Order was quashed and fees have not been charged since 2017.

However, in a consultation in 2024 the Conservative government explored reintroducing fees. The consultation said that requiring people to pay 'modest' fees would 'ensure users are paying towards the running costs of the tribunals and put its users on broadly the same footing as users of other court and tribunals who already pay fees, thereby ensuring cross-jurisdictional consistency'.[154] Moreover, fees would

> relieve some of the cost to the general taxpayer by requiring tribunal users to pay for the tribunal system, where they can afford to do so. In addition, modest fees may incentivise parties to settle their disputes early through Acas without the need for claims to be brought to an ET.

The proposed fee was £55 per claim, irrespective of type of claim or number of claimants. This was to be paid on issue of the claim; no separate hearing fee was proposed. Remission of fees for claimants with few savings and low income was proposed, as well as not requiring fee payments in relation to claims for redundancy payments from the National Insurance Fund. With the change in government, the fees question was not pursued. However, in October 2025 news reports indicated that the Labour government was considering introducing fees of £55,[155] which

[150] ibid, [68].
[151] ibid, [71].
[152] ibid, [72].
[153] ibid, [104].
[154] See: www.gov.uk/government/consultations/introducing-fees-in-the-employment-tribunals-and-the-employment-appeal-tribunal/introducing-fees-in-the-employment-tribunals-and-the-employment-appeal-tribunal.
[155] See: www.lawgazette.co.uk/news/labour-planning-to-bring-back-employment-tribunal-fees/5124634.article.

was thought to raise only £1.8 million towards the overall cost of £80 million of running the tribunal system. However, shortly afterwards the government made clear that it was not planning to reintroduce fees.[156]

Some participants in our research considered that it would be worthwhile reintroducing fees as a way of encouraging claimants to think twice before bringing a claim that was spurious or unmeritorious.[157] Several participants said that fees need to be at a level that is not too high so that it does not prevent claimants from bringing meritorious claims but is high enough to deter weak claims.[158] Many participants rejected the idea of having fees at all because of concerns about access to justice. They were also unconvinced that fees would filter out weak claims.[159]

B. Court Fees in Other UK Jurisdictions

Civil court fees are payable on all claims that are brought.[160] The fee level depends on the amount that is claimed, plus interest. In money claims the fees to issue a claim are as follows (Table 11.1).

Table 11.1 Issue fees in civil money claims[161]

Value of the claim	Fee
Up to £300	£35
More than £300 but no more than £500	£50
More than £500 but no more than £1,000	£70
More than £1,000 but no more than £1,500	£80
More than £1,500 but no more than £3,000	£115
More than £3,000 but no more than £5,000	£205
More than £5,000 but no more than £10,000	£455
More than £10,000 but no more than £200,000	5% of the value of the claim
More than £200,000	£10,000

[156] See: www.theguardian.com/money/2025/oct/08/david-lammy-rules-out-charging-workers-for-employment-tribunal-claims.

[157] Focus Groups: 12 November 2024, 20 November 2024 (12pm), 20 November 2024 (3pm); Survey answers.

[158] Focus Groups: 12 November 2024, 20 November 2024 (3pm); Survey answers.

[159] Focus Groups: 11 November 2024, 20 November 2024 (3pm), 10 December 2024 (1.30pm); Survey answers.

[160] See: www.gov.uk/government/publications/fees-in-the-civil-and-family-courts-main-fees-ex50/civil-court-fees-ex50.

[161] ibid.

A further fee is required for the hearing and depends on the track that the case has been allocated to (Table 11.2).

Table 11.2 Hearing fees in civil money claims[162]

Type and value of claim	Fee
Small claims track for claims up to £300	£27
Small claims track for claims between £300.01 and £500	£59
Small claims track for claims between £500.01 and £1,000	£85
Small claims track for claims between £1,000.01 and £1,500	£123
Small claims track for claims between £1,500.01 and £3,000	£181
Small claims track for claims more than £3,000	£346
Fast track claims	£619
Intermediate track or multi-track claims	£1,334

Court fees are also payable in the family courts.[163] To file an application for divorce, nullity or civil partnership dissolution, the fee is £612. An application for a financial order, other than by consent is £313 and if it is by consent it is £60.

A person may apply for remission of the fees – either before or after paying them – if they are eligible. Eligibility is determined by how much money they have in savings, their income and which benefits they receive.[164] The savings of a partner are also included in the calculations. An applicants must apply for fee remission for each fee separately.

C. Interim Conclusions

There is something almost existential for employment lawyers that the tribunal system should be a costs-free jurisdiction and be free at source. We think this principle is important for simple, low value claims: they deal with important rights but claims often yield limited monetary sums such that costs and fees would make it unviable to bring these claims. It would be wrong to shut people out of their right to access justice. We consider that no fees (or costs orders) should operate in cases allocated to Track 1. However, for other claims a fee system should be considered, particularly in Track 3 cases, as is the case for ordinary civil claims.

[162] ibid.
[163] ibid.
[164] See: www.gov.uk/get-help-with-court-fees.

IV. Conclusions

A system originally intended to provide quick, accessible justice for simple claims by workers is now dealing with a range of cases from the most simple to multi-day claims involving difficult legislation (see chapter one). In this chapter we have argued that principles which once resonated – in particular cheapness – do not work in the more complex cases. We therefore propose a costs regime for these difficult cases which mirror that in the civil courts, and a separate regime for the middle group of cases whereby a costs order may be made where a party has not engaged with dispute resolution opportunities (see chapter 13). The simplest cases would still generally be based on the principle that each side bears its own costs. However for any costs regime to work successfully, enforcement would have to be effective and we turn to this issue in chapter twelve.

Court fees are also a difficult issue. It is notable that fees are payable in civil and family proceedings which frequently involve equally basic rights where people have limited funds. We consider that fees should be considered for cases in Tracks 2 and 3, but should be set at a level that is appropriate for the track that the case is allocated to. We do not think fees should apply for cases on our proposed Track 1. However, we consider that any court fee should be set at a percentage of the sums claimed: this would ensure that parties carefully consider what their claim is really worth, thus encouraging settlement of claims by injecting realism into the parties' positions. The fees payable would be a relative measure of the time that will likely be taken in the tribunal hearing. A fee remission scheme would also be required.

12

Enforcement of Awards and Addressing Systemic Issues

I. Introduction

Having looked at the challenges in the pre-litigation and litigation stage in employment cases, we turn to the post-litigation phase. There are two specific issues which we think are problematic: ensuring awards made are actually paid in full; and ensuring the employer stops the unlawful behaviour in question not just in respect of the individual but also more generally in the workplace.

In respect of payment of awards, there is no point in having an employment tribunal system to adjudicate on employment rights if the awards that are made are not paid. A tribunal award cannot be directly enforced and claimants must use additional processes to enforce either an award or an Acas COT3 settlement agreement. There is no data on how many tribunal awards remain unpaid although one government study from 2013 suggests a large percentage of awards and COT3 settlements are not paid, possibly up to 50 per cent.[1] Moreover, recent media reports suggest that enforcement through one channel, the government enforcement scheme, has very limited success. We recognise that the Employment Rights Act 2025 proposes changes in the enforcement system that are positive, including the setting up of the Fair Work Agency (FWA). However, we think the role of the FWA could be expanded further (section II).

In respect of the second issue, addressing wider patterns of discriminatory or other behaviour, an employment tribunal may make a recommendation in discrimination claims requiring an employer to take steps to obviate or reduce the effect of matters addressed in the claim. However, the recommendation must be limited to addressing matters for the particular complainant and cannot be made more generally.[2] Participants in our research raised concerns about the effectiveness of individual claims in achieving systemic change. This is a subject that has also been raised by academic commentators, both in relation to the lack of data about tribunal claims that might be analysed to identify patterns of employer behaviour and the lack of any mechanism by which that analysis might take place

[1] See: www.gov.uk/government/news/government-considering-new-powers-to-tackle-non-payment-of-tribunal-awards.

[2] Equality Act 2010, s 124.

and be used to encourage, cajole or require employers to comply with the law (section III).

In addition, when considering what additional mechanisms might help to engender systemic changes, several participants highlighted the positive work of ombuds in different fields and the Independent National Whistleblowing Officer in Scotland because of the feedback loop between determining complaints and addressing systemic issues in a sector (section III.B). We have also considered the use of Reports to Prevent Future Deaths by coroners following an inquest to address issues revealed by the inquest (section III.C). We argue that claimants should be able to report the non-payment of an award to the FWA which should be empowered to help enforce the award, perhaps with penalties payable to the FWA. There also needs to be a means of systematically tracking and analysing data relating to COT3 settlements and tribunal awards. This would enable the FWA to monitor whether particular employers or sectors need additional advice, support or investigation.

II. Enforcement of Employment Tribunal Awards

A. The Current Position

An employment tribunal judgment or order takes effect from the day when it is given or made, unless the tribunal specifies otherwise. If the judgment or order is for the payment of money, a party must comply within 14 days of the date of the judgment or order, again unless the tribunal provides otherwise.[3] If the respondent fails to comply, a claimant has two options: asking the respondent to be fined and named online by the government, or enforcement through the civil courts. However, these options will be ineffective if the respondent business is no longer in existence due to insolvency or otherwise. The problem of 'phoenix' companies – where one entity is dissolved and an entirely new entity effectively takes over the business – is a serious difficulty but goes beyond the scope of this research.[4] For present purposes it is sufficient to note that delays in the employment tribunal system risk exacerbating the problem of non-payment because the company may no longer be in existence by the time that the claim is adjudicated.

Assuming that the business still exists, if a respondent fails to pay a settlement under a COT3 or an employment tribunal award, the claimant can fill out the

[3] Employment Tribunal Procedure Rules 2024 SI 2024/1155, r 64.

[4] A 2013 study by the Department for Business found that 'The most common reason for non-payment were that the employer against whom the claim was made was now insolvent (37%); however over half of claimants giving this as the reason believed that the company they had worked for was now trading again under a different name or at a different location': 'Innovation & Skills, Payment of Tribunal Awards: 2013 Study' (Crown Copyright 2013) 6. See: assets.publishing.service.gov.uk/media/5a7c469de5274a2041cf2e94/bis-13-1270-enforcement-of-tribunal-awards.pdf.

'Employment Tribunal penalty enforcement form' and send it to the Department for Business and Trade.[5] For COT3 settlements, the claimant can apply as soon as the deadline for payment has passed. For employment tribunal awards, the claimant must wait until the time in which the respondent could have filed an appeal has expired,[6] that is 42 days from the sending of the tribunal judgment.[7]

A warning notice will be issued to the respondent and, if they fail to pay within 28 days of that notice, they will be required to pay a penalty of 50 per cent of the original award amount plus 8 per cent interest per year. In addition, if the claimant has ticked the relevant box on the form, the respondent may also be publicly 'named and shamed' for failing to pay. The naming system applies only if the respondent has failed to pay an employment tribunal award (as opposed to a COT 3 settlement payment), and the sum(s) payable must be over £200. The objective of the naming scheme is 'to increase the rates of timely payment of employment tribunal awards through creating a new deterrent to employers for not paying'.[8]

Alternatively, a claimant can enforce COT3 settlements and tribunal awards through the civil courts. The usual method is the Fast Track Enforcement scheme.[9] The claimant completes the required form authorising a High Court Enforcement Officer (HCEO) to demand payment from the respondent. The HCEO will apply for the award to be enforced, apply for a writ of control, issue the writ of control and attempt to recover the monies owed. In other words, the HCEO will do what is required to try to recover the money. However, the claimant will have to pay the court fee of £80 to issue the writ of control. While that fee will be added to the amount that is owed by the respondent (together with interest on the award and the costs of the HCEO), if the monies are not recovered, then the claimant will not be reimbursed for the court fee. In addition, if there is only partial recovery of the monies, then part of that will be used to cover a proportion of the HCEO's fees.

A further alternative is for the claimant to apply to have the sums registered as a county court judgment. If the sums are not then paid, the claimant can then apply for a warrant which will result in a county court bailiff seeking to recover the money from the respondent. This costs £83.[10]

In Scotland, the claimant can apply to the Secretary of the employment tribunal in Scotland for an 'extract' of the judgment and can then instruct a sheriff

[5] See: www.gov.uk/government/publications/employment-tribunal-penalty-enforcement.

[6] Employment Tribunals Act 1996, s 37B(3)(c).

[7] Employment Appeal Tribunal Rules 1993 SI 1993/2854, r 3(3).

[8] See: www.gov.uk/government/publications/employment-tribunal-naming-scheme-guidance/employment-tribunal-naming-scheme-guidance.

[9] Different forms are used depending on whether enforcement is sought of a tribunal award (form EX727) or COT3 settlement (form EX728): www.gov.uk/government/publications/form-ex727-i-have-an-employment-or-an-employment-appeal-tribunal-award-but-the-respondent-has-not-paid-how-do-i-enforce-it and www.gov.uk/government/publications/form-n322b-application-for-an-order-to-allow-enforcement-of-a-decision-or-an-acas-settlement-form-cot3-that-does-not-require-permission-to-proceed.

[10] See: www.gov.uk/employment-tribunals/if-you-win-your-case.

officer. The sheriff officer will take steps to enforce the award against the respondent, known as 'diligence'.[11]

In reality, however, there are significant problems with enforcement of awards and these have persisted over many years. In *Unison*,[12] the Supreme Court noted that

> [a] study carried out by the Department of Business, Innovation and Skills, shortly before the introduction of fees, found that only 53% of claimants who were successful before the ET were paid even part of the award prior to taking enforcement action ('Payment of Tribunal Awards', 2013). Even after enforcement action, only 49% of claimants were paid in full, with a further 16% being paid in part, and 35% receiving no money at all.[13]

Academic research has found similar problems. Busby and McDermont say:

> A fundamental problem with the current system is the lack of an effective enforcement mechanism as demonstrated by our case studies. Many claimants are unaware that, even if a financial award is made in their favour, the ET cannot force the employer to pay up … This situation is not new: Citizens Advice has been reporting on the non-payment of ET awards since 2004 and continued to argue in 2013 that the state should play a proactive role in enforcing ET awards.[14]

Statistics are not available about how many employment tribunal awards go unpaid because no data is kept. However, some data is available in relation to the penalty enforcement scheme which depends on claimants choosing to pursue the monies owed to them and does not include those who use the county court judgment route of enforcement. In 2025, following Freedom of Information requests, news reports said that since 2016 more than 7,000 workers had used the penalty enforcement scheme but 'three quarters of them did not get their money. They asked for help to recover awards and legally binding settlements totalling more than £46m. Nearly £36m of that has gone unpaid'.[15] Moreover, even when fines have been issued 'only 109 of the more than 4,800 companies penalised since 2016 have paid those fines. The government has issued fines worth £9.6m but only collected £95,000 – less than 1%'.[16] No company has been 'named and shamed' despite 4,000 requests to do so.[17] As Busby and McDermont say 'It seems particularly unjust

[11] Employment Tribunals Act 1996, s 15(2).

[12] *R (on the application of Unison) v Lord Chancellor* [2017] UKSC 51.

[13] ibid, [36]. See also S Corby, 'British Employment Tribunals: From the Side-Lines to Centre Stage' (2015) 56 *Labor History* 161, 172–73.

[14] N Busby and M McDermont, 'Access to Justice in the Employment Tribunal: Private Disputes or Public Concerns?' in E Palmer et al (eds), *Access to Justice: Beyond the Policies and Politics of Austerity* (Hart Publishing 2016) 210, 229.

[15] See: www.thebureauinvestigates.com/stories/2025-10-02/revealed-thousands-of-rogue-bosses-have-failed-to-pay-tribunal-awards.

[16] See: www.thebureauinvestigates.com/stories/2025-10-02/employment-tribunals-scandal-of-toothless-scheme-to-punish-non-paying-bosses; and: www.bbc.co.uk/news/articles/cvgjk8qnx2yo.

[17] See: www.thebureauinvestigates.com/stories/2025-10-02/employment-tribunals-scandal-of-toothless-scheme-to-punish-non-paying-bosses.

that, having suffered the expense and stress of a hearing, a worker whose claim has succeeded (against the odds) finds that he or she has to take further legal action to get any money owed'.[18]

Our research participants also noted the delay caused by having to transfer matters from the employment tribunal to the county courts and suggested that tribunals should have the power to enforce their judgments. One survey participant suggested that there was a need to 'create an efficacious enforcement process so that successful claimants are compensated swiftly when they have won their case'.[19] Busby and McDermont suggest that there should be a way for HMRC to enforce unpaid tribunal awards, perhaps by awards being 'added to the recovery of unpaid tax where appropriate'.[20]

In conclusion, there are shocking levels of non-payment of awards and very real difficulties with the enforcement of awards. The current enforcement systems require claimants to take further (costly) steps to enforce awards with very limited success. We think that the FWA needs to take a significant role in this issue; we discuss this in the next section.

B. Enforcement in the Employment Rights Act 2025

The Employment Rights Act 2025 (ERA 2025) provides for the establishment of the FWA from April 2026 but it is anticipated that there will be a transition period before it is fully operational.[21] The FWA will absorb the functions of HMRC, the Gangmasters and Labour Abuse Authority (GLAA), the Health and Safety Executive (HSE) and the Employment Agency Standards Inspectorate (EASI) in relation to labour market enforcement.[22] It will be responsible for the employment tribunal penalty enforcement process.[23] The Office of the Director of Labour Market Enforcement will cease to exist.[24] The aim is to create a 'strong, recognisable single brand so workers know where to go for help', to provide a single place where employers can turn for help, and to 'improve efficiency by ensuring there is one leadership team to oversee work in line with a unified strategy'.[25]

The FWA will be an arm's length executive agency of the Department for Business and Trade and will have an advisory board utilising a social partnership

[18] Busby and McDermont (n 14) 210, 229.
[19] Focus Group, 11 November 2024.
[20] Busby and McDermont (n 14) 210, 229.
[21] See: www.gov.uk/government/publications/implementing-the-employment-rights-bill.
[22] As to which see ch 2. The GLAA will be abolished: s 151 Emloyment Rights Act 2025 (ERA 2025).
[23] sch 7, pt 1, para 13 ERA 2025.
[24] s 151 ERA 2025.
[25] Fair Work Agency factsheet: assets.publishing.service.gov.uk/media/67e3d1cedcd2d93561195bdf/fair-work-agency.pdf.

model with equal representation from businesses, trade unions and independent experts.[26] The FWA will be required to produce an enforcement strategy every three years and an annual report setting out their achievements.[27] The ERA 2025 provides that the FWA will have the powers that HMRC, the GLAA and EASI had in their enforcement work; this is a consolidating measure to ensure that there are no gaps in relation to different rights in their powers to, for example, require employers to provide information or to make an unannounced inspections.[28] The FWA will be able to require employers to make, for example, a Labour Market Enforcement (LME) undertaking and ask a court to make an LME order.[29] A breach of an LME order remains a criminal offence punishable by way of a fine or imprisonment.[30]

The regime for a notice of underpayment of the national minimum wage will remain, requiring employers to pay individuals specific sums where they have not paid the right amount and to pay a penalty to the government in respect of those underpayments.[31] However, in addition, the FWA will be able to enforce failures to pay holiday pay and statutory sick pay in the same way as in relation the national minimum wage by using notices of underpayment and penalty payments where these are not complied with.[32] The penalty must be paid within 28 days of the notice and will be 200 per cent of the sum specified in the notice of underpayment.[33] This is subject to a maximum of £20,000 and a minimum of £100 for each person who has been under paid.[34] That penalty is halved if the sums owed to the individuals are paid and half the penalty is paid before the end of 14 days from the day of the notice of underpayment.[35] The penalty is paid to the Secretary of State.

The ERA 2025 enables further rights to be enforced by the FWA if so provided for in regulations.[36] It is unclear which rights this might be applied to but we consider that it could usefully be extended to cover issues of unpaid wages, unlawful deduction from wages, and other non-payments of statutory payments such as statutory maternity pay.

A proposal to make directors personally liable for employment tribunal awards has not been pursued in the ERA 2025, despite featuring in the original

[26] s 96 ERA 2025.
[27] ibid, ss 97–98.
[28] ibid ss 99–105.
[29] ibid ss 122–32. See ch 2.
[30] ibid, s 142.
[31] ibid, s 106.
[32] ibid, sch 7, pt 1.
[33] ibid, s 110(1)–(4).
[34] ibid, s 110(5) and (6).
[35] ibid, s 111(4).
[36] ibid, sch 7, pt 2.

Green Paper.[37] We consider this to be a missed opportunity: the ability to make a director personally liable for an award that has been made would have significantly incentivised businesses to pay the award. It would also have given claimants a further avenue to pursue matters if the company failed to pay.

One measure in the ERA 2025 that is particularly promising is the introduction of the power for the FWA to recover costs against employers who have not complied with the law requiring them to pay a charge.[38] The method for calculating that charge remains unspecified but we consider that the ability for the FWA to charge non-compliant employers is central to the likely success of the FWA. As discussed in chapter three, funding state enforcement bodies is a significant challenge and has substantially limited their effectiveness. By charging employers where they are not compliant should have both a positive deterrent effect and enable the FWA to be far more effective by increasing their own resources.

The ERA 2025 also gives the FWA the ability to bring employment tribunal proceedings on behalf of a worker where the worker could bring a claim but appears not to be doing so.[39] This is a slightly odd provision because any compensation that is awarded goes to the worker and it is unclear why the FWA would pursue this avenue rather than directly enforce the relevant rights if they are within their ambit. While the provision in the ERA 2025 allows for the FWA to bring proceedings in relation to all rights, it seems unlikely that they would bring proceedings that were not related in some way to their other enforcement work. In addition, the FWA is empowered by the ERA 2025 to give legal assistance to any party to civil proceedings relating to employment law, trade union or labour relations law, and to recover costs if they are ordinarily recoverable.[40] This provision also goes beyond matters that are within the FWA's remit but we expect that the FWA would be unlikely to support claims that were not related to its remit in some way. The ERA 2025 also provides for the FWA to reclaim their expenditure out of any costs that are awarded to a party they support. This is significant and may facilitate claimants in seeking clarity on more complex points of law by pursuing claims to the higher courts, such as occurred in relation to holiday pay.

For the FWA to be able to conduct more enforcement than currently undertaken by the existing enforcement bodies, including the enforcement of employment tribunal awards and COT3 agreements, proper funding and resources will be required. In that regard, the picture does not seem particularly hopeful: in its response to the Business and Trade Committee report in May 2025, the government did not commit to providing more resources to the FWA than

[37] See: labour.org.uk/wp-content/uploads/2022/09/Employment-Rights-Green-Paper.pdf. Directors were sued personally by workers in the High Court for inducing a breach by the company of its obligations to pay the minimum wage in *Antuzis v DJ Houghton Catching Services Ltd* [2021] EWHC 971.

[38] s 146 ERA 2025.

[39] ibid, s 119.

[40] ibid, ss 120 and 121.

has been provided to the other enforcement bodies.[41] Instead, it focused on the increased efficiencies arising from the agencies in question all being under one roof together with the benefits of modern intelligence techniques. While the charging provisions described above are likely to help, we think that resources are likely to be a limiting factor going forward.

That said, some of the provisions of the ERA 2025 are promising. It makes sense to bring enforcement under one roof to support the sharing of intelligence and more efficient and effective working. It might be hoped that including the enforcement of non-payment of employment tribunal awards within its remit will help the FWA to identify employers who are not playing by the rules. The ability of the FWA to charge non-compliant employers will certainly help fund the work of the FWA and provide an incentive to employers to comply. However, this all depends on resources, and we are less optimistic about that.

We turn now to consider the second issue in this chapter: how systemic change might be delivered. We begin by looking at the current situation and its limits before seeing how change is delivered in other sectors, looking at the role of the Parliamentary and Health Service Ombudsman, and the Scottish equivalent.

III. Addressing Systemic Issues

A. The Current Situation

Sections 124(2)(c) and (3) Equality Act 2010 (EqA 2010) allows an employment tribunal to make a recommendation 'that within a specified period the respondent takes specified steps for the purpose of obviating or reducing the adverse effect on the complainant of any matter to which the proceedings relate'. However, before 1 October 2015 the EqA 2010 provided that a recommendation could be concerned with either the complainant or 'any other person' which allowed for much wider recommendations. If a respondent fails 'without reasonable excuse' to comply with an appropriate recommendation, then the tribunal may make a (further) award of compensation.[42]

Participants in our research had serious concerns about the impact of tribunal decisions on how businesses operate. Some participants said that different approaches were needed for different types of case. Some suggested that external enforcement bodies should be more involved, working alongside the employment tribunals, in complex cases of discrimination and whistleblowing.[43] In Scotland,

[41] Business and Trade Committee, *Make Work Pay: Employment Rights Bill: Government Response* (First Special Report of Session 2024–25, HC 932).
[42] Equality Act 2010, s 124(7) (EqA 2010).
[43] Focus Group, 10 December 2024 (1.30pm); Survey answers.

the work of the Independent National Whistleblowing Officer was described favourably and several participants suggested that these sorts of non-tribunal enforcement efforts should be increased.[44]

Hodges has raised similar concerns:

> The system does not systematically record data on cases against businesses or public employers that is fed back and used to trigger some regulatory or self-regulatory scrutiny of trends or problems with individual employers that could be prevented, addressed, or solved. ET judgments are now published online in all cases. They are freely searchable. It is possible to build up a picture of good and bad employers as well as serial litigants and other features. But this significant resource is not examined systematically by anyone, let alone an official who might be able to identify trends or clusters and who has power to intervene directly to achieve change.[45]

There are also significant problems with the data that are collected. Blackham, in her study of age discrimination, says that:

> The online publication of ET decisions potentially heralds a new era of accessibility and openness in tribunal decision-making. However, this new system is only as good as the data that is inputted into it. Many cases in this particular sample did not have full written reasons attached to the online record; ETs often deliver their decisions verbally, and written reasons are not always requested by the parties.[46]

Moreover, the tribunal judgment website 'remains difficult to navigate, with a fairly basic search function',[47] something which we also discovered. The search results are often inaccurate.[48]

Hodges notes that Acas uses its own data to inform debate but that there is no systematic analysis to enable systemic change. He asks:

> Could an award trigger an obligation that could be enforced through a civil sanction on the employer (or relevant individuals, such as the CFO) or be monitored by the ET, or another public body such as the Small Business Commissioner … ? But is there a better approach? A system that provides monitoring of compliance with settlements and awards, such as delivered by leading consumer Ombudsmen, should be effective and an easier process.[49]

Given these problems is there another way drawing on lessons from the ombuds system?

[44] Focus Group, 19 November 2024 (12pm).

[45] C Hodges, *Delivering Dispute Resolution: A Holistic Review of Models in England and Wales* (Hart Publishing 2019) 509.

[46] A Blackham, 'Enforcing rights in employment tribunals: insights from age discrimination claims in a new 'dataset' (2021) 41 *Legal Studies* 390, 408.

[47] ibid, 394.

[48] See ch 7, section IV.

[49] Hodges (n 45) 509.

B. Ombuds

i. Parliamentary and Health Service Ombudsman

Ombuds operate across a number of sectors. We discussed the Parliamentary and Health Service Ombudsman (PHSO) in chapter five as an ombud that is particularly well known and operates differently from most consumer sector ombuds because they seek to resolve matters first before formally investigating. However, if the complaint cannot be resolved, then the PHSO will investigate and determine whether to fully uphold, partially uphold or reject a complaint. Importantly for our purposes, if a complaint is fully or partly upheld then the PHSO can make recommendations to the organisation concerned to put things right. This may be in the form of an apology, financial recompense, or writing an action plan 'to prevent the same mistakes happening to someone else, address failures in its system and improve its service'.[50] As the PHSO says:

> It is a false economy and poor administrative practice to deal with complaints only as they arise and to fail to correct the cause of the problem. Learning from complaints, and offering timely and effective remedies, gives the best outcome in terms of cost effectiveness and customer service – benefiting the service provider, the complainant and the taxpayer.[51]

If the PHSO makes recommendations, then they will also 'follow up on them until they are acted on'. This is achieved by sending a letter reminding the relevant organisation that their recommendations must be acted upon and then identify the actions the PHSO will take if they are not completed. The PHSO does not have 'legal powers to enforce our recommendations' but may inform relevant regulators or as a last resort make a special report to Parliament.[52]

ii. Scottish Public Services Ombudsman and Independent National Whistleblowing Officer (Scotland)

The Scottish Public Services Ombudsman (SPSO) has a wide remit covering a variety of devolved public services in Scotland including council, health service, prisons, water and sewerage providers, Scottish government, universities and colleges. The SPSO is the final stage for complaints about those services. The process that the SPSO follows is the same as the PHSO in England.

The SPSO can make recommendations for redress dealing with individual or group harm. However, they may also make recommendations 'in relation to

[50] See: www.ombudsman.org.uk/organisations-we-investigate/putting-things-right#:~:text=Making%20recommendations,suffered%20damage%20to%20their%20reputation.

[51] PHSO Principles for Remedy: www.ombudsman.org.uk/about-us/our-principles/principles-remedy.

[52] ibid.

service improvement or complaints handling'.[53] That may involve recommending that an organisation should 'change a process' or 'put in place a procedure they should have had' in order to 'make sure that same thing doesn't happen to someone else'.[54] These recommendations are published and the SPSO states that they 'follow up rigorously on every recommendation to make sure it is carried out'.[55] Organisations 'usually comply' with its recommendations, but if they do not then the SPSO will draw public attention to this.[56]

The Independent National Whistleblowing Officer (INWO) is the final stage of the process for those raising whistleblowing concerns about the NHS in Scotland.[57] The SPSO has taken up the role and functions of the INWO. The aim of the INWO is 'to ensure everyone delivering NHS services in Scotland is able to speak out to raise concerns when they see harm or wrongdoing putting patient safety or service delivery at risk'.[58] The INWO will investigate complaints about how whistleblowing concerns have been handled and make recommendations, where relevant.

The ability of an ombud to make recommendations following an investigation and to follow up on their implementation is of particular interest. It enables real change to be engendered in the organisations that have been investigated. The publicity attached to a failure to comply with recommendations is also important. However, we consider that in the private sector there would need to be more 'teeth' to a failure to comply with recommendations, particularly in sectors that do not have a regulatory body that would otherwise take an interest in failures to comply with the law.

C. Reports to Prevent Future Deaths

Coroners have powers to issue reports for the prevention of future deaths (RPFD). Schedule 5, paragraph 7 Coroners and Justice Act 2009 provides that where a senior coroner conducting an investigation into a person's death finds circumstances creating a risk of other deaths and considers that 'action should be taken to prevent the occurrence or continuation of such circumstances, or to eliminate or reduce the risk of death created by such circumstances', the coroner must 'report the matter to a person who the coroner believes may have power to take such action'. The coroner may not make recommendations and 'can only raise concerns with the recipient of the report if they believe action should be taken

[53] See: www.spso.org.uk/sites/spso/files/communications_material/RedressPolicy.pdf.
[54] See: www.spso.org.uk/how-we-put-things-right.
[55] ibid.
[56] See: www.spso.org.uk/faq-categories/our-rules-and-powers#:~:text=Will%20the%20Ombudsman's%20recommendations%20be,other%20complainants%20know%20the%20outcome.
[57] The Public Services Reform (The Scottish Public Services Ombudsman) (Healthcare Whistleblowing) Order 2020.
[58] See: inwo.spso.org.uk/what-we-do.

to prevent future deaths'.[59] The person to whom the report is made must provide a response within 56 days from the day on which it was sent, unless the coroner grants an extension.[60] The response must contain:

a. details of any action that has been taken or which it is proposed will be taken by the person giving the response or any other person whether in response to the report or otherwise and set out a timetable of the action taken or proposed to be taken; or
b. an explanation as to why no action is proposed.[61]

The report, and response, must be sent to the Chief Coroner who may publish it and may send it to 'any person who the Chief Coroner believes may find it useful or of interest'.[62] The report and response is also sent to 'interested parties' which often includes the family of the deceased.

In 2024, 713 reports were issued, compared with 569 in 2023.[63]

RPFDs are not without their difficulties. The process has been criticised particularly in relation to 'inconsistent reporting, poor response rates, and difficulties in accessing and analysing' RPFDs.[64] Some academics have suggested that there needs to be a national system to develop guidelines and to sanction failed responses.[65]

However, while the coroner who wrote the report has no legal power to take any further steps to require compliance, the Chief Coroner tried a 'name and shame approach': at the end of 2024, the Chief Coroner published a list of organisations and government departments that had not provided a response to a report issued in 2024 within the statutory time limit. This was described as a 'badge of dishonour' for those organisations.[66] Thereafter a large number of responses were received, although in September 2025, the Chief Coroner noted that 16 reports were still outstanding.[67] Further, the lack of response to an RPFD may be used by regulatory bodies such as the Care Quality Commission or the General Medical Council to identify parties in need of investigation and intervention. Moreover,

[59] Para 4.2 Report of the Chief Coroner to the Lord Chancellor, Annual Report for 2024.

[60] Reg 29 The Coroners (Investigations) Regulations 2013 SI 2013/1629.

[61] ibid, reg 29(3) and (4).

[62] ibid, reg 28(5)(b).

[63] See: www.gov.uk/government/statistics/coroners-statistics-2024/coroners-statistics-2024-england-and-wales#prevention-of-future-death-reports; and: www.gov.uk/government/statistics/coroners-statistics-2023/coroners-statistics-2023-england-and-wales#prevention-of-future-death-reports.

[64] B Bremner, C Heneghan and G Richards, 'A systematic narrative review of coroners' Prevention of Future Deaths reports (PFDs): A tool for patient safety in hospitals' (2023) 28 *Journal of Patient Safety and Risk Management* 227. See also Q Zhang and G Richards, 'Lessons from web scraping coroners' Prevention of Future Deaths reports' (2023) 91 *Medico-Legal Journal* 142.

[65] Bremner, Heneghan and Richards (n 64).

[66] See: www.hilldickinson.com/insights/articles/avoiding-badge-dishonour-responding-prevention-future-death-regulation-28-reports.

[67] Chief Coroner's Annual Report 2024, para 4.6.

in litigation civil judges are likely to 'take an increasingly dim view' of a failure to respond.[68]

For the purposes of this book, the coroner's powers to issue an RPFD are significant because these reports identify systemic issues which the addressee is meant to deal with. While the current system holds great promise, it lacks enough backbone to ensure that RPFDs are responded to and changes are implemented. However, the coronial system shows that other jurisdictions, when faced with systemic issues, have a mechanism for flagging them and requiring action in response.

IV. Conclusions

There are very real problems in both the individual enforcement of employment tribunal awards and COT3 settlements and in achieving systemic change through the litigation process. We think that the FWA could be developed to achieve improvements in both.

It is quite wrong that employment tribunal judgments cannot be enforced more easily and quickly. The FWA should take a much stronger role in this: claimants should be able to make a simple report about the non-payment of an award to the FWA to trigger help enforcing that award and to enable targeted investigation by the FWA. We recognise, however, that this will take additional resources which are scarce. It may be that additional penalties should be imposed on non-compliant employers that are payable to the FWA to fund their work and to enable stronger enforcement of employment rights.

The FWA should also have a role in monitoring issues being brought to the Employment Resolution Service that we propose, being settled by a COT3 and where an employment tribunal award is made. This would allow the FWA to identify, through systematic tracking and analysis of the data, whether there are particular employers or sectors where their input is needed, whether through their investigatory powers or more informally to provide advice and support to employers. The FWA could deploy its powers to bring changes to particular sectors in similar ways to the ombuds, or involve regulatory bodies in certain sectors. However, data needs to be collected to enable a more systematic approach to these issues.

[68] See: www.dekachambers.com/2025/01/22/prevention-of-future-death-reports-what-you-need-to-know-in-2025/.

PART V

Recommendations and Methodology

In this book we have sought to explain the current system of dispute resolution, highlight the problems with its current operation as identified in the literature and through our empirical work. Our empirical research was based on a broad 'mixed methods-grounded theory' approach, utilising empirical data from a survey, focus groups and interviews. We drew extensively on publicly available data and material obtained from Freedom of Information (FOI) requests. We also cast our net wide in terms of our comparative analysis to achieve a deep and broad understanding of the issues in play and nuanced reflection on what a future system might look like (Appendix I).

Drawing on suggestions from our research participants, good practice from other parts of the UK and overseas and our own reflections, we have tried to 'grey sky' think about how the current system might be reimagined. In this final Part, we address a selection of the many reports that have made recommendations in the past; some of past recommendations are equally applicable now. We then set out our own recommendations. These fall into three parts: first, some simple changes that could be made to the current system; second, some more ambitious suggestions for changes in the current system; and third, a radical reimagining of how disputes are addressed. (These are intended to provide the framework for future discussions not a blueprint for reform: chapter thirteen.) We finish the book with some conclusions and some hopes and aspirations.

13

Recommendations Past and Present

I. Introduction

So far in this book we have broken down the dispute resolution process into its component parts – from initial grievance/disciplinary process through to early conciliation and then on to the formal litigation process and finally on to the enforcement of the awards. We have examined what works – and what does not – in order to consider what a reformed tribunal system might look like. We are, of course, not the first to examine this issue, not least because concerns about how tribunals, set up to deal with a few thousand cases each year (see chapter one), have long been groaning under the weight of tens of thousands of cases addressing ever more complex law in the era of AI. There have been a large number of reports making recommendations for reform. In this chapter we shall look at some of the key reports, considering their recommendations and highlighting those which coincide with some of the suggestions we are making (section II). In section III we summarise our key recommendations and produce a summary list of the main recommendations in section IV. Section V concludes.

II. Past Recommendations

A. Introduction

There have been a number of reports considering how to reform the employment tribunal system. We want to focus on three which speak to the points made by our research participants: the Gibbons Report, the Beecroft Report and the more recent Law Commission *Report on Employment Law Hearing Structures*. We briefly address other reports in section II.E.

B. The Gibbons Report

i. ADR

The Gibbons Report, *Better Dispute Resolution: A review of employment dispute resolution in Great Britain*, was published in 2007. It strongly supported early dispute resolution but considered that the statutory dispute resolution procedures set out in the 2004 Dispute Resolution Regulations[1] had had the opposite effect. The 2004 Regulations were introduced effectively to require disciplinary or grievance procedures to take place in the workplace prior to bringing proceedings. This was done to give employers an opportunity to consider the matter before a tribunal claim was submitted, thus enabling potential early resolution. While the Regulations were introduced with the best of intentions, there was considerable litigation as to what the provisions meant. Moreover, the Gibbons Report found that

> the procedures carry an unnecessarily high administrative burden for both employers and employees and have had unintended negative consequences which outweigh their benefits. Many businesses told the Review that they have caused an increase in the number of disputes.[2]

As we have seen from our own research, the effect of the procedures was to formalise disputes, escalating problems rather than solving them early and informally. Gibbons noted that the 'parties tend to get caught up in process rather than focusing on achieving an early acceptable outcome';[3] that the Regulations 'exacerbate and accelerate disputes' because of the 'the strong link between the internal procedures and employment tribunal proceedings'; that the 'parties tend to focus on ensuring all the provisions of the procedure are fulfilled, lest they are penalised later at an employment tribunal, rather than examining ways of resolving the underlying problem'; and that the Regulations created expectations of the case going to tribunal rather than incentives to resolution.[4] And so, similar to the situation we have today, this made disputes more likely to go to the employment tribunals, with all the costs and stress involved.

Gibbons also noted that the complexity of the procedures and the penalties for failing to follow them meant that both employers and employees tended to seek external advice earlier, making parties defensive and more likely to consider an employment tribunal from the outset.[5] He therefore proposed removing the 2004 Regulations and giving a stronger role to the Acas Code of Practice, with a 25 per cent uplift/reduction in compensation should the employer/employee not comply with it. However, we consider that the tendency to lawyer up early precipitated by the (now abolished) 2004 Regulations continues today. As we

[1] The Employment Act 2002 (Dispute Resolution) Regulations, which came into force on 1 October 2004, mandated that all employers must adhere to basic statutory procedures when handling dismissals, disciplinary matters, and employee grievances in the workplace. However, the Employment Act 2008 repealed the statutory dispute resolution procedures laid out in the Employment Act 2002 and introduced instead the more flexible procedure we have today guided by the Acas Code of Practice.

[2] M Gibbons, *Better Dispute Resolution: A Review of Employment Dispute Resolution in Great Britain* (March 2007) 8: www.mediationagency.com/pdf/DTI.pdf.

[3] ibid, 9.

[4] ibid, 25.

[5] ibid, 8.

have explained (in chapter four), this is not conducive to early resolution. We therefore agree with the Gibbons Report that there should be greater use of early resolution and alternatives to tribunals: mediation has 'the potential to be particularly effective in the context of employment disputes', and, more generally:

> [A]ll those with an interest in employment disputes agree that in many cases, the intervention of a third party – via Acas conciliation, mediation or another technique – offers the best way of achieving early resolution.[6]

As with our research, Gibbons saw parallels with family law dispute resolution. He was particularly keen on a

> greatly increased role for mediation; my attitude is based, as you know, on my knowledge of the use of mediation in resolving difficult family disputes, and also with some involvement in alternative dispute resolution through the civil courts. Encouraged by signs of success in the context of employment disputes elsewhere in the world, I commend increased use of mediation to employers, employees and practitioners in Great Britain.[7]

Gibbons thought that Acas could potentially have a positive role to play but that reductions in funding and limitations on the periods in which they have a duty to conciliate had adversely affected the level of Acas involvement. He said:

> Acas typically becomes involved after a tribunal application has been made, and is sometimes prevented from offering its services late on in the tribunal process. It may therefore miss both early and final opportunities for achieving settlement.[8]

Gibbons also emphasised that disputes should be resolved 'as early as possible', which would mean 'less disruption to workplaces and to individuals' careers, and reduced burdens on the resources of all concerned – employers, employees and the state'.[9] On the importance of early resolution, the report noted that:

> There is a window of opportunity for early resolution. Delay increases the likelihood of positions becoming entrenched and the dispute leading to formal processes, with significant financial costs to both parties and to the Government, and a serious impact on employers and employees in terms of lost time, stress and the likely breakdown of the employment relationship.[10]

He also noted the advantage of early resolution via non-formal routes in terms of remedies: that 'early resolution can also involve outcomes not available through the tribunal system such as a positive job reference, an apology and changes in behaviour'.[11]

[6] ibid, 38–39.
[7] ibid, 5.
[8] ibid, 9–10.
[9] ibid, 5.
[10] ibid, 23.
[11] ibid, 9.

ii. Problems with the Functioning of the Employment Tribunals

The Gibbons Report also considered the employment tribunal process itself. It noted that the employment tribunal procedure involves high costs for the parties and results in a lack of access to justice. The report says:

> Employment tribunals are considered too costly and complex for all involved … The Review heard that vulnerable employees can be deterred from accessing the tribunal system by the complexity of both the underlying law and tribunal process … The costs to parties and the state can be highly disproportionate to the value of the claim.[12]

It noted, too, that both employers and employees find the tribunal process expensive and stressful. For employees, the report noted that

> the overwhelming view of those the Review spoke to was that tribunals are increasingly complex, legalistic and adversarial making them a daunting experience for many. The burden of preparation and anxiety over what is to come can adversely affect health and strain relationships.[13]

The Gibbons Report identified reasons for this complexity: the complexity of the procedure and the law; the amount of resources and time spent on weak claims ('too many weak and vexatious claims are being allowed through the system'); and tribunals not consistently using the powers available to them in relation to efficient case management and awards of costs in cases of unacceptable behaviour.[14] It also reported on 'claims of inconsistency in case management and judgments'.[15]

iii. Gibbons' Recommendations

The report proposed three sets of recommendations that were 'deregulatory and simplifying' and which were meant to reduce costs to business and employees and the complexity of the system (as it was in 2007).[16] The first set of recommendations focused on the need to 'support employers and employees to resolve more disputes in the workplace', and to do so informally. This included, among other things, the repeal of the 2004 statutory dispute resolution procedures and the introduction of 'clear, simple, non-prescriptive guidelines' on grievances, discipline and dismissal.[17] The report also suggested incentivising the parties to use early dispute

[12] ibid, 8–9.
[13] ibid, 21.
[14] ibid, 9.
[15] ibid, 47.
[16] ibid, 5.
[17] ibid, 27. The report states in this regard that 'Acas provides a Code of Practice on disciplinary and grievance procedures, which has been widely used and is generally supported. The Review has been told that the Acas Code could be improved in a number of areas, for example in respect of early resolution, the needs of small businesses and best practice in disputes where employment has terminated. The guidelines which the Review is proposing should address these areas of concern'.

resolution including the available array of alternative dispute resoluton (ADR), such as in-house mediation and ENE.[18]

The second set of recommendations focused on ways to 'actively assist employers and employees to resolve disputes that have not been resolved in the workplace' – via means other than employment tribunals.[19] The report observed that 'many claims are settled "at the tribunal door", just before a hearing, no doubt because the imminence of the hearing concentrates the parties' minds on the realities of the situation'. Often, the report said, this is due to the parties' 'poor understanding of the realities of employment tribunals', with both claimants and respondents not appreciating the costs, stress and emotional upheaval involved in tribunal claims.[20] The report accordingly suggested measures including the introduction of a simple process to settle monetary disputes on issues such as wages, redundancy and holiday pay, without the need for tribunal hearings;[21] offering a free early dispute resolution service, including where appropriate, mediation,[22] before a tribunal claim is lodged; offering incentives to use early resolution techniques, with compliance having an impact on tribunal awards and cost orders – but it ruled out the introduction of a mandatory or near-mandatory approach to ADR;[23] and abolishing the fixed periods within which Acas must conciliate, 'ensuring that Acas can conciliate whenever appropriate' (it found that 'Acas conciliation not only starts too late, but ends too soon').[24]

As with our research participants' comments, Gibbons argued that there was a fundamental need for 'culture change', 'so that the parties to employment disputes think in terms of finding ways to achieve an early outcome that works for them, rather than in terms of fighting their case at a tribunal'.[25] Suggestions also related to the need to manage parties' expectations before they submit claims that could potentially be avoided, including by increasing the quality of advice to potential claimants and respondents, through an adequately resourced helpline and the internet (which would also highlight to them the advantages of ADR). The report recommended redesigning the employment tribunal application process, so that potential claimants accessed it through the helpline and received advice on alternatives when doing so.[26]

[18] ibid, 10, 28–30.
[19] ibid, 10–11.
[20] ibid, 34.
[21] ibid, 36.
[22] ibid, 38–39.
[23] ibid, 39–42. The report supports a 'voluntary approach' to the use of ADR: driving up the awareness of and demand for ADR services and ensuring an adequate and timely supply of ADR services. See: ibid, 41.
[24] ibid, 10–11, 35, 43.
[25] ibid, 38.
[26] ibid, 10–11, 36–38.

The third set of recommendations focused on ways to 'make the employment tribunal system simpler and cheaper for users and government'. Some of these issues were also discussed in our research:

1. The need to simplify employment law.
2. Simplifying the employment tribunal claim and response forms, removing requirements for unnecessary and legalistic detail, eliminating the 'tick-box' approach to specifying claims, and encouraging claimants to give a succinct statement or estimate of loss.
3. Making time limits easier for all to understand and apply, including by unifying the time limits on employment tribunal claims and the grounds for extension of those limits.
4. Giving employment tribunals enhanced powers to simplify the management of 'multiple-claimant' cases.
5. Encouraging employment tribunals to engage in active, early case management with consistency of practice in order to maximise efficiency.
6. Considering whether the employment tribunals have appropriate powers to deal with weak and vexatious claims and whether the tribunals use them consistently.
7. The need to use lay members more effectively in the tribunal system.[27]

We would agree with all of these recommendations.

C. The Beecroft Report

The Coalition government commissioned Adrian Beecroft to make recommendations on reforming employment laws with the aim of promoting economic growth and reducing regulatory burdens on businesses. His *Report on Employment Law* (October 2011) mainly deals with proposed changes to substantive employment laws and calls for different levels of deregulation. However, it also recommended introducing a fee for employees who apply to an employment tribunal. Of particular relevance to our study, is the report's recommendations on the 'employment tribunal process and awards'.[28]

The report found that employment tribunals 'are expensive, time consuming and personally stressful'.[29] The report notes that employers and employees share concerns about tribunals: both 'generally deeply dislike' tribunals. Their perception, according to the report, is that 'the rules are very complicated and there is a

[27] ibid, 11, 48–51.

[28] A Beecroft, *Report on Employment Law* (24 October 2011) 7: assets.publishing.service.gov.uk/media/5a79e70b40f0b670a8026456/12-825-report-on-employment-law-beecroft.pdf.

[29] ibid.

feeling that the outcomes are inconsistent because different panels take different views of similar cases'.[30]

The report noted that there was a need to reduce the number of cases that end up in an employment tribunal and that the government had (at the time of the report) announced its intention to implement a number of steps to address this issue, including a requirement to offer Acas-led conciliation (resulting in a recommendation that is binding on both parties) before an individual can apply to a tribunal; clarification of the likely levels of compensation on the tribunal application form; and extension of the unfair dismissal qualification period from one year to two years. The report also noted that there were plans (at that time) to increase the deposit and costs order limits as a way of deterring weak and vexatious claims.

D. Law Commission's Report on Employment Law Hearing Structures

While Gibbons and Beecroft focused particularly on reforms to the tribunal system with an emphasis on ADR, the Law Commission's *Report on Employment Law Hearing Structures* (April 2020) looked more at questions of jurisdiction. Its report addressed inefficiencies and complexities arising from the shared jurisdiction between civil courts and employment tribunals. It proposed a series of reforms aimed at improving access to justice, efficiency and coherence of tribunal processes.[31]

i. Jurisdiction and Time Limits

The Law Commission concluded that the tribunal's exclusive jurisdiction should remain as it is, because the special characteristics of employment tribunals make them a uniquely appropriate and effective forum for resolving these types of claim. The report also said that a shared jurisdiction would create unnecessary complexity and confusion. In addition, it referred, among other things, to the cost advantages of the employment tribunal and the accessibility of the system:

> Some consultees highlighted that, in contrast to civil courts, the informality of employment tribunals combined with the fact that they generally operate as a no-costs jurisdiction (and therefore claimants can bring a claim without the risk of being liable for the legal costs of defendants) make them more accessible to both parties.[32]

[30] ibid.

[31] Law Commission, *Employment Law Hearing Structures: Report* (28 April 2020): assets.publishing.service.gov.uk/media/5f47d2a2e90e07299030ceb6/6.6527_LC_ELHS-Main-Report_FINAL_WEB_210420__1_.pdf.

[32] ibid, 13.

Additionally, the Law Commission proposed extending the time limits for bringing all types of employment tribunal claims to six months, despite the fact that some consultees were concerned about the further delays that a longer time limit would cause in processing and dealing with claims which was contrary to the intended function of employment tribunals as 'speedy arbiters of disputes'.[33]

The report also proposed that the provisions relating to the extension of time should be harmonised so that time could be extended in all cases where the tribunal considers it 'just and equitable' to do so (ie, that the less strict test should apply).[34]

Chapter 4 of the Law Commission's Report proposed extending the jurisdiction of the employment tribunals, currently restricted by the Employment Tribunals Extension of Jurisdiction (England and Wales) Order 1994. It said that an employee should be able to bring a breach of contract claim in an employment tribunal while still employed, as well as where liability arises after employment has ended. They recommended that the time limit for breach of contract claims should be aligned with the unfair dismissal limit (itself increased to six months) and there should be an increase of the current £25,000 limit on the contractual jurisdiction in employment tribunals to £100,000. This would also apply to employers' counter-claims. Finally, the report recommended that jurisdiction should continue to be excluded from the employment tribunals in relation to claims by employers and that employers should not be able to counter-claim against employees and workers who have brought only statutory claims against the employer.[35]

ii. Orders

Chapter 8 of the Law Commission's Report deals with restrictions on the types of order which may be made in the employment tribunals, and examines the granting of injunctions, the apportioning of liability between respondents in discrimination claims, and the enforcement of tribunal awards. In relation to enforcement, the Report acknowledged the serious problem of non-payment of tribunal awards:

> [D]espite the range of enforcement possibilities available, it is clear that the enforcement of tribunal awards is not satisfactory. Claimants have to complete a new set of paperwork and pay additional fees. There are also decisions to be made about what form of enforcement is most appropriate. These difficulties are exacerbated by the fact that claimants have to engage with a new institution, which will not be familiar with the details of their case.[36]

[33] ibid, 14–15.
[34] ibid, 8.
[35] ibid, 8.
[36] ibid, 167.

However, the report said that granting the employment tribunals the same range of powers that the civil courts have to enforce orders would not address the numerous enforcement problems: the employment tribunals lack relevant expertise, and the additional resources that would be required and the increase in case load would not be justifiable.[37] Accordingly the report suggested the creation of a fast track for enforcement allowing the claimant to remain within the employment tribunal structure when seeking enforcement. It also recommended that the government should investigate the extension of the Department for Business, Energy and Industrial Strategy's penalty scheme,[38] for example by triggering it automatically on the issue of a tribunal award.[39]

E. Other Reports

The previous sections have highlighted the recommendations of some of the more recent reports on reforming the employment tribunal system. There have, of course, been a number of other reports. For example, Hepple et al in their report on the enforcement of equality legislation discuss:[40]

- Deposits and unmeritorious cases noting that the £150 deposit was generally considered by respondents to be an ineffective means of removing unmeritorious claims: 'The amount was too low to deter the determined vexatious litigant while at the same time being sufficiently high to deter a genuine litigant of limited resources'.[41]
- Interim relief referring to the potential benefits of interlocutory hearings for weeding-out cases. The report highlights the role of managing parties' expectations and providing some kind of authoritative assessment of the merits of the claim, themes we address as well. Hepple et al say: 'In our view, the only realistic measures are for tribunals to make more effective use of interlocutory hearings (IHAs) at which issues can be refined, and parties may realise the weakness of their claim or defence, and by greater use of existing powers to award costs where a party acts unreasonably'.[42]

[37] ibid.

[38] The Department for Business, Energy and Industrial Strategy employment tribunal penalty scheme was introduced in 2016, under which the government fines and publicly names respondents for late payments. See: ibid, 166.

[39] ibid, 10.

[40] B Hepple, M Coussey and T Choudhury, *Equality: A New Framework: Report of the Independent Review of the Enforcement of UK Anti-Discrimination Legislation* (Hart Publishing 2000). In an earlier report for Justice in 1987, Hepple and others recommended an inquisitorial approach in unfair dismissal claims and other straightforward matters and that legal aid should be provided for parties in more complex, particularly discrimination claims: B Hepple, *Industrial Tribunals*: A Report by Justice (1987).

[41] Hepple, Coussey and Choudhury (n 40).

[42] ibid, 93.

- Class actions and group litigation concluding that while the private class action used in the US could not be transposed to the UK, enforcement would be enhanced if the Equality and Human Rights Commission (EHRC) had the power to institute proceedings in its own name or jointly with individuals, where there is a common question of fact or law affecting a number of persons, whether identified or not. In addition, they recommended that the EHRC should be able to claim injunctive and declaratory relief or an order requiring compensation to be paid to a defined group of individuals; and that individuals who fall within the defined group should be able to register within a specified time, and, if they do so, to enforce any order for compensation to the extent of their own loss or injury.[43]
- Conciliation, mediation and arbitration concluding that the focus should be on mediation, which would be done by a new entity. They note that:

> One of the criticisms of the present system is that Acas have a duty only to promote conciliation but no duty to promote equal opportunities. They facilitate communication and the exchange of views between the parties but 'do not make decisions on the merits of the case nor impose or even recommend a settlement' … So far Acas has signalled a reluctance to attempt a more proactive approach aimed at reaching settlements which promote equal opportunities. They believe that this would undermine their neutrality … Accordingly, we would urge support for a privately-funded pilot project, initially perhaps in respect of sexual harassment cases. Consideration should also be given to a requirement for having third party independent mediation in employment cases incorporated into employment grievance procedures.[44]

The Law Society produced a discussion document in 2015 addressing whether there should be a single Employment and Equality Court, bringing together the matters that are currently addressed in the tribunal system and in the county and high courts.[45] As discussed in chapter nine, they recommended the use of four tracks for different complexity of case. In relation to the different tracks, they said:

> There would be a single application point and cases would be allocated to the appropriate level. Parts of the single jurisdiction would be based on civil litigation principles, and other sections would remain true to the tribunal principles of simplicity and accessibility. ADR exit points would be available throughout the system.[46]

[43] ibid, 95–97.
[44] ibid, 110, 112.
[45] Law Society, *Making employment tribunals work for all* (September 2015): consult.justice.gov.uk/digital-communications/review-of-fees-in-employment-tribunals/supporting_documents/lawsociety-discusisondocument.pdf.
[46] ibid 7–8.

Other authors have also written about the best way forward for tribunals. Hodges' work has been particularly influential on our thinking.[47] He recommends a 'simplified pathway'[48] and particularly rationalising the court–employment tribunal (ET) duplication:

> ETs should have exclusive jurisdiction. All employment disputes should be heard in the ET system … Cases involving complex issues of law and fact, such as in much commercial employment litigation, could be triaged into a more formal track.[49]

Hodges recommends a dispute resolution model with two basic elements, the first being a labour market regulator combining various surveillance and enforcement functions and second, an integrated labour ombudsman delivering the functions of information, integrated dispute resolution feedback and evidence based supportive intervention. In the second function,

> dispute resolution will be available from a body that fuses Acas and ETs with some extension to their modes of operation. The first objective should be assisting resolution in the workplace, in relation to which various options discussed above could be adopted, especially through provision of information and support. The second line would be through an integrated pathway as described above, involving triage, information gathering, case management, mediated negotiation and binding determination. The system would then go further, since the overriding objective is not only to achieve just outcomes in individual cases, but also to reduce the likelihood of similar or other problems arising in future through improving culture in workplaces.

He emphasises the need for a 'seamless or integrated pathway' between Acas and the ET:

> A simpler pathway can be created, which goes seamlessly through the stages of information, triage, mediated communication, decision, capture and feedback of data, and intervention to improve compliance and culture. The approach would take place in the policy context of a shift in culture away from an adversarial and polarising paradigm towards supporting Just Workplaces.[50]

He also thinks there should be feedback on patterns and trends that could be pursued by the regulatory authority or the ombudsman.[51]

F. Interim Conclusions

It is often noted that there is 'nothing new under the sun'. Recognition of the problems with the employment tribunal system date back at least 30 years and

[47] C Hodges, *Delivering Dispute Resolution: A Holistic Review of Models in England and Wales* (Hart Publishing 2019).
[48] ibid, 506–07.
[49] ibid, 506.
[50] ibid, 506.
[51] ibid, 516.

there is no shortage of ideas as to how to fix them. We have benefited very much from the work of our forebears. We turn now to consider our specific proposals.

III. Present Recommendations

A. Introduction

Having looked at some of the recommendations made in previous reports on addressing the challenges facing employment tribunals we return now to our recommendations. The simple recommendation is the need for financial resource – and lots of it – to pay for more judges, more legal officers and more employed (rather than agency) administrative staff. Greater flexibility in how the current resources are used would go some way to help so that leadership judges could decide how to use the resources they have rather than being constrained by the 'sitting day' unit of currency currently used for resource allocation. However, in these financially straitened times we recognise that addressing the issues with the employment tribunal system is not a government priority and the sums of money involved are unlikely to be delivered. Further, we think that it is not in anyone's interests to fight these cases all the way through an employment tribunal unless absolutely necessary. So the main focus of the recommendations is to emphasise the resolution of disputes at as early a stage as possible, to continue to offer regular opportunities for resolution away from court, and to create incentives for early resolution (section III.B).

However, cases will continue to go to tribunals. Where this happens we have a number of recommendations to make. They fall into three categories. The first are essentially improvements to the existing system (section III.C); the second concern more ambitious changes to the existing system (section III.D); the third concern radical reform to the existing system (section III.E). In summary, we think that:

- Greater differentiation of claims is needed, according to their value and complexity.
- Different claim forms are needed with greater guidance on their contents.
- There should be an approach to case management that becomes stricter and more formal as the value increases.

We also make recommendations about changes to the enforcement system (section V).

Our recommendations arise from an analysis that recognises the need for trade-offs between different issues and that seeks to balance the different needs of different actors in the system. Our recommendations are not intended to be a precise blueprint but, we hope, represent a package of ideas that are both radical and practical which can go a long way towards addressing the current, serious problems with the employment tribunal system at a time when more work will come its way from the Employment Rights Act 2025 (ERA 2025).

B. Pre-Litigation Resolution of Disputes

As we discussed in Parts I and II of the book, we think there needs to be a radical repositioning of employment disputes. Very many of these disputes are highly emotive and intrinsically relational. The loss of a job strikes at the heart of a person's identity and, of course, their source of income. The longer a dispute lasts, the more 'stuck' or 'entrenched' the parties become. Creative solutions that step away from a limited view of the financial value of a claim can be more productive for all the parties. Once this is recognised, then the importance of early and swift resolution away from the tribunal becomes obvious.

There was near unanimity among all participants in our research that the grievance procedure does not work: it does not help parties resolve disputes and instead it entrenches them in positions at an early stage, rather than allowing them to engage relationally to find creative solutions to problems. Similarly, employers move to use the formal disciplinary procedure too quickly because of a fear of being criticised for not addressing matters according to the detailed provisions in written policies at an early stage. We recognise that this may primarily arise as a perception that the organisation 'will be taken to tribunal' if they fail to follow the precise details of the policy, rather than the reality of what a tribunal would in fact do in a claim.

However, we think that employers – and particularly HR professionals – should be encouraged to step away from using policies and procedures as a shield in litigation and focus instead on resolving disputes on the ground. This is a role that trade union officials traditionally took in the workplace and there is now a need for others in the business, where trade union representation is limited, to do this instead. HR professionals and managers need to be much more willing to roll up their sleeves to try to resolve issues rather than focus on following policies to the letter. We think the role of HR professionals is ultimately contradictory: to protect the employer from claims, to introduce and manage policies, and to manage promotion exercises. This inevitably means there is little space for employment dispute resolution which may be in the employee's best interests (and the employer's in the longer term). A designated HR function – separate from the other HR functions – for a particular individual to act as mediator/ombuds in difficult cases in large workplaces would be a positive step forward. Employers could be incentivised to do this by being protected from a statutory uplift of compensation if the case subsequently goes to a tribunal.

Further, we recommend that the Acas Code should be amended to make it clear that parties must make attempts to resolve the issues informally before a claim is brought and that the formal steps should be used only where informal attempts to resolve matters are unsuccessful. This would apply to both employees and employers: employees would be expected to raise concerns and give the employer an opportunity to resolve them before bringing a claim; and employers would be expected to seek to address concerns meaningfully. Workplace mediation – whether facilitated by a designated independent staff member within the employer or by an external third party – should be strongly emphasised and encouraged. It may be that a voucher scheme for parties – particularly small businesses – to access mediation, like that in family law, could be established. We think that the uplift/reduction in damages is a helpful tool to give weight to the requirement to resolve matters before a claim is brought and it should be applied where informal resolution attempts have not been made. At present, lay people read the Code as requiring the steps to be followed; the wording needs to make it clear that this is not a requirement. A formal grievance procedure could be used, but only as a last resort, not the first resort. Acas guidance could be used to show how this process might work.

In addition, the Acas Code of Practice on Disciplinary and Grievance Procedures should be amended to specify that the disciplinary procedure should also be used as a matter of last resort. We are not suggesting that a disciplinary procedure should not be used. Indeed, in cases of potential criminal offences we anticipate that an employer would move immediately to a formal disciplinary procedure. However, there are many matters which currently go into a formal disciplinary procedure (eg, timekeeping, absence, insubordination) which could be addressed – at least initially – in a more informal manner. What we are advocating is essentially the rolling out of the practice in NHS Wales where there was a fundamental change in mindset so that the disciplinary process was used as a last, not the first, resort. This will have an impact on tribunals' consideration of the fairness of a dismissal: it would become unfair in many circumstances if informal resolution attempts had not been made before moving to the formal disciplinary process.

Alongside these technical changes, we recommend that an Employment Resolution Service (ERS) should be established. This body should be the first port of call for all employers and employees seeking information and advice about issues in the workplace. It should actively encourage, support and facilitate internal workplace mediation. It should also be the point of contact for employers and employees to access more formal processes. We consider that there would be real value to it being a department of the new Fair Work Agency (FWA).

We do not think that it should be part of Acas because we recommend that the ERS – particularly in its mediation role discussed below – should take a radically different approach to the current work of Acas. First, we think that when an employee/worker phones the ERS there should be an element of immediate triaging. Where the call is very simple then information and advice could be provided within that call. However, if the call is more complex we think that people should be given a separate appointment for, say, 30 minutes to allow more targeted and detailed information to be provided.

Second, the ERS should actively encourage, and where appropriate, facilitate workplace mediation.

Third, the ERS should operate as the single point of contact where, despite strong encouragement and support, the dispute cannot be resolved, and a claim is going to be brought. In those circumstances, the ERS should operate as a triage service. For example, where the issue concerns basic rights, we recommend that the ERS can report matters to the FWA for them to investigate and enforce those rights. Where the issues appear likely to be resolved easily, then they should have a phone conciliation service that the parties can access, similar to the phone service of the New Zealand Mediation Service and the pilot project in Scotland. Where matters are more complex, then parties should be offered an appointment with the mediation service. We consider that Acas should retain a role in relation to collective disputes. The process might look something like that outlined in Figure 13.1.

Figure 13.1 Flowchart of the new process

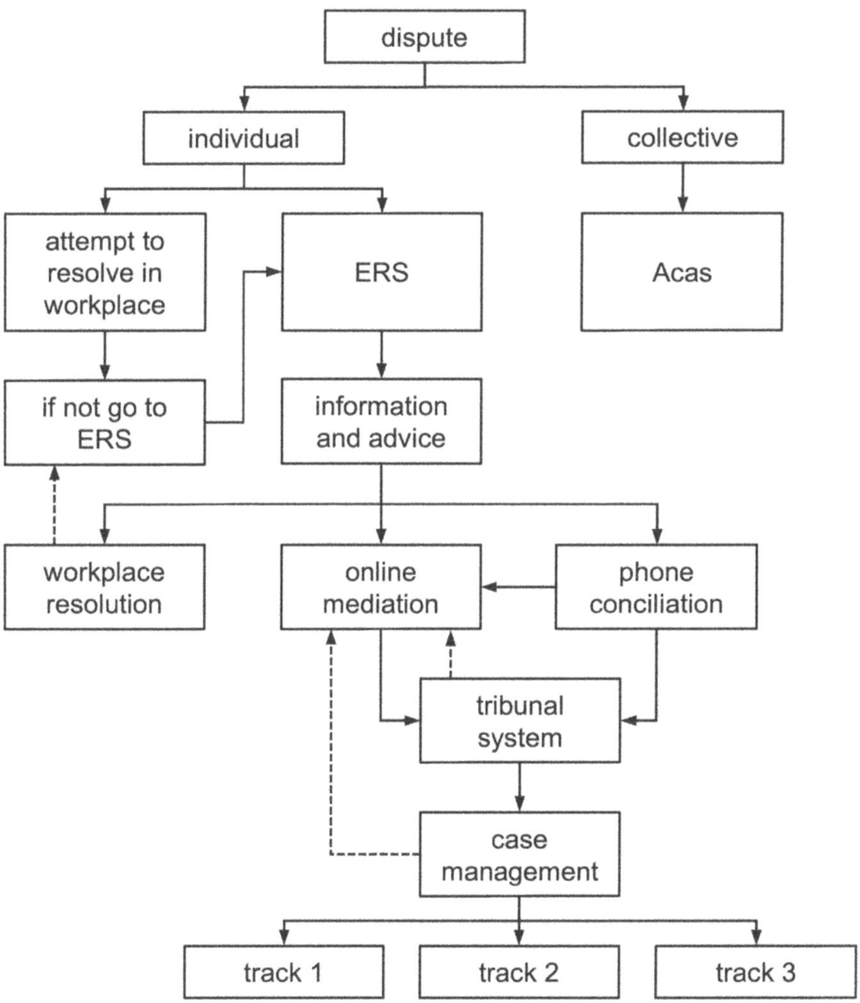

We recommend that the phone service would speak with the employee and then speak with the employer to try to resolve the issues. It would be primarily shuttle conciliation but might also include providing information to either party so that they can consider whether their position – as to what they are claiming, or the issues that are being raised against them – is sustainable. We would envisage this system to be used for simple matters such as non-payment of wages but it may also address a simple unfair dismissal claim.

For more complex matters, we recommend that the ERS provides a mediation service for parties. Parties should be asked to complete a simple form setting out the nature of the 'employment relationship problem'[52] and, most importantly, the resolution that they are seeking, or a response to the issues raised by the other party. We do not think that this form should require the parties to provide legal labels to the issues but should be kept as simple as possible for litigants in person to be able to express their concerns and the resolution they want. The reason to ask for some information is to assist the ERS to identify whether in person mediation would be more appropriate than online mediation, or whether a trauma-informed approach will be necessary. We recommend that the default is for the mediation session to be online. We recommend that the mediators are very experienced in employment law (eg, 20 years plus) so that they can provide clear reality testing. One possible pool of people who could work as mediators for the ERS are lay members of the employment tribunals who could be provided with mediation training. These are people with extensive practical experience in employment matters as well as in employment litigation and we think they would bring that knowledge to bear in mediations very successfully. Although lay members of the tribunal are traditionally on an employee or employer panel, we do not consider that this is relevant in the mediation context: we consider that they are likely to be sufficiently experienced to be impartial. Alternatively, a public appointments process could be used to identify experienced employment professionals. The quality of the mediators at the ERS will be crucial to its success.

We recommend that appointments with the online mediation service should be provided to parties very swiftly following their contact with the ERS: in both Australia and New Zealand offers of a meeting are made within a matter of weeks. We were struck by the emphasis that mediators in both Australia and New Zealand placed on their ability to resolve disputes through a short online mediation session of 90 minutes. The limited time frame for the session, together with the blend of having an element of reality testing, as well as being resolution-focused rather than problem-focused, seems to ensure that sessions are highly productive in achieving a resolution. Our view is reinforced by discussions with judges in those systems, who also said that a lot could be achieved in a focused session of 90 minutes. We consider that these points would be a helpful benchmark

[52] As in New Zealand, avoiding the language of 'claims': see ch 6.

for the ERS mediation service: appointments should be offered within six weeks of contacting the ERS and online sessions should be limited to 90 minutes. After a single online session, if the mediator considers that a further session would be helpful – whether in person or online – we recommend that this option is offered to parties.

It may be that as a result of the single online session, the mediator identifies that a different form of mediation will assist the parties. The ERS must be free to utilise the most suitable mediation style for the particular dispute. As we have noted, the New Zealand service operates a trauma-informed approach in some disputes. Transformational mediation – and even therapeutic mediation – may be appropriate in particularly high conflict matters or where the claimant remains employed. This will not be needed in very many employment disputes, but the ERS should have the flexibility to provide parties with the style of mediation that is necessary to resolve the dispute. Moreover, as we have noted, the mediation must include an element of reality testing.

It is crucial that parties are required to engage in trying to resolve disputes early. In public sector cases, the need for Treasury approval operates as a significant blockage to resolution. Careful consideration needs to be given to how internal government processes can be restructured so that they cease to be a stumbling-block for early resolution of claims. The government should be leading the way in resolving disputes with their employees to provide an example for other employers.

In relation to parties in all types of claim, we recommend that they are required to attend either a phone conciliation appointment or online mediation appointment before being permitted to bring a claim or defend a claim. Where conciliation or mediation is unsuccessful in resolving the dispute, the ERS should certify that the parties have attended to permit them to bring or defend a claim in the tribunal. It is imperative that both sides engage in this process; it is not a tick-box exercise. Failure to engage by claimants could lead to the claim being struck out, and by respondents that an award may be made against them.

Extending the limitation period for claims to six months was suggested by many participants in our research and is being introduced by the ERA 2025: we consider this to be sensible to enable proper time for alternative resolution processes to operate. Given the extension of limitation to six months, we think that on balance there would need to be a further 'pause' in limitation while the ERS mediation takes place: that would only take six weeks after six months, meaning a maximum period of 7.5 months.

A concern may be raised that by emphasising the early resolution of disputes, there is a risk of preventing the public condemnation of an employer or public vindication of workers' rights,[2] it denies the law of an educative role,[3] or that compromise would be used in place of justice and that there may be issues with Article 6 of the European Convention on Human Rights. We recognise these concerns. We would recommend that there is a good information sharing process between the ERS and the FWA so that the FWA can monitor whether a particular employer is – or employers within a particular sector or industry are – facing an unusually high number of issues with their staff. This would allow the FWA to intervene either via their investigatory powers or more informally to provide advice and support to employers. We also recognise that the delays in the tribunal system in some regions are now so serious – and likely to get worse after the ERA 2025 – that the Article 6 rights of the litigants stuck for many years in the system are likely to be undermined and so a balance needs to be struck between delivering justice in individual cases and justice delayed for the many others.

Finally, we recommend that in cases which cannot be solved via ERS mediation, the ERS issues a certificate for the cases to go to a tribunal. However, even in cases which go through the tribunal process, tribunal judges remain free to refer cases back to the ERS at any stage, with the consent of the parties, if it looks likely the parties have become open to a mediated resolution.

We turn now to our recommendations about the operation of the employment tribunal system as it stands at present. As noted above, our recommendations fall into three categories: more minor changes, more ambitious changes and more radical changes.

C. More Minor Changes to the Current System

In respect of more minor changes, we think one of the most important is to rewrite the claim forms. As noted in chapter eight, the ET1 and ET3 forms require parties to understand the legal labels for their claims and provide open text boxes in which they can set out a lengthy narrative. Moreover, many claimants struggle to limit their claims and for some, the existence of multiple tick boxes does not assist them to focus on their key claims. We would recommend that the ET1 and ET3 forms are replaced with new forms.

For the majority of claims, we think there is significant value to a system whereby claimants are only asked about questions that are relevant to the type of claim they are bringing, as in the claim form used in Ireland. Once the claimant has identified – in lay language – whether they are bringing a claim about the fact that they have lost their job, about things that have happened to them while they are working and/or about things that have happened since they lost their job, the form should ask specific questions about what their complaint is about. For example, they might be asked whether they are complaining about what happened, and when and who was present at the time. Each of those items should be given in separate boxes rather than as a single free-flow box. They would then be asked why they think each event happened.

While we recognise that legal labels need to be given to the actions complained of, we recommend that the form uses simple language, rather than the technical legal language. For example, by asking why the claimants thinks each event happened, this would identify whether the complaint is one of discrimination or whistleblowing or trade union detriment. Ideally, they would be asked to provide a short narrative (with a limit on the number of words/characters) rather than having boxes to tick. There are numerous, reliable and well-tested AI models (and not AI models that are generically and freely available which are known to cause ET1 claims to be made ever more complex and cover a wide variety of claims) that can summarise lengthy text into short narrative sentences. These should be used to ask follow-on questions. So, for example, if someone has said it was because they had previously raised a complaint, the form would open up to ask further questions about what the complaint was about and would ask questions to identify the elements of, say, a whistleblowing or victimisation claim.

At preliminary hearings, tribunal judges are adept at extracting this information from claimants and respondents who are litigants in person. We recommend that the structured questioning that is used at many preliminary hearings is used on the original forms with follow-up questions being asked depending on the answer given. Limited AI support would be able to assist with identifying the correct follow-up questions to ask.

The forms should also require parties to upload certain documents straight away. For example, for unfair dismissal claims, a party should be required to upload the dismissal letter and any disciplinary hearing notes; for victimisation claims, a party should be required to upload any document in which the protected act for a protected disclosure was made. For claims in easier cases (cases that we term Track 1 cases, considered further below), the documents that are uploaded should be everything that is likely to be required to determine the claim. We anticipate that experienced tribunal judges, working with the Ministry of Justice, would be able to identify the documents that are required in the majority of these types of case; the requirement to upload specific documents for certain types of claim could be built into the forms.

However, this will require proper technical support. Asking people to upload documents should not result in a folder of random files. The documents should be uploaded, clearly attached to specific questions so that when a judge comes to look at the claim form, or the response form, the documents are attached to the relevant question and can be identified quickly and easily. The technology architecture will be crucial for this to be workable.

Moreover, the form should include specific questions about the remedy that is sought and, where the remedy is financial, questions should be framed – as they are in financial remedy claims in the family courts – so that a schedule of loss can automatically be created. Once again, parties should be required to upload documents addressing the basic information such as uploading three months of wage slips in the previous job and information giving evidence of their current earnings. An early schedule of loss should assist in promoting earlier settlement of disputes.

We have considerable optimism that an AI model, like that used by Valla (discussed in chapter eight), might prove highly effective at producing a timeline and identifying claims from a narrative account of the issues. This would enable litigants in person to explain their claims or responses without having to deal with the complexities of the law. We recommend that this use of a commercial AI model is seriously considered as an alternative to reformulating the ET1 and ET3 forms. However, considerable testing of the AI model would be required to ensure that the legal claims identified from the narrative are accurate and most importantly, focused and refined.

There will be some cases where a simplified form is not appropriate. We anticipate that these claims will be brought as Track 3 cases (see below). For those cases, we consider that a formal claim form with a Particulars of Claim and response form with a pleaded Defence should be required.

In order to avoid the overlap of jurisdictions between ETs and the county court, we think that, like the Law Commission, there should be an increase of the current £25,000 limit on the contractual jurisdiction in employment tribunals to £100,000.

As noted in chapter twelve, there is a shocking level of non-payment of awards and COT3 settlements. We think that the FWA should be sufficiently resourced so that they can enforce payment of the full amount of a tribunal award or COT3 settlement, imposing a penalty for non-payment.

Further, in respect of Acas, while we have advocated that much of the individual work currently done by early conciliation should be carried out by a new Employment Resolution Service, if this is not possible, then Acas's approach to conciliation/mediation should be evaluative rather than facilitative. This is to help particularly litigants in person obtain a more realistic appreciation of their case.

D. More Ambitious Changes to the Current System

Our proposals for much greater use of ADR, including the establishment of an Employment Resolution Service, which would replace Acas' early conciliation function, would fall under the rubric of more ambitious change. We think grievance procedures cause greater harm than good; the language of grievance already sets up the two sides in opposition. We think the grievance procedure should be abolished and replaced with, for example, 'an expression of concern' document which would start a process where an HR mediator could step in.

For cases that go to an employment tribunal, we would also like a statement, enshrined in statute, that reminds lawyers that employment tribunals, especially in the less complex cases, are intended to be quick, cheap and accessible fora. Such a statutory provision has been used successfully in Australia and gives the judges/mediators statutory cover to adopt a proportionate response to employment claims. We would also like a statutory statement that says that there is a presumption that tribunals should be the last resort.

As noted above, there are real challenges in enforcing tribunal awards (see chapter twelve). We would recommend that tribunal awards should have the same status as a county court judgment and should be enforceable through the usual county court processes without first having to obtain a county court judgment. It may be that the ERS could also play a role in this regard, either signposting parties to the FWA to enforce payment or providing parties with support to engage with the county court enforcement teams if an award has not been paid within 28 days. We also consider that, in cases where the employment tribunal thinks non-payment is a risk, it should have the power to require parties to write to the tribunal by no later than two months after the remedy judgment to confirm that the sums ordered have been paid. Where the sums have not been paid, the tribunal would be able to list a further hearing to ascertain why they have not been paid and to impose a penalty for that non-payment. We would anticipate that this power would only be used where there were grounds for believing that there was a risk of non-payment.

In addition, we consider that the FWA could play a significant part in improving the employment landscape. First, data could be collected in relation to the claims that are successful before a tribunal so that it can then be analysed by the FWA to identify patterns in relation to the types of claim that are being upheld in relation to specific employers and/or sectors. Second, whenever there has been a non-payment of an award – whether this is identified by the FWA, the ERS or because the employment tribunal exercised their power to require confirmation of payment – the FWA should use this to consider investigating the employer. Both of these measures would enable more targeted investigation by the FWA to identify whether there are broader issues with particular employers and to provide support to them, or to provide targeted advice to employers in particular industries that are dealing with a number of claims of a particular type.

E. Most Radical: Use of Different Tracks

We know the extent to which the current system is under strain. While our original hypothesis was that the low value cases were blocking the system, in fact our evidence shows it is the high value/high complexity cases mainly involving discrimination/detriment which are slowing up the other more straightforward cases. Our most radical proposals are therefore to introduce a tracking mechanism, as in the civil courts. We would hope that, with more focused information on the ET1 and ET3 forms, the claims that are being brought might be clearer. Once they have been received by the tribunal service, we recommend that they are allocated to one of three tracks administratively. All three tracks would remain in the employment tribunal system which has the specialist expertise to deal with these matters. Employment tribunal judges already deal with highly complex cases; some also sit in the Employment Appeal Tribunal. We see no need for Track 3 cases to be transferred to the generalist High Court.

Throughout the process, irrespective of which track the claim has been allocated to, we recommend that non-court dispute resolution is encouraged and that judges should readily send cases back to the ERS mediation service where they consider that further efforts should be made to resolve the claim. The New Zealand experience indicates that the readiness on the part of judges to send cases back to the mediation service has influenced the public perception of the importance and success of mediation. In addition, as we note below, there should be regular points in the process where mediation must be considered by the parties. Placing non-court dispute resolution at the heart of the legal system has been the direction of travel across the UK legal landscape since the Woolf reforms: that needs to be reinforced in the employment tribunal system.

Figure 13.2 A three-track system

Track 1	Track 2	Track 3
• claims for <6mths earnings or up to £20k whichever is the lowest. • legal officer first and if this does not resolve the issues then to a judge; 3 hours max • no fee/no costs • limited paperwork eg 25-50 pages	• claims for <2yrs' earnings • legal officer first, if no resolution then Judge for directions • ENE (half day); • max 5-day hearing with strict case management; • strict limits on bundles and WS • oral judgment. • fees? • limited costs regime	• ≥2yrs earnings / particular complexity / at C's choice / multiple claims. • closely case managed by same judge • private mediation & private ENE or 1 day court ENE if not • procedure akin to CPR esp re. disclosure, bundles and WS • fees? • full costs regime

i. Track 1

We recommend that claims for less than six months' earnings or up to, say, £20,000 are placed on Track 1, unless there are very good reasons why not. The paperwork submitted should be no more than 25–50 pages. This would include cases that are currently on the short track but may also include simple unfair dismissal claims and other matters on the standard track. By using this track, claimants would be choosing to limit their claims to less than six months' earnings, or say £20,000, whichever is the lower, but have their claims resolved more rapidly and informally than is currently possible within the tribunal system.

These cases should be considered by a legal officer who should make contact with the parties to establish whether the matter can be resolved. They should use a facilitative approach to try to assist in the resolution of the claim. We anticipate that, with additional legal officer resource, very many of these claims would not require a hearing before a judge: while there may be additional resource initially, this is likely to reduce sitting days that are taken up by Track 1 cases.

Assuming it cannot be resolved, the legal officer should identify whether any further disclosure is required or whether witness statements are needed but this should be the exception rather than the norm. Directions should be made, using non-technical language. Claims should be listed for an online hearing before a judge alone, utilising an inquisitorial approach. The hearing should be listed for no more than three hours and should be 'quick, informal and avoid unnecessary technicalities', as we identified from the Australian FWC process, and inquisitorial and informal, like the New Zealand Employment Relations Authority. It should be made clear that damages for claims allocated to this track will be limited to six months' earnings. The judgment should be given orally, with parties having the ability to apply (and pay for) a transcript if required.

Given the sums involved, we do not consider that a fee should be payable or that a costs regime should operate. Essentially, Track 1 should operate like the Fair Work Commission in Australia or the Employment Relations Authority in New Zealand, providing swift informal justice in simple cases brought and defended by litigants in person. There should be a statutory provision specifying that the hearing is intended to be informal and seek swift resolution to the dispute.

ii. Track 2

Claims that are for more than six months but less than two years, or up to £80k earnings, should be allocated to Track 2. Upon receipt of these claims, the legal officer should contact the parties to establish whether the matter can be resolved. The expectation with Track 2 cases should be that the parties have used the online mediation service of the ERS. Where they have not, the legal officer should have the power to send the case back to attempt online mediation.

Assuming the case cannot be resolved, the legal officer should refer the case to a judge to provide directions. We recommend that very strict case management is used in Track 2 cases. The judge should have the power to require parties to limit their cases to their five or ten best points or to require parties to manage the evidence such that the case can be heard in a maximum of five days. Judges should be able to strike out claims and order deposits more readily. This will also require the application of strict limits on the volume of documents and number of witnesses that may be relied upon in Track 2 cases. We recommend that Presidential Guidance is produced on what the usual limits should be for different cases.

An ENE hearing should then be listed before a judge for half a day unless the parties confirm that a private ENE hearing has been conducted. The documents, witness statements and bundle should be prepared ahead of the ENE hearing.

If the case does not resolve, a hearing should be listed to determine the claim. That hearing should take place within a specific listing time: the speed of the determination will be a critical feature in encouraging the use of Track 2 and act as a trade-off to the stricter case management process.

We recommend that an oral judgment should be given. If a party wishes to obtain a written record of the judgment, they should be required to pay for a transcript of the judgment as in the civil courts, rather than having a right to written reasons without any cost.

Our view is that once claimants are seeking more than the equivalent of six months' pay, a requirement to pay fees should be considered, on the basis of being a percentage of the value that is awarded. Alternatively, the use of a penalty – payable to the FWA by respondents where an award is made that is greater than any offers made prior to the hearing – may be a means of addressing the cost to the system of these claims and acting as an incentive to parties resolving matters.

We think that claimants should be allowed to choose between bringing their case as a Track 2 case or a Track 3 case. In making that choice, they must decide whether they wish to be subject to very rigorous case management and a maximum number of hearing days. If they choose to be subject to that more limiting approach, we consider that they should not then generally be subject to costs.

However, where offers have been made after the ENE hearing and those offers are not beaten by the claimant or respondent subsequently, we consider that this should be a basis for the judge to consider making a costs award. The ENE hearing – whether provided by the tribunal service or privately – will have provided considerable benefits to the parties in hearing from an independent third-party about the likely merits of their claims. That allows them to make sensible offers in light of that view and rejecting offers having had a view from an independent judge should, we consider, usually sound in limited costs. We recommend that costs in those circumstances should be more limited than an award of all the costs incurred by a party; one option might be to restrict the costs payable to a percentage of the value of the claim, particularly if an offer is rejected and then not beaten at a subsequent tribunal. So, for example, if the tribunal awards £15,000, but the respondent's offer had been £20,000 then a costs award of, say 10% of the final award may be ordered. Once again, this should ensure that parties take a considered view of both the sums they are claiming and the value of offers that are made.

iii. Track 3

Claimants should be able to opt into Track 3. These claims would be for claims seeking more than two years' earnings or for claims where the claimants do not want to be subject to the strict case management approach in Track 2.

We consider that these claims will require close case management by the same judge throughout the life of the case in so far as this is feasible. The judge should be able to refer a case back to the ERS at any time, if they consider that mediation would assist. Directions should be made, with sanctions following a failure to comply. We would recommend that in these trials, the judge case managing the claim should determine the extent to which disclosure and witness statements should be limited and that the trial should operate under the strict rules of evidence and procedure akin to the Civil Procedure Rules. Case management should be guided by proportionality, with the importance of that principle enshrined in statute. We would expect these cases to be heard by more experienced employment judges who were ticketed to do so. A written judgment would usually be produced after a Track 3 trial.

It must also be recognised that these cases are likely to be the most emotionally charged and so we would recommend that there is a direction requiring parties to engage in non-court dispute resolution. We recommend that there are mandatory touch points in the litigation process where non-court dispute resolution must be considered by the parties and with the tribunal. We anticipate that the non-court dispute resolution would often take the form of a private mediation: this may range in style depending on the nature of the dispute. However, we think that there is real value in encouraging parties to pursue private ENE, like the private financial dispute resolution hearings in family law. These have the benefit of giving the parties clarity as to the relative merits of their cases and an opportunity to put their case before an independent third-party, with more time and in perhaps more convivial surroundings than at a court-based ENE. Where a private ENE has not been conducted, we recommend that a one-day ENE hearing is listed by the tribunal after disclosure and witness statement exchange, as a final opportunity to avoid the trial. Where non-court dispute resolution processes have not been engaged with, costs should be considered.

Track 3 claims would operate much as multi-track claims do in the civil courts. Therefore, we consider that a court fee should be payable, calculated as a percentage of the value claimed. In addition, we recommend that a full costs regime should apply. We think that it should be issue based. Anecdotally, we were told of representatives who add discrimination or whistleblowing claims to otherwise simple unfair dismissal matters in order to try to obtain greater compensation when the merits of those claims are limited. In those circumstances, where the discrimination or whistleblowing claims fail, costs should be payable by the claimant even where their unfair dismissal claim succeeds. While recognising that introducing a costs regime represents a significant change to the status quo in the tribunal system, we consider it necessary and proportionate given the resources required for these claims both for the judiciary and the parties.

Moreover, this would have several advantages. First it would enable a structure akin to the Part 36 regime under the Civil Procedure Rules to operate which would incentivise non-court dispute resolution. Consideration would have to be given as to how issues relating to a claimant seeking a declaration or reinstatement or re-engagement would be factored into the Part 36 equivalent regime. However, creative solutions to the dispute would thereby be encouraged. Given the requirement to have an ENE hearing, parties would have received an impartial, independent view of the merits of the claim prior to the trial enabling offers to be made that could be weighed considering the view. In addition, having a full costs regime would enable the use of conditional fee arrangements and after the event insurance. This would have the benefit of enabling parties to be legally represented in claims that are, by their nature, likely to be complex and lengthy. At present, we think that the lack of a costs regime in complex claims is itself a barrier to accessing justice for many people: they cannot obtain legal representation without significant upfront costs, they cannot use conditional fee agreements, and are often forced to litigate very complex matters alone.

We recommend that claims involving more than ten people should usually be managed as Track 3 cases. In these cases, we consider it imperative that a designated judge case-manages these claims throughout, as occurs currently. Depending on the number of claimants, we would recommend a multi-day ENE hearing. Specific rules should be developed to manage multiple claims, particularly relating to the selection of test claimants and addressing disclosure proportionately.

iv. Choice of Track Allocation

For claims that might sit within either Track 1 or Track 2, we recommend that the parties should have the opportunity to say which track they consider to be most suitable on the application form. However, the decision as to whether the case is allocated to Track 1 or Track 2 should be a judicial decision; this would primarily be based on the value sought but complexity or other factors, such as controversy or the sensitivity of the subject area, may mean that a case should be heard on a different track. In addition, if the value or complexity of a claim changes, parties should be able to apply to the tribunal to change track.

For claims that might sit within either Track 2 or Track 3, we consider that this should be at the choice of the claimant. The corollary of the claimant having the choice of track is either accepting a limit on their claim so it can be addressed within a proportionate degree of resources and with a cap on the amount of compensation that can be awarded, or accepting that the usual costs rules will apply. We recommend that claimants should have the benefit of clear information and advice from the ERS about the different approaches in each track.

Two matters will need to be carefully considered with the tracking approach. First, an equality impact assessment will need to be carried out to ensure that there is no disproportionate impact on certain groups in utilising the tracks. Second, consideration should be given to when the track allocation decision takes place. Our initial view is that it should occur on receipt of the claim and response forms because it will determine the nature and rigour of the case management process. However, it may be that the track allocation, at least as between Track 2 and Track 3, could take place after a first preliminary hearing, to allow clarification of the case prior to allocation.

By utilising the tracking approach (the relatively few) claims that are currently heard in the civil courts could be brought into Track 3 in the employment tribunal. If there was a wish to have a single jurisdiction, this could easily be achieved, although the participants in our research did not consider the divided jurisdiction to be particularly problematic.[53]

IV. Summary of Recommendations

In this final section we try to summarise our suggestions:

Emphasis on Alternative Dispute Resolution (ADR)

1. The Acas Code of Practice on Disciplinary and Grievance Procedures should be amended to make it clear that there is no requirement to follow a formal grievance procedure before bringing a claim to the tribunal. It should be emphasised that parties must make attempts to resolve the issues informally. The uplift/reduction in damages should be retained but applied only where informal resolution attempts have not been made. Grievances should be renamed as, for example, 'matters of concern'.
2. The Acas Code of Practice on Disciplinary and Grievance Procedures should be amended to specify that the disciplinary procedure should be used as a matter of last resort in most cases.
3. An Employment Resolution Service should be established. This body should be the first port of call for all employers and employees seeking information and advice about issues in the workplace. It should provide comprehensive information and advice, with longer appointments where more complex advice is required. It should also actively encourage, support and facilitate internal workplace mediation.
4. Where further assistance is required, the Employment Resolution Service should operate as a triage service directing enquiries to the Fair Work Agency for matters of enforcement of basic rights, to a phone conciliation service for issues that appear to be possible to resolve straightforwardly or to an online mediation service staffed by experienced and highly capable mediators.
5. Parties should be required to attend either a phone conciliation appointment or online mediation appointment according to the complexity of the matter. These sessions should be resolution-focused, rather than problem-focused, and should include an element of 'reality testing', rather than being purely facilitative. The specific type of mediation should be tailored to the circumstances of the case. Where required, such as in certain discrimination matters, the mediation should follow a 'trauma informed' approach or transformative mediation approach.

[53] See Figure 1.3 (ch 1). Focus Group, 13 November 2024.

6. Where conciliation or mediation is unsuccessful in resolving the dispute, the Employment Resolution Service should certify that the parties have attended to permit them to bring or defend a claim in the tribunal. However, judges should readily send cases back to the Employment Resolution Service for further mediation.

More Minor Changes to the Current System

7. The ET1 and ET3 forms should be remodelled. Questions should avoid legal labels, use simple language and be specific and precise. Previous answers should determine the questions that are asked next so that they are dependent on the claims that are brought. Answer boxes should be restricted to a certain number of words to help parties remain focused on key issues. Specific questions about remedy should be asked so that a schedule of loss is produced at the outset. Parties should be asked to upload certain documents according to the claims made.
8. An AI model to convert a narrative into a timeline of events and specific legal claims should be carefully evaluated.
9. The approach of Acas to conciliation/mediation should be evaluative rather than facilitative.
10. There should be an increase of the current £25,000 limit on the contractual jurisdiction in employment tribunals to £100,000.
11. The Fair Work Agency should be properly resourced to enable them to enforce tribunal awards and COT3 settlement payments, and impose a penalty for non-payment.

More Ambitious Changes to the Current System

12. The grievance procedure should be abolished and replaced with, for example, 'an expression of concern' document which would start a process where an HR mediator can step in.
13. There should be statements, enshrined in statute, that tribunals, especially in the less complex cases, are intended to be quick, cheap and accessible fora as well as a statutory presumption that tribunals should be the last resort.
14. Tribunal awards should have the same status as county court judgments and be enforceable accordingly. Tribunals should have the power to require parties to confirm to them that awards have been paid, with the possibility of imposing a penalty where they are not.
15. Proper data should be collected as to the types of claim that are successful, and where awards are not paid, to enable the Fair Work Agency to investigate and/or advise and support particular employers or those operating in particular sectors.

Most Radical Changes to the Current System

16. Cases should be allocated to one of three tracks by a legal officer. Non-court dispute resolution should be actively encouraged on every track.
    a. Track 1 should deal with claims for less than six months' earnings. This track would deal with matters informally, with little additional documentation than that lodged with the claim and response forms and would be heard online before a judge for no more than three hours.
    b. Track 2 would deal with claims for more than six months' earnings and less than two years' earnings. Standard directions should be given with strict limits on the number of pages for a bundle and the length of witness statements. Track 2 cases should be subject to rigorous case management whereby the judge can require parties to pick their best five or ten points, or to limit the case so that it can be heard within a maximum of five days. Strike outs and deposit orders should be more readily used. A half day early neutral evaluation hearing should be listed before a judge after exchange of witness statements. Consideration should be given to court fees being payable, as a percentage of the value of the claim. The judgment should be given orally, with parties required to pay for a transcript of the judgment if they seek it. Where offers made after the early neutral evaluation hearing are not beaten, this should usually result in a costs award limited to a percentage of the value of the claim.
    c. Track 3 would deal with claims for more than two years' earnings or where the claimant chooses to bring their claim under this regime. These claims should, where possible, be case managed by the same judge throughout the life of the case. Directions should be made with sanctions for non-compliance. Mandatory touch points should operate throughout the litigation process when parties and the tribunal are required to consider non-court dispute resolution. Mediation – including transformative mediation – should be encouraged, together with private early neutral evaluation hearings. After witness statement exchange, a one-day early neutral evaluation hearing should be held, unless a private early neutral evaluation hearing has been conducted. Orders for disclosure, bundles and witness statements should follow the Civil Procedure Rules with limits determined by the judge case managing the claim. A court fee, as a percentage of the value of the sum claimed, should be payable. A full costs regime should operate on an issue basis, including provisions equivalent to Part 36. These claims should be heard by experienced judges with the appropriate ticket and a written judgment should be produced.

17. Claims involving ten or more claimants should usually be managed as Track 3 cases. Specific rules should be developed to manage these claims including rules about the selection of test claimants and addressing disclosure proportionately.

V. Conclusions

We recognise that the tribunal system is facing a large number of serious challenges – most importantly the volume and complexity of cases and insufficient resources to address them. Cases in some regions are now being listed for 2029, four years after the date of writing this book. This is not just an issue about cost, although concerns about the financial and emotional costs of litigation should not be underestimated, but it is about the rule of law. Justice delayed is very much justice denied.

The advent of the Employment Rights Act 2025, if it really is to have the transformative effect the government hopes, needs to be accompanied by an effective system of dispute resolution. Adding an estimated 15 per cent more claims[54] into an already overloaded system will leave many rights unenforced and individuals disappointed. The Employment Rights Act 2025 must be accompanied by serious reform to the current system. The introduction of the Fair Work Agency is a start but its limited jurisdiction will not be sufficient to address the serious issues facing the tribunal system.

However, following a review of the whole system we think that there are a number of ways that those challenges can be addressed. Reform is needed not just of the tribunal process but much earlier. In brief, reform is needed at the beginning, the middle and end of the process.

First, the beginning. We have suggested ways of keeping cases out of the tribunals altogether: by encouraging more proactive involvement of HR in resolving disputes and not just having recourse to procedures which seem to entrench both sides. We think there are ways of encouraging employers to resolve disputes in the workplace through a combination of financial incentives and statutory language. We also think that a new body could be set up, the Employment Resolution Service, taking a very different approach from that of Acas, and adopting a more proactive approach. It should be the first port of call for all employers and employees seeking information and advice about issues in the workplace and it should actively encourage, support and facilitate internal workplace mediation. This has proved highly successful in Australia and New Zealand. The Employment Resolution Service should provide a phone

[54] See: assets.publishing.service.gov.uk/media/6842fa6e4d039a010411f076/employment-rights-bill-economic-analysis.pdf, para 61.

conciliation and online mediation service that is mandatory before a claim can be brought, or responded to, before the employment tribunal.

Second, the middle. If the case does go to the tribunal, we have a number of ideas as to how to streamline the processes. Most radically, we have proposed a case tracking system which adopts a different approach depending on the value and complexity of the case. If this is not feasible, we have made various suggestions for improving the current functioning of the tribunals, ranging from making changes to the claim form to imposing much more emphasis on alternative dispute resolution (ADR). This has proved very successful in family law.

Third, the end. There is still a very high level of non-compliance with tribunal awards and the current process for securing compliance is difficult. We have therefore proposed simpler access to the county court system for enforcement of judgments and better use of data to improve the processes for engendering systemic change.

The current system does not give claimants or respondents true access to justice: in those regions where there are long delays, waiting for many years for a claim to be heard is not justice. Even where the delays are not so long, we are not sure that so many cases should be going to tribunal. Litigation is expensive, financially and emotionally. We think many cases would be better resolved through ADR. This is the principal message of our book. We hope that the blueprint we are recommending might change the approach to ADR and enable parties to obtain resolution of their disputes – whether through ADR or through adjudication – at a speed and cost that is proportionate to the issues involved.

Appendix 1: Methodology

I. Overview

This appendix sets out the methodology 'that we have' used in our research to address the question: 'What can realistically be done to address the problems of an employment tribunal system which can no longer deliver on its original objectives of informal, speedy, accessible access to justice'. We have adopted a 'mixed methods-grounded theory' approach[1] (i) to address the broad and comprehensive nature of the issues that have arisen; and (ii) to focus on the data rather than seek to test a prior theory. The combination of these two approaches is 'particularly complementary'.[2] Employing a variety of methodologies is a pragmatic approach[3] which 'combines both qualitative and quantitative research methods to understand a research problem'.[4] This approach seeks a more nuanced understanding of the law and legal processes in the context of complex socio-legal interactions.[5]

Underpinning the book is, of course, traditional legal analysis of legislation and rules of procedures in employment law. However, the book also draws on empirical research, looking at the various issues with the current employment dispute resolution system in the UK. Empirical legal research is a valuable tool when considering the existing operation of dispute resolution systems and its redesign, as it can shed important light on how procedural rules operate in practice,[6] what changes are needed, and how existing legal provisions could be better used.[7]

The book also adopts a comparative approach, not in the traditional sense of trying to understand another legal system or jurisdiction but rather to look at how other jurisdictions tackle similar problems and to consider whether those jurisdictions might offer ideas for solutions to the problems experienced

[1] J Creswell and V Plano Clark, *Designing and Conducting Mixed Methods Research* (Sage 2018); M Howell Smith, W Babchuk, J Stevens, A Garrett, S Wang and T Guetterman, 'Modelling the use of mixed methods-grounded theory: developing scales for a new measurement model' (2020) 14 *Journal of Mixed Methods Research* 184.

[2] Howell Smith et al (n 1), 184.

[3] Creswell and Plano Clark (n 1) 37.

[4] A Blackham, 'When law and data collide: the methodological challenge of conducting mixed methods research in law' (2022) 49 *Journal of Law and Society* S87, S89.

[5] L Nielsen, 'The Need for Multi-Method Approaches in Empirical Legal Research' in P Cane and H Kritzer (eds), *The Oxford Handbook of Empirical Legal Research* (Oxford University Press 2010) 952, 955.

[6] C Menkel-Meadow and B Garth, 'Civil Procedure and Courts' in P Cane and H Kritzer (eds), *The Oxford Handbook of Empirical Legal Research* (Oxford University Press 2010) 680.

[7] M Partington, 'Empirical Legal Research and Policy-making' in P Cane and H Kritzer (eds), *The Oxford Handbook of Empirical Legal Research* (Oxford University Press 2010) 1003.

by the employment tribunal system in the UK. Consequently, we explore dispute resolution in other UK jurisdictions including family law, as well as looking to employment dispute resolution in several Commonwealth jurisdictions.

This chapter outlines the methodology used in our empirical research (section II), the research process (section III), including the comparative work we undertook, before concluding (section IV).

II. The Empirical Research

A. Quantitative Research

When conducting quantitative empirical legal research, it is common practice to rely on observational datasets, that is, existing sources of data. Quantitative data is used to draw inferences – applying known facts to formulate generalisations about broader patterns.[8] While much has been written about the difficulties in the employment dispute resolution system, and practitioners are well aware of many of the problems, this stage in the research was essential to provide insight into the key issues that are causing the current system to fail to meet its fundamental aims.

In our research, the quantitative stage involved collating publicly available data relating to employment tribunal claims, employment appeal tribunal appeals, and other mechanisms of enforcing workplace rights. This data enabled us to reach broad inferences about the fundamental issues at play in the employment tribunal system and other enforcement mechanisms. Our analysis of this data allowed us to identify the growth in claims, the extent of the backlog in cases, the relative proportions of certain types of claim, the use of strike out and deposit orders, and the relative successes of cases.

When considering the use of proper sampling of data in our research, we noted that, unsurprisingly, 'researchers should collect as much data as resources and time allow because basing inferences on more data rather than less is almost always preferable'.[9] However, the data that was publicly available in some areas was relatively limited. Consequently, we identified when it was not practically possible to collect data across all time periods and utilised carefully chosen sampling that would seek to avoid any biases towards a particular research assumption.[10] Our sampling decisions in the current research have been made to meet these requirements: where possible, we collected all publicly available data, in some circumstances we had to limit this to the data available from the

[8] L Epstein and A Martin, 'Quantitative Approaches to Empirical Legal Research' in P Cane and H Kritzer (eds), *The Oxford Handbook of Empirical Legal Research* (Oxford University Press 2010) 904–05.

[9] ibid, 910.

[10] ibid.

last five years (particularly where we were extracting data from annual reports), and in other contexts we had to limit it to two years (eg, in relation to High Court employment case load where we had to extract data manually from the case database). In addition, Freedom of Information (FOI) requests had to be circumscribed to ensure they were reasonable, increasing the likelihood they would be responded to.

B. Qualitative Research

The second stage of the empirical research was the qualitative research which sought to deepen and broaden the understanding of the issues in play. In this phase, we conducted an online survey of practitioners, ran focus groups and undertook 'snowball' interviews. The aim of the approach utilised in the qualitative research phase was that it was as comprehensive as possible, engaging with relevant users, practitioners and policy-makers in a semi-structured interview process in order to go beyond existing preconceptions (both ours and theirs), to uncover the way the system operates in practice, how it could be changed going forwards and assessing the different trade-offs that were in play.

C. The Complementarity of Quantitative and Qualitative Research

It is well acknowledged that quantitative and qualitative data can be complementary with the right research design. While quantitative data generally provides information on the degree to which some feature is present, qualitative methods can be used to draw out more meaningful interpretation of the data, including a more exploratory, explanatory and descriptive understanding of the nature of a social phenomenon.[11] In the present research, after gathering quantitative data that uncovered general patterns in the issues in employment dispute resolution, the qualitative data has provided a much deeper understanding of the particular challenges and potential solutions identified by those who are most familiar with the system.[12] Qualitative data is particularly important in the current context of dispute resolution, since it is relevant to think not only about the official proceedings that have taken place (which can be captured to some extent by quantitative data), but about the various indirect effects of the law, actions parallel to legal

[11] L Webley, 'Qualitative Approaches to Empirical Legal Research' in P Cane and H Kritzer (eds), *The Oxford Handbook of Empirical Legal Research* (Oxford University Press 2010) 928.

[12] As noted by Menkel-Meadow and Garth (n 6) discussing the use of empirical research for devising reforms in civil procedure and courts (697): 'Counting the number of trials does not directly respond to the question of "how much public or private justice is enough?"'.

enforcement,[13] and occurrences prior to formal legal action, including cases that do not mature into the submission of a claim.[14] These types of 'off the record' dynamics are not captured by any of the institutional records, requiring qualitative methodologies such as interviews to reveal them.[15] More generally, it has been recognised that undertaking qualitative research after quantitative research may be useful 'so that the nuances of and mechanisms underlying the themes that have emerged during the quantitative phase may be examined in more detail'.[16]

As to the specific research question examined in this study, it is one which renders qualitative research particularly fitting. Indeed, the answer to the question as to the 'right' arrangements for employment dispute resolution is not an objective one that can simply be answered relying on the raw data we gathered.[17] This is because the 'answer' involves considerations that cannot be judged according to any 'objective' or numerical measurement, but is one which requires a more context-specific, socially-grounded evaluation.[18] Furthermore, this issue entails numerous trade-offs between different, sometimes conflicting, considerations. Different desirable goals for dispute resolution systems, such as the efficiency or the speed of the process, access to justice, procedural justice, truth ascertainment, and achieving justiciable outcomes, can be in tension with one other.[19] Balancing such a trade-off inevitably involves subjective assessments by the different stakeholders of the system, and must be examined in the relevant social and cultural contexts.[20] And so, while existing research points to numerous considerations

[13] As Barmes writes, in relation to her empirical research on behavioural conflict at work in the UK: 'The starting point that I would argue cannot be emphasized enough is that a great many people who experience problems at work, whether about behaviour or other things, do not turn to law and lawyers. While the majority reacts in some way, what they do often does not invoke law and there is a non-negligible minority who do nothing at all … It is necessary, therefore, to be alert to law's influence beyond the immediate outcomes of individual enforcement action to encompass, first, the indirect, systemic effects of some individuals asserting legal rights, and second, organizational responses independently of enforcement attempts. My qualitative analysis of judgments and my interview study directly investigated the possibilities by examining the operation in practice of employment rights adjudication and the reception of law into organizations': L Barmes, *Bullying and Behavioural Conflict at Work: The Duality of Individual Rights* (Oxford University Press 2015) 11–12.

[14] According to existing empirical research, much adjudication occurs outside courts: S Anleu and K Mack, 'Trial Courts and Adjudication' in P Cane and H Kritzer (eds), *The Oxford Handbook of Empirical Legal Research* (Oxford University Press 2010) 546.

[15] H Kritzer, 'Claiming Behavior as Legal Mobilization' in P Cane and H Kritzer (eds), *The Oxford Handbook of Empirical Legal Research* (Oxford University Press 2010) 265–66.

[16] Webley (n 11) 933.

[17] Menkel-Meadow and Garth (n 6) explains, in relation to empirical research on ADR (600): 'In ADR some criteria of quality measurement for some factors, such as efficiency, can be quantitative, while other factors – fairness, availability of tailored and flexible solutions, and the degree of self-determination in such processes – resist quantitative measurement and must be assessed in a more qualitative fashion'.

[18] See, eg, Menkel-Meadow and Garth (n 6) 690–91 (in relation to the 'optimal' level of civil litigation); R Macdonald, 'Access to Civil Justice' in P Cane and H Kritzer (eds), *The Oxford Handbook of Empirical Legal Research* (Oxford University Press 2010) 494, 501–02, 509–10 (in relation to the measurement of 'access to justice').

[19] Menkel-Meadow and Garth (n 6) 680–81.

[20] *cf* ibid, 691.

that ought to be taken into account in reimagining the employment dispute resolution system, the key question is how to realise them in practice, particularly given that resources are inevitably limited. Qualitative interviews with a wide range of people allowed us to assign weight to these criteria in the context of the operation of this particular system.

III. Our Qualitative Research Process

A. Survey

The first stage of the qualitative research was to identify the main issues that are problematic in the system. For this, we reviewed the literature identifying existing studies in this area to come up with a list of potential issues to consider.[21] This array of potential problems was then summarised in a simple and generalised online survey to see which of the potential problems were relevant, in practice, in the present UK employment dispute resolution context.[22]

In terms of the sampling techniques chosen for the survey, the primary technique was of 'purposeful sampling', that is, where researchers 'seek out key people or events that are likely to provide rich sources of information or data'.[23] In light of the scope of our research question, we opted to reach a broad group of stakeholders in the UK employment dispute resolution system, representing different segments of users and practitioners, including solicitors, barristers, members of the judiciary,[24] trade union representatives, HR professionals, and lawyers and legal advisers working in the not-for-profit sector.[25]

[21] On the role that literature and theory play in shaping the empirical research agenda and framing the questions addressed by empirical work, see: S Deakin, 'Labor and Employment Laws' in P Cane and H Kritzer (eds), *The Oxford Handbook of Empirical Legal Research* (Oxford University Press 2010).

[22] As explained by Nielsen (n 5) 953: 'Surveys provide a snapshot of a system or population at a particular moment in time and thus can supply comprehensive measurement of attitudes and demographic characteristics'.

[23] ibid, 934.

[24] On the value of qualitative research involving lay and professional judges in yielding insights about the functioning of mixed tribunals, see: N Vidmar, 'Lay Decision-Makers in the Legal Process' in P Cane and H Kritzer (eds), *The Oxford Handbook of Empirical Legal Research* (Oxford University Press 2010) 644. On the value of qualitative research examining trial court judges' approaches to their work, see: Anleu and Mack (n 14) 563–66. The authors explain (ibid, 566): 'Information obtained directly from judges provides important insights into the perceptions, experiences and approaches of the judicial officer, who remains the central participant in the trial court. Examining the trial court and adjudication from the vantage point of the judge enables identification of the variety of factors – organizational, professional, legal, and individual – that can affect the process of adjudication and decision-making'.

[25] As explained by Webley (n 11) 934, 'A well designed study will usually also provide findings that capture a broad range of experiences rather than those from only a few people or situations. The findings will be representative in the sense of capturing the range or variation in a phenomenon, but not in the sense of allowing for the estimation of the distribution of the phenomenon in the population as a whole'.

The link to the survey was sent out to the members of the Employment Lawyers Association (ELA) (mailing list of 6,610 members), the Industrial Law Society (ILS) (mailing list of 850 members) and to the over 100 members of the Employment Legal Advice Network (ELAN). There will have been duplication across the three mailing lists. In addition, we made extensive use of social media to recruit survey participants. The survey was open from Friday 18 October to Friday 19 December 2024. We received 193 complete substantive responses.[26]

Of the 193 participants, 149 individuals were solicitors, 23 were barristers, five worked in HR, four in the judiciary, and two were trade union representatives. Ten participants identified as 'other'. As to where they worked, 37 individuals indicated they worked in a city law firm with a substantial employment team, 29 worked in regional firm with a substantial employment team, 23 worked in a regional firm with a small employment team, 22 worked in a boutique employment firm, 14 worked in a city law firm with a small employment team, 11 worked in specialist employment chambers, seven worked in a generalist chambers with an employment team, another seven worked as in-house lawyers, six worked for a charity, five worked as sole practitioners, three worked in a trade union, and 29 identified as working in 'other'.

There was a range of professional experience: 18 individuals indicated that they had 0–5 years of professional experience; 23 had 5–10 years of professional experience; 26 had 10–15 years of professional experience; 28 had 15–20 years of professional experience; and 98 had over 20 years of professional experience. While there was a predominance of practitioners working in London and the surrounding area, 85 participants were not London based: there were 23 in the Midlands, 13 in North-West England, 12 in North-East England, 10 in South-West England, eight in the East of England, seven in Scotland, five in Wales, five on the South Coast, and two in Northern Ireland.

One hundred and eighty-seven individuals indicated what percentage of their practice involved claimant or respondent work: 26.2 per cent of participants indicated that over 50 per cent of their practice involved working for claimants with 14.97 per cent stating that their practice was 100 per cent claimant-focused; 64.17 per cent of participants indicated that more than 50 per cent of their work was for respondents of which 34.22 per cent had entirely respondent practices; and 6.95 per cent of participants said that they had a practice that was evenly split between claimant and respondent work. Six participants did not indicate what percentage of their practice involved claimant or respondent work; this appears to have been because they were acting as mediators or as judges.

[26] A total of 217 participants responded to the survey. However, some responses were blank, provided only contact details or declined to agree to us storing the relevant data. Once these entries were removed, there were 193 completed responses. Some data cleansing was required so that answers fitted into the relevant category of, for example, barrister or judge, or as to the type of firm/chambers the person worked from.

The responses from the survey helped us to narrow down the long list of potential problems identified in the literature to the issues in the current system that practitioners considered were significant.[27] The results of the survey then, in turn, served as the basis for how we constructed the semi-structured interviews and focus groups that followed.[28]

B. Focus Groups and Interviews

For the focus groups and interviews, 'purposeful sampling' was combined with a 'snowball sampling technique', that is, when the participants identified additional participants whom they considered would be helpful for the purposes of the study.[29] Together, purposeful sampling and snowball sampling were used to supplement each other, ensuring the empirical data was representative of the varied and numerous stakeholders of the employment dispute resolution system, and that interviewees reflected a range of backgrounds, covering different roles, professional background and expertise, as well as geographical distribution.

The focus groups and interviews proceeded on a semi-structured basis so that the discussion remained flexible and open ended. The results of the survey helped us to steer the conversation with all the participants around common themes that, at least initially, were identified as relevant. Both the list of guiding questions and the people we chose as interviewees were influenced by the survey's responses,[30] reflecting a research design that accommodated changing conditions, perceptions and findings.[31] In this way, the issues identified by the survey were explored in an in-depth manner, drawing on the experiences of key stakeholders representing a wide variety of users of the system.

More specifically, people were invited to sign up to the focus groups through the emails to ELA, ILS and ELAN members. In addition, we considered the spread of professional role and geographical location of participants and invited people to join groups where there was insufficient representation. We met with 60 people during 15 focus groups. Then we undertook eight interviews with

[27] The starting point for the survey analysis can be broadly described as a 'classical content analysis', where '[r]esearchers read the text to pull out emerging themes, attempting to make them as specific as possible by analyzing how they are used, the limits of their use, the context within which they appear, and so on. Once these themes solidify, they become "codes" which may then be counted and considered in relationship with other codes': Webley (n 11) 942–43.

[28] On the design of qualitative empirical research by combining these kinds of complementary methods, see: Webley (n 11) 932–33. See also: Nielsen (n 5) 953–54.

[29] Webley (n 11).

[30] Glaser and Strauss describe such a process as 'theoretical sampling', that is, 'the process of data collection for generating theory whereby the analyst jointly collects, codes, and analyzes his data and decides what data to collect next and where to find them, in order to develop his theory as it emerges': B Glaser and A Strauss, *Discovery of Grounded Theory: Strategies for Qualitative Research* (Routledge 1999) 45.

[31] Webley (n 11) 932.

different team members at Acas, the Office of the Director of Labour Market Enforcement, Department for Business and Trade, YESS (an employment dispute resolution charity), and the Employment Legal Advice Network (ELAN) (a network of employment law advice charities).

By conducting individual and group interviews of practitioners and users of the employment dispute resolution system, our empirical research allowed us to gain access to the experiences and perceptions of the relevant stakeholders of the system. Focus groups, in particular, foster conversations between interviewees and interviewers, in a way that can contribute to bringing about insights and solutions that would not have been reached otherwise. Interviews, similarly, allow the interviewee to elaborate on their views, including the reasons for the responses.[32] These features render them particularly useful, as we have aimed to explore how the resolution of employment disputes might best be achieved.

In order to deepen and broaden our understanding of how disputes are addressed in other UK jurisdictions and overseas, we conducted 23 interviews with family law practitioners (a range of barristers, solicitors and mediators); staff at the Aneurin Bevan University Health Board; team members at Valla, a commercial company using AI to help claimants to bring proceedings; members and retired members of the Australian Fair Work Commission; staff at the Australia Women's Legal Centre; practitioners in Singapore; the Head of the Employment Relations Authority New Zealand, and the National Manager of the Employment Mediation Service New Zealand; as well as academic colleagues in Birmingham University and Bristol University, the University of Sydney, the University of Melbourne and Victoria University of Wellington.

Finally, we were able to speak with the President of the Employment Appeal Tribunal; the Presidents of the Employment Tribunals (England and Wales, Scotland and Northern Ireland); and a small group of regional employment judges to explore their perceptions of the current system and the potential (and challenges) with the recommendations we were considering making. We also discussed the recommendations with senior practitioners in a Chatham House event in London and with civil servants from various government departments and subsequently with the CBI, TUC and various trade unions, and with those advising Charlie Mayfield on his *Keep Britain Working Review*.[33]

C. Analysing the Data

In order to analyse this data, we have drawn on what can be termed the (adaptive) 'grounded theory method'. While Glaser propounds a strict grounded theory methodology, Charmaz takes a flexible guidelines approach which

[32] ibid, 936–37.
[33] *Keep Britain Working – Final Report*: assets.publishing.service.gov.uk/media/6909fac488a98da87e292282/keep-britain-working-review-final-report.pdf.

recognises the constructivist nature of theory that develops from the data.[34] The important element of the grounded theory methodology is that the theory emerges or is constructed from the data. It 'involves developing theory as the research proceeds rather than testing a hypothesis posited in advance'.[35] According to Glaser and Strauss, when generating theory by joint collection, coding and analysis, there are not two distinct processes. Rather, researchers

> must be looking for emergent categories, reformulating them as their properties emerge, selectively pruning [their] list of categories while adding to the list as the core of [their] theory emerges, along with developing his hypotheses and integrating [their] theory – in order to guide [their] theoretical sampling at each step of the way.[36]

This approach allowed us 'to seek an understanding of an area, by developing and refining a theory as more is learned about the area'[37] thus allowing us not to be confined to any of the preconceptions and intuitions resulting from existing research in this field. Further, it enabled us to be open to exploring the best direction for the future of the employment dispute resolution system, in light of our evolving understanding of the problems in and possible solutions for the system.

Our approach was *adaptive* grounded theory which uses prior theories as 'orienting devices' and 'combines the use of extant theory with the development of theory from research findings'.[38] According to this approach, while researchers may begin the research with a partial framework regarding the structure and processes in the situations that are studied, they should 'also be sufficiently theoretically sensitive so that [they] can conceptualize and formulate a theory as it emerges from the data'.[39]

This approach has been reflected in the current study throughout the survey as well as the focus groups and interviews. Our starting point was influenced by the literature review of existing studies, which helped us, initially at least, to frame our understanding of the issues. However, the results of the survey influenced the way in which we constructed the focus groups and semi-structured interviews. This ultimately led us to consider the parallels between family law and employment law.

D. Comparative Understanding

Having identified the problems with the current employment dispute resolution system, we looked at other areas of domestic law with similar characteristics to

[34] Glaser and Strauss (n 30); B Glaser, 'Constructivist grounded theory?' (2002) 3 *Forum Qualitative Social Research* 3(3); K Charmaz, *Constructing Grounded Theory* (Sage Publications 2014) 16.
[35] Glaser and Strauss (n 30) 101. See also: Webley (n 11) 944.
[36] Glaser and Strauss (n 30) 72.
[37] Webley (n 11) 944.
[38] D Layder, *Sociological Practice: Linking Theory and Social Research* (Sage 1998) 24.
[39] Glaser and Strauss (n 30) 45–46.

employment law to explore how they operated and whether we could learn from them. Our focus was on systems that are characterised by a high number of litigants in person, low cost–high volume claims as well as systems involving complex litigation. Our data led us particularly to explore, and undertake a series of interviews with practitioners involved in, family law cases involving financial disputes. However, our analysis ranged across issues including personal injury claims, commercial court work, disciplinary processes at the Aneurin Bevan NHS Trust, the work of ombuds and the use of AI. We were able to interview staff at Aneurin Bevan, at Valla and colleagues in Cambridge investigating AI in legal judgments.

From there, we looked to jurisdictions abroad and drew on relevant international practice. We identified countries internationally whose systems appear to offer considerable advantages, or elements that were of interest. Through various networks of academics, practitioners and our own personal research contacts, we sought to identify the successes and failures of other systems via interviews with key stakeholders, practitioners and academics in those countries to identify best practice that we might draw on.

IV. Conclusions

Taken together, each of the research methodologies has its own strengths and weaknesses but, with the right research design, they can provide important complementary data in addressing the research question. This is particularly important in the context of research on dispute resolution: trial courts are multi-dimensional and changing institutions, and adjudication is a complex process. Understanding their roles and significance requires many different kinds of ongoing empirical legal study.[40] Therefore, this set of methodologies can be seen as reflecting the multiple dimensions required for such an analysis, examining them on micro, meso and macro levels. As such, the quantitative research provides data on general tribunal activity and trends over periods of time and across jurisdictions, while the surveys and interviews provide more fine-tuned data at the organisational and individual level, revealing how employment tribunals, courts and adjudication operate in practice, as well as the perceptions and attitudes of particular research subjects.[41] Each of these methodologies sheds light on aspects of our research that cannot be obtained by the other methodologies, and each 'contributes, in different ways, to advancing knowledge about the nature, role, and reality of trial courts and adjudication'.[42]

[40] Anleu and Mack (n 14) 567.
[41] See further, ibid, 547.
[42] ibid, 567.

INDEX

www.ingramcontent.com/pod-product-compliance
Ingram Content Group UK Ltd.
Pitfield, Milton Keynes, MK11 3LW, UK
UKHW020906190926
475560UK00010B/298

9 781509 990535